JOSHUA

THE OLD TESTAMENT LIBRARY

Editorial Advisory Board

Richard D. Nelson

JOSHUA

A Commentary

Westminster John Knox Press
Louisville, Kentucky

© 1997 Richard D. Nelson

Book design by Jennifer K. Cox

8/00

First edition
Published by Westminster John Knox Press
Louisville, Kentucky

This book is printed on acid-free paper that meets the American National Standards Institute Z39.48 standard. ⊗

PRINTED IN THE UNITED STATES OF AMERICA

97 98 99 00 01 02 03 04 05 06 — 10 9 8 7 6 5 4 3 2 1

Library of Congress Cataloging-in-Publication Data

Nelson, Richard D. (Richard Donald), date.
    Joshua : a commentary / Richard D. Nelson. — 1st ed.
    xvii, 310p.   cm. — (The Old Testament library)
    Includes bibliographical references and indexes.
    ISBN 0–664–21941–1 (alk. paper)
    1. Bible. O.T. Joshua—Commentaries. I. Title. II. Series.
BS1295.3.N45   1997
222'.207—dc21   97–8356

CONTENTS

PREFACE

Thanks are owed to the Lutheran Brotherhood for providing financial support for this project, and to the Board of Directors of Gettysburg Lutheran Seminary for granting me a sabbatical on which to complete this volume.

The translation of Joshua is my own. Biblical quotations generally are from the NRSV unless otherwise noted. Citations from Qumran and from Mishnaic and related literature follow the standard abbreviations. Certain words and phrases in the translation are enclosed in brackets. These represent portions of the Masoretic text absent from the Old Greek version and judged to be expansions of the earliest recoverable text.

ABBREVIATIONS

AB	Anchor Bible
AnBib	Analecta Biblica
AOAT	Alter Orient und Altes Testament
ANEP	*The Ancient Near East in Pictures Relating to the Old Testament,* ed. J. Pritchard, Princeton, 1969
ANET	*Ancient Near Eastern Texts Relating to the Old Testament,* ed. J. Pritchard, Princeton, 1969
ATANT	Abhandlungen zur Theologie des Alten und Neuen Testaments
ATAT	Arbeiten zu Text und Sprache im Alten Testament
ATD	Das Alte Testament Deutsch
BA	*Biblical Archaeologist*
BASOR	*Bulletin of the American Schools of Oriental Research*
BBB	Bonner biblische Beiträge
BBET	Beiträge zur biblischen Exegese und Theologie
BETL	Bibliotheca ephemeridum theologicarum lovaniensium
Bib	*Biblica*
BibOr	Biblica et orientalia
BHS	*Biblia Hebraica Stuttgartensia,* Stuttgart, 1977
BJS	Brown Judaic Studies
BN	*Biblische Notizen*
BWANT	Beiträge zur Wissenschaft vom Alten und Neuen Testament
BZ	*Biblische Zeitschrift*
BZAW	Beihefte zur Zeitschrift für die alttestamentliche Wissenschaft
CahRB	Cahiers de la Revue biblique
CBC	Cambridge Bible Commentary
CBQ	*Catholic Biblical Quarterly*
CD	Damascus Document
ConBOT	Coniectanea biblica, Old Testament
DH	Deuteronomistic History
E	English (where verse numbers differ from the Hebrew)
EB	Echter Bibel
ETR	*Etudes théologiques et religieuses*

FB	Forschung zur Bibel
FOTL	The Forms of the Old Testament Literature
FRLANT	Forschungen zur Religion und Literatur des Alten und Neuen Testaments
GTA	Göttinger theologische Arbeiten
HAR	*Hebrew Annual Review*
HAT	Handbuch zum Alten Testament
HSM	Harvard Semitic Monographs
IB	*Interpreter's Bible*
IEJ	*Israel Exploration Journal*
JANESCU	*Journal of the Ancient Near Eastern Society of Columbia University*
JNES	*Journal of Near Eastern Studies*
JNSL	*Journal of Northwest Semitic Languages*
JQR	*Jewish Quarterly Review*
JPSV	Jewish Publication Society Version
JSOT	*Journal for the Study of the Old Testament*
JSOTSup	Journal for the Study of the Old Testament Supplement Series
JSS	*Journal of Semitic Studies*
KB³	*Lexicon in Veteris Testamenti libros,* L. Koehler and W. Baumgartner, 3d ed.
LXX	Septuagint (the Greek version tradition as a whole)
LXX^A	Codex Alexandrinus
LXX^B	Codex Vaticanus
MT	Masoretic Text
NAB	New American Bible
NCB	New Century Bible
NICOT	New International Commentary on the Old Testament
NIV	New International Version
NJB	New Jerusalem Bible
NRSV	New Revised Standard Version
OBO	Orbis biblicus et orientalis
OBT	Overtures to Biblical Theology
OG	Old Greek (earliest recoverable Greek version)
OL	Old Latin version
Or	*Orientalia*
OTL	Old Testament Library
OTS	*Oudtestamentische Studiën*
PEQ	*Palestine Exploration Quarterly*
PJ	*Palästina-Jahrbuch*
RB	*Revue biblique*
REB	Revised English Bible

S	Syriac
SBS	Stuttgarter Bibelstudien
SBLMS	Society of Biblical Literature Monograph Series
SBLSCS	Society of Biblical Literature Septuagint and Cognate Studies
SBLSS	Society of Biblical Literature Semeia Studies
ScrHier	Scripta hierosolymitana
SEA	*Svensk exegetisk årsbok*
Sem	*Semitica*
SJOT	Scandinavian Journal of the Old Testament
ST	*Studia Theologica*
STDJ	Studies on the Texts of the Desert of Judah
T	Targum
TA	*Tel Aviv*
TDOT	*Theological Dictionary of the Old Testament,* ed. G. Botterweck and H. Ringgren, Grand Rapids, 1977–
ThWAT	*Theologisches Wörterbuch zum Alten Testament,* ed. G. Botterweck et al.
TynBul	*Tyndale Bulletin*
TZ	*Theologische Zeitschrift*
UF	*Ugarit-Forschungen*
V	Vulgate
VT	*Vetus Testamentum*
VTSup	Vetus Testamentum Supplements
WBC	Word Bible Commentary
WMANT	Wissenschaftliche Monographien zum Alten und Neuen Testament
ZAW	*Zeitschrift für die alttestamentliche Wissenschaft*
ZDPV	*Zeitschrift des deutschen Palästina-Vereins*

SELECT BIBLIOGRAPHY

I. Commentaries

Boling, R. *Joshua,* AB 6, Garden City, N.Y., 1982.
Bright, J. "The Book of Joshua," *IB* II, New York, 1953.
Butler, T. *Joshua,* WBC 7, Waco, Tex., 1983.
Fritz, V. *Das Buch Josua,* HAT I/7, Tübingen, 1994.
Görg, M. *Josua,* EB 26, Würzburg, 1991.
Gray, J. *Joshua, Judges, Ruth,* NCB, London, 1967.
Hertzberg, H. *Die Bücher Josua, Richter, Ruth,* ATD 9, Göttingen, 1953.
Miller, J., and G. Tucker. *The Book of Joshua,* CBC, Cambridge, 1974.
Noth, M. *Das Buch Josua,* HAT I/7, Tübingen, 1953.
Soggin, J. A. *Joshua: A Commentary,* OTL, Philadelphia, 1972.
Woudstra, M. *The Book of Joshua,* NICOT, Grand Rapids, 1981.

II. Monographs

Aharoni, Y. *The Land of the Bible,* Philadelphia, 1979.
Auld, A. G. *Joshua, Moses and the Land,* Greenwood, S.C., 1980.
Blenkinsopp, J. *Gibeon and Israel,* Cambridge, 1972.
Cortese, E. *Josua 13–21. Ein priesterschriftlicher Abschnitt im deuterono-mistischen Geschichtswerk,* OBO 94, Göttingen, 1990.
Floss, J. *Kunden oder Kundschafter? Literatur-wissenschaftliche Untersuchung zu Jos 2,* Teil 1, ATAT 16, St. Ottilien, 1982; Teil 2, ATAT 26, 1986.
Greenspoon, L. *Textual Studies in the Book of Joshua,* HSM 28, Chico, Calif., 1983.
Hawk, L. *Every Promise Fulfilled: Contesting Plots in Joshua,* Louisville, Ky., 1991.
Holmes, S. *Joshua: The Hebrew and Greek Texts,* Cambridge, 1914.
Kallai, Z. *Historical Geography of the Bible,* Leiden, 1986.
Kang, S. *Divine War in the Old Testament and in the Ancient Near East,* BZAW 177, Berlin, 1989.

Koopmans, W. *Joshua 24 as Poetic Narrative,* JSOTSup 93, Sheffield, 1990.

Kuhnert, G. *Das Gilgalpassah: literarische, überlieferungsgeschichtliche und geschichtliche Untersuchungen zu Josua 3–6,* Mainz, 1982.

Margolis, M. *The Book of Joshua in Greek,* Paris, 1931–38; Philadelphia, 1992.

Miller, P. *The Divine Warrior in Early Israel,* HSM 5, Cambridge, Mass., 1973.

Mitchell, G. *Together in the Land,* JSOTSup 134, Sheffield, 1993.

Mölle, M. *Der sogenannte Landtag zu Sichem,* FB 42, Würzburg, 1980.

Mullen, E. *Narrative History and Ethnic Boundaries: The Deuteronomistic History and the Creation of Israelite National Identity,* SBLSS, Atlanta, 1993.

Na'aman, N. *Borders and Districts in Biblical Historiography,* Jerusalem Biblical Studies 4, Jerusalem, 1986.

Noth, M. *The Deuteronomistic History,* JSOTSup 15, Sheffield, 1981.

Otto, E. *Das Mazzotfest in Gilgal,* BWANT 107, Stuttgart, 1975.

Polzin, R. *Moses and the Deuteronomist,* New York, 1980.

Schäfer-Lichtenberger, C. *Josua und Salomo: Eine Studie zu Autorität und Legitimität des Nachfolgers im Alten Testament,* VTSup 58, Leiden, 1995.

Schmitt, G. *Der Landtag von Sichem,* Arbeiten zur Theologie I/15, Stuttgart, 1964.

———. *Du sollst keinen Frieden schliessen mit den Bewohnern des Landes,* BWANT 91, Stuttgart, 1970.

Schwienhorst, L. *Die Eroberung Jerichos: exegetische Untersuchung zu Josua 6,* SBS 122, Stuttgart, 1986.

Stern, P. *The Biblical Ḥerem: A Window on Israel's Religious Experience,* BJS 211, Atlanta, 1991.

Svensson, J. *Towns and Toponyms in the Old Testament with Special Emphasis on Joshua 14–21,* ConBOT 38, Stockholm, 1994.

Wijngaards, J. *The Dramatization of Salvific History in the Deuteronomic Schools,* OTS 16, Leiden, 1969.

Winther-Nielsen, N. *A Functional Discourse Grammar of Joshua,* ConBOT 40, Stockholm, 1995.

Younger, K. *Ancient Conquest Accounts: A Study in Ancient Near Eastern and Biblical History Writing,* JSOTSup 98, 1990.

III. Articles or Chapters

Anbar, M. "The Story about the Building of an Altar on Mount Ebal: The History of its Composition and the Question of the Centralization of the Cult," *Das Deuteronomium,* ed. N. Lohfink, BETL 68, Leuven, 1985, 304–9.

Beek, M. "Joshua the Savior," *Voices from Amsterdam,* ed. M. Kessler, SBLSS, Atlanta, 1994, 145–53.

Begg, C. "The Function of Josh. 7:1–8:29 in the Deuteronomistic History," *Bib* 67 (1986): 320–34.

Bird, P. "The Harlot as Heroine: Narrative Art and Social Presumption in Three Old Testament Texts," *Semeia* 46 (1989): 119–39.

Boling, R. "Levitical History and the Role of Joshua," *The Word of the Lord Shall Go Forth*, ed. C. Meyers and M. O'Connor, Winona Lake, Ind., 1983, 241–61.

Brekelmans, C. "Joshua v 10–12: Another Approach," *OTS* 25 (1989): 89–95.

———. "Joshua 24: Its Place and Function," *Congress Volume Leuven 1989*, ed. J. Emerton, VTSup 43, Leiden, 1–9.

Coats, G. "The Ark of the Covenant in Joshua: A Probe into the History of a Tradition," *HAR* 9 (1985): 137–57.

———. "The Book of Joshua: Heroic Saga or Conquest Theme?" *JSOT* 38 (1987): 15–32.

Coogan, M. "Archaeology and Biblical Studies: The Book of Joshua," *The Hebrew Bible and Its Interpreters*, Biblical and Judaic Studies 1, ed. W. Propp, Winona Lake, Ind., 1990, 19–32.

Culley, R. "Stories of the Conquest: Joshua 2, 6, 7, and 8," *HAR* 8 (1984): 25–44.

Feldman, S. "'Sun Stand Still' — A Philosophical-Astronomical Midrash," *Proceedings of the Ninth World Congress of Jewish Studies*, ed. C. Goldberg, Jerusalem, 1986, 77–84.

Fensham, F. "The Treaty Between Israel and the Gibeonites," *BA* 27 (1964): 96–100.

Fritz, V. "Die sogenannte Liste der besiegten Könige in Josua 12," *ZDPV* 85 (1969): 136–61.

Giblin, C. "Structural Patterns in Joshua 24:1–25," *CBQ* 26 (1964): 50–69.

Grintz, J. "The Treaty of Joshua with the Gibeonites," *JAOS* 86 (1966): 113–26.

Halbe, J. "Gibeon und Israel: Art, Veranlassung und Ort der Deutung ihres Verhältnisses in Jos IX," *VT* 25 (1975): 613–41.

Halpern, B. "Gibeon: Israelite Diplomacy in the Conquest Era," *CBQ* 37 (1975): 303–16.

Hawk, L. "Strange Houseguests: Rahab, Lot, and the Dynamics of Deliverance," *Reading Between Texts: Intertexuality and the Hebrew Bible*, ed. D. Fewell, Louisville, Ky., 1992, 89–97.

Holladay, J. "The Day(s) the Moon Stood Still," *JBL* 87 (1968): 166–78.

Jobling, D. "The Jordan a Boundary: Transjordan in Israel's Ideological Geography," *The Sense of Biblical Narrative: Structural Analyses in the Hebrew Bible II*, JSOTSup 39, Sheffield, 1986, 88–134.

Kaminsky, J. "Joshua 7: Holiness Violation and Corporate Punishment," *Corporate Responsibility in the Hebrew Bible*, JSOTSup 196, Sheffield, 1995, 67–95.

Kearney, P. "The Role of the Gibeonites in the Deuteronomistic History," *CBQ* 35 (1973): 1–19.

Kloppenborg, J. "Joshua 22: The Priestly Editing of an Ancient Tradition," *Bib* 62 (1981): 347–71.

Koopmans, W. "The Poetic Prose of Joshua 23," *The Structural Analysis of Biblical and Canaanite Poetry*, ed. W. van der Meer and J. de Moor, JSOT-Sup 74, Sheffield, 1988, 83–118.

Liver, J. "The Literary History of Joshua IX," *JSS* 8 (1963): 227–43.

Lohfink, N. "The Deuteronomistic Picture of the Transfer of Authority from Moses to Joshua," *Theology of the Pentateuch*, Minneapolis, 1994, 234–47.

Margalit, B. "The Day the Sun Did Not Stand Still: A New Look at Joshua x 8–15," *VT* 42 (1992): 466–91.

Marx, A. "Rahab, Prostituée et Prophétesse: Josue 2 et 6," *ETR* 55 (1980): 72–76.

Mayes, A. "Deuteronomy 29, Joshua 9, and the Place of the Gibeonites in Israel," *Das Deuteronomium*, N. Lohfink, BETL 68, Leuven, 1985, 321–25.

McCarthy, D. "An Installation Genre?" *JBL* 90 (1971): 31–41.

———. "Some Holy War Vocabulary in Joshua 2," *CBQ* 33 (1971): 228–30.

———. "The Theology of Leadership in Joshua 1–9," *Bib* 52 (1971): 165–75.

Möhlenbrink, K. "Die Landnahmesagen des Buches Josua," *ZAW* 56 (1938): 238–68.

Moran, W. "The Repose of Rahab's Israelite Guests," *Studi sull' Oriente e la Bibbia: G. Rinaldi,* ed. G. Buccellati, Genoa, 1967, 273–84.

Nelson, R. "Josiah in the Book of Joshua," *JBL* 100 (1981): 531–40.

Newman, M. "Rahab and the Conquest," *Understanding the Word: Essays in Honor of Bernhard W. Anderson,* ed. J. Butler et al., Sheffield, 1985, 167–81.

Noth, M. "Überlieferungsgeschichtliches zur zweiten Hälfte des Josuabuches," *Festschrift F. Nötscher,* BBB 1, 1950, 152–67.

Orlinsky, H. "The Hebrew *Vorlage* of the Septuagint of the Book of Joshua," VTSup 17 (1968): 187–95.

Ottosson, M. "Rahab and the Spies," *DUMU-E2-DUB-BA-A: Studies in honor of A. Sjöberg,* ed. H. Behrens et al, Philadelphia, 1989, 419–27.

Peckham, B. "The Composition of Joshua 3–4," *CBQ* 46 (1984): 413–31.

———. "The Significance of the Book of Joshua in Noth's Theory of the Deuteronomistic History," *The History of Israel's Traditions: The Heritage of Martin Noth,* ed. S. McKenzie and M. Graham, JSOTSup 182, Sheffield, 1994, 213–34.

Peterson, J. "Priestly Materials in Joshua 13–22: A Return to the Hexateuch?" *HAR* 4 (1980): 131–45.

Porter, J. "The Background of Joshua 3–5," *SEA* 36 (1972): 5–23.

———. "The Succession of Joshua," *Proclamation and Presence,* ed. J. Durham and J. Porter, Richmond, 1970, 102–32.

Robinson, R. "The Coherence of the Jericho Narrative: A Literary Reading of Joshua 6," *Konsequente Traditionsgeschichte,* OBO 126, ed. R. Bartelmus et al., Fribourg, 1993, 311–35.

Rofé, A. "The Editing of the Book of Joshua in the Light of 4QJosh^a," *New Qumran Texts and Studies,* STDJ 15, ed. G. Brook and F. Martinèz, Leiden, 1994, 89–104.

———. "The End of the Book of Joshua according to the Septuagint," *Henoch* 4 (1982): 17–36.

———. "The History of the Cities of Refuge in Biblical Law," *Studies in the Bible,* ScrHier 31, Jerusalem, 1986, 205–39.

———. "Joshua 20: Historico-Literary Criticism Illustrated," *Empirical Models for Biblical Criticism,* ed. J. Tigay, Philadelphia, 1985, 131–47.

Rösel, H. "Anmerkungen zur Erzählung vom Bundesschluss mit den Gibeoniten," *BN* 28 (1985): 30–35.

———. "Erwägungen zu Tradition und Geschichte in Jos 24: ein Versuch," *BN* 22 (1983): 41–46.

———. "Die Überleitungen vom Josua- ins Richterbuch," *VT* 30 (1980): 342–50.

Roth, W. "Hinterhalt und Scheinflucht: der stammespolemische Hintergrund von Jos 8," *ZAW* 75 (1963): 296–304.

Rowlett, L. "Inclusion, Exclusion and Marginality in the Book of Joshua," *JSOT* 55 (1992): 15–23.

Sawyer, J. "Joshua 10:12–14 and the Solar Eclipse of 30 September 1131 B.C.," *PEQ* 104 (1972): 139–46.

Saydon, P. "The Crossing of the Jordan, Jos. chaps. 3 and 4," *CBQ* 12 (1950): 194–207.

Schäfer-Lichtenberger, C. "Das gibeonistische Bündnis im Lichte deuteronomischer Kriegsgebote: zum Verhältnis von Tradition und Interpretation in Jos 9," *BN* 34 (1986): 58–81.

Seidel, H. "Der Untergang Jerichos (Jos. 6)—Exegese ohne Kerygma?" *Theologische Versuche* 8 (1977): 11–20.

Smend, R. "Das Gesetz und die Völker: ein Beitrag zur deuteronomistischen Redaktionsgeschichte," *Probleme biblischer Theologie,* ed. H. Wolff, Munich, 1971, 494–509.

Snaith, N. "The Altar at Gilgal: Joshua 22:23–29," *VT* 28 (1978): 330–35.

Sperling, S. "Joshua 24 Re-examined," *HUCA* 58 (1987): 119–36.

Stone, L. "Ethical and Apologetic Tendencies in the Redaction of the Book of Joshua," *CBQ* 53 (1991): 25–36.

Sutherland, R. "Israelite Political Theories in Joshua 9," *JSOT* 53 (1992): 65–74.

Thompson, L. "The Jordan Crossing: *Sidqot* Yahweh and World Building," *JBL* 100 (1981): 343–58.

Tov, E. "The Growth of the Book of Joshua in the Light of the Evidence of the LXX Translation," *Studies in the Bible,* ScrHier 31, ed. S. Japhet, Jerusalem, 1986, 321–39.

———. "Midrash-Type Exegesis in the LXX of Joshua," *RB* 85 (1978): 50–61.

Tucker, G. "The Rahab Saga (Joshua 2): Some Form-Critical and Traditio-Historical Observations," *The Use of the Old Testament in the New, and Other Essays: Studies in Honor of W. F. Stinespring,* Durham, N.C., ed. J. Efird, 1972, 66–86.

Tunyogi, A. "Book of the Conquest," *JBL* 84 (1965): 374–80.

Van Seters, J. "Joshua 24 and the Problem of Tradition in the Old Testament," *In the Shelter of Elyon,* ed. W. Barrick and J. Spencer, JSOTSup 31, Sheffield, 1984, 139–58.

———. "Joshua's Campaign of Canaan and Near Eastern Historiography," *SJOT* 4 (1990): 1–12.

Vogt, E. "Die Erzählung vom Jordanübergang, Josue 3–4," *Bib* 46 (1965): 125–48.

Walton, J. "Joshua 10:12–15 and Mesopotamian Celestial Omen Texts," *Faith, Tradition, and History,* A. Millard et al., Winona Lake, Ind., 1994, 181–90.

Weinfeld, M. "The Extent of the Promised Land—the Status of Transjordan," *Das Land Israel in biblischer Zeit,* ed. D. Strecker, GTA 25, Göttingen, 1983, 59–75.

Wenham, G. "The Deuteronomic Theology of the Book of Joshua," *JBL* 90 (1971): 140–48.

Wilcoxen, J. "Narrative Structure and Cult Legend: A Study of Joshua 1–6," in *Transitions in Biblical Scholarship,* ed. J. Rylaarsdam, Chicago, 1968, 43–70.

Younger, K. "The 'Conquest' of the South (Jos 10, 28–39)," *BZ* 39 (1995): 255–64.

Zakovitch, Y. "Humor and Theology or the Successful Failure of Israelite Intelligence: A Literary-Folkloric Approach to Joshua 2," *Text and Traditions: The Hebrew Bible and Folklore,* ed. S. Niditch, Atlanta, 1990, 75–104.

Zevit, Z. "Archaeological and Literary Stratigraphy in Joshua 7–8," *BASOR* 251 (1983): 23–35.

INTRODUCTION

1. The Character and Relevance of Joshua

The book of Joshua describes the invasion, conquest, and division of the land of Canaan by Israel, pictured as a unified national group organized into twelve tribes and under the resolute leadership of Joshua, successor to Moses. Although the book is clearly the product of multilayered tradition and a process of literary growth, the final canonical form can be understood as a self-contained and coherent literary whole. The subject matter falls into neat halves, covering military conquest in chapters 1–12 and then in chapters 13–24, settlement and life in the land. The story line is initiated by speeches of Yahweh and Joshua in chapter 1. Joshua is organized primarily by geography. An east to west crossing into Canaan (chaps. 2–5) is followed by military campaigns directed at the center (chaps. 6–8), south (chaps. 9–10), and north (chap. 11), concluded by a summary list (chap. 12). The division of the land first covers the east Jordan tribes (chap. 13), then the central tribes (chaps. 14–17), then the peripheral and non-geographic tribes (chaps. 18–21). Joshua achieves its ultimate goal in three concluding sections intended to promote Israel's fidelity in the land. These take the form of a cautionary narrative (chap. 22) and two parenetic addresses (chaps. 23–24).

According to Jewish reckoning, Joshua is the first of the four books of the Former Prophets, along with Judges, Samuel, and Kings. This perception accurately reflects the book's thematic connection to what follows, the story of Israel's life in the land. At the same time, this traditional designation inappropriately detaches Joshua from Deuteronomy as the last book of the Torah. It is obvious that the reader of Joshua is expected to be thoroughly acquainted with both the narrative and legal portions of Deuteronomy. The final form of the book is clearly marked off from its context as a self-contained unit, beginning with the installation of Joshua as successor to Moses (1:1–6) and closing with his death and burial (24:29–31). At the same time, the introductory formula "after the death of Moses" (1:1) couples the book to a more comprehensive periodization of the Former Prophets by means of the same expression (Judg. 1:1; 2 Sam. 1:1; 2 Kings 1:1). Seen in an even wider perspective, Joshua serves as a central component in the overall narrative sequence of Genesis through Kings. The book realizes story elements introduced as early as Gen. 9:25–26;

10:15–19; and 12:1–3 that come to their decisive closure in the last chapters of 2 Kings.

Joshua is not just a plotted narrative, but a book of mental maps. The dominant map is the territory of all twelve tribes, who completely fill up the land (chaps. 15–19), but a contrasting cognitive map restricts the true land of inheritance to the territory west of the Jordan. This latter conception lies behind the view that crossing the Jordan was a step of exceptional consequence (chaps. 3–4) and is one of the presuppositions for the narrative of 22:10–34 (esp. v. 25). In addition, two other, more expansive maps are also present. One is the "land that remains" in 13:2–6, which consists of claimed but unconquered territory in Philistia and Phoenicia. This territory corresponds to the remainder of the Egyptian province of Canaan. The other is the expansionistic aspiration of Josh. 1:4, picked up from Deut. 11:24, which claims the distant Euphrates as the northern boundary of Israel's promised land. This last cognitive map seems to derive from the language of royal myth (1 Kings 5:1 [4:21E]; Ps. 72:8). The utopian notions of the "land that remains" and of the Euphrates border infuse the book of Joshua with the flavor of unredeemed promise. The reader is offered alternate interpretations for Israel's unfulfilled expectations. On the one hand, these can be seen as hopeful indications of greater things to come (13:6b; 17:18; 23:5). Yet the incomplete conquest is also judged to be the result of Israel's disobedience or military inability (15:63; 16:10; 17:12–13) and is seen as the basis for future threats to Israel's well-being (7:12; 23:12–13).

Joshua touches a raw nerve in most modern readers, who recoil from its chronicle of a brutal conquest of an indigenous population, deliberate acts of genocide against them, and the colonization of their ancestral land. North American readers, as well as those from other parts of the globe, all too easily recognize parallels with their own national stories of immigration, bloodshed, settlement, and cultural conflict. Moreover, the concept of a Divine Warrior who fights the battles of one nation at the expense of others seems incompatible with enlightened notions of religion. Joshua is inevitably a product of its own age and culture, and this should not be denied or glossed over. At the same time, Joshua deals with issues that still concern its contemporary readership, especially questions involving the identity of those who see themselves as the people of the God of Israel. How are God's gifts of peoplehood to be interpreted and valued? What are the responsibilities of peoplehood? What does it mean that many of God's longstanding promises have been kept, while others seem unfulfilled? What is the relationship of the people of God to the land that has been entrusted to their care?

2. Joshua and History

Joshua is fundamentally a theological and literary work. Hardly any of the material it preserves is of the sort that can be directly used for historical reconstruction (for details, see "Formation of the Book" and "Form Criticism" below). Joshua's traditional tales display a folkloristic character and a strong etiological inclination. Their themes of divine war and conquest served to build and strengthen Israel's group identity and to explain features of geography and social life, but do not necessarily reflect genuine memories of Israel's origins. The overall narrative structure of invasion and total conquest is the contribution of the authorial and redactional process and not something dictated by the earliest forms of the constituent tales. Only the geographical lists and boundaries can be considered as credible historical sources, witnessing to actual administrative structures, although from a period later than Israel's first emergence in the land. It should come as no surprise, therefore, that Joshua's account of a large-scale invasion of Canaan by Israel cannot be supported by the archaeological evidence.

The Merneptah Stele (about 1210 B.C.E.) documents that a people called Israel existed in Palestine at the end of the 13th century B.C.E. However, little can be said with any certainty about how Israel actually came into being as an identifiable ethnic and cultural entity.[1] One thing has become increasingly clear, however. The archaeological record does not support Joshua's story of a conquest by a people arriving from outside Palestine. Some cities important to the biblical story of conquest (Jericho, Ai, Heshbon) were not occupied in a significant way in the Late Bronze II period (LB II; about 1400–1200 B.C.E.). They could not have been the victims of an Israelite conquest that would coordinate with the start of the Iron I period (about 1200–1000 B.C.E.). It cannot be determined just who caused the destruction of other cities such as Bethel, Hazor, or Lachish, but there are several likely candidates besides Israel. Moreover, these devastations were not followed quickly by settlement that can be identified as Israelite. Finally, many LB II urban sites were not destroyed at all in the transition into the Iron I period.

Archaeologists tend to connect the emergence of Israel with the inauguration of hundreds of small unfortified Iron Age I settlements founded in the late 13th and early 12th century, primarily in the central hill country. These testify to the influx of settlers into previously unoccupied areas not under the control of the Late Bronze Age Canaanite urban centers. Because the pottery of these settlements exhibits strong continuity with that of LB II Canaan and because the associated epigraphic finds utilize the Canaanite alphabet, there is no reason to see these pioneers as infiltrators or invaders from somewhere outside Palestine.

1. For what follows, see M. Coogan, "Archaeology and Biblical Studies: The Book of Joshua," *The Hebrew Bible and Its Interpreters,* Winona Lake, Ind., 1990, 19–32; W. Dever, *Recent Archaeological Discoveries and Biblical Research,* Seattle, 1990; I. Finkelstein, *The Archaeology of the Israelite Settlement,* Jerusalem, 1988; N. Lemche, "Sociology, Text and Religion as Key Factors in Understanding the Emergence of Israel in Canaan," *SJOT* 5 (1991): 7–18; T. Thompson, *Early History of the Israelite People from the Written and Archaeological Sources,* Leiden, 1992.

These villages lack any sort of elitist architecture such as exceptionally large houses, suggesting a simple, egalitarian social structure. Other distinguishing cultural features seem to have been determined by the demands of agricultural life in the highlands: "four room" courtyard houses, rock-hewn cisterns, hillside terraces, and large "collar-rim" jars appropriate for the storage of agricultural products. All this suggests that the emergence of Israel was an indigenous development, related to economic, social, and demographic transformations occurring within the borders of Palestine itself. The Late Bronze Age urban culture of Canaan suffered profound dislocations, associated in part with the increasing weakness of Egypt, Canaan's former imperial master. The rapid influx of new settlers into the highlands may represent the peaceful infiltration of former pastoralists settling down to agriculture. The more likely option is that they were elements of the indigenous peasant population of Palestine attracted to new economic opportunities in the highlands and/or disaffected by life dominated by the economic and political power of the Canaanite city-states.

Thus Palestine seems to have been home to two parallel cultures in the early Iron Age, each occupying a different geographic and economic niche. In the lowlands was the established, elitist culture of the city-states with their kings and chariots. At the same time, an alternate social system was developing in the highlands. This was an egalitarian, rural village culture, without the social stratification that comes with being organized as a state. It depended on a largely self-contained economy based on farming and herding. The stories in the book of Judges seem to reflect the lifestyle and social organization of this society.

It was this highland group that came to identify itself as Israel. The origins of their sense of shared identity remain obscure, but the archaic poetry preserved by their descendants (Exodus 15, Judges 5) suggests that a shared devotion to Yahweh played an important role in this process of ethnic formation. Another factor would have been the forging of systems of affinity between extended families, endogamous clans, and eventually territorially based tribes. Traditions of common military activity with the support of Yahweh, like those preserved in Joshua, doubtless played an important role in Israel's process of self-identification and differentiation. Certainly some limited armed conflict between these two societies can be assumed to have taken place, as evidenced by the Song of Deborah (Judges 5). However, the concept of an invasion and conquest of Canaan by Israel, either of the comprehensive sort recounted in Joshua or the more piecemeal and limited type suggested by Judges chapter 1, must be excluded on the basis of the evidence.

Joshua's true historical value consists in what it reveals about the social and ideological world of those who told these stories, collected and redacted them, and then read the resulting literary product. Joshua is a historical witness to what later generations believed had happened to their ancestors. The needs of an increasingly centralized monarchy would have favored the growth of a unified narrative of origins. Any such narrative was bound to tell of a unified invasion and successful conquest from the outside, for that would be the best way to coordinate Israel's presence in and claim on the land with its deeply-rooted tradition of an exodus from Egypt and its poems and tales of Yahweh as Divine Warrior. It is common for traditions of national origin to speak of immigration from another place, as Israel itself was aware (Genesis 10; Amos 9:7). Israel's early "xenophobic" martial poetry (Josh. 10:12b–13a; Exod. 15:13–17; Judg. 5:19–21) likely played an important role in shaping a self-understanding founded on the notion of conquest. Victories over vanished peoples provided a natural explanation for the ruined cities that dotted the landscape. The social stratification and ethnically mixed nature of the monarchic state (Gen. 9:26–27; 2 Sam. 21:1–6; 1 Kings 9:20–21; Ezek. 16:3) could be readily explained in terms of older peoples dominated by new invaders. Contemporary tribal demography was traced back to an initial territorial allotment at Yahweh's command and under Yahweh's control.

3. Formation of the Book

Joshua employs a wide range of materials to tell its story: divine war narratives, folktales with an etiological background, deuteronomistic sermons, border descriptions, city lists, and so forth. These disparate materials are not always in complete agreement. For example, the Rahab story seems to prepare for a different sort of conquest of Jericho than the one actually recorded. The list of kings in chapter 12 does not correspond to the preceding conquests. Joshua's great age prompts both his distribution of the land and his final words to the nation (13:1 and 23:1). The book ends with two unrelated final speeches of Joshua in chapters 23 and 24. All this is evidence that the final shape of Joshua is the product of a complex process of literary formation. The history of this formation has been described in different ways.[2]

The starting point for understanding Joshua's literary history is the deuteronomistic language found in those portions of the book that give it its most

2. The classic source-critical approach is represented by K. Möhlenbrink, "Die Landnahmesagen des Buches Josua," *ZAW* 56 (1938): 238–68, and W. Rudolph, *Der 'Elohist' als Erzähler von Exodus bis Josua,* BZAW 68, Giessen, 1938, 165–253. S. Mowinckel, *Tetrateuch-Pentateuch-Hexateuch,* BZAW 90, Berlin, 1964, 12–16, 33–76, traces J and P in Joshua, the latter especially in the geographic lists of chapters 13–21. E. Otto, *Das Mazzotfest in Gilgal,* BWANT 107, Stuttgart, 1975, 26–95, unravels Yahwistic and deuteronomistic strands stemming from an ancient Gilgal ceremony throughout chapters 1–12. M. Rose, *Deuteronomist und Jahwist: Untersuchungen zu den Berührungspunkten beider Literaturwerke,* ATANT 67, Zurich, 1981, proposes that the conquest material was shaped by a proto-deuteronomist and that this early deuteronomistic layer is older than the J material in the Tetrateuch. Joshua underwent a J-like redaction, deuteronomistic redaction, and a P-like redaction. Other studies are reviewed by A. G. Auld, *Joshua, Moses and the Land,* Greenwood, S.C., 1980, 88–98.

distinctive shape and direction. This deuteronomistic redactional presence is visible throughout much of Joshua, but noticeably absent from the description of land distribution (chaps. 13:1–21:42 apart from 14:6–15). These deuteronomistic elements associate the story of Joshua with the larger topic of Israel's national existence as the people of Yahweh. Deuteronomistic language is most apparent in those sections that speak of obedience to the law and the theological significance of the conquest. It seeks to link Joshua's conquest to the previous account of Moses as military leader and lawgiver and to the future story of Israel in the land (1:1–18; 8:30–35; 12:1–6; 21:43–22:6; 23:1–16). This deuteronomistic material represents more than just a series of isolated expansions or incidents of retouching, but is a comprehensive redaction or act of authorship. By it Joshua has been made part of a larger account of the story of Israel in the land that stretches from Deuteronomy to 2 Kings. That is to say, 1:1–12:24; 21:43–22:6; 23:1–16; 24:28–31 make up a portion of the Deuteronomistic History (DH).[3]

The DH form of Joshua treats conquest and occupation as a matter of dutiful obedience to Yahweh's command given to Joshua as successor to Moses. This is set forth in a transitional speech of Yahweh that looks back to Moses and forward to Joshua's leadership (chap. 1). The two and a half tribes east of the Jordan take a prominent role throughout. The nation carefully pauses along the way to set up memorial stones as witnesses to future generations (chap. 4) and to build an altar and read the law at Shechem in obedience to Deuteronomy (8:30–35). When the conquest is completed and the land has rest from war, Joshua distributes the land according to tribal allotments (11:23; 12:7–8; 21:43–45), although this procedure is not actually described in DH, nor are any geographic details reported. After the east Jordan tribes are sent home (22:1–6) and just before his death, Joshua delivers a transitional speech (chap. 23), interpreting what has just taken place and preparing for the grim story of disobedience which follows in Judges and Kings. Some have proposed dividing DH in Joshua into more than one deuteronomist.[4] However, unlike the situation in Judges or Kings, evidence is lacking in Joshua for a second deuteronomist with a theological viewpoint different from DH or using a distinct vocabulary. The only possible exception might be the addition of chapter 24.

---

3. M. Noth, *The Deuteronomistic History,* JSOTSup 15, Sheffield, 1981, 5–8, 36–41, and *Josua,* HAT I/7, Tübingen, 1953, 7–10. Noth lists other DH passages as 2:9b, 10b, 11b; 3:2–4, 6–10; 4:6, 7, 10aB, 12, 14, 21, 22, 24; 5:4–7; 6:4, 5, 8, 12b–13a, 26; 8:1, 2a; 9:9bB–10, 24, 27b; 10:1, 2b, 25; 11:12, 15, 21–23; 14:6–15 (eliminating some detail). M. Weinfeld, *Deuteronomy and the Deuteronomic School,* Oxford, 1972, 344, suggests adding the formulaic language in 10:8, 25–40; 11:8, 11, 14. B. Peckham, "The Significance of the Book of Joshua in Noth's Theory of the Deuteronomistic History," *The History of Israel's Traditions: The Heritage of Martin Noth,* JSOTSup 182, Sheffield, 1994, 213–34, reviews the place of Joshua in Noth's theory, traces subsequent developments, and criticizes the entire enterprise as fallacious.

4. The most influential proposal in this direction has been that of R. Smend, "Das Gesetz und die Völker: ein Beitrag zur deuteronomistischen Redaktionsgeschichte," *Probleme biblischer*

A second and earlier organizational pattern is visible beneath the DH structure, the horizon of which does not extend much outside the story of conquest victories. The individual narratives of chapters 2–11 are linked together in a way that is completely independent of any deuteronomistic interest or language. Thus the initial spy story (chap. 2, a traditional way to launch a conquest) is attached to the fall of Jericho (chap. 6) by the figure of Rahab, while the Jordan crossing story also links to Jericho through the processional role of the ark (chaps. 3–4). At the same time, the application of the *ḥērem* ban on Jericho leads to the story of Achan, which in turn has been interleaved with the tale of the conquest of Ai (chaps. 7–8). The conquests of Jericho and Ai motivate the Gibeonites to seek a treaty (chap. 9), which in turn is the cause of war with the Jerusalem coalition (chap. 10). News of Israel's successes also leads to victory over a northern coalition under Jabin king of Hazor (chap. 11). The resulting whole has been cemented together by a series of notices describing the fearful reaction of the inhabitants of the land, especially the kings. They hear about Israel and their exploits, they are afraid, and they react. This theme is first brought up by Rahab (2:9–10a, 11a, 24), then repeated at 5:1 with reference to all the Amorite kings. In 9:1–3 it motivates both a hostile alliance of all the kings and the parallel ruse of the Gibeonites. In 10:1–2 and 11:1–2 news of Israelite success also leads to coalition attacks. The same general motif also appears in 6:1, 27. In this way a group of discontinuous stories have been interlocked together into a larger written narrative, one that had an independent existence before being later incorporated into DH.

In this pre-deuteronomistic version of Joshua, Yahweh gives victory to Israel in attacks on the keystone cities of Jericho and Ai, news of which leads to the formation of two ill-fated coalitions, first in the south, then in the north. The enemies are the kings of the old Canaanite city-state system, and Israel's victory over them is complete. Yet at the same time, those elements of the local population who react with prudence and good judgment, that is, Rahab and the Gibeonites, survive the debacle, and their descendants still continue to exist as ethnic communities only partially integrated into Israelite society. In contrast, disobedient Israelite elements represented by Achan and his family, perish.

Theologie, Munich, 1971, 494–509, who traces a nomistic DtrN subsequent to the original historian (1:7–9; 13:2–6; chap. 23). A division between pre-exilic and exilic editions is carried out quite thoroughly by R. Boling, *Joshua,* AB 6, Garden City, N.Y., 1982. He assigns Rahab, interest in east Jordan tribes, cultic matters, and the farewell of chapter 23 to Dtr2. His division between Dtr1 and Dtr2 also encompasses chapters 13–22. Other examples of this approach are A. Mayes, *The Story of Israel between Settlement and Exile,* London, 1983, 40–57; M. O'Brien, *The Deuteronomistic History Hypothesis: A Reassessment,* OBO 92, Göttingen, 1989, 67–81; B. Peckham, *The Composition of the Deuteronomistic History,* HSM 35, Atlanta, 1985, 7–9, 21–68. V. Fritz, *Josua,* HAT I/7, Tübingen, 1994, 3–4, analyzes Joshua into a rather sparse deuteronomistic historian, followed by later deuteronomistic and priestly redactors (RedD, the equivalent of Smend's DtrN, and RedP). Evaluation of all such proposals hinges on how much tension and complexity the critic is prepared to allow in the ideological opinions of biblical authors and editors.

There is a distinct etiological flavor to this pre-deuteronomistic book of Joshua. It describes the origin of great city ruins, the existence of non-Israelite groups, place names, and grave markers. Although the tales told are about an Ephraimite hero and take place mostly in Benjaminite territory, the editorial outlook is distinctly Judahite (for example 10:16–41; 11:2, 16; note the key role played by the ark). Nevertheless, pre-deuteronomistic Joshua claims to be the story of "all Israel," and its geographic coverage represents all parts of the land west of the Jordan. The Red Sea event hovers in the background, as a cause of the enemy's fear (2:10a; cf. 5:1 and significantly Exod. 15:13–16) and as a template for the Jordan crossing.[5]

A third complex of material comprises the narrative of land allotment in chapters 13–19, along with information about the cities of refuge and the levitical cities (chaps. 20–21). Here the redactional picture is less clear. The most reasonable conclusion to draw from the duplication of the phrase about Joshua's advanced age in 13:1 and 23:1 is that what follows 13:1 was inserted into the DH form of the book at a later date. While Joshua's old age is a perfectly appropriate motive for his last words, it seems less pertinent to the task of land division. Certainly having two different scenes motivated by the pressure of Joshua's advanced age would be unlikely in a story line created by a single author or editor. Evidently part of 23:1 was copied and carried forward to provide an attachment point for the insertion of supplementary geographic data between the end of chapter 12 and the DH summary statement of 21:43–45.

This geographic information rests on source material, some of which originally had an administrative purpose. This is certainly true of the district system behind 15:20–62 and 18:21–28. On the other hand, much of this material seems to have been concocted by scribal erudition on the basis of traditions and source lists of uncertain origin. With the exception of the artificial system of levitical cities in chapter 21, there is nothing intrinsically "priestly" about any of this geographic material,[6] nor, with the exception of 14:6–15 and the MT version of chapter 20, is it perceptibly deuteronomistic. This geographic data also underwent amplification after it was inserted (e.g., the insertion of 13:2–6, chaps. 20 and 21, and perhaps 14:6–15; 15:13–19; 19:49–50). Some narrative bits (15:13–19, 63; 16:10; 17:11–13) and some geographic details (19:29–30, 42) are also found in Judges chapter 1. The question of literary dependence at this point is disputed, although there is evidence of reciprocal influence. The existence of a common source is a possibility.

Yet another problem is raised by the presence of a second farewell speech in chapter 24. This chapter has been the focus of an extraordinary amount of

---

5. Again this analysis follows Noth, *Josua*, 11–13. Noth termed this author the *Sammler* ("collector" or "compiler") and proposed a date around 900 B.C.E. In Noth's view, this *Sammler* also contributed 10:40–42 and 11:16–20.

6. As doggedly insisted by Mowinckel, *Tetrateuch-Pentateuch-Hexateuch*, 51–76.

scholarly attention.[7] Nearly everything about it is controversial, including whether or not deuteronomistic language is present and whether it reflects genuine tradition or is an artificial literary composition.

Finally, there are aspects of the final form of Joshua that are priestly in language and outlook. The classic notion that the Pentateuchal source P can be found in Joshua still has its supporters,[8] and the presence of some P-like language is undeniable in chapters 13–21. Eleazar as co-leader beside Joshua (14:1–2; 19:51; 21:1–2) and the tent of meeting (18:1; 19:51) point to a desire to include priestly details into the story of land distribution. Joshua 13:21b–22 seems to have been taken from Num. 31:8, and there is a literary relationship of some sort between Josh. 17:2–6 and Num. 26:29–33; 27:1–11. A special problem is raised by Josh. 22:9–34, a narrative in which P-like language is present (vv. 9, 19, 22, 29), and Phinehas and the tabernacle are important to the story in its present form. P-like touches outside of chapters 13–22 (e.g., 3:4; 4:19; 9:15b, 18–21) definitely indicate that priestly redactional interests played a role in the creation of the final form of Joshua. To go so far as to link this minor redactional activity with the Priestly writing in the Pentateuch, however, is to go beyond the evidence.

4. Form Criticism

From the perspective of form criticism, Joshua as a whole may be classified as historiography. As such it is a systematic account of Israel's past intended to build and strengthen group identity and to explain the contours of its readers' present. Joshua utilizes sources (popular stories, geographic lists, etc.) and traces cause and effect over time. Of course as is typical in biblical history writing, the sources are used uncritically and Joshua's concept of historical causation is primarily theological (e.g., 11:20) rather than political or economic.

The raw materials that stand behind the written form of Joshua can be classified into genres, permitting at least something to be said about their pre-literary history and intention. The sources used to compile the pre-deuteronomistic book of Joshua (chaps. 2–11) derive from the storytelling tradition of the people. These tales were often perpetuated and retold in connection with

---

7. Two important studies are G. Schmitt, *Der Landtag von Sichem,* Arbeiten zur Theologie I/15, Stuttgart, 1964, and M. Mölle, *Der sogenannte Landtag zu Sichem,* FB 42, Würzburg, 1980. For a thorough review of scholarship, see W. Koopmans, *Joshua 24 as Poetic Narrative,* JSOT-Sup 93, Sheffield, 1990, 1–95.

8. See J. Blenkinsopp, "The Structure of P," *CBQ* 38 (1976): 275–92, who points out the striking use of "subdue the land" in both Gen. 1:28 and Josh. 18:1. Also see E. Cortese, *Joshua 13–21: Ein priesterschriftlicher Abschnitt im deuteronomistischen Geschichtswerk,* OBO 94, Göttingen, 1989, and J. Peterson, "Priestly Materials in Joshua 13–22: A Return to the Hexateuch?" *HAR* 4 (1980): 131–45.

places and landmarks (a city mound, a valley, a grave cairn). There is some-times an association with a place name (Gilgal, Foreskins Hill, Valley of Achor, Ai). Etiological concerns are visible, although the recognition of etiol-ogy hardly exhausts the intention or purpose of these narratives. Conquest nar-ratives about Jericho and Ai explained the presence of imposing city ruins. Di-vine Warrior tales glorified Yahweh by celebrating victories at Beth-horon and the waters of Merom. Stories stimulated by supposed gravesites were re-counted about Achan in the Valley of Achor and the five kings at Makkedah. The trickster tales of how Rahab and the Gibeonites shrewdly seized their op-portunity to survive concentrate on interethnic relationships. A narrative about a numinous appearance to Joshua near Jericho (5:13–15) breaks off too abruptly to be classified, but clearly stems from an earlier tradition of some sort. More minor genres also appear: the genealogy of Achan, the doxological poetic fragment of 10:12–13, geographic descriptions (10:40–41; 11:16–17). More difficult to classify is the narrative of the Jordan crossing in chapters 3–4. Although often asserted to be cult legend involving ceremonies practiced at Gilgal, the central focus is the miraculous crossing of the Jordan by the ark, while many of the supposedly cultic details are redactional supplements. Per-haps the precursor tale was something like an "ark legend," similar to the miraculous and triumphant progress of the ark recounted in 1 Samuel 4–6 and 2 Samuel 6.

The issue of etiology is controversial. On the one hand it is clear that the mere presence of a "to this day" testimony formula means little. These are of-ten redactional comments rather than original narrative components,[9] although their presence may sometimes be an accurate editorial recognition of a story's etiological character. Etiological concerns must be sought out in the essential shape of a narrative, and they are undeniably present in Joshua. Such narratives were told in order to help people come to terms with a landscape full of ancient city ruins, the neighboring presence of alien populations, and other social and geographic realities. Once Israel came to believe that they had entered the land as conquerors, imposing city ruins like Jericho, Ai, and Hazor would naturally come to be explained as evidence of a conquest achieved with the aid of Yah-weh. The original social location of these stories in a peasant society may be indicated by how often "kings" serve as the antagonists.[10]

---

9. B. Childs, "A Study of the Formula 'Until this Day,'" *JBL* 82 (1963): 279–92; B. Long, *The Problem of Etiological Narrative in the Old Testament*, BZAW 108, Berlin, 1968; Van Dyke, "The Function of So-called Etiological Elements in Narratives, *ZAW* 102 (1990): 19–33. The for-mula usually intends to bolster the trustworthiness of the story to which it is added and to heighten its entertainment value. It indicates to the reader that the narrative is still significant now, not just a matter of antiquitarian interest.

10. On this topic more generally, see L. Rowlett, "Inclusion, Exclusion and Marginality in the Book of Joshua," *JSOT* 55 (1992): 15–23.

However, recognition that etiology played some role in the origin and transmission of a given narrative does not mean that etiology was its only purpose. Nor does this imply that etiology was always the most important reason for a story's continued existence in the culture. Other more significant functions of such narratives would have focused on social and community matters. Thus the Achan story provides a warning. The Rahab and Gibeonite stories help ease ethnic tensions. The conquest stories praise Yahweh. More generally, these tales would have built national pride and bolstered Israel's claim to its territory. It is this fact which best explains the appearance of such stories in Joshua, for the overall intention of the book is to strengthen national identity and assert Israel's possession of its ancestral lands. Joshua as a whole is an etiology in the sense that it seeks to disclose how the people who called themselves Israel came to be who they were and where they were.

Whether the DH version of the book utilized additional oral or traditional sources beyond those available in the pre-deuteronomistic book is less clear, although the literary composition of chapter 23 employs the testament form. One may point to the written genre of "list" in 12:9–24, most of which represents an independent source used by DH. The post-DH final form of Joshua includes five narratives with similar plots supporting land tenure: 14:6–15; 15:13–19; 17:4–6; 17:14–18; 21:1–3 (a literary imitation). These may be labeled "land grant narratives." Chapter 24 is best seen as a purely literary composition.

The final form of Joshua also added toponym lists and boundary descriptions in chapters 13–21. Of these, 15:20–62 plus 18:21–28 is unquestionably a genuine administrative document, while chapter 21 is just as clearly an artificial scribal composition, although the first part (vv. 13–18) represents a source list of some kind. The other geographic materials are a mixture of border descriptions and city lists. The prehistory and interpretation of this material has been the subject of much study.[11] To the degree that these materials once may have had administrative functions, one can postulate that border descriptions would have regulated relations between tribes, while city lists would have facilitated the collection of taxes and the utilization of forced labor and military resources. However, the actual origin of these toponym lists may instead reflect scribal erudition. Perhaps they served as exemplars for students to copy, in the way that such pedagogic lists were used in other ancient Near Eastern cultures. Whatever their pedigree, these lists and border descriptions were

---

11. The most accessible comprehensive discussions are those of Y. Aharoni, *Land of the Bible,* Philadelphia, 1979, 232–62, 298–305, 347–56; and Z. Kallai, *Historical Geography of the Bible,* Leiden, 1986, 99–476. This commentary devotes relatively little space to the problem of the identification of city sites (toponymy) or to the disputed placement of boundaries. Attention is paid instead to the literary organization of these geographic descriptions and their literary and ideological function within Joshua. An appendix lists the modern Arabic names and map reference numbers of those indentifications that are undisputed or highly probable.

preserved and organized in a scribal environment, enriched with summary totals, clarified by the insertion of verbs between the border points, and glossed with explanatory data. In their present form they are literary exercises in cognitive mapping, performed for social and ideological purposes. Like the conquest narratives of the foregoing chapters, these geographic materials strengthened national identity and asserted Israel's secure possession of its ancestral lands. It is instructive to compare these Joshua texts to Ezek. 45:1–8; 47:13–48:29. The ideological map given in Joshua is certainly more realistic than that of Ezekiel, but the literary and theological purposes are similar.

5. Literary Analysis

Diachronic analysis is not the only way for an interpreter to encounter Joshua. Literary factors such as plot, point of view, the play of language, reader response, and the coherence of the final form of the book also require attention.[12] Several literary studies of Joshua have appeared in recent years.[13] These studies have wrestled with the book's most obvious incongruities. For example, the conquest is asserted to be complete and the enemy totally exterminated (1:3–6; 10:40–42; 11:16–23; 21:43–45), yet both alien nations and unpossessed land remain (13:2–6; 15:63; 16:10; 17:12–13; 23:4–5, 7, 12–13). Israel is asserted to have been completely obedient to Yahweh and the law (24:31), yet clear examples of disobedience stand out (the oath with Rahab, Achan, the covenant with Gibeon). Viewed historically, of course, this ambiguity is the result of the book's growth and development involving confident non-deuteronomistic stories being overlaid by DH's more guarded viewpoint from the perspective of deuteronomic law and the upcoming story of Israel's disobedience. This was overlaid in turn by optimistic geographic materials and then further glossed by negative reports of incomplete conquest. Yet the reader

12. Historical-critical and literary approaches should not be treated as mutually exclusive or antagonistic methods of interpretation. Each makes valid attempts to answer a different set of questions. Experience shows that insights from one method often illuminate one's use of the other. It is often possible to coordinate voices and perspectives discovered in a biblical text by synchronic methods with watershed events in Israel's history. Conversely, recognition of diachronic layers in a text should not undermine appreciation for the literary effect and artistry of its final, canonical form.

13. L. Eslinger, *Into the Hands of the Living God,* JSOTSup 84, Sheffield, 1989, 25–54, sees the book as deeply ironic and Yahweh as a not entirely positive character. L. Hawk, *Every Promise Fulfilled: Contesting Plots in Joshua,* Louisville, Ky., 1991, describes an enigmatic book with two positive plots of obedience and national integrity opposed by two counter-plots of disobedience and fragmentation. R. Polzin, *Moses and the Deuteronomist,* New York, 1980, 16–24, 84–91, 117–27, traces a narrative voice of rigid obedience modified by a second voice of more moderate tolerance. Rowlett, "Inclusion, Exclusion and Marginality in the Book of Joshua," uses Foucault's theory of power as an exercise in social control to discover that Joshua intends to facilitate a process of state building.

of the final complex whole needs some sort of interpretive framework to come to terms with this multifaceted ambiguity. In all such literary readings of Joshua, however, the book remains necessarily open-ended and enigmatic. As is often true of biblical literature, it is up to the reader to hear and appraise the contradictory messages and then create from them a pattern of meaning that relates to the reader's particular situation.

The final, canonical form of Joshua offers the reader a reasonably coherent plot. The book begins and ends with interpretive speech (chaps. 1 and 23–24), as well as with transitions of leadership from Moses to Joshua and then from Joshua to succeeding generations. The narratives of chapters 2–11 are woven together by links between story pairs (Rahab-Jericho; Jordan crossing-Jericho; Jericho-Achan; Achan-Ai; Rahab-Gibeon; south coalition-north coalition), by the theme of hearing and fearing (2:9–10a; 5:1; 9:1–3; 10:1–2; 11:1–2), and by the organizing device of central, southern, and northern campaigns. At the same time, a somewhat muddled calendar of two seven-day periods (1:10–11; 3:1–3, 5; 4:19; 5:10; 6:15) holds crossing, passover, and Jericho together. The narrative progress is punctuated by cultic actions at Gilgal (chap. 5) and Shechem (8:30–35). These illustrate Israel's conscientious obedience to the commands that accompanied Yahweh's initial promises in chapter 1.

Joshua reports the conquest in four subplots: Jericho, Ai, south coalition, north coalition. The first two focus on "impregnable" cities, the other two on alliances. In spite of their substantial differences, the four subplots also exhibit similarities. The objects of Israel's hostile action are twofold: enemy kings and enemy cities. Often the coordinated fates of both are highlighted. All four subplots speak of the difficulties inherent in Israel's task (6:1; 7:2–5; 10:3–5, 6b; 11:1–5). These challenges are countered by statements of assurance from Yahweh (6:2; 8:1–2, 18; 10:8, 19; 11:6). Yahweh and Joshua give instructions (6:3–7; 8:2, 4–8, 18; on booty: 6:18–19; 8:2; 11:6b). Victory is won by varying proportions of divine and human effort, sometimes involving the divine war motif of dawn (6:15; 8:10; 10:9) and marvels done by Yahweh (6:20; 10:11–14). Commands about booty are explicitly obeyed (6:24; 8:27; 11:14). The totality of victory is emphasized by language about fire (6:24; 8:19, 28; 11:11), slaughter (6:21; 8:22, 25–26; 10:10–11, 20, 28, etc.; 11:8, 11–12, 14), and ruin (6:26; 8:28; 11:10). The fate of the kings receives special attention (6:2; 8:2, 29; 10:16–18, 22–27; 11:10, 12). A testimony formula may seek to validate the story by reference to some present reality (6:25; 8:29; 10:27). The literary effect of this reiteration of motifs is to suggest the inevitability and totality of Yahweh's victory, something also implied by the patterned repetition of 10:28–39 and the methodical list of 12:9–24.

The summary of chapter 12 terminates the first narrative movement, that of military conquest. The list of defeated kings emphasizes the scope of victory and prepares for a second narrative movement (chaps. 13–21) in which geographic catalogs are presented in a narrative framework describing land distribution. The preceding movement is oriented towards action and mobility and tells of foundational triumphs. This second movement is more static and describes the shape of idealized tribal settlement patterns. Whereas the first movement is predominantly optimistic, the second admits to shortfalls in Israel's realization of total conquest. Other narratives about land allocation are interspersed into this second movement, in which promises are kept and problems are solved (Caleb, Othniel, the daughters of Zelophehad, extra land for Joseph, a grant to Joshua). This second movement is enclosed in a rough way by the brackets of Joshua's old age (13:1; 23:1) and the evaluative brackets of 11:23 and 21:43–45. Joshua's charge to and dismissal of the east Jordan tribes (1:12–18; 22:1–6) form an even wider set of brackets that holds the first and second movements together.

The story of the altar built by the east Jordan tribes (22:9–34) functions as a parenetic summary similar in purpose to chapters 23–24, albeit in narrative rather than sermonic form. It reflects on questions of continued national unity and loyalty to the single sanctuary of a single people, questions unavoidably raised by tribal allotment and dispersal. Like the two later summaries, it looks to the future by raising the specter of punishment for disobedience (vv. 20, 31). Joshua concludes with an exploration of the meaning of the conquest in chapter 23, followed by a second summary in chapter 24 reflecting on the implications of the entire election tradition of Genesis through Joshua. The book's overall move from optimism to pessimism is completed by the threats of these last two chapters, which prepare for the calamities to follow in Judges and Kings.

Joshua son of Nun remains the chief unifying factor throughout (see "The Figure of Joshua" below), but his leadership role is somewhat diluted in the second half of the book by the appearance of the priests Eleazar and Phinehas (14:1; 17:4; 19:51; 21:1; chap. 22). From a literary standpoint, however, Yahweh is the most prominent character. The plot line emerges from promises made by Yahweh (1:3, 6; 5:6; 21:43, 45; 23:14) and Yahweh's purposes in history (11:20). These events are the direct outgrowth of Yahweh's earlier acts of exodus and Red Sea crossing (2:10; 4:23; 5:2–9; 9:9; 24:4–7, 17). Yahweh both installs Joshua as leader and is present with him throughout (1:9; 3:7; 4:14). As Divine Warrior, Yahweh engages in battle and wins all victories as the one who "fought for Israel" (10:14; 23:10), or withholds victory when it suits the divine purpose (7:1–5). Through the mechanism of the lot, Yahweh guides the process of land division (14:2; 15:1; 18:11, etc.). A significant offstage character is Joshua's predecessor Moses, whose example of leadership and legacy of lawgiving powerfully influences the course of events and the reader's evaluation of Joshua. Moses' name appears almost sixty times in Joshua, and more subtle allusions to him may be intended in 5:15 and 24:25–26.

6. Theological Themes

The book of Joshua is a literary production designed to create and support the identity of the people it calls "all Israel."[14] They are the people of Yahweh the Divine Warrior. They are the rightful masters of the land of Canaan. They are a people formed by the demands of the law given through Moses. The book seeks to give its readers the courage to meet whatever current challenges are brought on by their identity as Yahweh's people. It also seeks to communicate hope for a future fulfillment of Yahweh's promises. Various literary and rhetorical strategies are used to achieve these purposes: celebrations of the Divine Warrior's victories, narratives about obedience, disobedience, and land grants, verbal maps of claimed territory, sermons urging compliance with the law. Stories told in different places by different segments of the population have been gathered together as the common achievement of "all Israel" (3:17; 8:15, etc.) under the common leadership of one leader (1:17; 3:7; 4:14; 6:27) at one time (10:42). The invocation of enemies and a sharp distinction between "them" (Amorites, Canaanites) and "us" ("all Israel") have always been effective ways to forge a shared sense of identity. The book of Joshua is a witness to the power of a shared story to generate, define, and defend a community. Five aspects of this theological story deserve further exploration: the land, the conquest, Israel's enemies, the practice of *ḥērem,* and obedience to the law of Moses.

Land

The theological importance of the land to Israel's sense of identity can hardly be overestimated.[15] Canaan is Yahweh's land (22:19, 32) and it is a good land (5:6, 12; 23:13, 15, 16). Yahweh's gift of the land is the core plot action of Joshua, constituting an arc of promise and fulfillment that begins in 1:2–6. This promise had originally been made to Israel's ancestors (1:6; 5:6; 21:43–44), and its realization is referred to persistently (2:9, 24; 3:10; 5:12; 10:40–42; 11:16–17, 23; 12:7–8; 14:15b; 21:43–45; 23:4–5; 24:13, 28). Because it was none other than Yahweh the Divine Warrior who granted the land, Israel had an inalienable right to it, unless Yahweh himself should choose otherwise (23:13, 15–16;

---

14. For Joshua's role in building national identity within the context of DH, see E. Mullen, *Narrative History and Ethnic Boundaries: The Deuteronomistic History and the Creation of Israelite National Identity,* SBLSS, Atlanta, 1993, 87–119. Instructive in this regard are numerous parallels between Joshua and the foundation accounts of Greek colonies traced by M. Weinfeld, "The Pattern of the Israelite Settlement in Canaan," *Congress Volume Jerusalem 1986,* VTSup 40, Leiden, 1988, 270–83.

15. W. Brueggemann, *The Land: Place as Gift, Promise, and Challenge in Biblical Faith,* OBT, Philadelphia, 1977; N. Habel, *The Land Is Mine,* OBT, Minneapolis, 1995.

24:20). For exilic and post-exilic readers, the land represented both fulfilled promise and defaulted legacy, simultaneously a sign of Yahweh's fidelity and Israel's infidelity. The land was the center of ethnic identity and the object of both regret and hope.

Use of the sacred lot to distribute the land (14:2; 19:51) communicates that the authority of Yahweh stands behind Israel's settlement patterns. These are not merely a result of historical contingency, but further tokens of Israel's authentic claim on Palestine. When apportioned by lot, the land became Israel's "inheritance" (*naḥălâ*, 11:23), a word used almost fifty times from chapter 13 on. As "inheritance," what was initially transferred by Yahweh's act of land grant was passed down through the family as a central focus of group identity.

In deuteronomistic thought, "rest" (*nwḥ* hiphil, *menûḥâ*) signifies Israel's unthreatened possession of the land. Promised by Deut. 12:9–10, the achievement of rest begins with the conquest (Josh. 1:13, 15; 21:44; 22:4; 23:1), but culminates in David's victories (2 Sam. 7:1, 11; 1 Kings 8:56). A second phrase, "the land had rest from war" (11:23; 14:15; root *šqṭ*), communicates the peace experienced in the land after Yahweh's victory and prepares for the use of this expression in Judges.

Conquest

The conquest theme is not the only way the Hebrew Bible conceptualizes Israel's right to possess the land. Sagas recounting the patriarchs' travels through Canaan, their establishment of sanctuaries, and stories about their tombs, all promoted Israel's claims to the land. In Gen. 31:19–54 territorial strife between Israel (Jacob) and Syria (Laban) leads to the erection of a boundary marker. What one might term a poetic approach is represented by the motif of Yahweh's planting Israel in the land like a vine or tree (Exod. 15:17; 2 Sam. 7:10; Ezek. 17:22–23; Ps. 80:9–12 [8–11E], and Amos 2:9–10 for "unplanting" the Amorites). The tribal blessings seem to have been another traditional way to tie elements of Israel to the land (compare Gen. 49:13–15; Deut. 33:12, 20–23, 28). A more mythic concept is presented by Deut. 32:8–9, where the world's nations are assigned to their respective gods and their boundaries are thereby fixed. Israel was given as Yahweh's "portion" (*ḥēleq*) and "inheritance" (*naḥălâ*). The parallel to the language of Joshua is striking. Another way of claiming land is embodied in Num. 21:27–30, where Israel's acquired title to territory north of the Arnon is documented by a traditional song recalling a previous Amorite victory over Moab. Jephthah uses similar reasoning in Judg. 11:14–27. Nevertheless, understanding Israel's ownership of the land in terms of a conquest tradition became the most common pattern. Conquest stories are told in Genesis 34, Numbers 13–14, 21, 32, and Judges 1, 17–18. The conquest is referred to in Pss. 44:3–4 [2–3E]; 78:54–55; 105:44; 135:10–12;

136:17–22. Exodus 15:13–17 links the terror of the foe and Israel's settlement directly to the Red Sea event (compare Ps. 114:1–3). This ideology of conquest was always vital to Israel because their hold on the land was always at risk. The book of Judges recalls that external threats were characteristic of Israel's earliest history. During the monarchy, the territory east of the Jordan was imperilled by Moab, while Syria threatened the north. The collapse of the kingdom of Israel disconnected everything north of the kingdom of Judah from native political control, and subsequent pressure from Assyria on Judah led to additional losses of land on the west. With the fall of Judah, Edomite incursions alienated large tracts to the south. After the restoration, the disparity between the restricted geography of contemporary reality and the more extensive claims made by tradition remained acute. Against this bleak background, Joshua's conquest tales must have encouraged readers in every generation. Even the Maccabees found inspiration in them.[16] It is likely that Joshua concentrates so intensely on the region of Benjamin precisely because it was so often the focus of territorial disputes. Early on, Benjamin was under Philistine pressure, then an arena of struggle between Judah and Israel, and still later encompassed the border between Judah and the Assyrian provinces.

To extol Yahweh as the Divine Warrior was to engage in doxology (Exod. 15:1, 3). This was a common form of religious and political expression in the ancient Near East.[17] Recounting tales of conquest was a way of praising Yahweh's power and graciousness. In this sense then, the book of Joshua is a theological confession, summarized in the creedal statement: "Yahweh fought for Israel" (10:14, 42; 23:3, 10). Comparison with the Mesha Inscription (*ANET* 320–21) is instructive in this regard. The two works share concepts and vocabulary, notably the roots *ḥrm*, *grš*, *yrš*. Both speak of enemy kings, divine commands to conquer, votive gifts, enumeration of the enemy, slave labor, and the names of towns claimed by conquest. There are major differences, of course, in that Mesha speaks of building projects and is referring to recent events rather than a tradition about the distant past. The striking point is that

16. 2 Macc. 12:15. A corollary of this circumstance is that the dating of the post-DH portions of Joshua to almost any period is at least conceivable. A radical example of late dating is J. Strange, "The Book of Joshua: A Hasmonean Manifesto?" *History and Traditions of Early Israel,* VTSup 50, Leiden, 1993, 136–41. Chapters 13–19 leave a vacuum in the Samaritan territory of central Ephraim/Manasseh and concentrate on Judah, Galilee, and east of the Jordan, the traditional "three lands of the Jews" (cf. *m. Sheb.* 9:2). This suggests that proposals for a very late date for this material at least deserve a hearing.

17. S. Kang, *Divine War in the Old Testament and in the Ancient Near East,* BZAW 177, Berlin, 1989; P. Miller, *The Divine Warrior in Early Israel,* HSM 5, Cambridge, 1973; M. Weinfeld, "Divine Intervention in War in Ancient Israel and in the Ancient Near East," *History, Historiography and Interpretation,* Jerusalem, 1983, 121–47; M. Weippert, " 'Heiliger Krieg' in Israel und Assyrien. Kritische Anmerkungen zu Gerhard von Rads Konzept des 'Heiligen Krieges im alten Israel,' " *ZAW* 84 (1972): 460–93.

both texts are theological reviews of the past intended to celebrate and substantiate ownership of national territory and to honor the national god. Modern readers experience discomfort with the notion of divinely directed conquest. We naturally read Joshua against the background of the Crusades, colonial conquests in the Americas, Africa, and Asia, and the physical and cultural destruction of indigenous peoples by aggressive outsiders. To us Joshua may sound like a theological justification for the forceful appropriation of land that rightfully belongs to others. Certainly a hermeneutic of suspicion is not out of place here, especially since the ideology of Joshua has been used to justify such policies in North America, South Africa, and the Middle East.[18] However, the interpreter also needs to remember that the communities who formulated and read Joshua were groups always threatened by the loss of their land, or even landless exiles hoping for its restoration. It was most often Israel who was victimized as an indigenous people menaced by politically and technically superior outside forces. In Joshua, this superiority is illustrated by enemy kings with iron chariots and cities with impregnable walls. Israel perceived that its culture and religion were being endangered by hostile outsiders and alien groups with whom they shared the land. The book of Joshua was part of their reaction to this threat.

The Enemy

The concept of the enemy is expressed in terms of nations and city-state kings. In the DH form of the book, the nations appear in a stereotypical list of six or seven (3:10; 9:1; 11:3; 12:8; 24:11; compare Exod. 3:8 etc.; Deut. 7:1; 20:17).[19] Otherwise they are generally termed Amorites and Canaanites, though without much geographic consistency (5:1; 7:7, 9; 10:5–6, 12; 17:16, 18; 24:12, 15, 18). "Canaanite" is the usual term for those who remain after the conquest (13:3–4; 16:10; 17:12–13; Geshurites and Maacathites in 13:13, Jebusites in 15:63). Ideologically the extermination of the nations glorifies Yahweh as warrior and promotes Israel's claim to the land. Conversely, their continued existence functions simultaneously as an opportunity (13:6; 17:18; 23:5), as a danger (23:7, 12; 24:15), and as a potential source of threatened punishment (23:13). The multifaceted ideological function of these enemy nations explains how the deuteronomistic level of Joshua can simultaneously affirm

18. F. Deist, "The Dangers of Deuteronomy: A Page from the Tradition History of the Book," *Studies in Deuteronomy,* VTSup 53, Leiden, 1994, 13–29.

19. T. Ishida, "The Structure and Historical Implications of the Lists of Pre-Israelite Nations," *Bib* 60 (1979): 461–90. For an analysis of the theological and literary role of the enemy in Joshua, see G. Mitchell, *Together in the Land,* JSOTSup 134, Sheffield, 1993, 122–84. These names probably reflect the social and political conditions of the period of composition rather than genuine historical memory. See N. Lemche, *The Canaanites and Their Land,* JSOTSup 110, Sheffield, 1991; Rose, *Deuteronomist und Jahwist,* 215–220; J. Van Seters, "The Terms 'Amorite' and 'Hittite' in the Old Testament," *VT* 22 (1972): 64–81.

that every foe met in battle was destroyed (1:5; 11:20; 21:44), while some nevertheless survived as a danger and threat (chap. 23). The first assertion glorifies the faithfulness of Yahweh and looks back to the promises of Deuteronomy. The second explores the theme of disobedience and penalty and looks forward to the story told in Judges and Kings.

Joshua suggests that it was the kings of Canaan who were the primary enemy. This is apparent in chaps. 8, 10–12, but elsewhere as well. Even if some peoples and territory remained unsubdued, the book insists that all Amorite and Canaanite kings were obliterated. Perhaps there is some memory of the breakdown of Canaan's political structure as a city-state system in this pattern, but ideologically it reflects the mythic language found in Pss. 2, 48, 72, where Yahweh's enemies are foreign kings. It may also echo the antimonarchic, peasant social location of the original storytelling tradition.

The Ban (*Ḥērem*)

The enemy is treated as *ḥērem,* something devoted to destruction.[20] Rather than understanding this institution primarily as a sort of vow or sacrifice, a proper understanding of *ḥērem* must begin with seeing it as one of the categories in Israel's cultural classification system, not unlike the categories "holy" or "unclean."[21] If something or someone falls into the classification *ḥērem,* he, she, or it is a possession of Yahweh and therefore not to be used by humans. Because *ḥērem* is to be withdrawn from general use, everything classified as such must either be destroyed or given over to the priests or the temple treasury (6:19, 24; Num. 18:14; Ezek. 44:29). Like impurity or holiness, *ḥērem* was a potentially contagious quality (6:18; 7:12; Deut. 7:26) that needed to be handled circumspectly. Divine war was not the only possible context for a thing or person being treated as *ḥērem,* as Lev. 27:21, 28–29 demonstrate.

The fruits of Yahweh's victories were naturally Yahweh's property and therefore susceptible to falling into the category of *ḥērem.* In a culture in which war captives often became slaves of the victors, any elements of the enemy population which were considered as *ḥērem* would have had to be killed in order to prevent this from happening. This would also be true of any livestock that might happen to fall into the *ḥērem* category. However, precisely what in the way of captured wealth was supposed to be treated as *ḥērem* is handled differently in different biblical texts. The most expansive application of the category is described at Jericho: all the people and all the booty are *ḥērem.* Obviously from a narrative point of view, only this exceptionally unrestricted version of *ḥērem* could be used

---

20. The most recent full-scale study is P. Stern, *The Biblical Ḥerem: A Window on Israel's Religious Experience,* BJS 211, Atlanta, 1991. Also see N. Lohfink, "*ḥāram,*" *TDOT,* V, 180–99 and M. Malul, "Taboo," *Dictionary of Deities and Demons in the Bible,* Leiden, 1995, 1559–65.

21. R. Nelson, *Raising Up a Faithful Priest,* Louisville, Ky., 1993, 17–38.

to lead into the Achan story. The only other examples of treating inanimate valuables as *ḥērem* are Deuteronomy's policies towards an apostate Israelite city (Deut. 13:16–18 [15–17E]; cf. Exod. 22:19 [20E]) and pagan cult objects (Deut. 7:25–26).

According to Deuteronomy, in warfare against non-Israelite cities in the land of promise "everything that breathes" was to be categorized as *ḥērem* (Deut. 20:16–17; Josh. 10:40; 11:11, 14).[22] Obviously the entire human population of these cities was to be massacred (compare Deut. 7:2; Josh. 8:26; 10:28–39), but whether livestock was also to be treated as *ḥērem* is less clear. Domestic animals were indeed *ḥērem* according to the opinion behind 1 Samuel 15 and Josh. 6:21, but not according to DH's own reading of Deuteronomy (Deut. 2:34–35; 3:6–7; Josh. 8:2, 26–27; 11:11, 14). In the cases of Rahab's family and the Gibeonites, the usual requirements of *ḥērem* are short-circuited by the counter-requirement that oaths must remain inviolate. This total slaughter of the enemy, appalling to the modern reader, is celebrated in Joshua as exemplary obedience to the commands of Yahweh (10:40; 11:12, 15, 20).

Obedience

Yahweh commands Joshua not only to fight but to obey (1:7–8). Compliance with the book of the law (8:30–35; implicitly in 8:29 and 10:27; 23:6; 24:26) and the commands of Yahweh and Moses (1:13; 4:10; 9:24; 10:40; 11:12, 15, 20; 13:6; 14:2, 5; 17:4; 21:2, 8; 22:2, 5) are a constant theme. A number of plots are shaped on the pattern of command and subsequent obedience, including the Jordan crossing (chaps. 3–4), Jericho (chap. 6), and Ai (chap. 8). Circumcision and passover are observed in the proper manner (5:2–12). At the first opportunity Joshua observes the directives of Deut. 11:29–30 and 27:1–13, at least approximately (8:30–35). This public written display of the law emphasizes its importance and makes it accessible to all. Joshua's solemn reading of the law imposes the demand for obedience on the entire social structure of Israel. Yet if much of the book asserts Israel's obedience, the issue of disobedience is also explored in the narratives about Achan (chap. 7), the Gibeonites (chap. 9), and the altar of the east Jordan tribes (chap. 22). The two final addresses of Joshua challenge the Israel of the future, that is the readers of the book, to obey the most important mandate of all, to worship Yahweh and Yahweh alone (23:6–8, 11, 16; 24:14, 23). The plot of Joshua as a whole illustrates the deuteronomistic parenetic formula that obedience leads to success and disobedience to ruin.

---

22. Deuteronomy's policy for "far off" cities that resisted was to put all adult males to the sword, while the women, children, livestock, and wealth could be utilized as booty (Deut. 20:12–14). The category of *ḥērem* does not seem to come into play in this case at all.

7. The Figure of Joshua

The plot of Joshua stretches out between the death of Moses and the death of Joshua, who begins as the servant of Moses ("attendant," 1:1), but at the end is called "servant of Yahweh" (24:29). Traditions about Joshua are most substantially anchored to the site of his inheritance and burial at Timnath-serah in Ephraim (19:49–50; 24:30), a grave that later textual developments (LXX 21:42D; 24:30A) and general Palestinian practice suggest would have been the object of popular veneration. 1 Chronicles 7:27 provides Joshua with an Ephraimite genealogy. Because chapters 2–9 center on the territory of Benjamin, Joshua is often thought to be a somewhat later addition to these stories, perhaps as a unifying element added in the first stage of collecting and writing. As an Ephraimite hero, he may have been most originally at home in the Divine Warrior narrative centered on Ephraimite Beth-horon (10:10–14). Tradition also knows him as a faithful spy with Caleb, but a critical reading of the texts involved (particularly 14:6–8; Num. 13:30–31; Deut. 1:34–36) suggests that he was a latecomer to this role as well.[23]

Joshua is presented as the successor to Moses (1:5; 3:7; 4:14) who emulates the pattern of Moses in several ways.[24] Crossing the Jordan recapitulates the Red Sea event (4:23). Joshua's encounter with the commander of Yahweh's army echoes the burning bush experience (5:13–15 and Exod. 3:2–5). He repeats Moses' function as intercessor (7:6–9 and Deut. 9:25–29). He holds up his sword against the enemy much as Moses holds up his arms (8:18 and Exod. 17:11). Their parallel roles as conquerors and then distributors of the land are evident when 12:1–6 and 13:8–33 are read in parallel with 12:7–24 and chapters 14–19. However, Joshua does not take over Moses' office as lawgiver (with the possible exception of 24:25), but instead consistently points back to the law which Moses gave as the standard for national fidelity (1:7–8, 13; 4:10; 8:30–35; 11:12–15; 22:2; 23:6). Like Moses, Joshua sometimes speaks as a prophet (6:26; 7:13; 24:2).

Joshua is also presented as a royal figure, one who particularly resembles Josiah. This becomes evident when one compares:

> 1:6–9 to Deut. 17:18–20 and 1 Kings 2:1–4, the royal standard of courage and obedience

---

23. The classic study of Joshua's place in the conquest tradition is A. Alt, "Josua," *Kleine Scriften* I, Munich, 1953, 176–92. For the notion that Joshua is secondary to many Pentateuchal texts, see M. Noth, *A History of Pentateuchal Traditions,* Chico, Calif., 1981, 175–77.

24. See J. Porter, "The Succession of Joshua," *Proclamation and Presence,* Richmond, 1970, 102–32. For a comparison to Elisha, see C. Schäfer-Lichtenberger, " 'Josua' und 'Elischa': eine biblische Argumentation zur Begründung der Autorität und Legitimität des Nachfolgers," *ZAW* 101 (1989), 198–222, and "Josua und Elischa—Ideale Typen von Führerschaft in Israel," *Wünschet Jerusalem Frieden,* Frankfurt, 1988, 273–82.

1:7 and 23:6 to 2 Kings 22:2, the royal standard of undevi-
ating integrity
5:10–12 to 2 Kings 23:21–23, royal sponsorship of a correct
passover
8:30–35 to 2 Kings 23:2–3, royal leadership in pledging loyalty to the law

In the context of Deuteronomy through 2 Kings, the figure of Joshua serves as
a forerunner for the ideological role played by later kings, and especially for
the expansionistic and reforming policies of Josiah.[25] As his name seems to
signify (Sir. 46:1), Joshua was the ideal "savior," who not only won battles and
secured possession of the land, but was able to hold the people to perfect loyalty his whole life (24:31). In this way he serves to prepare for the military de-
liverers who follow in Judges (3:9, 15).[26]

8. Text

The Masoretic (MT) and Old Greek (OG) texts of Joshua offer substantially
different readings in many places. Although the Greek is about 5 percent
shorter, both the MT and OG text forms are expansionistic in the sense that
each contains scribal additions, harmonizations, and developments not found
in the other. Both also show mechanical haplographies (omissions triggered by
similarities in the beginning or end of words and phrases) and other typical
scribal errors. In recent years it has become clear that the Greek version of
Joshua is a dependable translation of a form of the Hebrew text with textual
value at least equal to that of MT.[27] Two almost universally accepted OG readings are the restoration of eleven names in the town list of Judah (after 15:59)
and the levitical cities of Reuben in 21:36–37.

By Old Greek is meant the earliest recoverable form of what is popularly

---

25. R. Nelson, "Josiah in the Book of Joshua," *JBL* 100 (1981): 531–40. For an extensive
study of the figure of Joshua, including a comparison to Solomon, see C. Schäfer-Lichtenberger,
Josua und Salomo: Eine Studie zu Autorität und Legitimität des Nachfolgers im Alten Testament,
VTSup 58, Leiden, 1995, 190–224, 356–64.

26. For this suggestion and for the understanding of Joshua in later biblical literature, see M.
Beek, "Joshua the Savior," *Voices from Amsterdam,* SBLSS, Atlanta, 1994, 145–53. See also D.
McCarthy, "The Theology of Leadership in Joshua 1–9," *Bib* 52 (1971): 165–75.

27. S. Holmes, *Joshua: The Hebrew and Greek Texts,* Cambridge, 1914; H. Orlinsky, "The
Hebrew *Vorlage* of the Septuagint of the Book of Joshua," *Congress Volume Rome 1968,* VTSup
17 (1968), 187–95; A. G. Auld, "Joshua: the Hebrew and Greek Texts," *Studies in the Historical
Books of the Old Testament,*VTSup 30, 1979, 1–14, and "Textual and Literary Studies in the Book
of Joshua," *ZAW* 90 (1978): 412–17. Also see S. Silipä, "The Septuagint Version of Joshua 3–4,"
*VIIth Congress of the International Organization for Septuagint and Cognate Studies, Leuven
1989,* SBLSCS 31, Atlanta, 1991, 63–74.

called the Septuagint (LXX).[28] Once inner-Greek corruptions, translational misunderstandings and strategies, and obviously tendentious alterations have been isolated from this reconstructed OG, it must be valued on par with MT in establishing the earliest recoverable text of Joshua. Close examination shows the translation to be faithful, although not mechanically literal. With rare exceptions, the Greek translator of Joshua did not abbreviate, so that OG readings shorter than MT must be given full credence as witnesses to a shorter (and thus most likely better) Hebrew text. An obvious caveat, of course, is that OG remains a translation and thus cannot be turned back into Hebrew with total confidence. The responsible critic will be hesitant to reconstruct a text on the basis of uncertain retroversions. Apart from this, however, MT ought not be treated *in Joshua* as an intrinsically better text than OG. One has a "textual problem" anytime witnesses disagree, not just when MT is seen as problematic in some way. Conversely, the text critic must avoid the temptation of defending obviously expansionistic or midrashic OG readings based on some notion of its innate superior character.[29]

The text-critical principles followed here are the standard ones. Except where there is a likelihood of mechanical haplography, the shorter or more difficult reading is judged to be the earliest recoverable one. Because in the case of Joshua one is in the fortunate position of having two divergent forms of the text to work with, one is able to achieve a text earlier than that offered by either MT or OG by means of the relatively simple expedient of eliminating the scribal expansions of each. The resultant critical text can hardly be claimed to be the "original text," but it is at least a text closer to what would have been in the hands of the book's earliest readers. Often there is little to choose between minor alternatives (presence or absence of *waw,* singular or plural) and in such cases it is best to follow MT. Place names, of which there are many in Joshua, are especially fluid, and again MT should be evaluated as superior because of its ongoing connection with the geography of Palestine.

The text notes are intended to reveal the logic behind the critical text upon which the translation is based and are intended to provide enough information to guide interpreters in making their own evaluation of the evidence. These notes usually state which variant has been chosen and provide a rationale for the choice. Assumptions of mechanical haplographies are explicitly delineated. On

28. In establishing the OG on the basis of the complex LXX evidence, I have generally followed the masterly work of M. Margolis, *The Book of Joshua in Greek,* Paris, 1931–38; Philadelphia, 1992. See also C. Benjamin, *The Variations between the Hebrew and Greek Texts of Joshua, Chapters 1–12,* Philadelphia, 1921; and L. Greenspoon, *Textual Studies in the Book of Joshua,* HSM 28, Chico, Calif., 1983.

29. See E. Tov, "Midrash-Type Exegesis in the LXX of Joshua," *RB* 85 (1978): 50–61, and "The Growth of the Book of Joshua in the Light of the Evidence of the LXX Translation," *Studies in the Bible,* ScrHier 31, Jerusalem, 1986, 321–39.

the other hand, many uncomplicated or less important MT expansions that are not present in OG have simply been bracketed in the translation without further explanation. This procedure has reduced what would otherwise have been an excessive number of text notes and permits the reader to keep track of MT more easily. For both practical and theological reasons, many interpreters of Joshua will wish to focus on MT without much regard to text critical issues. *Text given in brackets represents MT material absent from OG and judged not to have been part of the earliest recoverable text.*

In chapters 5, 6, 20, and 24, the divergence between OG and MT is so great that the differences between the two are best seen as a matter of divergent recensional development rather than ordinary textual variation. That is to say, editorial changes or revisions have been introduced into one form of the text but not in the other.[30] In these cases both the earliest recoverable text (designated as the "unrevised text") and the alternate text that has undergone redaction or modification (called the "revised text") are translated and receive commentary. MT represents such a revised text in Josh. 5:2–9; 6:1–15; and 20:1–9 over against OG, which preserves a shorter, more original unrevised text. The situation is reversed at the end of chapter 24, where OG witnesses to a midrashic "revised text," and MT retains the earliest recoverable form.

Qumran Cave IV preserved fragments of two Joshua manuscripts that offer important readings.[31] The most striking surprise is that 4QJosh[a] positions the reading of the law at Shechem (and thus presumably the whole pericope of 8:30–35) immediately before 5:2–7 and thus immediately after the Jordan crossing, in strict obedience to the command of Deut. 27:2.

---

30. For this concept, see E. Tov, *Textual Criticism of the Hebrew Bible,* Minneapolis, 1992, 313–49.

31. 4QJosh[a] is edited by E. Ulrich and 4QJosh[b] by E. Tov in *Qumran Cave 4: Discoveries in the Judaean Desert* XIV, Oxford, 1995, 143–52 and 153–60. For an evaluation of their place in the textual evidence, see L. Greenspoon, "The Qumran Fragments of Joshua: Which Puzzle Are They Part of and Where Do They Fit?" *Septuagint, Scrolls and Cognate Writings,* SBLSCS 33, Atlanta, 1992, 159–94.

JOSHUA

Preparations
Joshua 1:1–18

Yahweh Charges Joshua

1:1 After the death of Moses [the servant of Yahweh][a] Yahweh said to Joshua son of Nun who had been the attendant of Moses, 2 "Moses my servant is dead. Now get up, cross [this] the Jordan, you and all this people, to the land which I am going to give them [to the Israelites]. 3 I have given over every place on which the sole of your foot will step, just as I promised Moses: 4 From the wilderness and [this] the Lebanon as far as the great river, the Euphrates River, [the whole land of the Hittites] and as far as the great Western Sea will be your territory. 5 No one will resist you your entire life. I will be with you just as I was with Moses. I will not abandon you or forsake you. 6 Be brave and strong, for you will cause this people to inherit the land which I swore to their ancestors to give them.

7 Only be [very] brave and strong, being careful to do just what[b] Moses my servant commanded you. Do not deviate from it right or left, so that you may be successful everywhere you go. 8 This law book should not disappear from your mouth. Think about it day and night so that you may be careful to act in accordance with everything written in it. Then you will make your journey prosperous and will succeed.[c] 9 Surely I have commanded you to be brave and strong. Do not be alarmed or terrified, for Yahweh your God[d] is with you everywhere you go."

Joshua Charges the People

10 Then Joshua commanded the officers of the people, 11 "Pass through the middle of the camp and command the people: 'Get rations ready for yourselves, because within three days you will be crossing this Jordan to go and take over the land which Yahweh your God is going to give you to take it over.'"[e]

12 To the Reubenites, Gadites, and half tribe of Manasseh Joshua said, 13 "Remember the command which Moses the servant of Yahweh gave you: 'Yahweh your God will give rest for you and give you this land.' 14 Your wives, children, and cattle will live in the land which he

has given you,[f] but you will cross over organized for war[g] ahead of your kinfolk — valiant warriors[h] all — and help them, 15 until Yahweh[i] gives rest like yours to your kinfolk and they too take over the land which Yahweh your God is going to give them. Then you will return to the land which belongs to you [and you will take it over],[j] which Moses [the servant of Yahweh] has given you toward the east across the Jordan."

The Eastern Tribes Respond

16 They answered Joshua, "We will do everything you have commanded us and will go anywhere you send us. 17 Just as we obeyed Moses [thus] we will obey you. Only may Yahweh your God be with you as he was with Moses! 18 Whoever obstinately opposes your orders and does not obey your words in regard to anything you might command will be executed. Only be brave and strong!

a. Bracketed material represents MT readings not present in OG and judged not part of the earliest recoverable text.

b. Follows OG. MT expands with *kol hattôrâ* to read "according to the whole law which." The masculine gender of "from it" is evidence that MT represents an expansion.

c. Follows MT, retained here as a moderately cumbersome deuteronomistic formula. OG has a shorter text.

d. Use of the third person for Yahweh suggests that one could understand everything from "do not deviate," in v. 7 until the end of v. 9 as a quotation of Moses rather than of Yahweh (cf. 8:31). The MT expansion to v. 7 muddles this question. The translation considers Yahweh as the speaker throughout.

e. OG lost "to take it over" by haplography involving the start of the next verse: *lr[šth wlr]'wbny.*

f. Follows OG. MT changes the grammatical subject with a harmonistic expansion from v. 15: "Moses has given you across the Jordan."

g. "Organized for war" (*hămušîm*, also 4:12; Judg. 7:11) is literally "arranged by five/fifty," that is, either divided into units of fifty soldiers each (2 Kings 1:9; Isa. 3:3) or having an overall disposition into five sections (center, two wings, advance and rear guard).

h. "Valiant warriors" (*gibbôrê haḥayil*) are fighters of the highest valor and competence (8:3; 10:7; Judg. 6:12; 11:1; 1 Sam. 16:18).

i. Follows MT. OG has a dittography, "your God" (*'lhykm*), before "your kinfolk" (*l'ḥykm*).

j. MT *wyrštm 'wth* is a dittography of the previous word *yrštkm.*

The introduction to the book of Joshua is constructed as a series of four speeches (vv. 2–9, 10–11, 12–15, 16–18). It was composed by DH to inaugurate the era of conquest under the new leader Joshua. The concentration of deuteronomistic language is high throughout,[1] and dependence on Deut. 7:24; 11:24–25; and 17:18–19 is evident. The suggestion that the structure and language of some sort of traditional "installation genre" is present in this text[2] is difficult to prove, given the repetitious and circuitous character of deuteronomistic style. However, there is a definite royal flavor to this chapter, probably the result of a desire on the part of DH to create parallels between the figures of Joshua and Josiah.[3] Yahweh's charge in vv. 1–9 is paralleled by 1 Kings 2:2–4 and seems to have been composed along the general lines of an enthronement or royal installation.[4] To meditate on the book of the law epitomizes the deuteronomistic royal ideal (v. 8; Deut. 17:18–19). Another royal-sounding element is the pledge of uncompromising obedience by the eastern tribes (vv. 16–18). Yahweh's promise to the entire community is concentrated so that it rests on the military success of a single individual (the second person singular of v. 5), producing another parallel between Joshua and the office of the king (compare David in 2 Sam. 7:9–10). Like Josiah (2 Kings 22:2) and the ideal king of Deut. 17:20, Joshua is not to deviate from obedience to the right or left (v. 7). Unlike Saul (1 Sam. 16:14), but like David (1 Sam. 16:18) and Hezekiah (2 Kings 18:7), Joshua's leadership and authority will be legitimated by Yahweh's presence (vv. 9, 17).

The introductory phrase "after the death of Moses" marks the transition to a new era of leadership (Judg. 1:1; 2 Sam. 1:1; 2 Kings 1:1). In the larger horizon of DH, Yahweh's address to Joshua (vv. 1–9) functions as one of the editorial speeches that structure and unify the whole work (Deuteronomy 1–3, Joshua 23, 1 Samuel 12, 2 Samuel 7, 1 Kings 8).[5] These speeches look backward and forward to reflect on the significance of events reported by DH. From a literary standpoint such speeches give an author the chance to address readers directly in order to provide motivations for the characters and to frame the issues at stake. By fading behind the speeches of authoritative characters, an author gains the appearance of greater objectivity. DH used this technique to guide readers into adopting a particular theological interpretation of Israel's history in the land. Here Yahweh's programmatic speech points forward toward the goal of total military success. Achievement of this goal will be summarized by 11:23; 12:7–24; and 21:43–45. At the same time, Israel's success is set into the context of obedience to the law, in accordance with the chief axiom of deuteronomistic theology.

---

1. Weinfeld, *Deuteronomy and the Deuteronomic School,* 336, 339, 342–44, 346.

2. N. Lohfink, "The Deuteronomistic Picture of the Transfer of Authority from Moses to Joshua," *Theology of the Pentateuch,* Minneapolis, 1994, 234–47; D. McCarthy, "An Installation Genre?" *JBL* 90 (1971): 31–41.

3. Nelson, "Josiah in the Book of Joshua."

4. G. Widengren, "King and Covenant," *JSS* 2 (1957): 12–17; E. Nielsen, "Some Reflections on the History of the Ark," *Congress Volume Oxford 1959,* VTSup 7, Leiden, 1960, 70–72; Porter, "The Succession of Joshua," 107–18.

5. Noth, *The Deuteronomistic History,* 5–6.

The main themes of the book, in both its DH and final form, are launched by Yahweh's introductory speech:

> v. 2 (crossing) points to chaps. 3–4, 22
>
> vv. 3–6, 9 (conquest) point to chaps. 2, 6, 8, 10–12
>
> v. 6 (allotting the land) points to 11:23; 12:1–6; chaps. 13–21
>
> vv. 7–8 (obedience to the law) point to 8:30–35; chaps. 5, 7, 9, 23–24

The three other speeches (vv. 10–11, 12–15, and 16–18) likewise introduce several themes and interests of the book which follows. National claims on ancestral territory are supported (vv. 13–15). Israel is promised "rest" and possession of the land (v. 15). There is a call to faith, courage, and strength in a time of crisis (v. 18). The interchange between Joshua and the east Jordan tribes inaugurates the book's thesis that "all Israel" cooperated together to effect a unified conquest (3:7; 4:14; 8:15; 10:29; etc.).

Although other conquest traditions were apparently in existence (Num. 21:1–3; Genesis 34; Judges 1), DH shares the perspective of the pre-deuteronomistic book of Joshua and the older Jericho and Gilgal traditions of chapters 2–6 that Israel entered the land from the east by crossing the Jordan. This was of course also required by the rhetorical setting of Deuteronomy as a pre-invasion speech in the plains of Moab. In fact, Deuteronomy provides both the starting point for the book of Joshua (the death of Moses, Deut. 34:5; location east of the Jordan) and the goals of its plot. These goals are to cross the Jordan, take over the land, and achieve rest (cf. Deut. 9:1; 11:31; 12:10). Joshua thus starts with the assumption that its readers have already read Deuteronomy. The core of Deuteronomy (chaps. 5–28) and the DH portions of that book (in chaps. 1–3, 31, and 34) set up the themes and roles that are explored in these four prefatory speeches. The figure of Joshua has already been introduced (Deut. 1:38), and readers have been prepared for his transition to leadership (Deut. 3:21–22, 26–28; 31:1–8). Readers have already heard Yahweh's charge to Joshua to be "brave and strong" in order to bring to fulfillment the promise of a national homeland (v. 6; Deut. 3:28; 31:6–8, 23). They have also encountered the law book (Deut. 31:9–13) and know what to expect from the eastern tribes (Deut. 3:18–20). Moreover, they know that Israel has already failed at conquest because of fear and disobedience (Deut. 1:19–45). Therefore both human courage and divine presence will be indispensable for any future success.

A new stage in the drama, prepared for by Deuteronomy, is now triggered by the death of Moses. Joshua is presented as the successor to Moses.[6] A rich network of connections extends back into the past to coordinate the figure of

---

6. Porter, "The Succession of Joshua," 102–32.

Joshua with that of Moses: Joshua as the attendant of Moses (v. 1), Yahweh's promise to Moses (vv. 3–4; Deut. 11:24), Yahweh's presence with Moses (vv. 5, 17; Deut. 2:7), and the people's obedience to Moses (v. 17). Each of these Mosaic themes is now shifted onto Joshua. Moses was Yahweh's servant (vv. 2, 7), and at the end of the final form of the book, Joshua will be given the same title (24:29).

There is special emphasis on one particular item of continuity, the book of the law commanded by Moses, which Joshua is to obey (vv. 7–8). This law book is already known to readers as the law spoken by Moses after the defeat of Sihon and Og (Deut. 1:3–5), subsequently written down to be read every seven years to the assembled nation (Deut. 31:9–13), and stored beside the ark (Deut. 31:24–26). To follow this law in all its particulars (Deut. 31:12; 32:46) without deviation (Deut. 5:32; 17:11, 20; 28:14) and to keep it persistently in the foreground of one's consciousness will assure success in the coming conquest. This represents a central tenet of Deuteronomy's theology (Deut. 5:33; 6:6–9, 24–25). Once the Jordan is crossed, the law is to be obeyed (Deut. 11:31–32), and Joshua will prove to be a model of such obedience (5:10; 8:29, 30–35; 10:27). A counter-theme of disobedience will also emerge in the narratives about Achan (7:11), the treaty with the Gibeonites (9:14), and the altar built by the eastern tribes (22:10–20). Moreover, warnings about the consequences of disobedience are pivotal to Joshua's farewell speeches (chaps. 23 and 24). However, the topic of disobedience really becomes dominant only in Judges (Judg. 2:10–3:6). In the larger redactional scheme of DH, Joshua illustrates the correlation between obedience and success, while Judges follows with the contrasting association between disobedience and disaster.

Joshua's central theme is the gift of the land. The verb *ntn* "give" appears in this context eight times in chapter 1, with Yahweh and Moses (once) as subject. "To give the land" represents fundamental confessional language throughout the book (2:9, 14, 24; 5:6; 8:1; 9:24; 18:3; 22:4; 23:13, 15, 16; 24:13). The special quality of life in the land given by Yahweh is "rest" (root *nwḥ;* 1:13, 15). "Rest" is the security established by the defeat of the enemy (Deut. 12:10; 25:19). Such "rest" will be the consummation of this campaign and of Joshua's career (21:44; 22:4; 23:1). Another key word central to Joshua is "take over" (*yrš* qal, "to possess by virtue of conquest," vv. 11, 15). This, along with the hiphil of the same root ("dispossess," "destroy or drive out in order to take possession") will be used more than twenty times in the narratives to follow.[7]

Some of the book's internal ideological tensions begin to emerge in this first chapter as well. Conquest as an almost effortless procession in which Yahweh does nearly everything (chaps. 3–4, 6) is suggested by vv. 3, 5, and 11,

---

7. N. Lohfink, "*yaraš*," *TDOT* IV, 371–76.

whereas the hard realities of human combat in partnership with the divine warrior (chaps. 8, 10–11) loom in v. 14. Victory and possession of the land are the
subject of repeated promise, but also seem to be contingent on obedience to the
law (vv. 7–8). There is also tension between the promise of complete success
and the reality that some peoples and territory would still remain to be conquered. This is the case in the DH edition of Joshua (chap. 9; 23:4–7, 12–13)
and to a much greater extent in the final form (13:2–6, 13; 15:63; 16:10;
17:12–13). In this regard, Yahweh hints even here at a disparity between the
expansive land of promise (v. 4) and what will turn out be the more narrow
land of actual occupation (v. 3).

These four speeches provide a theological orientation to the narratives that
follow. Readers of various historical periods are invited to ponder the relationship between divine promise and gift over against human faith and action.
In the context of their own present challenges and crises, these readers are
urged to respond with courage, with trust in Yahweh's promises and presence,
and in obedience to the law. They are assured that possession of the land, although perhaps now endangered or lost or about to be retrieved, remains a matter of long-standing divine promise. They are called to national solidarity,
submission to divinely appointed leadership, obedience to the law, and self-
sacrifice for the good of the whole people. This introduction, first configured
for the DH form of Joshua, proved appropriate as well for the expanded final
form of the book and for readers experiencing the challenges of defeat, exile,
and foreign domination.

[1–9] Yahweh speaks to Joshua in an unmediated way as had formerly been
the case with Moses. This seems to have already been a feature of the source
material used by DH (4:1; 5:2; 6:2; 7:10; 8:1). The designation of Joshua as
Moses' "attendant" (v. 1) is traditional (Exod. 24:13; 33:11; Num. 11:28) and
is used here to help authenticate the transition from Moses to Joshua. Similar
examples are 1 Sam. 3:1 (Samuel) and 1 Kings 19:21 (Elisha).

Yahweh's first directive begins a pattern that is repeated several times in
Joshua. Divine command (vv. 2–9) is followed by Joshua's own corresponding directives (vv. 10–15) and then by Israel's subsequent obedience. Variations on this threefold pattern can be found in chapters 3, 4, 6, and 8.[8] Yahweh's speech equips Joshua with instructions, as well as motivations and
resources for carrying them out. There are imperatives to action: ("get up,
cross," v. 2) and obedience ("do not deviate," "be careful to act," vv. 7–8), as
well as to courage ("be brave and strong," "do not be alarmed or terrified," vv.
6a, 9a). These imperatives are supported by reassuring indicatives of promise,
along with a geographical description of the goal (vv. 3–5, 6b, 9b). The same
motivational themes will continue to appear as the book unfolds: Yahweh's

---

8. Compare 3:7–8 (divine command), 9–13 (Joshua's directive), 14 (obedience). The same
pattern is repeated in 4:1–8; 4:15–18; 6:2–8; and 8:1–17.

presence with Joshua (3:7; 4:14; 6:27), courage grounded by promise (8:1; 10:8, 25; 11:6), and obedience to the law (8:31; 22:5; 23:6).

Joshua's assignment has two aspects to it, both already prepared for in Deuteronomy. First, he is commanded to cross over and lead the people into the land (v. 2; Deut. 1:38; 3:21, 28; 31:3, 7, 23). Second, as a consequence of this, he is to put Israel in possession of the land (hiphil of *nḥl;* v. 6; Deut. 1:38; 3:28; 31:7).[9] The completion of this second task is only briefly noted in the DH form of Joshua (11:23; 12:7; 23:4). Joshua's greater role in the partition of the land in the final form of the book is a redactional expansion of his second task (13:6–7; 14:1; 19:51).

Much of vv. 3–9 was composed on the basis of Deut. 7:24; 11:24–25; and also reflects 31:6–8 (DH). Thus vv. 3–5a were created on the basis of Deut. 11:24–25, while vv. 5b–6, 9 follow the model of Deut. 31:6–8. The charge of vv. 7–8 is formed on the royal instruction of Deut. 17:18–19. A shift to second person plural in vv. 3–4 extends the motivation of these verses to the whole nation (and to the readers). Then v. 5 returns the address back to Joshua alone, converting the plural of the source (Deut. 11:25) to a singular. To walk over a stretch of land (v. 3) may have been a way of making a legal claim to it. This is suggested by Gen. 13:17 and the importance of shoes in legal customs involving real estate (Deut. 25:9–10; Ruth 4:7–8).

Verse 4, based on Deut. 11:24, gives a generalized territorial description of the "from . . . to" type.[10] The text of this seems to be corrupt both here and in Deuteronomy. The south to north extent is given first: from the wilderness (here the Negeb and not the eastern desert, compare Deut. 1:7) via the Lebanon to the Euphrates. Then a second axis of the territory is traced from an unspecified east locality towards the west at the Mediterranean. This represents the most expansive form of Israel's traditional land claim (Gen. 15:18; Deut. 1:7). Hegemony up to the Euphrates may have been realized by the imperialist ambitions of the United Kingdom, but even then only as loose control over tributary and associated states (2 Sam. 8:3–12; 1 Kings 5:1, 4 [4:21, 24E]; 8:65). The territory actually conquered and occupied according to Joshua (10:40–41; 11:16–17, 21–22; chaps. 13–19) represents the more limited reality of the kingdoms of Judah and Israel.

Verse 5 is filled with the language of divine war and reflects the situation of Deut. 20:1–4, which is a set-piece example of an uplifting speech made to

9. For the assertion that Joshua is installed here as one who would divide up the land among the tribes as in chapters 13–19, see Lohfink, "The Deuteronomistic Picture of the Transfer of Authority," 234–47. This argument rests on the assumption that *nḥl* hiphil must be always be understood as "divide as an inheritance" as in Deut. 21:16. The more general translation "cause to inherit" is preferable in Deut. 1:38; 3:28; 31:7; Josh. 1:6. See KB[3], 648, and E. Lipiński, "*naḥal*," *ThWAT* V, 346, 352–54, who proposes as a translation "to transform a right of general ownership into an exclusive right as a share of an inheritance," [my translation], 344.

10. For example 13:3–4; Exod. 23:31; Num. 13:21; 2 Sam. 24:2 and so forth.

troops on the eve of battle. In DH, Moses has already given several comparable speeches using similar language (Deut. 1:29–31; 2:24–25; 31:1–6; with
3:21–22 and 31:7–8 directed to Joshua). These encouraging speeches consist
of stock rallying cries ("be brave and strong," "do not be alarmed or terrified")
and encouraging promises ("I have given," "no one will resist," "I will not
abandon or forsake"). Yahweh's pledge to be "with" the combatants is also
part of divine war ideology (cf. Judg. 6:12; 1 Sam. 17:37). Yahweh's speech
evokes for the reader the bold spirit and fervor of the narratives that follow and
anticipates the repeated summons to courage in the remainder of the book (8:1;
10:8, 25; 11:6). As the plot unfolds, this call for courage on the part of Israel
will contrast with the enemies' chronic terror (2:9, 24; 5:1; 10:2).

Verse 7 is introduced by particle *raq*, introducing a note of contingency to
the promise of v. 6. Joshua and the reader are to consider what has just been
promised in light of the issue of obedience. In this verse the imperatives of v.
6 are somewhat oddly redirected from the realm of warfare into another sphere,
that of obedience to the law. The traditional summons to bravery in battle is
converted into a call for courage in obeying the precepts of Deuteronomy.
Verse 7 takes up "be brave and strong" from v. 6 almost as a quotation for further elaboration. Then v. 9a repeats the same phrase, thus forming an *inclusio*
or envelope to enclose the theme of obedience. Finally v. 9b returns to the previous theme of boldness in warfare.[11] The closest parallel to this line of thought
is 1 Kings 2:1–4 (DH), where the situation is comparable. David gives advice
to his successor in a speech with a similar structure and nearly identical content. The question of obedience to the book of the law is a central theme of DH,
one which will continue to reappear (e.g., 8:31; 22:5; 23:6).

[10–11] The impact of Yahweh's speech results in two directives by Joshua
(vv. 10–11 and 12–15). First he instructs the entire nation by means of the officers to prepare for the campaign. These officers have already been introduced
by Deut. 1:15, where they also have a military function. Their employment
here roughly follows the divine war procedures of Deut. 20:5–9. Verse 11 provides a three-day timetable for the events to follow, and these same officers
will reappear "at the end of three days" to give further instructions (3:2). After this they fade into the role of passive audience (8:33; 23:2; 24:1). Chapter
2 has its own parallel three-day schema (2:16, 22), and the reader must assume
that somehow these two run concurrently.

This first speech by Joshua helps orient readers to the narrative situation.
The scene is the same as that of Deuteronomy, an address to those about to
cross over and occupy the land (Deut. 6:1; 7:1; 8:1; 9:1; 11:8, 11, 31). By pick-

---

11. Clearly v. 9 returns to the content of v. 6 and gives the motive for what v. 6 requires. Thus
vv. 7–8 are often taken to be a later interruption of the original line of thought and the connection
between vv. 6 and 9. See Lohfink, "The Deuteronomistic Picture of the Transfer of Authority,"
239–41.

ing up the language of divine promise that he has just heard (verb *ntn*, vv. 3, 6), Joshua also propels the story forward into the action of chapter 3. The command to prepare provisions is in some tension with 5:11–12. Here the emphasis is on obedient preparation for an arduous journey. The point of 5:11–12 is that the benefits of Canaan were enjoyed by Israel even before the first battle was fought.

[12–15] Disjunctive word order foregrounds the eastern tribes as a new topic.[12] Both they and the reader are urged to remember the events reported in Deut. 3:12–22, and an extensive reuse of language from there reinforces the connection. Moses provides the guarantee for these tribes as the one who mediated Yahweh's promise and gave them their land. The theme of "rest" (your present rest, your kinsfolk's imminent rest) holds this section together and points forward to 21:44; 22:4; 23:1.[13] Giving rest (*nwḥ* hiphil) is defined as giving a homeland (vv. 13, 15).

Viewing these two-and-a-half tribes as a distinct entity accords with deuteronomistic convention, but raises disturbing questions for the reader about their place in the national story.[14] Although an integral part of the idealized tribal system and of the united and northern monarchies, their territory was not "Canaan" in the traditional sense reflected in either Egyptian texts (Amarna Letters; also *ANET* 254, 478) or the Hebrew Bible (Num. 34:2, 10–12; Deut. 32:49). This concern with the eastern tribes will surface again at the Jordan crossing (4:12–13), in the summary of 12:1–6, in the introduction to land allotment (13:8–32), and ultimately in the conflict related in chapter 22. Here in chapter 1, these tribes are highlighted in order to emphasize the "all Israel" theological schema of Joshua. All groups engage in a unified conquest coordinated by a single leader. They also represent a continuing claim on eastern territories that had been lost to Moab in the mid-ninth century and to Assyria after 732 B.C.E.

[16–18] The introductory cycle of communication concludes with the response of the eastern tribes, who serve here as a sort of Greek chorus speaking the mind of the whole people. They indicate an absolute willingness to follow Joshua, backing up their consent with a reference to the standard of their past obedience to Moses and with a call for the death penalty for any recalcitrants (compare Deut. 13:11 [10E]; 17:12). This last statement foreshadows Achan's fate (7:25; 22:20).

12. The literary relationship between Joshua's version and that of Numbers chapter 32 is complex and disputed. See M. Noth, *Numbers: A Commentary,* OTL, Philadelphia, 1968, 234–39.

13. The classic exposition of the theme of rest remains G. von Rad, "There Remains Still a Rest for the People of God," *The Problem of the Hexateuch and Other Essays,* New York, 1966, 94–102.

14. M. Weinfeld, "The Extent of the Promised Land—the Status of Transjordan," *Das Land Israel in biblischer Zeit,* GTA 25, Göttingen, 1983, 59–75; D. Jobling, "The Jordan a Boundary: Transjordan in Israel's Ideological Geography," *The Sense of Biblical Narrative,* JSOTSup 39, Sheffield, 88–134.

However, the double use of *raq* ("only," vv. 17, 18) potentially restricts their enthusiasm and introduces some tension into the plot. This particle implies that the second statement, introduced by *raq,* is more foundational and important than the first statement, although both are true. The syntax asserts: "A is true, but B is even more important." The first use of *raq* (v. 17) emphasizes their wish that Yahweh be with Joshua just as promised in v. 5, but also inserts a subtle note of contingency into their pledge of obedience. Once again Moses serves as the yardstick by which Joshua is measured. The second use of *raq* (v. 18) is both a wish and an echo of Yahweh's command (vv. 6, 7), but again sounds an element of reservation. The first caveat, that of Yahweh's presence with Joshua, returns in 3:7 and 6:27, where his success resolves any uncertainty. The second issue, courage, is raised again after the Ai debacle (8:1) and will be broadened into a challenge to the whole community in 10:25. The rhetorical strategy is powerful. Raising slight questions about Yahweh's presence and Joshua's courage makes the subsequent demonstration of these realities all the more convincing.

Rahab
Outsmarts the Scouts
Joshua 2:1–24

Caught in the Trap

2:1 Joshua the son of Nun [secretly][a] sent two young[b] scouts from Shittim saying, "Go, look over the land, especially Jericho." The two young men set out and came to Jericho and came[c] into the house of a prostitute named Rahab and lay down there. **2** The king of Jericho was told, "Some men have come here [tonight][d] from the Israelites to scout out the land." **3** So the king of Jericho sent word to Rahab, "Send out the men who came to you [who came to your house][e] tonight, for they have come to scout out [all] the land." **4** But the woman took the [two][f] men and hid them[g] and then said, "Of course the men came to me, but I did not know where they came from.[h] **5** When it was time to close the gate at dark the men left. I do not know where they [the men] went. Chase [quickly] after them, for you might catch up with them!" **6** Now she had[i] taken them up to the roof and had hidden them in the woody flax[j] laid out for her on the roof. **7** The men[k] pursued them on the Jordan road above the fords and the gate was shut.[l]

Rahab's Stipulations

As soon as the pursuers went out after them 8 and before they lay down, she came up to them on the roof. 9 She said to the men, "I know that Yahweh has given the land to you and that terror concerning you has fallen on us [and that the whole population of the land has melted with fear before you],[m] 10 because we have heard how Yahweh dried up the water of the Red Sea before you when you came out of Egypt and what you did to the two kings of the Amorites who were on the other side of the Jordan, to Sihon and Og whom you devoted to destruction. 11 We heard and our hearts melted, and no one's courage could rise again because of you, because Yahweh your God is God in heaven above and on earth below. 12 Now swear to me by Yahweh, because I have dealt loyally with you that you too will deal loyally with my father's house [and give me a token of good faith].[n] 13 Save the life of my father and my mother and my brothers [and my sisters] and everything they have and deliver my life from death."[o] 14 The men said to her, "Our life in exchange for yours [pl] [if you do not tell this business of ours]! When Yahweh gives us the land, we will deal loyally and faithfully with you [sg].[p]

Escape from the
Trap and Renegotiation

15 Then she lowered them [on a rope] through the window [for her house was on the face of the wall for she was living inside the wall].[q] 16 She said to them, "Go to the hill country[r] so that the pursuers do not encounter you. Hide yourselves there for three days until the pursuers return and afterwards you may go your way."

17 The men said to her, "We shall be absolved from this[s] your oath [which you made us swear]. 18 Look, when we come into the land,[t] you shall tie this crimson [cord of][u] thread in the window through which you lowered us and gather your father, your mother, your brothers, and your whole family into the house with you. 19 Anyone who goes out the doors of your house into the street will bear the blame for his death, but we shall be absolved. We shall bear the blame for the death of anyone who is with you in the house if a hand is laid on him. 20 But if you [sg] tell this business of ours, then we are absolved from your oath [which you made us swear]. 21 She said, "It will be as you have said." She sent them away and they went.[v] Then she tied the crimson cord in the window.

Mission Accomplished

22 They went and entered the hill country and stayed there for three days until the pursuers returned.[w] The pursuers had searched along the whole road but did not find them. **23** The two young men[x] turned back and came down from the hill country. They went across [and they came] to Joshua the son of Nun and told him everything that had happened to them. **24** They said to Joshua, "Certainly Yahweh has given the whole land into our power. Moreover, the entire population of the land has melted with fear before us."

a. MT expansion absent in OG and Syr. MT represents a revision which emphasized secrecy, moving "by night" from v. 3 to v. 2 and anticipating v. 20 by expanding v. 14.

b. Follows OG reading "young men" (*nĕ'ārîm*) *for* MT *"men"* (*'ănāšîm*) here and in v. 23. This same variation occurs at 6:22, although at 6:23 both OG and MT retain "young men scouts." The MT revision may have been intended to diminish the sexual implications of the original.

c. Follows OG. MT lost *šny hn'rym lyryḥw wyb'w* through haplography caused by the repetition of *wyb'w*.

d. OG has "tonight" in v. 3. MT moved the word to v. 2 to emphasize the secrecy motif and to reduce sexual implications.

e. Follows S. MT presents a grammatically smoothed conflation of two variant readings: "who came (in)to you" (S) and "who came to your house" (OG). Syriac preserves the more difficult, offensive, and morally ambiguous original.

f. Omitted by OG (here LXX[A]) and V.

g. The singular object suffix must be taken as plural as the versions do. *Ṣpn* implies "hide to protect" (Exod. 2:2). In v. 6, *ṭmn* signifies "hide by burying" (Josh. 7:21).

h. Follows MT. OG lacks "but I did not know where they came from," but this does not have the character of a scribal or redactional expansion. It seems to be an important part of Rahab's defense and is retained for that reason.

i. The subject-first sentences of vv. 6–7 are somewhat perplexing, but can be understood as emphatic and contrastive, highlighting each subject in turn: "but *she* had (flashback perfect) taken up . . . but *the men* pursued . . . and *the gate* was shut."

j. "Woody flax" is a construct ("flax of wood") indicating make-up or nature. The flax stalks have not yet been processed.

k. Since "men" everywhere else refers to the spies, an alternate translation for v. 7a would be "as for the men, they pursued them."

l. Follows OG, resolving the lack of a direct object marker before "gate" by taking the verb as a passive and construing the last part of v. 7 with v. 8. The grammatically problematic MT can be explained as a corruption of an original *whš'r šgr wyhy k'šr yṣ'w* ("and the gate was shut and it happened as soon as they went out"). The *waw* of *wyhy* was erroneously read with *šgr* to create a perfect plural. This facilitated the corruption of the remaining *yhy* into *'ḥry*.

m. MT expansion anticipating v. 24 and creating a cross reference to Exod. 15:15b–16a.

n. MT expansion anticipating v. 18 and providing an interpretation of the crimson thread.

o. Both text traditions expanded this verse. MT added "sister(s)." OG added "my father's house" and "all my house." OG "deliver *my* [MT "our"] life from death" is taken here as the original, more difficult reading.

p. The two text traditions diverge.

OG	MT
The men said to her, "Our life in exchange for yours [pl]!" She said, "When Yahweh gives you the city, deal loyally and faithfully with me."	The men said to her, "Our life in exchange for yours [pl]! If you [pl] do not tell this business of ours, when Yahweh gives us the land we will deal loyally and faithfully with you [sg]."

MT expands the spies' speech, anticipating v. 20 and converting their agreement into a carefully guarded promise contingent on the behavior of Rahab and her family. This connects with the MT revision's concern for secrecy. In OG Rahab speaks instead, accepting their unconditioned oath by restating their obligation. Perhaps the change in persons in OG was an attempt to recover sense after a misreading of *lānû* "to us" as *lākem* "to you." Although "city" may be appropriate for Rahab's viewpoint and "land" for the spies' perspective, "city" here appears to be a pedantic OG correction, as in v. 18.

q. Follows OG in omitting "on a rope" and v. 15b. The suggestion that OG is rationalizing the problem of Rahab's house being on the wall which later falls flat presumes recognition of a logical problem ignored by generations of readers. It is more likely that the rope and wall are explanatory additions. MT offers a conflated doublet of two alternate explanations: "for her house was on the face of the wall" and "for she was living inside the wall." Of these, V preserves only the first. The ancient reader presumably would have been able to draw the implied conclusion about the use of a rope and the exterior position of her window in a casemate wall without the MT glosses.

r. "To the hill country" is in emphatic position as the direction opposite from that taken by the pursuit.

s. The apparently masculine form of the demonstrative pronoun is problematic and should be vocalized as a feminine *hazzōh*. For the translation "absolved" see Gen. 24:41; Deut. 24:5; 1 Kings 15:22. Alternate translation: "This is how we will fulfill the oath" (NAB, NJB).

t. OG corrects "land" to "the outskirts of the city," but MT is appropriate from the scouts' perspective.

u. Omitted with OG as a doublet or expansion from v. 21, although the construct "cord of thread" could be taken to mean "a tight weave of threads." OG precedes with "you will give the sign," presumably based on a misreading of the direct object particle as *'wt*.

v. OG lost several words through haplography, from *wylkw* in v. 21 to *wylkw* in v. 22. The loss may have been bolstered by a feeling that Rahab's action would be premature at this point.

w. OG lost "until the pursuers returned" through haplography: *ym[ym 'd-šbw hrdp]ym*.

x. See note b.

The commissioning and setting out of the two spies, along with their return and report (vv. 1, 23–24), frame three dialogues staged in three different settings. In vv. 3–5, Rahab converses with the king's delegation, while the spies are in hiding. In vv. 8–14, Rahab negotiates with the spies on her roof. In vv. 16–21, her concluding dialogue with them takes place. This last interchange is staged somewhat awkwardly, with Rahab up in the window and the spies on the ground, or perhaps even still hanging outside! In between and around these three conversations a tense adventure is played out. The spies fall into danger (vv. 1–2), are hidden and become trapped at the same time (vv. 6–7), escape the city (v. 15) and their pursuers (v. 22), and finally return in safety (v. 24).

The Rahab story has attracted a great deal of attention in recent decades.[1] In order to understand the movement of the narrative, it is vital to note that Rahab is in firm control in the first two dialogues, but that the spies take control of the conversation in the third. As we shall see, Rahab is dominant while the men are in her house because, although she has saved them from immediate danger, they still remain imperiled and trapped. It is only when they are safely outside the city wall that they can modify the demands Rahab has placed upon them.

Another way of considering the shape of this plot is to think of two parallel and contrasting stories, that of the spies and that of the king's men, which touch only at the focal point of Rahab. The men commissioned (*šlḥ*) by the king dialogue with Rahab, hear what she claims not to know, are sent away by her with instructions, go toward the Jordan in active quest, and return in abject failure. The men commissioned (*šlḥ*) by Joshua hear instead what Rahab knows (contrast v. 9 with vv. 4–5), are sent away by her with instructions, go in the opposite direction toward the hills to hide passively, and return with their mission successfully accomplished. Rahab is the only meeting point of these two groups, and her actions are fundamental to the success of one and the failure of the other.[2]

The Rahab story exhibits syntactical abruptness (especially vv. 6–8) and narrative irregularities, such as the clumsy notion of negotiating up through the window (vv. 15–21), the awkward reference to "this crimson thread" (v. 18), and alleged doublets (vv. 4 and 6). The language is overfull and repetitious in places (vv. 10, 17–20). There are narrative gaps, such as the absence of any ex-

---

1. In addition to the studies cited, see also F. Abel, "L'anathème de Jéricho et la maison de Rahab," *RB* 57 (1950): 321–30; P. Bird, "The Harlot as Heroine: Narrative Art and Social Presumption in Three Old Testament Texts," *Semeia* 46 (1989): 119–39; R. Culley, "Stories of the Conquest: Joshua 2, 6, 7, and 8," *HAR* 8 (1984): 30–35; M. Ottosson, "Rahab and the Spies," *DUMU-E2-DUB-BA-A. Studies in Honor of A. Sjöberg,* Philadelphia, 1989, 419–27; G. Tucker, "The Rahab Saga (Joshua 2): Some Form-Critical and Traditio-Historical Observations," *The Use of the Old Testament in the New and Other Essays: Studies in Honor of W. F. Stinespring,* Durham, N.C., 1972, 66–86; N. Winther-Nielsen, *A Functional Discourse Grammar of Joshua,* ConBOT 40, Stockholm, 1995, 105–62.

2. A. Marx, "Rahab, Prostituée et Prophétesse: Josue 2 et 6," *ETR* 55 (1980): 72–76.

planation of how the spies' mission was compromised. These complications have naturally given rise to various theories involving multiple sources or redactions.[3] Although there can be no doubt that the text has had a complicated prehistory, the approach taken here will concentrate on the narrative's present form, while observing how the originally independent narrative has been modified to function as part of the larger plot of Joshua.

There are strong reasons to conclude that some form of the Rahab story once existed independent of its present context. Chapter 2 creates a noticeable break in the expected movement from chapter 1 (command to cross) to chapter 3 (the crossing). The three days of 2:16, 22 can be correlated with the chronology of 1:11 and 3:2 only with difficulty, if at all.[4] Although tied redactionally to the fall of Jericho (6:17b, 22–26), the Rahab story is fundamentally independent of it. Chapter 2 certainly envisions the capture of Jericho, but hardly in the miraculous way reported by chapter 6, which fails to pick up the motif of the crimson thread and does not take into account the implied location of Rahab's house, which would have been destroyed in the wall's collapse. Obvious deuteronomistic language is confined to Rahab's confessional speech (vv. 10b, 11b; compare Deut. 4:39), which has strong connections to the DH review of history in Deut. 2:26–3:17 and the parallel speech of the Gibeonites (9:9–10). The unifying theme for the pre-deuteronomistic book of Joshua is present in vv. 9a, 10a, 11a, 24a. Israel's adversaries have heard the news and reacted (5:1; 9:1–3; 10:1–2; 11:1; 2:10a duplicates 4:23). Thus the Rahab narrative can be thought of as functioning in at least three systems of meaning: on its own as a tale told in Israel, as the first episode in the pre-deuteronomistic book, and as part of the larger sweep of DH.

In the *first system of meaning,* as a self-contained tale, this narrative tells of a clever act of treachery by Rahab. By her astute grasp on reality and quick thinking, she is able to assure the safety of her family and the continued existence of her descendants. A briefer example of this sort of tale is found at Judges 1:23–26, where a disloyal citizen of Luz betrays the way into his city.

---

3. H. Hertzberg, *Die Bücher Josua, Richter, Ruth,* ATD 9, Göttingen, 1957, 20–21 finds two traditions: vv. 13–16 in which Rahab dominates, and vv. 17–21 where the spies take the lead. J. Floss, *Kunden oder Kundschafter? Literatur-wissenschaftliche Untersuchung zu Jos 2,* ATS 16, St. Ottilien, 1982, 71–81, 171–72, 205, sees the earliest literary stage as vv. 1–3, 4c–6, 15, 16, 22–23, and traces behind this an oral story of Rahab's rescue of her accused customers. Fritz, *Josua,* 33–41 supposes the original story to be vv. 1–3, 4b–7, 15–17a, 18–19, 21–23. F. Langlamet, "Josué II et les traditions de l'Hexateuque," *RB* 78 (1971): 163–64, gives a tabular overview of earlier critical theories.

4. A sufficiently flexible reader may choose to take 1:11 as day 1, 3:1 as day 2, and 3:2 as day 3, with the entire spy story enclosed within this period. Their adventure in Jericho and flight to the hill country would have taken place on day 1 and their report to Joshua on day 3. The crossing itself on 10 Nisan happens on day 4 (3:5; 4:19). However, chapter 3 presents its own complications to this pattern.

Possibly this earlier story told of an entry point or weak spot in the defenses marked by Rahab with her crimson cord to facilitate entrance into the city. This would explain the spies' rather strange demand for secrecy for their compromised mission (v. 20). The placement of the cord on the *outside* of the wall makes it more understandable as a signpost for attackers and less appropriate as a "recognition signal" for troops who have already overrun the city. There are folktale parallels from classical sources in which harlots play similar roles in memorable conquests.[5] Of course, no story of internal treachery could have been originally connected to the tale of Jericho's miraculous collapse in chapter 6. Another suggestion is that in its pre-literary form the story told of a prostitute's customers being rescued by her when falsely accused of spying. This would have subsequently been converted by its framework (vv. 1 and 23b–24) into a story of spies sent by Joshua in connection with the conquest.[6]

The prehistory of the Rahab story must remain a matter of speculation. Probably the original narrative focused on local and tactical questions. How was the city compromised? How was the Rahab clan saved? It was later redaction that reframed it into a national and strategic perspective. Joshua as leader of united Israel sends spies from the military bivouac at Shittim, who discover the defeated mood of the population and thus certify Yahweh's gift of the land. The espionage aspects of the plot are unquestionably limited to Joshua's commission and instructions, the king's words, and the message eventually conveyed (vv. 1–3, 23b–24). According to both Joshua and the king of Jericho, these two are to survey enemy territory (vv. 1–3). However, their mission is short-circuited, and they do not really spy so much as bring back a report of the enemy's consternation, a fact learned solely from Rahab. Perhaps it is in this sense, possibly with a touch of irony, that they are termed "messengers" in a later reference to them (6:25).

Therefore the primary Rahab story was not really a spy narrative. It only operates inside the framework of one, for the course of espionage is immediately derailed by v. 1b into quite another sort of tale. The underlying narrative problem is not the collection of information and its delivery to Joshua, but rather the danger these hapless young men get themselves into. The plot interest centers on how Rahab safeguards them and in the process extracts an important concession to rescue herself and her family. Here we can recognize a typical ethnological saga in which a wily ancestor helps herself and her kinfolk through shrewdness and presence of mind. She does so by shielding imperiled visitors and forcing from them a promise of future protection. Rahab is a trickster. She seems to help the king, but tricks him. She seems to aid the spies, but

---

5. A. Windisch, "Zur Rahabgeschichte, zwei Parallelen aus der klassischen Literatur," *ZAW* 37 (1917–18): 238–68. For example, a courtesan of Abydos enabled her home city to be retaken by her countrymen.

6. Floss, *Kunden oder Kundschafter?* I, 71–79, 215–17.

traps them. At this level the saga provides an etiology for the continued existence of a non-Israelite group, the "house of Rahab" in or near Jericho (6:25). Of course the etiological formula there is redactional,[7] but it is nonetheless an accurate reflection of the story's earlier function. Of course, as Israel retold the saga, its center of gravity would be less and less the survival of Rahab's family and more and more her protection of the spies and her aid in expediting the conquest. Although the continued existence of Rahab's clan may not have been too pressing a concern for greater Israel, the larger issue of the presence of alien peoples would remain important into the monarchy and long afterward.

This "hospitality to strangers in danger" plot type is also reflected in the similar story of the two angels who visit Lot in Sodom (Gen. 19:1–23). Threatened by the men of the doomed city, whose blind groping parallels the futile pursuit of the king's men, these two angels/messengers (compare Josh. 6:25) become the objects of Lot's attempts to protect his guests. But in the end they offer protection from the coming catastrophe to their host and his family (note the resemblance of 6:23b to Gen. 19:16b). A further intriguing correlation is that Rahab's name echoes the "public square" (*rĕhôb*), a component shared by both the Sodom and Gibeah narrative type scenes (Gen. 19:2; Judg. 19:15, 17, 20).[8] In folktales fugitives often find shelter and protection with a sympathetic woman. One is reminded of how the spies Ahimaaz and Jonathan, on their way to report to David, were hidden in a cistern that their hostess covered with grain, and how she went on to misdirect their pursuers (2 Sam. 17:18–21). A similar tale, but with a reversed ending, is that of Sisera and Jael (Judges 4 and 5).[9]

Rahab's story is saturated by an atmosphere of sexuality. This undercurrent of ambiguous sexual innuendo begins with the spies' act of "lying down." Is this intercourse (Gen. 19:33, 35) or perhaps just preparing for sleep (2 Kings 4:11)? Both the king and Rahab also use the similarly ambiguous language of "going in to" her (vv. 3, 4; Gen. 6:4, Judg. 16:1 and often). Perhaps Rahab's name itself ("wide") may harshly hint at her profession.[10] A *bêt rĕhôb* may signify a brothel (as hinted in Isa. 57:8; Ezek. 16:24, 31). In the earliest recoverable text the spies

---

7. Childs, "A Study of the Formula 'Until This Day,'" 286, 292.

8. Parallels with the Lot story are explored by L. Hawk, "Strange Houseguests: Rahab, Lot, and the Dynamics of Deliverance," *Reading between the Texts: Intertexuality and the Hebrew Bible*, Louisville, Ky., 1992, 89–97. He finds a common five-element plot sequence and suggests that Joshua 2 is a reflection on the Sodom story. For similarities in vocabulary see Langlamet, "Josué II et les traditions de l'Hexateuch," 180–83.

9. Here too the fugitive is hidden, lying down under cover, vulnerable to the power of a woman, caught in a refuge that turns out to be a trap. Moreover, the sexual is not far from the surface of Jael's story. Consider the tent peg as a reverse rape and the "between the legs" language of Judg. 5:27.

10. H. Barstad, "The Old Testament Feminine Personal Name Rahab: An Onomastic Note," *SEA* 54 (1989): 43–49. As a sentence name it could be taken as "[The god] has opened [the womb]."

are "young men" (vv. 1, 23), doubtless vulnerable to sexual temptation, and they come to Rahab at night (v. 3). Even the crimson thread (vv. 18, 21) may have sexual connotations.[11]

Thus within the first system of meaning, working as an independent tale, the story is an etiology for the continued presence of the "house of Rahab" as a foreign group living in Israel's territory. The pivotal role of Rahab's astute, decisive scheme and the large amount of time spent describing negotiations are consequences of this etiological focus. Her scheme explains this group's survival, and the negotiations provide the foundation for their legal status as protected foreigners. Joshua 6:24–25 indicates that this group existed as a alien presence, "outside the camp of Israel," although the etiological formula itself is little more than a literary convention. In spite of the curse of 6:26, Jericho apparently continued to be inhabited (Judg. 3:13; 2 Sam. 10:5). Admittedly intriguing suggestions that this Rahab group engaged in some sort of cultic prostitution[12] or that she was an oracle priestess and her roof a cultic shrine[13] are without textual foundation.

The story of the Gibeonites represents a parallel. They too have heard about the exodus and east Jordan conquests and with a wily stratagem secure a place in the new order. The agreements made in each story are similar in shape (prologue, stipulations, sanctions, sign).[14] The continued existence of distinct ethnic groups within the social and political framework of Israel is a well-documented phenomenon (13:13; 15:63; 16:10; 17:12–13). Preserving and retelling this story would have provided the Rahab group with a measure of security as resident aliens under covenant protection. The treacherous slaughter of the Gibeonites by the nationalist Saul (2 Sam. 21:1–5) indicates that such security could not be taken for granted.

Yet one must ask how a narrative presumably first preserved by the house of Rahab, in which Israelites serve as hapless pawns of her clever plot, could have become popular enough in Israel to emerge as part of their own history of conquest. One possible answer is offered by a social and political reading of the story.[15] The landless Israelites, their peasant descendants, and the clan of Rahab stand together in a social sense as marginalized groups over against Jericho's king, who represents the centralized power of the royal establishment.

11. It is as an image for a woman's lips in Cant. 4:3. The women in the birth scene of Gen. 38:28 also have a crimson thread handy, perhaps indicating that it was an item of feminine finery.

12. G. Hölscher, "Zum Ursprung der Rahabsage," *ZAW* 38 (1919–20): 54–57; Mowinckel, *Tetrateuch-Pentateuch-Hexateuch,* 13–15.

13. J. Heller, "Die Priesterin Rahab," *Communio Viatorum* 8 (1965): 113–17.

14. K. Campbell, "Rahab's Covenant; a Short Note on Joshua 2:9–21," *VT* 22 (1972): 243–44.

15. M. Newman, "Rahab and the Conquest," *Understanding the Word: Essays in Honor of Bernhard W. Anderson,* Sheffield, 1985, 167–81; P. Horn, "Josue 2:1–24 im milieu einer 'dimorphic society,'" *BZ* 31 (1987): 264–70, illustrates this sort of social reading with parallels from Mari and the Code of Hammurabi.

Viewed according to such a paradigm, this narrative reveals itself as a typological antiestablishment story, gleefully told by the lower classes out of the hearing of their "betters." The king's minions are easily deflected by a woman's misdirection. The landless gain land (the word itself is used seven times) and a marginal group traced back to a prostitute acquires a future. The Rahab clan and the peasant class in Israel, both at odds with centralized power structures, would each have had reason to enjoy this story.

Within the *second system of meaning,* that is, within the horizon of chapters 2–11, the narrative functions as a story of spying. It is common in biblical tradition for a spying mission to prepare for conquest (7:2; Numbers 13; Deut. 1:22–25; Judg. 18:2–10).[16] The ultimate narrative goal of such stories is often the delivery of the spies' report and the nature of the reaction to it (7:3; Num. 13:25–14:4; Deut. 1:25b–28; Judg. 18:8–10). That is undeniably the case here, where morale is a central focus (as in Num. 13:28–33; Judg. 18:9–10). Although in Deut. 1:28 it was Israel's hearts that melted, now the tables are turned.

Rahab's speech points forward to Jordan crossing (compare 4:23) by referring to the Red Sea (v. 10). Her negotiations for the survival of her family link this story further forward to the fall of Jericho in chapter 6. Yet the spies' report encompasses the "whole land" (v. 24), not just Jericho, so that the Rahab narrative also serves as the first step of the entire conquest extending through chapter 11. The conquest theme is underscored by the use of divine war language such as "terror" and "melt." (vv. 9, 11).[17] Instead of the usual holy war oracle giving assurance (as Judg. 18:5–6), however, here it is Rahab rather than Yahweh who asserts the divine will and the terror of the foe. It was at this level that the Rahab folktale was framed into a pre-conquest spy story, even though the formula at 6:25 shows a continued editorial recognition of its original etiological intent. The pre-deuteronomistic book of Joshua reused Rahab's story to assert a theological and nationalistic proposition: this land is ours because Yahweh, the divine warrior, has given it to us. The presence of alien groups in our midst does not undermine this fact in any way. Indeed the wisest of their ancestors recognized the truth about Yahweh, and the hearts of all of them melted with fear. Thus the reader is intended to embrace and be sustained by Rahab's perception of Yahweh and Yahweh's gift, especially because she shows herself to be so insightful and astute. The success of her wise plan gives authority to her words in vv. 9–11, so that the reader is induced to believe them.

---

16. S. Wagner, "Die Kundschaftergeschichten im Alten Testament," *ZAW* 76 (1964): 255–69; A. Malamat, "The Danite Migration and the Pan-Israelite Exodus Conquest: A Biblical Narrative Pattern," *Bib* 51 (1970): 1–16; Langlamet, "Josué II et les traditions de l'Hexateuque," 331–36. For a comparison with Judges chapter 18, see Rose, *Deuteronomist und Jahwist,* 146–51. Is it simply coincidence that the spies of Num. 13:21 go as far as *Rehob* (compare "Rahab") and that the town scouted by the Danites was under the control of Beth-*rehob* (Judg. 18:28)?

17. D. McCarthy, "Some Holy War Vocabulary in Joshua 2," *CBQ* 33 (1971): 228–30.

Within the *third system of meaning,* that of DH, the spy story becomes the story of a conversion. Here interest centers on Rahab's renowned confession of faith. Her confession gives DH a chance to tie together the conquest west of the Jordan with the previous story of victories east of the Jordan. She also first introduces the theme of *ḥērem* (devotion to destruction, v. 10) that helps to hold together chapters 6, 7, 10, and 11, and illustrates Israel's obedience to Deuteronomy. In the DH version of her speech, Rahab's motivation is not just fear, but a confessional recognition of who Yahweh really is. She asserts Yahweh's overwhelming control over the fate of nations. Rahab reminds us of Naaman the Syrian, whose profession of faith is not dissimilar (2 Kings 5:15). From the perspective of DH, Rahab's conviction that "Yahweh has given the land" echoes what Yahweh has already told Joshua (1:2–3). When reported to him, it corroborates the divine promise. Rahab's words also confirm the pledge of Deut. 2:25, made in the context of the victory over Sihon and Og, that Yahweh would spread terror whenever enemy peoples hear of Israel.

Setting this tale into its wider deuteronomistic context also exposes for the first time a puzzling tension with which the reader must wrestle throughout the book of Joshua. Can the spies' oath to Rahab and Joshua's later confirmation of it be squared with Deuteronomy's prohibition of making covenants with the nations in the land of promise (Deut. 7:2)? The entire population of "near" cities inside the promised territory (Deut. 20:16–18) are supposed to be exterminated. Bound up with this is the further paradox that any acknowledgment that foreign groups such as Rahab and the Gibeonites continued in the land seems to contradict the contention that Israel's triumph was absolute (e.g., 11:16–20, 23; 21:44).

At the widest canonical level, the New Testament presents Rahab as an ancestor of David and Jesus (Matt. 1:5) and as an example of faith and faithful works (Heb. 11:31; James 2:25). 1 Clement points to her as a model of belief and hospitality, while allegorizing the red thread as a type of Christ's saving blood (1 Clem. 12:1, 8). In Jewish tradition she married Joshua and became an ancestor of several prophets.[18]

At all three levels it is Rahab, and not the ill-fated spies, who is at the center of this story. She is the only character with a name. She uses her disreputable profession to cover her claim of innocence and protect the spies. With prudence she sees the coming crisis and seizes the opportunity of the moment to overcome it. Like Abigail she perceives emerging contours of power and allies herself with them. Like Jael with her tent peg or the woman of Judg. 9:53 with her millstone, she uses the common stuff of the womanly world to meet the threat. Her flax covers her guests, her crimson thread safeguards her family. Because Joshua is addressed to the world of men in a patriarchal society,

18. *b. Meg.* 14b; M. Beek, "Rahab in the Light of Jewish Exegesis," *Von Kanaan bis Kerala,* AOAT 211, Neukirchen-Vluyn, 1982, 37–44.

("your wives, children, and cattle" 1:14; 23:12), much of this narrative's pungency rests in the circumstance that it is a woman who dominates the story. In this sense she is like Judah's daughter-in-law Tamar or (dare we say) Delilah, who also traps her amorous enemy caller. Like the crafty midwives of the exodus, she gains a house and a name in Israel (compare Exod. 1:15, 21). Rahab the foreign harlot seems to play a role in the masculine and military plot of Joshua something like that played by Jael in Judges. Her story gives notice that sometimes Yahweh's will is accomplished not by the glorious institution of divine war or by military superstars, but by the quick-thinking, perceptive faith and decisive action of the bit players in the drama: an alien prostitute, the midwives in Egypt, a nomadic housewife, a migrant farm worker from Moab, a pious widow named Judith.

Thus the national story of enemy fear and the conviction that conquest is Yahweh's gift is leavened by a personal and family story. This is a tale of a woman who is both cunning trickster, securing her family's future, and praiseworthy host, protecting her endangered guests in accordance with ancient norms of hospitality. In the midst of the virile game of war, with its masculine adventures in espionage, one woman seizes opportunity from the jaws of crisis and, by a shrewd and assertive use of the unusual freedom offered by her unenviable profession,[19] saves both herself and her family. She traps and pressures these young spies to extract what she wants: life and a future. Rahab acts wisely because she perceptively discerns the deeper truth of the situation. She has a vision of the future that God is bringing, a future she can trace out of the present situation (vv. 9–11). Thus the larger national epic and the smaller personal vignette converge on the same point. A clear head and a perceptive recognition that it is Yahweh who is in charge of events leads to life and salvation.

[1–3] Verse 1 introduces the characters and the locale. Shittim (also 3:1; location uncertain) is the traditional east bank staging point both in the Tetrateuch (Num. 25:1) and Micah 6:5. The phrase "the land, especially Jericho" implies that Jericho is the key to Canaan, both strategically and in the plot of the chapters to follow (note 8:2; 9:3; 10:1). Verse 1 and vv. 23b–24 form an outer narrative frame that connects this story to the larger plot. Although some have interpreted Joshua's act of sending spies immediately after hearing Yahweh's promise as disbelieving or weak behavior, the text itself provides no hint of this. In the Hebrew Bible spying preceeds conquest almost as a matter of course. Moses himself did the same thing immediately after receiving Yahweh's promise (Deut. 1:21–23). Joshua's repetition of this procedure in 7:2 does introduce a story of defeat, but the debacle at Ai had another cause altogether.

Although these two are assigned the task of looking over the target of Israel's attack, they will instead return to Joshua with a report of the enemy's state of

---

19. The narrative does not judge Rahab for her prostitution, but rather utilizes it to make the story work. Josephus was more sensitive and made her the proprietor of an inn (*Ant.* 5.1.2).

mind and a theological conclusion. Perhaps there are two spies because they will be functioning as witnesses. As "young men" (corrected text and 6:23) the reader may suspect that their approach to espionage may be somewhat hapless. "Lying down" in a harlot's house is an ambiguous move, one further exploited by the narrator with the sexual innuendo of "came in/came into" (vv. 3–4). On the other hand, a case can be made that they have picked a perfect place for their undercover work. Mesopotamian parallels suggest that Rahab could be thought of as operating an inn at the city gate, where she could keep track of comings and goings, perhaps with an obligation to report suspicious strangers.[20] In any case, strangers would not be conspicuous at Rahab's house and could pick up the latest news there. In the end, her occupation will turn out to be essential to their survival. For Rahab, at least, being a prostitute meant having economic and social independence. The house is hers (not some man's) and she is the one who takes responsibility for her family—brothers and father included. The two meanings of "house" as building and as family are intertwined in the story. What happens in her house (vv. 1, 18, 19) means safety for her father's house (*bêt 'āb* "family," vv. 12, 18).

Now that the reader's interest has been piqued, v. 2 introduces the narrative problem. Tension rises rapidly. The secret is betrayed. The king knows everything about the spies' origin and mission. This precipitates them abruptly into the role of endangered guests in a hostile city, like the angels in Sodom or the Levite at Gibeon, or more ominously, like Sisera hiding out in the tent of Jael. Rahab herself is confronted both by the king's men (v. 3) and by a personal crisis. They tell her that her guests are spies. They demand she hand them over, using language similar to that employed to pressure Lot and the old Ephraimite of Gibeon into betraying their guests (Gen. 19:5; Judg. 19:22).

[4–7] Rahab adroitly turns the crisis to her own advantage. First (*waw*-consecutive) she hides the Israelites, then tells her story. She begins with what is presumably the truth ("the men came . . . I did not know") and then moves into falsehood (the men left . . . I do not know") in order to deflect the pursuit from her house to outside the city (v. 5). Her reply picks up each important point made by the king:

> "The men came to you."
>   Yes, "the men came to me."
> "Men have come from the Israelites."
>   But "I did not know where they came from."
> "Send out the men" (hiphil of *yṣ'*).
>   But "the men left" (qal of *yṣ'*).

20. D. Wiseman, "Rahab of Jericho," *TynBul* 14 (1964): 8–11; Code of Hammurabi 109, *ANET*, 170.

Repeating the delegation's sexual implications ("came into/to"), she uses her prostitution as protective coloring to claim innocence and, repeatedly, ignorance. From a professional standpoint she can hardly be expected to care where these customers came from or where they went. She urges the king's men to chase her false lead. The narrator indulges in irony here. The supposition of the king's men is stated as though it were fact: "the men pursued them." So far, so good, but the gate's closing (vv. 5, 7) sounds an ominous note for the alert reader.

The disjunctive syntax of vv. 6–8 has a retarding effect on the action. It is best to take v. 6 as retrospective and thus contemporary to v. 4. The delay in revealing just how she has hidden the spies creates narrative tension during her long reply. Where did she hide them? *Why* did she hide them? Will a search be made? Will she betray them? With this delayed exposition, the narrator has saved the negative aspects of the spies' situation until v. 6, revealing to the anxious reader the uncomfortable facts of just where and how she has hidden them. They are passive and helpless, submerged under a mound of flax. Their assignment had been to "dig up" (vv. 2, 3 *ḥpr*); instead they are "buried" (*ṭmn*). Probably there is some humor intended in their situation. Two men from a military expedition find themselves deeply enmeshed in the domestic textile domain of womanhood. Nor is her roof a particularly good hiding place, if one considers what happened to Bathsheba and David's wives (2 Sam. 11:2; 16:22). Rahab has hiden the spies in a place of dubious safety and undignified discomfort.

Verse 7 makes their situation even more desperate. The king's patrols now block their way back to Joshua, and of more immediate concern, the gate has been shut. Rahab has both saved them and trapped them, to her ultimate advantage. Their supposed "deliverance" by Rahab has left them vulnerable and helpless. They are not like Samson, who when caught is a similar trap, could simply pull up the city gates and walk away (Judg. 16:1–3)! Thus the reader discovers that the narrative problem set forth in v. 2 has by no means been resolved. As far as the plot is concerned, these spies have hit bottom and are ready for a new stage — negotiations with the woman who has both saved and entrapped them.

[8–14] Still passive, they are about to lie down again,[21] but Rahab remains in charge of the situation. In the preamble to her proposal (vv. 9–11), Rahab starts with prudent fear and moves to a positive faith in Yahweh. The Rahab

---

21. Much scholarly discussion has centered on the discrepancy between v. 1, where the scouts lie down or go to sleep, and v. 8, which reports they had not done so yet. For a review of positions, W. Moran, "The Repose of Rahab's Israelite Guests," *Studi sull' Oriente e la Bibbia: G. Rinaldi,* Genoa, 1967, 273–84, who proposes that v. 1 is proleptic of v. 8. The simplest explanation is that the men did lie down in v. 1, were relocated by Rahab in v. 4 (of which v. 6 is a flashback), and had not yet settled down again in v. 8.

of this speech is not distant from the cunning woman of the earlier folk-tale, for her eyes are open to the evidence of coming reality. More perceptive than Jericho's king, she discerns the deeper truth behind current events. She draws the empirical conclusion from them that Yahweh is god of heaven

and earth. She speaks for the population of the land, but at the same time disassociates herself from them. Her words provide the spies with the content for their later report to Joshua: "Yahweh has given the land to you . . . our hearts melted." Her emphasis on fear echoes the divine warrior tradition (cf. v. 9 with Exod. 15:15b-16a), and she utilizes the creedal language of Deuteronomy. Yet her words, for all their deuteronomistic flavor, remain appropriate to the ancestor of a group who would remain outside Israel's camp (6:23). Yahweh remains "*your* God." She is not the Gentile convert that later tradition would make of her, but rather one of those foreigners in the Hebrew Bible whose acknowledgment that Yahweh is God underscores the self-evident power and glory of Yahweh (Balaam, Naaman, Nebuchadnezzar, Darius).

This motif of the believing foreigner creates a sharp contrast to Rahab's own introduction of the *ḥērem* motif (v. 10). The incongruity implicit in Joshua's exceptional treatment of Rahab is further highlighted in 6:17. Within the limits of the Rahab story, the question is whether the survival of her family undermines Israel's claim on the land and Yahweh's promise. The narrative insists that, rather than putting Israel's rightful possession of the land into doubt, the continued existence of Rahab's clan actually supports their claim, for she herself confessed that Yahweh gave Israel the land. Israel's territorial rights are based on the authority of "God in heaven above and on earth below" (v. 11). Concern for the land envelopes the first dialogue: "I know that Yahweh has given the land to you (v. 9) . . . When Yahweh gives us the land (v. 14)."

The goal of her long prologue is reached in vv. 12–13. Her "request" for protection for herself and her family is explicitly grounded on her demonstrated loyalty (*ḥesed*) as a host to her guests, which has created a reciprocal obligation (cf. Gen. 21:22–24). But the reader has also not forgotten the spies' precarious predicament of being caught in her trap. The shut gate, patrols on the Jordan road, and their position buried under flax on the roof play an implied but unquestionable role in coercing their agreement to her terms. Certainly she could still betray them and claim they had discovered their ridiculous hiding place on their own! Therefore their open-ended and unconditioned (in the earliest recoverable text) promise (v. 14) begins with a plea that recognizes their continuing danger: save our lives and we will save yours. They duplicate her choice of words (cf. their v. 14 with her vv. 9, 12, and 13), for she is in control of the situation. It is absolutely appropriate that they will later refer to this as "*your* oath" (vv. 17, 20; cf. Gen. 24:8). Their obligation of covenant loyalty is to Rahab herself (v. 14b, second person singular), but the lives of her family are drawn into the balanced equation of the Israelites' oath of self-cursing (v. 14a, second person plural). For the language of their oath, compare 1 Kings 20:39, 42; 2 Kings 10:24.

[15–21] The narrative tension now relaxes. Since the men have agreed to her terms, Rahab next[22] handily solves the problem of the closed gate and their exposed position. Lowering people through windows seems to have been a standard narrative motif (1 Sam. 19:12; Acts 9:25). Scenes of women up in windows or on walls conversing with men below may reflect another stereotypical narrative situation (2 Sam. 20:16–21; 2 Kings 9:30–31). Once more the men are the passive beneficiaries of her actions. Even when they are outside (v. 16), Rahab remains very much in charge, giving these inept secret agents detailed instructions on how to avoid capture. She dictates their route and schedule. By doing this she also effectively prevents them from carrying out their original assignment as spies.

The gate problem is solved, the problem of the pursuit is solved, but what about their uncomfortably open-ended oath? It is only when they are out of the trap in which Rahab had entangled them that the spies can seize the conversational initiative (vv. 17–20). Now they are in a position to hedge their oath with conditions and details. The repetition of "absolved from your oath" (by which they mean the self-cursing oath of v. 14) encloses their words in an envelope of self-protection (vv. 17a, 20b). The complex verbal formulation, the identifying sign of the crimson thread, and the careful restriction of her family to the confines of her house are all intended to protect the spies from bloodguilt and to reduce the reader's disquiet. A breach of secrecy on Rahab's part would terminate the agreement. Of course the king already knows their identity and mission, but now they have something else to hide, namely the escape plan Rahab has contrived for them.

Although "*this* crimson thread" (v. 18) sounds as though they are providing her with it (as a gift of a bit of feminine finery?), this seems awkward from the standpoint of staging. Perhaps the reader is meant to suppose that Rahab has just lowered them by her (perhaps very feminine and sexy) crimson thread, presumably intended as a touch of humor.[23] This understanding could explain the MT's strengthening gloss "cord of " (note u). Another pos-

---

22. Note the *waw*-consecutive. W. Martin, "'Dischronologized' Narrative in the Old Testament," *Congress Volume Rome 1968*, VTSup 17, Leiden, 1969, 182, takes vv. 15–16 as a flashback.

23. For other suggestions of humor, Y. Zakovitch, "Humor and Theology or the Successful Failure of Israelite Intelligence: A Literary-Folkloric Approach to Joshua 2," *Text and Traditions: The Hebrew Bible and Folklore*, SBLSS, Atlanta, 1990, 75–98.

sibility is that a red thread was already hanging out her window as a conventional sign for a house of prostitution.[24] The "bloodguilt" formula of v. 19 (literally "blood upon one's head," here translated "bear the blame for one's death") belongs to the juridical sphere. It simultaneously fixes blame on one party and exculpates the other, while declaring the judgment of death (2 Sam. 1:16; 1 Kings 2:37).

[21–24] Rahab agrees to their modified terms with a laconic couple of words, perhaps demonstrating a wise person's skill in balancing speech and silence. Yet even now she retains the initiative and sends them off. Repeated language (vv. 16 and 22; "there for three days until the pursuers return") shows how carefully they follow her directions. Although her display of the cord (now a *tiqwâ* rather than a "thread") in the window is technically premature, it is the appropriate place for the narrator to assure us that she has taken this last prudent, expectant step. One suspects word play here with another sort of *tiqwâ*, "expectation, hope."

With vv. 23–24 the spy story once more envelopes Rahab's story. The plot movement, which has descended through the misadventures of these luckless young spies to their ultimate humiliation trapped under Rahab's flax, then moved upwards through their escape and undetected stay in the hills, now returns to its starting point in Joshua son of Nun. The reader appreciates the ironic repetition of *māṣā'* in vv. 22 and 23: the pursuers never could "find" them, but the spies report instead on what did "find them" ("happen to them"). They give Joshua a report entirely based on Rahab's words and interpret the situation with a faith statement also derived from her.

The Rahab story, as a preliminary act in the drama of conquest, is about the power of knowledge. The protective wall by which the king of Jericho sought to safeguard information is breached as a preview to the disintegration of Jericho's physical wall. However, the knowledge that Israel needs to have in order to participate in this particular sort of conquest is not of the sort usually collected by military intelligence. Rather it concerns the terror that is the weapon of the divine warrior and the realization that Yahweh, as God of heaven and earth (cf. 3:11), has predetermined Israel's victory. It is the sort of knowledge that gives Israel the courage to act and the confidence to believe. This knowledge is first perceived by Rahab ("I know," v. 9) and then passed on to Joshua. The enemy's state of mind points forward to 5:1; 6:1; 9:1–3; 10:1–2; 11:1–5. The Divine Warrior's power over heaven and earth will be shown at the Jordan, at Jericho, and in the skies over Gibeon (10:11, 12–14).

24. J. Asmussen, "Bemerkungen zur sakralen Prostitution im Alten Testament," *ST* 11 (1957): 182. Less likely suggestions have pointed to the supposedly protective implications of red, as in the blood on the doorposts in the first passover or to the use of the verb "tie" (*qšr*) in contexts involving alliance or covenant (e.g. Gen. 44:30; Deut. 6:8; 1 Sam. 22:8).

Crossing the Jordan
Joshua 3:1–17

Final Instructions

3:1 Joshua got up early[a] in the morning. They marched out of Shittim, came to the Jordan [he and all the Israelites] and stayed overnight there before crossing. **2** At the end of three days the officers passed through the middle of the camp. **3** They commanded the people, "As soon as you see the ark of the covenant of Yahweh your God and the levitical priests carrying it, then you will march out from your places and follow it—**4** (However, let there be some space between you and it, about two thousand cubits wide.[b] Do not come near it!)—so that you may know the way you should go, because you have never passed this way before."

5 Then Joshua said to the people, "Sanctify yourselves, for tomorrow Yahweh will do wonderful things among you." **6** Next Joshua said to the priests, "Lift up the ark of the covenant and pass in front of the people." So they lifted up the ark of the covenant and went in front of the people.

7 Yahweh said to Joshua, "Today I will begin to make you great in the opinion of all Israel, so that[c] they may know that I will be with you just as I was with Moses. **8** You are to command the priests who carry the ark of the covenant, 'As soon as you come to the bank of the Jordan, stand still in the Jordan.'"

9 Joshua said to the Israelites, "Come here and listen to the words of Yahweh your God. **10** [Then Joshua said] In this way you will know that 'God Who Lives' is among you and will completely dispossess[d] before you the Canaanites, Hittites, Hivites, Perizites, Girgashites, Amorites, and Jebusites. **11** Here is the ark of the covenant! The Lord of the whole earth is going to cross [in front of you] in the Jordan.[e] **12** [And now] take twelve men for yourselves from the Israelites,[f] one man per tribe. **13** As soon as [the soles of] the feet of the priests who are carrying the ark of Yahweh, Lord of the whole earth, rest in the water of the Jordan, the water of the Jordan will be cut off. The water coming down [from above] will stand still [as a single heap]."[g]

Marching Across

14 When the people marched out from their tents to cross the Jordan, with the priests carrying the ark of the covenant[h] in front of the people, **15** and as soon as those carrying the ark came to the Jordan and the feet of the priests carrying the ark were dipped into the water's edge—now the

Jordan had completely overflowed its banks as during the harvest season[i] — 16 then the water of the Jordan coming down from above stood
still. It rose up as a single heap very far off in Adam (the city next to
Zarethan),[j] and the water going down to the Sea of Arabah (the Salt Sea)
was cut off completely.[k] The people crossed opposite Jericho. 17 So the
priests carrying the ark of the covenant of Yahweh stood firmly[l] on dry
land in the middle of the Jordan while all Israel was crossing over on dry
land, until the whole nation finished crossing the Jordan.

   a. Alternate translation based on the root meaning of the verb as "shoulder": "broke
up camp early" (compare NJB). See B. Waltke and M. O'Connor, *An Introduction to
Biblical Hebrew Syntax,* Winona Lake, Ind., 1990, 27.4b.
   b. Follows MT. OG has '*mdw* "stand still" for *bmdh* "in distance."
   c. Here '*ăšer* indicates purpose as in Deut. 4:40.
   d. For the contention that *yrš* hiphil in this context (Yahweh as subject, alien people as object; 13:6; 23:5, 9, 13) connotes "destroy so someone else can possess," see N.
Lohfink, "*yaraš*," *TDOT* VI, 374–75 and "Die Bedeutung von hebr. *jrš, qal* und *hif.*,"
BZ 27 (1983): 14–33. The traditional translation "drive out" (NRSV, REB, NJB) leaves
room the possibility that the expelled population might continue to live elsewhere. Because Lohfink's proposal does not seem to be either excluded or demanded by the evidence, this translation opts for the more neutral "dispossess."
   e. This translation takes seriously the definite article with *běrît.* Alternate translation following the Masoretic punctuation: "the ark of the covenant of the Lord of the
whole earth."
   f. Follows OG "sons of Israel." MT "tribes of Israel" attempts to clarify an unclear text.
   g. Follows the shorter OG, *hmym hyrdym y'bdw.* MT supplements from v. 16, creating some puzzling grammar in the process. "Coming down" (*hayyōrĕdîm*) puns on
the name Jordan.
   h. The construct noun with the article here and in v. 17 is curious but not impossible (examples: 1 Kings 14:24; 2 Kings 23:17). This anomaly probably resulted from a
redactional expansion of the ark's title.
   i. Follows OG *kymy qṣyr* as the shorter text and supported by 4QJosh[b] *bymy.* MT
adds a letter to *k* make *kl ymy qṣyr* "all the harvest season." In OG the water has risen
as though it were harvest time. In MT it actually is harvest time and the overflow always occurs throughout this period. OG and a corrector of 4QJosh[b] both offer an explanatory addition: "wheat" harvest.
   j. "In Adam" follows MT Kethib. The distinctive OG reading ("over a very wide
area as far as the edge of Kiriath-jearim") may perhaps be retroverted to *bm'd 'd 'šr qṣ
k'rtn* (the name as LXX[B]). Through several visual errors this could have been a corruption of MT *b'dm h'yr 'šr mṣd ṣrtn* (Holmes, *Joshua: the Hebrew and Greek Texts,*
23). Thus OG indirectly supports the Kethib rather than the Qere, "from Adam."
   k. An asyndetic verbal hendiadys as in Ps. 73:19, the auxiliary verb having an adverbial function.
   l. OG lacks "firmly" (*hākēn,* infinitive absolute used as adverb, see note b on 4:3),
but MT is the preferred difficult reading.

The convolutions of chapters 3 and 4 result from the concentration of a large number of themes into the narrow nexus of Jordan crossing. Too many topics have been crammed into too constricted a narrative space so that the thematic threads have tangled and knotted. Successive commands by different characters stack up. The disposition of memorial stones competes for attention with the dominant plot line of Yahweh stopping the Jordan to make crossing possible. The text seeks simultaneously to enhance the standing of Joshua, to include various personnel, to define the processional order, to boost the wonder of the event, and to explore its theological meaning.

The most obvious complications in chapter 3 are:

> an apparent chronological discrepancy between vv. 1, 5 ("overnight," "tomorrow") and vv. 2–4 ("three days")
> the awkward placement of the first part of v. 4
> no reported execution of the command of v. 5
> the awkward placement of v. 12 and its delayed follow-up (not until 4:2)
> the ark carriers stand at the edge of the river (vv. 8, 13, 15), but also in the middle (v. 17)
> the waters are "cut off," but also "stand still"
> the complex, overfull sentence in vv. 14–16
> inconsistent nomenclature for the ark

The logical digressions and persistent reiterations in chapters 3 and 4 are undoubtedly the result of a complicated history of composition and redaction, but no hypothesis to unravel the history of their formation has met with general acceptance. The two predominant approaches have been either to treat the text as an interwoven combination of two self-contained narratives[1] or to postulate a simpler precursor text which has undergone successive redactions.[2]

---

1. Classically by Möhlenbrink, "Die Landnahmesagen des Buches Josua," 254–58. More recently, T. Butler, *Joshua*, WBC 7, Waco, 1983, 41–42, proposes a catechesis about the ark cutting the water plus a cultic confession about guidance across the river. Otto, *Das Mazzotfest in Gilgal*, 26–57, suggests a Gilgal source and a deuteronomistic source. E. Vogt, "Die Erzählung vom Jordanübergang, Josue 3–4," *Bib* 46 (1965): 125–48, traces a war narrative and a cultic procession.

2. Classically by Rudolph, *Der "Elohist" von Exodus bis Josua*, 169–78. Other proposals are those of Boling, *Joshua*, 179–81; C. Keller, "Über einige alttestamentliche Heiligtumslegenden II," *ZAW* 68 (1956): 85–97; Fritz, *Josua*, 43–56; J. Maier, *Das altisraelitische Ladeheiligtum*, BZAW 93, Berlin, 1965, 18–32; Noth, *Josua*, 25, 27, 31–32; J. Soggin, "Gilgal, Passah und Landnahme: Eine neue Untersuchung des kultischen Zusammenhangs der Kap. III–IV des Josuabuches," *Congress Volume 1965*, VTSup 15, Leiden, 1966, 263–77. The most intricate of these reconstructions are those of F. Langlamet, "La traversée du Jourdain et les documents de l'hexateuque," *RB* 79 (1972): 7–38, who uncovers five successive layers and J. Dus, "Die Analyse zweier Ladeerzählungen des Joshuabuches (Jos 3–4 und 6)," *ZAW* 72 (1960): 107–34, who isolates six independent traditions. There is a review of scholarship in Otto, *Das Mazzotfest in Gilgal*, 104–20.

Most recent interpreters insist that the two-source approach is untenable because the stoppage of the flow of the river is reported only once (3:16) and reversed only once (4:18). Apart from this reasonable conclusion, however, any generally acceptable comprehensive solution to this compositional tangle is probably unattainable.[3]

Nevertheless one can at least indicate with some confidence the contributions of DH to chapter 3. The original designation "carriers of the ark" (v. 15a) has been supplemented from a deuteronomistic perspective by "the levitical priests" (v. 3) and then simply by "the priests" (vv. 13, 14, 15, 17; 4:9, 10, 18). This factor explains the incessant participial formula "the priests carrying the ark," otherwise uncalled for because there are no other priests involved from whom this group needs to be distinguished. DH has added these priests as markers of legitimacy here and in chapter 6 in order to emphasize Joshua's obedience to Deut. 10:8 (compare Deut. 31:9, 25).[4] Other deuteronomistic contributions are the appearance of these priests in vv. 6, 8, and the long title "the ark of the covenant (of Yahweh)" (vv. 3, 6, 8, 11, 14, 17), in contrast to the simpler original usage of vv. 13, 15. The three-day chronology and "the officers" of vv. 2 connect back to the concerns of DH in 1:10–11. Joshua's correlation to Moses in v. 7 (and 4:14) was first asserted in 1:5, 17. The list of nations in v. 10 is also deuteronomistic (Deut. 7:1; 20:17).[5] Thus most or all of vv. 2–4 and 6–10, consisting primarily of commands, predictions, and theological explanations, are a contribution of DH.

The main narrative line of what remains (vv. 1, 5, 11, 13–17) seems substantially to embody the original story. The chronology of vv. 1 and 5 hangs together and v. 11 makes good sense as a follow-up to v. 5. Grammatically vv. 14 and 15a are temporal clauses which introduce the main sentence of v. 16. The ark, which appears abruptly, is certainly part of this pre-deuteronomistic material. The conception of the ark is non-deuteronomistic. Rather than being associated with Mosaic law (8:33–35; Deut. 31:25–26), here it is carried in the vanguard of the marching people. This same procedure will be followed in chapter 6, but after that the ark will play no further military role. In v. 11 the ark is flatly equated with Yahweh (cf. 6:7, 8, 13), much as in the ancient fragment Num. 10:35. Another non-deuteronomistic traditional item is the divine epithet "Lord of the whole earth (or land)" (vv. 11, 13).

3. Abandoning the quest to unravel a history of composition, B. Peckham, "The Composition of Joshua 3–4," *CBQ* 46 (1984): 413–31, discovers a baroque thematic structure that completely overpowers the narrative plot. For a reading that understands the irregularities as shifts in temporal perspectives and points of view, see Polzin, *Moses and the Deuteronomist,* 94–99. P. Saydon, "The Crossing of the Jordan, Jos. chaps. 3 and 4," *CBQ* 12 (1950) 194–207, remarkably finds no significant irregularities.

4. DH acted similarly in 1 Kings 8:1–13. See R. Nelson, "The Role of the Priesthood in the Deuteronomistic History," *Congress Volume Leuven 1989,* VTSup 43, Leiden, 1991, 134–35, 144.

5. For an exhaustive analysis of these lists, T. Ishida, "The Structure and Historical Implications of the Lists of Pre-Israelite Nations, *Bib* 60 (1979): 461–90.

Beyond a recognition of deuteronomistic redaction and the conspicuous gloss of v. 4a, further attempts to reconstruct the literary history of chapters 3–4 are probably doomed to failure. It is more productive to examine the narrative shape of these two chapters when read together as a literary whole. In its present form the story is not governed by the reporting of successive events in a smooth chronological flow. Instead there is a pattern of narrative action (obedience and miracle) interwoven with associated speech (command, prediction, and explanation). Although the resulting logic and narrative flow is disjointed, by using moderate effort the reader actually has no trouble making sense out of the story line. The basic pattern of chapters 3 and 4 is one of scene setting (3:1–2) followed by command and prediction (3:3–13) followed by obedience and miracle (3:14–17; 4:11–19). The ark enters the water at the river bank and triggers a miraculous halt in the river's flow (3:15). Then the ark moves (at least in the reader's mind) to the middle (3:17), where it remains as the people cross. The reader must presume that the processional priority of the ark (3:3, 14; 4:11) is naturally discontinued while the people cross. Finally the ark crosses from the middle to the far bank (4:11, 18).

There are really two interconnected stories here. The report of memorial stones (4:1–10, 20–24) can be distinguished from the plot of miraculous crossing (3:1–17; 4:11–19) and is necessarily secondary to it. That is to say, the primary story of crossing works very well on its own, but the ancillary story of stones cannot exist by itself. These two story lines are connected by the anticipatory verse 3:12, the repetitive linkage of 4:1, and shared language such as "middle of the Jordan," "cut off," and "cross." Although the people themselves finish their crossing in 3:17 and 4:1, the priests and ark still remain in the river bed. At this point, time is frozen (in part through a resumptive repetition of 3:16b–17 by 4:10–11a) while 4:1–14 explores in a tighter focus details of the crossing event and the matter of the memorial stones. Then narrative time is unfrozen by 4:15, with the command for the priests to come up out of the Jordan. This literary technique of freezing time and shifting perspective is almost cinematic in its effect. A similar approach to the problem of telling simultaneous stories can be found in 1 Kings 20:16–21. The memorial stones story will be covered in the exposition of chapter 4.

The basic plot of the crossing story is simple. Its two foundational pillars are 3:15–16 and 4:18, which describe the onset and termination of the marvel. Those who carry the ark dip their feet into the overflowing Jordan, and the water coming down stands still while the water going further down is cut off. The people cross. When those who carry the ark come up from the middle of the Jordan and their feet touch dry ground, the water returns to its place and runs as before outside its banks. A bracketing framework to this core is provided by 3:1 and 4:19: the people march out from Shittim to cross, then come out of the Jordan to a new encampment at Gilgal. The narrative circle is complete.

Almost everything else in the text points to this simple core plot line, either as a command to be obeyed, as a prediction to be fulfilled, as an explication of significance, or as a clarifying repetition. What results is an intricate network of unifying threads. Sometimes these become so dense that they impede the movement of the plot. For example, chapters 3 and 4 are linked together by speech/action bonds (3:7 to 4:14; 3:11 to 4:11; 3:12 to 4:1–2; and 4:6–7 back to 3:16). These speeches initiate actions by means of command and prediction, and also explain the significance of what happens. The actions themselves consist of human obedience and divine miracle. An inner circle of speeches focus on the story at hand:

> 3:3, command: follow the ark
> 3:4, explanation: the way is unknown
> 3:5a, command: sanctify yourselves
> 3:5b, prediction: wonderful things
> 3:6, command: lift the ark and go in front
> 3:8, command: stand still in the Jordan
> 3:11, explanation: the Lord of the earth is crossing
> 3:13, prediction: the water will stop
> 4:16–17, command: come out of the Jordan

Similarly, an outer circle of (deuteronomistic) sentences splices the narrative into the larger story of Joshua: 3:2, 7, 9–10; 4:12–14. Yet another set of phrases connects what happens at the Jordan back to the exodus experience (3:16 "single heap" like Exod. 15:8; 3:17 "dry land" like Exod. 14:21; perhaps the date in 4:19). This correlation is also made forcefully by 4:22–23.

Commands are given first by the officers (to the people; 3:3–4), then by Joshua (to the priests; v 6a), then by Yahweh (to the priests via Joshua; v. 8), then by Joshua again (to the Israelites; vv. 9–13). Some of these commands are explicitly executed:

> v. 3 by v. 14: the people march out after the ark
> v. 6a by vv. 6b and 14: the priests pick up the ark and go
>   before the people
> v. 8 by vv. 15, 17: the priests stand in the Jordan

The people's actions are perfectly obedient to divine command. This is a warranty of success in deuteronomistic theology. It also resonates with the larger command/obedience structure of Joshua as a whole (see, e.g., chaps. 6, 7, and 13). However, the call for the people to sanctify themselves (v. 5a) is never picked up and the selection of the twelve tribal representatives (v. 12) is held off until chapter 4.

Constant repetition is another important unifying factor. These repetitions connect reported events to the central plot movement, introduce new elements, and keep the story from bogging down completely. Thus 3:14 repeats 3:3 and 6 (marching with the ark in front) in order to move into 3:15–16. Verse 3:17

restates 15–16 and then goes on to introduce the new notion of the "middle of the Jordan," which is needed both to tell the story of the memorial stones and to move the action forward again at 4:18. Joshua 4:10–11, as a resumptive repetition of 3:16b–17, restarts the story after the excursus about the stones. It also introduces the important new information that everything commanded about the stones has been completed and that the ark crosses after the people have finished, something that prepares for 4:18. The whole composition is also held together by the reiteration of two key words: *'br* "cross" and *'md* "stand." "Cross" in various meanings occurs in 3:1, 2, 4, 6, 11, 14, 16, 17, and thirteen more times in chapter 4. "Stand still" is found with both the ark carriers and the water as subject: 3:8, 13, 16, 17 (and 4:10), tying together Israel's obedience and Yahweh's miracle.

The text aims to convey the importance of the Jordan crossing as a pivotal event. The solemn call for sanctification (3:5) is one indication of this (compare Exod. 19:10). The ideological focus is on Israel's national identity and their claim to the land. Both center on Yahweh's act. Yahweh in association with the ark, as "God Who Lives" and as "Lord of the whole earth/land," was with Israel when they crossed the symbolic boundary of the Jordan into the land. Yahweh dispossessed seven nations of the former inhabitants for their sake. The truth of this assertion is authenticated by an awe-inspiring standstill of the Jordan's flow, by which Yahweh's presence with Israel is demonstrated (v. 10). During the monarchy and Persian period, this text would underscore Israel's rightful possession of Canaan. In the years of exile or diaspora, when the people were no longer in the land, it would proclaim that their powerful God was still among them, not just as the local deity of the territory they had once controlled, but as "Lord of the whole earth" and as "God Who Lives."

Assyrian campaign reports sometimes stressed military achievement by reporting the successful crossing of flooded rivers. Here the Jordan is not just a factor of military terrain, but an ideological symbol (compare 22:19, 24–25).[6] It represents the boundary between landlessness and settled peoplehood. The act of "crossing" can mean a hostile encroachment into another's territory and a way of making a land claim (Gen. 31:52; Judg. 11:18–20). Crossing the Jordan means to begin to take control of the land Yahweh is giving (1:1, 11). It is appropriately described as a watershed event, designated as such by miracle and the erection of memorial stones. The importance of the crossing is also signaled by the presence of the ark.[7] Use of traditional vocabulary implies that it ought to be evaluated just as highly as the paradigmatic saving act at the Red

6. Jobling, "The Jordan a Boundary." See also A. Hulst, "Der Jordan in den alttestamentlichen Überlieferungen," *OTS* 14 (1965): 162–88. In chapter 22 the dividing Jordan is ideologically bridged by signs of unity: altar, cult participation, kinship language. The Jordan was no actual barrier to commerce and travel (Gen. 32:11; Josh. 2:7; 2 Sam. 17:22).

7. For the role of the ark see G. Coats, "The Ark of the Covenant in Joshua: A Probe into the History of a Tradition," *HAR* 9 (1985): 137–57.

Sea.[8] The Jordan crossing also takes on confessional significance in 24:11; Ps. 66:6; and Micah 6:4–5. The profound significance of crossing the Jordan is highlighted in a more subtle way by echoes of the Divine Warrior's mythic creation victory over the chaotic Sea/River (Ps. 114:3, 5).[9]

In the context of DH the crossing is also an incident of major significance. Deuteronomy was spoken as a prologue to DH by Moses "beyond the Jordan" in anticipation of new realities soon to unfold when the Jordan was crossed (Deut. 1:1, 5–8; 31:3–5). Now the history of Israel in the land under the authority of the book of the law (Deut. 31:9–13) can begin. Crossing the Jordan also links Joshua to Moses as the focus of Yahweh's saving presence (1:5, 17; 3:7; 4:10; 6:27). It is appropriate to mark this pivotal event with opportunities to educate future generations in good deuteronomistic fashion (4:6–7, 21–22; cf. Deut. 6:20–25) and to follow it by dutiful obedience to the law (chap. 5).

[1–4] Renewed movement begins a new narrative, presented as the consequence of the spies' report to the camp at Shittim (*waw*-consecutive) and also as the natural continuation of 1:18. Getting up early signals zeal in pursuing the task at hand (cf. 6:12; 7:16; 8:10). These deuteronomistic "officers" are also introduced at the key moments of 8:33; 23:2; and 24:1. Two competing chronologies surface here. One night in the new camp, followed by Yahweh's miracle on the next day seem to be envisioned by vv. 1 and 5. In contrast, the intervening v. 2 (DH) describes the three-day period earlier prepared for by 1:11. The three days already consumed by the spies (2:22) are apparently intended to be equated with this waiting period.[10]

Although the role of the ark as a vanguard is not a deuteronomistic notion, the idea that Yahweh crosses over in front of the nation is in line with Deut. 9:3. Verse 4b provides a motive for the ark's role in harmony with Deut. 1:33: the people must be shown the way. The disjunctive and emphatic syntax of v. 4a interrupts the connection between v. 3 and the rest of v. 4 and introduces an extraneous (probably priestly) concern about the ark's perilous holiness. Such a 900 meter separation would make the envisioned crossing scene impossible. It was on the basis of this verse and Num. 35:5 that the distance for a "Sabbath day's walk" was determined.

[5] Although this isolated call for sanctification is often cited as evidence

---

8. The water rose in a single "heap" (v. 16; Exod. 15:8; Ps. 78:13) and the people crossed on "dry land" (v. 17; Exod. 14:21; compare 2 Kings 2:8, which also takes place near Gilgal). "Wonderful things" (v. 5) implies the feats done against Egypt (Exod. 3:20; Ps. 78:11; 106:22; compare Exod. 34:10).

9. O. Kaiser, *Die Mythische Bedeutung des Meeres in Ägypten, Ugarit und Israel,* BZAW 78, Berlin, 1959, 135–40; R. Schmitt, "Meerwunder- und Landnahme-Traditionen," *TZ* 21 (1965): 260–68.

10. For two seven-day periods in chapters 1–6 see J. Wilcoxen, "Narrative Structure and Cult Legend: A Study of Joshua 1–6," *Transitions in Biblical Scholarship,* Chicago, 1968, 60–64.

that these chapters represent a sort of "cultic script,"[11] holiness was also a requirement in the ideology of divine war (Deut. 23:15 [14E]; 1 Sam. 21:5). "Tomorrow" points to the single night chronology of v.1, but could also be part of a routine formula of sanctification (7:13; Num. 11:18). The expression "among you" associates vv. 5 and 10.

[6–10] The deuteronomistic theme of what people can "know" from Yahweh's actions (vv. 7 and 10; cf. Deut. 7:9; 9:3) will return in 4:22, 24. The syntax of v. 8 is disjunctive, emphasizing the leadership role of Joshua (*you* and not someone else). Joshua's role as mediator of divine command (v. 8) is clear in the phrase "Yahweh said to Joshua" (v. 7; cf. 1:1; 4:1, 15; 5:9; 6:2; and the like). Verse 9 serves to emphasize and solemnize the divine word to follow. The title "God who lives" (v. 10) has a confessional ring to it and is also found in 1 Sam. 17:26; Ps. 42:3, 9 [2, 8E]; 84:3 [2E]; Hos. 2:1 [1:10E]. As a poetic title denoting God as active and present,[12] it is used by Deut. 5:26 with reference to the voice of the Horeb experience. Here the living God is the One who will be alive and active in the coming events of conquest.

[11] It is unclear whether "Lord of the whole earth/land" (also v. 13) is to be understood narrowly as suzerain of the land of Canaan or universally as ruler of the entire earth. On the one hand, the context of land claim suggests the more narrow interpretation as the land of Canaan, as does the deuteronomistic usage of *kol hā'āreṣ* (6:27; 10:40; 11:16, 23; Deut. 11:25; 19:8). On the other hand, the universal meaning "earth" is also within the orbit of deuteronomistic thought (Deut. 10:14; Josh. 2:11). Universal dominion is implied by this expression in Ps. 97:5; Micah 4:13; Zech. 4:14; 6:5. In this text either the local or universal sense would make the same point: the God who is crossing with Israel has both the power and the right to endow them with the land. A non-Israelite origin for this title is sometimes suggested.[13]

[12] The imperative mood abruptly and fleetingly returns to interject a new topic, one which anticipates 4:2. In the present form of the text, this isolated command creates suspense and signals that there will be more to this story than the report of a miraculous crossing.

[13–16] Everything works according to divine plan. The "wonderful things" promised in v. 5 are first anticipated (v. 13), then reported (vv. 14–16), then summarized (v. 17). There is a chiasm between vv. 13 and 16: "cut off" and "stand still," then "stood still" and "was cut off." There is also word play between the water that stands and the ark carriers who also "stand" (vv. 8, 17; 4:10). What is meant by "stand" is described in v. 16: the water "coming down"

---

11. Suggestions that a Gilgal liturgical ceremony lies behind chapters 3–5 or 6 are taken up in the exposition of chapter 4.

12. H. Ringgren, "*ḥayah,*" *TDOT*, V, 338–40.

13. See the scholars and texts cited by F. Langlamet, *Gilgal et les récits de la traversée du Jourdain*, CahRB 11, Paris, 1969, 112–15.

from upstream is halted. Because of this the water that would have flowed downstream is "cut off." Although the two different verbs could indicate the presence of earlier sources, in the present form of the text they describe a single image. The waters were cut off because they stood still.

Verses 14, 15, and the first part of 16 form a complex single sentence that has the effect of retarding the action into slow motion. The actions of the people and the priests and the state of the Jordan are all syntactically subordinated to form the temporal backdrop for the real center of narrative interest, the cessation of the water (v. 16; *waw*-consecutive). The language seeks to accent the miracle: "very far off," "completely." The wide geographic sweep of the omniscient narrator reaches upstream to Adam[14] and all the way down to the river's mouth. The circumstantial sentence v. 15b also increases the wonder and is mirrored in the description of 4:18. High water blocks any thought that one of the Jordan fords (2:7, 23) was utilized. Springtime flooding would also coordinate with 4:19 and 5:10. A subject first sentence (last four words of v. 16) returns the narrative focus back to the people, where it began in v. 14. "Opposite Jericho" reminds the reader of the goal of their march.

[17] Verse 17 is an overview and summary of two simultaneous actions, standing and crossing. The last part of v. 17 is repeated by 4:1a to "freeze the action" and introduce the new topic of the stones. The concurrent circumstances of standing and crossing remain in force until the people's crossing is completed, that is, until 4:10–11 restarts the action. A key word is repeated: the priests are standing "on dry land" (and what is more, "firmly" and in the middle of the Jordan), while the people are also crossing "on dry land." The miracle is certified; the crossing was not over a ford, but on dry land. The people are now identified as a "nation" (*gôy;* 5:6 [MT], 8; 10:13), perhaps indicating that crossing the Jordan to become a landed people has meant a change in national status.[15]

Completing the Crossing
Joshua 4:1–24

Twelve Memorial Stones

4:1 When the whole nation had finished crossing the Jordan, Yahweh said to Joshua, 2 "Take for yourselves [twelve] men from the people, one man

---

14. Near the mouth of the Jabbok at T. ed-Damiyeh 201167. The location of Zarethan is uncertain.

15. A comparable transformation in status may be indicated in Exod. 19:6 and Deut. 26:5. See R. Clements, "*gôy,*" *TDOT,* II, 428–31, and A. Cody, "When Is the Chosen People Called a Goy?" *VT* 14 (1964): 1–6.

per tribe. 3 Command [pl] them [saying], 'Choose and take up for your-selves [from right here]ᵃ from the middle of the Jordan [from where the feet of the priests stood]ᵇ twelve firmly set stones and bring them across with you and put them down in the camp where you stay tonight.'" 4 Joshua summoned the twelve men he had appointed from the Israelites, one man per tribe. 5 He [Joshua] said to them, "Cross in the presence of [the ark of] Yahweh [your God] to the middle of the Jordan and each of you lift up a stone on his shoulder to equal the number of the tribes of the Israelites, 6 so that this may be a sign among youᶜ that your children may ask in the future, 'What are these stones to you?' 7 Then you shall tell them that the water of the Jordan was cut off before the ark of the covenant of Yahweh when it crossed over [in the Jordan. The water of the Jordan was cut off].ᵈ These stones will be a memorial to the Israelites forever." 8 Then the Israelites did just as Joshua commanded and lifted twelve stones from the middle of the Jordan, just as Yahweh had said to Joshua, equal to the number of the tribesᵉ of the Israelites, and crossed with them to the camp and put them down there.

9 And twelve stonesᶠ Joshua set up in the middle of the Jordan where the feet of the priests carrying the ark of the covenant had stood. They are still there today.

Finishing the Crossing

10 Meanwhile the priests carrying the ark were standing in the middle of the Jordan until everything was finished which Yahweh had com-manded Joshua to tell the people [according to everything which Moses commanded Joshua].ᵍ The people crossed quickly. 11 As soon as the whole people had finished crossing, the ark of Yahweh crossed, with the priests being in front of the people.ʰ

12 The Reubenites, Gadites, and the half tribe of Manasseh crossed over organized for war ahead of the Israelites, just as Moses had told them. 13 [About] forty thousand armed for war crossed in the presence of Yahweh for battle to [the plains of] Jericho. 14 On that day Yahweh made Joshua great in the opinion of all Israel. So they revered him just as they had reveredⁱ Moses his whole life.

15 Yahweh said to Joshua, 16 "Command the priests who are carrying the ark of the testimony to come up out of the Jordan." 17 So Joshua com-manded the priests, "Come up out of the Jordan." 18 When the priests car-rying the ark of the covenant of Yahweh came up from the middle of the Jordan, the soles of the priests' feet touched the dry ground,ʲ and then the water of the Jordan returned to its place and ran as before completely out-side its banks. 19 The people came up out of the Jordan on the tenth day of the first month and camped at Gilgal on the eastern border of Jericho.

Memorial Stones at Gilgal

20 Joshua set up in Gilgal those twelve stones which they had taken from the Jordan. 21 He said to the Israelites,[k] "When[l] your children ask you,[m] 'What about these stones?' 22 you will inform your children [saying], 'Israel crossed this Jordan on dry ground.' 23 For[n] Yahweh your God dried up the water of the Jordan before you until you crossed over, just as Yahweh your God did to the Red Sea, which he dried up before us until we crossed over, 24 so that all the peoples of the earth might know that Yahweh's power is great, so that you[o] may always revere Yahweh your God."

a. MT expansion attempting to clarify the situation of the stones, absent from OG and 4QJosh[b].

b. MT expansion from v. 9, absent in OG and probably 4QJosh[b] because of space considerations. To translate what remains, the puzzling *hākîn* is construed as an infinitive absolute relating to "stones," in agreement with the LXX translator (see note 1 on 3:17).

c. "A sign among you" follows MT. There is no obvious explanation for OG, "a sign set forever." Margolis, *Joshua in Greek,* 52, characterizes "forever" as a "free addition."

d. Absent in OG and V. MT represents an expansion ("in the Jordan") followed by dittography ("The water of the Jordan was cut off").

e. "Equal to the number of the tribes" follows MT. There is no obvious explanation for OG, "at the completion of the crossing."

f. Since there is no definite article, it is most natural to understand these as a second set of stones. The OG translator characterized them as "other stones," as did V.

g. MT expansion, perhaps based on Deut. 27:4.

h. Follows MT. OG offers instead *wh'bnym lpnyhm,* "the stones being in their presence," another attempt to clear up confusion over the stones. Alternate translation: "the ark crossed with the priests to the head of the people" (compare NJB, REB, and NAB).

i. Follows MT. OG lacks *'šr yr'w 't,* "they had revered," apparently to create a smoother translation.

j. Usually this verb means "separate." An alternate translation would be "pulled themselves loose onto dry ground." See KB[3], 695.

k. Follows MT. OG has a haplography, *bglg[l wy'mr 'l bny yśr']l l'mr.*

l. Apparently this *'ăšer* is to be taken either temporally or conditionally (cf. Deut. 11:27; R. Williams, *Hebrew Syntax: An Outline,* Toronto, 1976, 469).

m. Follows OG. MT expands and "corrects" to "in the future when your children ask their parents."

n. This curious initial *'ăšer* must be taken as explicative, "in that" or "for" (Williams, *Hebrew Syntax,* 468). Joshua explains why parents are to give the foregoing response.

o. This is often repointed as an suffixed infinitive construct, "that *they* may fear." However, the Masoretic vocalization as a second person perfect fits deuteronomistic usage and context, as shown by K. Aryaprateeb, "A Note on YR' in Jos. IV 24," *VT* 22 (1972): 240–42.

Chapter 4 is part of the same narrative unit as chapter 3, and the plot expectations created by 3:1, 7, and 12 are realized here. The situation set up in 3:15–16 is reversed by 4:18. The march that begins with 3:1 concludes with 4:19. The key verb "cross" continues to dominate, joined by the verb "finish" (*tmm*, 3:16, 17; 4:1, 10, 11). The narrative jumble displayed by chapter 3 also persists. Complications caused by the text's tangled history of composition include:

> memorial stones interrupt the primary story of crossing and compete with it for narrative attention
> two groups of stones, one on shore (vv. 3–5, 8) and one set in the river bed (v. 9)
> the men "deposit" the stones in an unnamed camp in v. 8, but in v. 20 Joshua "erects" them in Gilgal
> two scenes of catechesis, one focusing on "cutting off" (vv. 5–7) and the other on "drying up" (vv. 21–24)
> vv. 1 and 10–11 report the completion of the crossing prematurely (cf. vv. 12–13, 16–18).
> various uses of *lipnê* create confusion over the order of the procession (4:5, 11, 12, 13; cf. 3:6)
> an unexpected appearance of the eastern tribes (v. 12) and the isolated placement of vv. 13 and 14
> v. 11 reports that the ark crossed out of the middle of the Jordan, but it is still there in v. 18
> inconsistent nomenclature for the ark as in chapter 3

The primary narrative of crossing begun in chapter 3 reaches its conclusion in 4:18–19. However, before this conclusion is reached, the plot line is "frozen" and broken by the inclusion of an ancillary plot involving memorial stones. This plot line starts when 4:1 repeats the last phrase of 3:17. The crossing plot is subsequently "unfrozen" by a resumptive repetition of 3:16b–17 by 4:10–11a. In this way the story of the stones is presented as taking place at the same time as the conclusion of the people's crossing and while the ark is still located in the river bed. At the conclusion of the crossing story (v. 19), vv. 20–24 direct attention for a second time at the twelve stones and present an alternate interpretation of their significance.

As is the case in chapter 3, there is a pattern of speeches which initiate the actions and comment on their meaning. Once again the actions consist of human obedience and divine miracle.

> v. 2, command: appoint twelve men (obeyed in v. 4)
> vv. 3, 5, command: take twelve stones (obeyed in v. 8)
> vv. 6–7, explanation: this is a sign
> v. 14, explanation: Joshua is made great (3:7)

vv. 15–17, command: come out (obeyed in v. 18)
vv. 21–24, explanation: like the Red Sea

Again as in chapter 3 there are links to the larger story of Joshua: the eastern tribes, Jericho, Joshua's reputation, the date, Gilgal. The comparison to the Red Sea made explicitly in 4:21–24 echoes significant vocabulary choices that implicitly make the same comparison in 3:16–17.

The concerns of DH are present in vv. 12 (compare 1:12–15), in v. 14 (compare 1:5, 17), and in the addition of priests as the carriers of the ark. DH's expanded terminology for the ark in vv. 7, 9, 18 (and v. 5 MT) contrasts with the simpler and presumably original wording of vv. 10 and 11.[1] Another characteristic deuteronomistic interest is the education of future generations (vv. 6–7 and 21–24; Deut. 6:20–25; Exod. 12:26–27). Verse 24 clearly exhibits deuteronomistic language (cf. Deut. 4:10; 14:23; 17:19). Perhaps the competing vignettes of vv. 6–7 and 21–24 represent successive redactions of DH.

With moderate effort a cooperative reader can produce a plausible narrative scenario out of this admittedly muddled text. Verses 1–8 take place while the ark is in the stream bed and at the conclusion of the people's crossing. Verse 9 refers to a second set of stones. Once these commands are all fulfilled and the people have hastened across, the ark also moves across. This action is stated in a general way in v. 11. It is described fully in vv. 15–18, but only after a "flashback" which provides further information on the crossing (vv. 12–13) and a comment on its significance (v. 14). The narrative arc which began with 3:15–16 is finally completed by 4:18. Verse 19 then fixes the time and place of the crossing and introduces the locale of Gilgal. The stones which the men had "put down" in v. 8 are now "set up" here by Joshua, and their significance is explored further. This same cooperative reader will be induced to understand *lipnê* in vv. 5 and 13 as "in the presence of" (as in this translation) rather than indicating priority in the order of procession as in 3:6, 14.[2]

This narrative has often been interpreted as a festival legend for a liturgy supposedly celebrated in Gilgal. It has been thought to relate to a springtime procession with the ark that reenacted the Jordan crossing in association with the Red Sea event. This suggested ritual is also sometimes thought to have encompassed the observance of circumcision and passover from chapter 5. The core of chapters 3 and 4 is thus understood to be a foundation legend for the sanctu-

---

1. The expression for the ark in v. 16 is P-like and may be associated with the first part of 3:4 and other priestly-sounding material in Joshua.

2. Some translators also manage to construe the circumstantial clause in 4:11 in the same way, as "in the presence of" (NIV). REB, NAB and NJB take this to mean that the ark and the priests returned after crossing to their original position as first in the order of march. Because v. 12 is a flashback, the expression there certainly must be taken in light of 1:14 (and Deut. 3:18) to mean priority in the order of procession.

ary at Gilgal and its cult.[3] While attractive, this whole notion is unlikely, primarily because the oldest narrative level of chapters 3 and 4 tells a story of miracle and crossing, but not one of priests, stones, or catechetical instruction. The memorial stones are part of an ancillary plot fitted into the primary story. The exodus associations (3:13, 16–17; 4:21–23), the presence of priests (DH), and teaching the young[4] are all redactional rather than part of the primary substratum of the story. The apparent springtime season functions in a narratival way to enhance the wonder (3:15) and to connect the story to the larger plot of Joshua (4:19 to 5:10, 12). Conversely, whatever etiological interests are present really focus on the twelve stones, not on the crossing of the ark. There can be little doubt that some elements of this narrative, especially the stones, were originally associated with the sanctuary of Gilgal, the importance of which is clear from 1 Sam. 11:14–15; Hos. 4:15; 9:15; 12:12 [11E]; Amos 4:4; 5:5. The name Gilgal ("circle") hints at a ring of standing stones, which may be referred to in Judg. 3:19. However, to gather elements from all the stages of the redactional growth of this text and then repackage them into a reflection of an otherwise unknown liturgical activity is methodologically unsound. This text as it stands exerts no discernable effort to legitimate Gilgal as a cultic place or to encourage or explain the celebration of any ritual action there. The closest parallel to this tale of the ark's progress from Shittim to Gilgal is the Ark Story (1 Samuel 4–6; 2 Samuel 6), which traces its adventures from Shiloh to Jerusalem.

Several levels of proclamation occur simultaneously. The narrative intends to exalt Joshua as model and hero (v.14), to remind readers of Yahweh's saving deeds in giving the land, to hold up the Jordan crossing as foundational to Israel's identity and faith, and to encourage obedience and fidelity to Yahweh. Such a text must have been meaningful to audiences proud of their national heritage, but also to those under stress from outside dangers or experiencing the threat of apostasy. Later readers who thought in categories of exile and return

3. This suggestion is represented classically by H.-J. Kraus, "Gilgal, ein Beitrag zur Kultusgeschichte Israels," *VT* 1 (1951): 181–99, and *Worship in Israel,* Richmond, 1965, 152–65. Other forms of the cultic script thesis are presented by Keller, "Über einige alttestamentliche Heiligtumslegenden, 85–97; Otto, *Das Mazzotfest in Gilgal,* 167–98; J. Porter, "The Background of Joshua 3–5," *SEA* 36 (1972): 5–23; Soggin, "Gilgal, Passah und Landnahme"; J. Wijngaards, *The Dramatization of Salvific History in the Deuteronomic Schools, OTS* 16, Leiden, 1969, 3–7, 90–93, 113–27; Wilcoxen, "Narrative Structure and Cult Legend." See also G. Kühnert, *Das Gilgalpassah: literarische, überlieferungsgeschichtliche und geschichtliche Untersuchungen zu Josua 3–6,* Mainz, 1982.

4. For arguments that these catechetical children's questions are literary creations rather than traditional genres and that the two examples in Joshua chapter 4 are redactional, see H.-J. Fabry, "Spuren des Pentateuchredaktors in Jos 4,21ff," *Das Deuteronomium,* BETL 68, 1985, 351–56. This counters the view that their life setting was in cultic practice, as proposed by J. Soggin, "Kultätiologische Sagen und Katechese im Hexateuch," *VT* 10 (1960): 341–47, and J. Loza, "Les catéchèses étiologiques dans l'Ancien Testament," *RB* 78 (1971): 481–500.

would be encouraged to hope that Yahweh's former deeds, recounted to each succeeding generation, might still hold the key to their future and that national restoration was still possible. Verse 24 sets Israel's continued fidelity into the context of the nations, who themselves may come to know Yahweh's power. This universal perspective echoes the theology of Second Isaiah and Ezekiel.

The act of retelling this story, something built right into the text itself (vv. 6–7, 21–24), would perform the social function of reinforcing peoplehood.[5] The Jordan is not just an item of geography, but part of a symbolic system. It represents the boundary between being a landless people and being a nation that possesses a homeland. A "rite of passage" means a change in status. To cross the Jordan boundary meant a transformation into nationhood. The move from Shittim to Gilgal was a saving act of Yahweh (Micah 6:5), initiated and empowered by Yahweh. To retell the story of crossing was to reinvigorate identity and esteem, to reinforce and objectify peoplehood, and to build the unity of the nation. Telling and hearing this story would create self-understanding and identity. The audience would come to see itself as twelve tribes forged into a single nation. Understood in this way, the text is less an etiology for a circle of stones than an etiology for the group identity of Israel.

Thus the story of crossing is a foundational myth of transition from a past time of promise to a present time of fulfillment, a journey from desert chaos to landed order, from Moses to Joshua, from desert manna to the produce of the land (cf. 5:12), from outside the land to inside it. Integral to Israel's identity was its claim on Canaan, for to cross the Jordan was to become a landed people whose land was specifically the territory west of the Jordan (3:10; 4:13; 22:19). Even the two and a half eastern tribes cross westward into Canaan in solidarity with the rest of Israel. As is typical of all biblical story, Israel's foundational transformation is told in a thoroughly theocentric way. It is the power of Yahweh that performs this great transmutation into peoplehood, a power keyed into the text by mythic overtones. The chaotic Sea/River may be an insurmountable barrier for humans, but the Divine Warrior cuts it and crosses through it in the form of the ark. Here the mythic and the "historical" merge and work together, a merger of creation theology and salvation theology comparable to that of Second Isaiah (compare Isa. 43:16–19).

[1–8] The last words of 3:17 are repeated in order to introduce a concurrent side plot. The "until" of 3:17 becomes the "when" of the ancillary plot. The course of the main plot is suspended until the commands about the stones are followed (v. 10). In light of 4:1, the description seems to envision a backtracking from west to east on the part of the twelve porters. In an earlier form of the text the verb *nwḥ* hiphil (vv. 3, 5) may have referred to the permanent

---

5. For what follows, see L. Thompson, "The Jordan Crossing: *Ṣidqot Yahweh* and World Building," *JBL* 100 (1981): 343–58.

installation of these stones on the bank (cf. 2 Kings 17:29; Isa. 46:7), in contradiction to v. 20. In the present context, however, the verb must be taken to indicate a temporary arrangement (cf. 6:23; Gen. 39:16; 1 Sam. 6:18). Gilgal is not mentioned in regard to these stones until v. 20. The somewhat obscure *hākîn* ("firmly") of 4:3 affords a word play involving 3:17 (*hākēn* "firmly") and 4:4 (*hēkîn*, "appointed").

The stones are taken to be a sign and memorial of a recited narrative of saving history, one limited at this point to the ark's crossing and the cutting off of the water before it. For Deuteronomy's concept of "sign," see Deut. 6:8; 11:18; 28:46, and for the similar notion of "memorial," see Exod. 13:8–9. Perhaps at one time the narrative about crossing the Jordan served as an etiology for these stones. However, in its present form the narrative does not exist for the sake of the stones, rather the stones support the narrative by giving it meaning and significance. They show that this story is foundationally important for future generations, that is, for the readers themselves. Perhaps originally the twelve standing stones at Gilgal reflected astral concepts, but in this text the number twelve echoes the strong "all Israel" interest of book as a whole and seems to reflect Deut. 1:23. From the standpoint of DH, the erection of these stones may have been intended as a partial fulfillment of what Deut. 27:2–3, 8 commanded to take place on the day Israel crossed into the land. However, the complete realization of Deut. 27:2–13 is delayed until Ebal and Gerizim are reached in 8:30–35.[6]

[9] A disjunctive, object-first sentence introduces some (other?) stones as a new topic. Now the middle of the Jordan, which has been the literary link between the location of the ark (3:17; 4:10, 18) and the source of the memorial stones (4:3, 5, 8), is itself spotlighted by the placement of stones. Exactly what is intended is obscure. Is the text describing a processional causeway or the rocks of a ford exposed at low water? A redactional testimony formula seeks to undergird the reliability of the narrative.

[10–11] The people now finally finish the crossing, something that has been proleptically announced twice already (3:17; 4:1). Another advance takes place when the completion of the crossing from the end of 3:17 is converted in 4:10 to the completion of obedience to Yahweh's command. This change takes into account what has been reported in vv. 2–9. Elements of 3:16b–17 are repeated by 4:10–11a in a different order with altered grammar in order to "restart" the frozen narrative action of crossing. This is a classic example of *Wiederaufnahme*, a literary indication of inserted, discursive, or simultaneous material.[7] However, the syntax shows a subtle change in focus when the narrative restarts. In 3:17 the priests were the subjects of the main verb, while a

6. This is true in MT and OG. 4QJosh[a] places 8:30–35 before 5:2.

7. S. Talmon, "The Presentation of Synchroneity and Simultaneity in Biblical Narrative," *Studies in Hebrew Narrative Art Throughout the Ages*, SchHier 28, Jerusalem, 1978, 9–26.

participle indicated that Israel was crossing simultaneously. Now in 4:10 the priests recede a bit into the background as the subject of a participle, while the people take center stage as the subject of the main verb. As in 4:1, the "until the nation finished" of 3:17 has become the "when the people finished" of 4:10. The excursus is over. A similar perspective shift is created by the omission of both occurrences of "dry land" present in 3:17. This focuses attention on the completion of the crossing rather than on the wonder of the miracle. The action moves up to speed as the people cross "quickly." "Quickly" also communicates the large size of the multitude involved.

In v. 11 the plot advances a step further when the ark's crossing is reported. In light of vv. 15–18 this seems premature, but in context it may be taken to mean that the ark moves from the center to the west edge of the stream bed. The reader then must assume that v. 18 backtracks a bit with "the middle of the Jordan" before reporting that the priests actually leave the water. The lame circumstantial clause at end of v. 11 seeks to recapture the processional order that puts the ark first (3:6, 11; but see text note h).

[12–13] A flashback reports that the eastern tribes have done what Moses commanded and Joshua reiterated (1:14; Deut. 3:18; note ḥămušîm "organized for war"). This interest reappears in 12:6; 13:8–32; and chapter 22. The subject-first sentence of v. 13 is most naturally taken as a reference to the same group. The military expression "armed" (ḥālûṣ) connects back to the eastern tribes in Deut. 3:18 (and Num. 32:20–32). It also points forward to Jericho (6:7, 9, 13).

[15–19] The restart of the crossing action, initiated by vv. 10–11, is picked up again with a return to a characteristic command/action sequence. Verses 15–17 represent the command phase and v. 18 the action phase. Verse 18 reports an item-by-item reversal of what happened in 3:15–16. The ideological reference to the exodus continues with ḥārābâ "dry ground" (3:17; Exod. 14:21).

The subject-first syntax of v. 19 returns the focus to the people. From a literary standpoint, this solemn date formula indicates the closure of one period of Israel's story and the opening of another. It also connects chapters 3 and 4 into a larger narrative frame, pointing forward to the passover of 5:10 (cf. Exod. 12:3 and 6).[8] As a geographic marker, v. 19 advances the story to the locale of chapter 5 and points further ahead to chapter 6. Gilgal as a crossing point is found in other biblical contexts (2 Sam. 19:16, 41 [15, 40E]), in one case with a corresponding miracle (2 Kings 2:1, 8). Gilgal will continue to be the headquarters for Israel (9:6; 10:6–7; 14:6).

[20–24] A disjunctive emphatic object-first sentence reintroduces the stones. The erection of stones is associated with covenant making in Exod.

---

8. According to Wilcoxen, "Narrative Structure and Cult Legend," 60–64, from 1:10–11 to passover can be counted as seven days, with the siege of Jericho occupying another seven.

24:4 (twelve stones) and Josh. 24:26. Like Elijah's reconstructed altar of twelve stones (1 Kings 18:31–32), the number twelve stresses the prototypical unity of "all Israel."

Verse 21 repeats the question of v. 6, but this time the answer coordinates Jordan crossing with the Red Sea event. Once again this is not so much an etiology for the stones as it is a literary technique for explaining their significance. The correlation with the Red Sea event is supported by vocabulary choice: *yabbāšâ* (v. 22, "dry ground," Exod. 14:22 P), the verb from the same root (v. 23), and "mighty hand" (v. 24; trans. as "your power is great," cf. Exod. 13:9; Deut. 4:34–35; 7:17–19; 11:2–4). The ark of v. 7 has disappeared from this second explanation. The focus instead is on the crossing of the people. "Drying up" has taken the place of "cutting off." The literal echo of Rahab's confession of 2:10 in v. 23 produces a syntactically rough connection between vv. 22 and 23. The difference in generations is carefully distinguished in Joshua's speech: *we* crossed the Red Sea, *you* crossed the Jordan. The logic of *ka'ăšer* ("just as") coordinates the miracle of the Jordan with that of the Red Sea, and by extension the leadership of Joshua with that of Moses (cf. 1:5, 17; 3:7; 4:14). This correlation between the Jordan and the Red Sea is not only typological, but mythic (cf. Pss. 66:6; 114:3). It is a way of saying that crossing the Jordan was a prototypical, foundational event for Israel.[9]

Verse 24 is thoroughly deuteronomistic in language and outlook. It universalizes the horizon of the crossing event to include all peoples (1 Kings 8:42, 60; 2 Kings 19:19), but then narrows the final focus to Israel's abiding fidelity to its God Yahweh (Deut. 5:29; 6:2). The Jordan crossing ends on the same note as the Red Sea event, Israel's fear of Yahweh (Exod. 14:31 J).

Beginning
in the New Land
Joshua 5:1–15

Reaction of the Kings

5:1 When [all] the kings of the Amorites across the Jordan [to the west] and [all] the kings of the Canaanites near the sea heard that Yahweh had dried up the water of the Jordan before the Israelites until they[a] had crossed, their hearts melted and there was no longer courage in them because of the Israelites.

9. Exodus 15:14–17 confirms this traditional connection between Yahweh's triumph at the Sea and Israel's "crossing" (verb *'br*) and occupation of the land. On the other hand, one should note that there is no actual "crossing" in the J description of the Red Sea event or in the description of the exodus in Deuteronomy.

Circumcision[b]

2 At that time Yahweh said to Joshua, "Make yourself flint knives

UNREVISED TEXT	MT REVISION
and sit[c] and circumcise the Israelites.	and circumcise *again* the Israelites *a second time.*[d]
3 So Joshua made flint knives for himself and circumcised the Israelites at Foreskins Hill.	3 So Joshua made flint knives for himself and circumcised the Israelites at Foreskins Hill.
4 This is the manner[e] in which Joshua circumcised[f] the Israelites:	4 This is the reason Joshua circumcised: *all the people who went out of Egypt, the males, all the warriors, had died in the wilderness on the way when they went out of Egypt.*
5 all who were born on the way and all those uncircumcised[g] when they went out of Egypt, these Joshua circumcised.[h]	5 *For all the people who went out were circumcised, but* all *the people* who were born *in the wilderness* on the way when they went out of Egypt *had not been circumcised.*
6 For Israel journeyed forty[i] years in the wilderness. Therefore many of them were uncircumcised,[j]	6 For *the Israelites* journeyed forty years in the wilderness *until the whole nation perished,*

the warriors who went out from Egypt, who had not obeyed Yahweh, to whom Yahweh had sworn that he would never show them the land that Yahweh had sworn to their ancestors to give to us—a land flowing with milk and honey. 7 Their children whom he had set in their place—Joshua circumcised them, for they were uncircumcised because they had not circumcised them on the way.[k]

8 When they [the whole nation] had finished being circumcised they stayed in their place in the camp until they recovered. 9 Then Yahweh said to Joshua, "Today I have rolled away from you the disgrace of Egypt." So the place is still called Gilgal today.

Passover

10 The children of Israel encamped in Gilgal[l] and celebrated the Passover on the fourteenth day of the month in the evening on the plains of Jericho.[m] 11 They ate the produce of the land [on the day after the Passover]—

unleavened bread and roasted grain—on that very day. 12 The manna stopped [on the day after] when they ate the produce of the land, and there was no longer manna for the Israelites. So they ate the yield of the land of Canaan that year.

The Commander
of Yahweh's Army

13 When Joshua was by Jericho he looked up and saw [and behold] a man standing before him with a drawn sword in his hand. Joshua went up to him and said to him, "Do you belong to us or to our enemies?" 14 He said, "No.[n] I am the commander of the army of Yahweh. Now I have arrived!" Then Joshua fell flat on his face and worshipped[o] and said to him, "What is my lord saying to his servant?" 15 The commander of the army[p] of Yahweh said to Joshua, "Take your sandals off your feet, because the place where you are standing is holy." [And Joshua did so.][q]

a. Follows Qere and OG, T, S. Kethib "we crossed" was caused by a visual confusion of *m* and *nw*.

b. 4QJosh[a] precedes v. 2 with the pericope about Joshua's altar, 8:[30–33] 34–35, joined by an editorial transition relating to the Jordan crossing. This placement is more logical in that it obeys the command of Deut. 27:2–8 precisely and coordinates the Ebal altar with the other ritual matters of circumcision and passover. For this reason it is also less likely to be original than the order of MT or OG.

c. Follows OG: *wšb w*. MT has *wšwb* in harmony with its assertion that this circumcision was a "second" one.

d. Line length suggests that 4QJosh[a] omits "a second time" along with OG.

e. *Dābār* is construed as "manner" in the original and "reason" in the revision.

f. OG translates as "purified."

g. *wkl h'rlym*, represented in OG as *kai hosoi pote aperitmētoi ēsan*.

h. That is '*lh ml yhwš*', which OG expands with "all." Because MT *l' mlw* is graphically similar, the revision may have been initiated or facilitated by a misreading.

i. Follows MT. OG "forty-two" is probably the result of a dittography: '*rb'ym [wšnym] šnh*.

j. That is, *lkn 'rlym hyw rbym mhm*. The retroversion of the OG conjunction *dio* is uncertain. If it represents *kî* (rather than *lākēn*) the meaning could be "because" or "indeed."

k. Follows MT. For v. 7b OG has "because those who were born on the way were uncircumcised," perhaps *ky 'rlym hyw hylwdym bdrk*. It is unclear which represents the preferable reading, although OG provides a better chiastic parallel to the earliest recoverable text of v. 5.

l. Follows MT. OG shows a haplography from "Gilgal" in v. 9 to "Gilgal" in v. 10.

m. Follows MT. OG has a doublet and an expansion here: "across the Jordan on the plain."

n. Follows MT, which has the more difficult reading. OG *lw* "to him" assimilates to the formula of vv. 13b and 14b. The commander's "no" is best understood as "neither," that is, that he represents a third force in the conflict, the army of Yahweh. J. Soggin, "The Negation in Joshua 5:14 (Emphatic *Lamed*)," *Old Testament and Oriental Studies,* BibOr 29, Rome, 1975, 219–20 and *Joshua,* 77, attempts to understand this as an emphatic *lamed,* "indeed." This disregards the shape of Joshua's question as giving two mutually exclusive choices.

o. Follows MT. OG omitted "and worshipped" to avoid an offense against piety.

p. Follows MT. OG omission of "army" is probably a matter of translational variation.

q. MT expansion like that of 10:23.

Chapter 5 consists of four clearly defined units: reaction (v. 1), circumcision (vv. 2–9), passover (vv. 10–12), and numinous appearance (vv. 13–15). The first two segments and the last are defined by prominent temporal markers that seem to indicate redactional joins. Two warlike sections encompass two ritual segments, and the ritual pair is held together by the location of Gilgal. Major issues of textual divergence involving the second and third units complicate matters further. Application of standard text-critical principles reveals that the MT of vv. 2–9 and 10–12 represents revisions of the earliest recoverable text. These revisions reflect an interest in harmonization and concerns about orthodoxy.[1]

A cultic origin or setting in life for this chapter has sometimes been suggested. Such proposals connect circumcision and passover at Gilgal to a ceremony reenacting the Jordan crossing that supposedly lies behind chapters 3 and 4.[2] However, any reconstruction of a ritual of circumcision and passover at Gilgal is fatally undercut by the recognition that the connection between chapter 5 and chapters 3 and 4 is purely redactional ("at that time," v. 2). Here circumcision is anchored to the larger story of exodus (vv. 2–9) and passover is connected to the themes of wilderness manna and the settlement of Canaan (vv. 10–12). These associations are literary rather than the result of some original overarching cultic *Sitz im Leben.* The appearance of the heavenly commander is even more loosely attached ("when Joshua was by Jericho," v. 13) and really points forward to the conquest of Jericho.

In the overall plot of Joshua, this chapter continues the theme of transition found in chapter 1 (from Moses to Joshua) and chapters 3 and 4 (from east to west of the Jordan). The boundary river has been crossed and the enemy kings terrorized (v. 1). Now Israel engages in further "rites of passage," moving from the shame of uncircumcision to circumcision and from wilderness manna to a settled agricultural economy. Upcoming campaigns are initiated by the fear of

---

1. For further details on the textual situation, see Holmes, *Joshua, the Hebrew and Greek Texts,* 28–31, and Auld, "Joshua: the Hebrew and Greek Texts," 9–10. For a vigorous denial that OG represents a better text than MT or that MT is the result of an orthodox revision, see D. Gooding, "Traditions of Interpretation of the Circumcision at Gilgal," *Proceedings of the Sixth World Congress of Jewish Studies,* Jerusalem, 1977, I, 149–64. 4QJosh[a] generally supports the longer MT.

2. See the exposition of chapter 4.

the kings and legitimated by the appearance of the heavenly commander. Each of the four units touches on the theme of the land. Verse 1 details the geography of its inhabitants. Verses 2–9 explore both the dangers of disobedience and Yahweh's promise of the land of milk and honey. Verses 10–12 describe the transition to the diet and economy of Canaan. Finally vv. 13–15 introduce conquest themes and identify at least one piece of the land as holy. These highly disparate materials are held together almost solely by the Jordan/Gilgal/Jericho locale, which also provides their primary attachment to chapters 3–4. Again this attachment is self-evidently one of literary composition, not evidence of a pre-literary liturgical recitation.

[1] This verse is a pre-deuteronomistic redactional tie between crossing into the land and the ensuing warfare with the kings. On the one hand, it serves as a conclusion for the Jordan crossing, reflecting the language of 4:23 and the content of 4:24 ("all the peoples . . . might know"). Yet the grammar of an introductory temporal phrase points to a new start. The verse looks forward to the struggles that follow. Its language connects to the organizing principle of the pre-DH form of Joshua (2:10a, 11a; 9:1; 10:1; 11:1) and reflects Divine Warrior ideology (Exod. 15:14–16). Here the Amorites are taken to be the inhabitants of the highlands (as also 10:5–6; Deut. 1:44) and the Canaanites those who live by the coast. The MT additions seek to avoid any confusion between these Amorites and Sihon and Og (2:10; 9:10; 24:8).

[2–9] The shorter, unrevised text, (substantially that of the OG without its own obvious expansions), speaks of two groups who needed to be circumcised: all those born in the wilderness and also those who had not been circumcised when they left Egypt. The two uncircumcised groups are presented in a chiastic pattern:

> A: all who were born on the way (v. 5)
> > B: all those uncircumcised when they went out of Egypt
> > (v. 5)
> > B': many of them were uncircumcised, the warriors who
> > went out of Egypt (v. 6)
> A': they had not circumcised them on the way (v. 7)[3]

There is no emphasis in the unrevised text that Joshua's circumcision was a repetition of an earlier practice (as opposed to v. 2 MT). The text's primary focus is on the new generation born "on the way," (first part of v. 5, v. 7). Those uncircumcised at the time of the exodus are mentioned only incidentally (second part of v. 5, v. 6). The thematic phrase "on the way" designates this new generation and brackets the explanation of Joshua's act (vv. 5 and 7).[4]

---

3. OG has a perfect parallel: "those who were born on the way." See text note k.

4. The unrevised version of the story has a puzzling internal contradiction. Yahweh's oath against the old generation indicated that they would not see the land (v. 6). How could some of

The repeated language of vv. 2 and 3 continues the command-obedience structure of chapters 3 and 4. To sit while circumcising is said to be an Egyptian practice (*ANEP*, 629). In any case, it would be the appropriate posture for circumcising adults. The final disposition of these knives will be the topic of the OG text at 21:42D and 24:30A. That these are flint knives may derive originally from the Joshua grave tradition witnessed to by these OG texts, but also reflects the ingrained conservatism of ritual. Perhaps this notice was intended as a polemic against the use of metal knives (compare Exod. 4:25; 20:25). "Foreskins Hill" is most likely an undeveloped geographical etiology (compare Judg. 15:17), but alternately could refer more generally to all those places where foreskins were customarily buried or covered with earth.[5]

The narrative action takes place in vv. 3, 8–9. Verses 4–7 represent an explanatory section in non-narrative syntax, with at least vv. 5–6 apparently being a contribution of DH. "Went out of Egypt," "obeyed Yahweh," and "land flowing with milk and honey" are consistent with deuteronomistic language, and the forty wilderness years is clearly a deuteronomistic concept (Deut. 2:7; 8:2, 4; 29:4 [5E]). Yahweh's oath of punishment in v. 6 points back to Deut. 1:34–40. Another classic deuteronomistic theme is the contrast between disobedient and obedient generations (vv. 6–7; Deut. 2:14–16; Judg. 2:10). Possibly v. 6 implies that at least part of their disobedience consisted precisely in their failure to be circumcised (see text note j), which in turn suggests that the "disgrace" of v. 9 was their insubordinate uncircumcised state.

The narrative action picks up again in v. 8 and concludes with a somewhat forced[6] etiological notice, which seems to be a redactional touch.[7] The verb *tmm* "finish" continues the important sequencing role it has played in 3:16, 17; 4:1, 10, 11. The "disgrace of Egypt" may refer to the uncircumcised state of those who left Egypt (in line with a possible understanding of v. 6). This interpretation is supported by Gen. 34:14. Or perhaps the humiliation of Egyptian slavery is intended or the invective and insult Israel suffered from the Egyptians (Ezek. 16:57; 1 Sam. 17:26; 25:39).[8]

The theme of new beginnings and the crossing of new frontiers continues. The contrast of the two generations encapsulates Israel's transition from disobedience to obedience, from Yahweh's sworn threat to fulfilled promise, and

---

them still be around to be circumcised by Joshua (v. 5)? Probably the notion that the punishment applied only to those over a certain age (Num. 32:11) is assumed. The logical disturbance seems to have been caused by the injection of a deuteronomistic theme into v. 6 (Deut. 1:34–35; 2:14).

5. R. Gradwohl, "Der 'Hügel der Vorhäute' (Josua V 3)," *VT* 26 (1976): 235–40.

6. Neither the verb *gll* nor the question of "disgrace" play any part in the narrative. Even "Gilgal" is mentioned only in the larger context (4:19–20; 5:10). The figurative usage "roll away disgrace" is also found in Ps. 119:22.

7. Childs, "A Study of the Formula 'Until This Day,'" 285.

8. E. Kutsch, "*ḥārap* II," *TDOT* V, 209–15.

from the wilderness to the land of milk and honey. Circumcision also marks Israel's transition by setting aside the disgrace of the past. It is presented as a rite of passage from being an itinerant people "on the way" (vv. 5 and 7) to a people settled in the land. Once more readers have their national identity reinforced and energized. The striking "us" of v. 6 includes the readers also as recipients of Yahweh's promise and as members of the new generation that Yahweh has set in place instead of the old one (v. 7). This theme of a new start would be meaningful for pre-exilic readers undergoing a revitalizing reformation, but also for exilic or post-exilic readers looking forward to improved circumstances. Another effect of this section would be to encourage fidelity in the practice of circumcision. It also introduces a sober warning about the effects of disobedience, a theme that will play out in chapter 7.

[2–9 MT] The MT revision alters the story to improve its logic and orthodoxy by judicious additions, (notably vv. 4–5a), omissions (in v. 5, note g), and reformulations (see text notes c, h, j). It carefully specifies that all the men of war had perished in the wilderness (vv. 4, 6). Moreover, it insists that all Israel had been circumcised at the point of the exodus; no one came out uncircumcised (v. 5a). Perhaps this sensitivity arose from a desire to emphiasize that all those who would participate in the upcoming passover were circumcised (Exod. 12:44–48), although the text itself never advances passover as a motivation for Joshua's circumcision. Because that earlier generation had all perished (v. 6), now the new generation (and they alone) needed to be circumcised (v. 7). Lest there be any further misunderstanding, this newly circumcised generation explicitly encompasses the entire nation (v. 8). Since the exodus generation had all been circumcised, this circumcision of those born on the way is asserted to be a "second" one (v. 2). It is a "second time" in the sense of being a reimposition of the rite after it had lapsed after the "first time." The revised text sharpens the differentiation between the old disobedient generation (by the addition of vv. 4–5a) and the new obedient generation (by a revision of v. 5b). This contrast is set up as a chiasm (v. 5):

A: they were circumcised
  B: all the people who went out
  B': but all the people who were born in the wilderness
A': had not been circumcised

The MT revision also uses a word play between vv. 6 and 8 involving the verb *tmm* to highlight the contrast between the two groups: "the whole nation perished . . . the whole nation had finished." Yet these two contrasting groups are nonetheless woven together by a common story. This is accentuated by repeated phrases: "all the people," "went out from Egypt," "in the wilderness on the way," and the use of the word *gôy* for both groups (vv. 6 and 8; see 3:17 and 4:1). The inclusion of "the males" in v. 4 may be a cross reference to Gen. 17:10–14.

[10–12] This is a compact narrative consisting of five *waw*-consecutive verbs. It begins abruptly with a repetition of the language of 4:19, as though the previous story had not been related. Most translations turn this into a subordinate temporal clause. Four uses of the preposition *b* depict the setting: "in Gilgal," "on the fourteenth day," "in the evening," "on the plains of Jericho." This last phrase is a geographic reminder that this event stands between crossing and attack. There are intriguing word plays between "in the evening" and "on the plains" and "produce" in vv. 10–12a (*bāʿereb, bĕʿarbôt, mē ʿăbûr*). The verb "eat" is pivotal, used three times. Verse 12 first looks back ("the manna stopped"), then looks forward into the indefinite future with a circumstantial clause ("there was no longer manna"). This latter expression subtly echoes the description of the psychological state of the enemy in 2:11 and 5:1 ("there was no longer courage"). Verse 12b explains the uncommon term "produce" from vv. 11 and 12a with a more common word and specifies the land in question as precisely the land of Canaan. "In that year" calls to mind that this change ends the forty-year history of wilderness manna.

Without doubt this text reflects a complicated prehistory, the details of which are elusive. Two themes interact in a complex way. The minor theme of passover is explored alongside the major theme of transition from manna to agricultural produce. The relationship between these two themes has been complicated by the circumstance that "unleavened bread" is mentioned as one of the two products of the land (v. 11). Although this naturally brought to mind for later readers the festival of unleavened bread that was eventually conjoined with passover in the history of Israel's worship (Lev. 23:5–6), this potential connection is really actualized only on the level of the MT revision. In the earliest recoverable text, unleavened bread has only a literary and not a cultic connection to passover. This means that theories that locate the ceremonial eating of unleavened bread in the supposedly distinctive cultic practice of Gilgal must be set aside.[9]

Like vv. 2–9, this foundational passover coordinates the initial settlement of the land with later Israel's ritual practice. That this is a national passover (rather than a family or local celebration) supports the "all Israel" theme of the book. Passover here seems to be primarily coordinated with priestly and deuteronomistic interests. The allusion to 4:19 and the P-like reference to the date highlights the temporal move from the tenth to the fourteenth day, while allowing

---

9. For Kraus, *Worship in Israel*, 161–65, this text demonstrates the union of the unleavened bread and passover rituals at Gilgal. Otto, *Das Mazzotfest in Gilgal*, 57–65, 175–91, denies that such a union was possible, but proposes an unleavened bread pilgrimage ritual there. G. Kühnert, *Das Gilgalpassah: literarische, überlieferungsgeschichtliche und geschichtliche Untersuchungen zu Josua 3–6*, Mainz, 1982, discovers a combination of a nomadic Israelite passover (the desert festival requested of Pharaoh) combined with a borrowed Canaanite custom of first fruits as unleavened bread and roasted grain.

for a conventional three-day healing period. This may also reflect the circumstance that the tenth was the day the passover victim was selected and the fourteenth was the day it was killed (Exod. 12:3, 5). "On that very day" in v. 11 is a priestly expression.[10] Deuteronomistic language and interests, in which the date of the fourteenth plays no role (see Deut. 16:1), are more prominent. Joshua celebrates a centralized national passover like the one envisioned in Deuteronomy 16 and carried out by Josiah (2 Kings 23:21–23). The passovers of Joshua and Josiah thus mark fundamental historical turning points in DH. The "in the evening" (*bāʿereb*) of v. 10 reflects the specifics of Deut. 16:4, 6, rather than the "between the two evenings" found in P texts. Use of the verb *ʿśh* with passover as its object, although usually associated with P, is also found in both Deut. 16:1 and 2 Kings 23:21. Therefore, this section represents an important structural element in DH and one of the ways that Joshua has been paralleled with the figure of Josiah.[11]

Coordinated with this first passover in the land is the end of the manna. The cessation of manna as a sign of Israel's passage from wilderness to the settled land is also found in Exod. 16:35, a text which has a literary relationship of some sort to this section.[12] Dependence on manna is at some variance with DH's notion of provisions in 1:11, but the manna story is clearly part of deuteronomic tradition (Deut. 8:3, 16).

Unleavened bread and roasted grain are specified as representative of the produce of the land (v. 11). Both are foods of disordered circumstances and time pressures, involving uncomplicated preparation. Quickly prepared and easily transported, roasted grain was a natural food for a military encampment (1 Sam. 17:17; 25:18; 2 Sam. 17:28). For the same reason it is a typical "first fruit" (Lev. 2:14; 23:14, which shares the phrase "that very day" with v. 11; Ruth 2:14), a concept unsurprisingly part of the background of this description of Israel's first dependence on Canaan's crops. Deut. 26:1–2 also connects the offering of first fruits with Israel's entrance into and possession of the land. Moreover, there is a natural connection between passover and first fruits (the coordination of Lev. 23:5–8 and 9–14; cf. Exod. 23:15–16). Again because of its short preparation time, unleavened bread was a food of haste and thus of emergency hospitality (Gen. 19:3; 1 Sam. 28:24; perhaps 2 Kings 23:9). It is a perfectly natural menu item for the first day of a new situation. The first bread from Canaan's crop would necessarily be unleavened. Unleavened bread in this text originally had nothing to do with the ritual eating of unleavened bread

---

10. Priestly interests in Joshua may also be noted in 3:4; 4:15, 19.

11. Nelson, "Josiah in the Book of Joshua." It must be admitted that Joshua himself is not actually mentioned in this unit. Israel is the subject of the verbs.

12. Rose, *Deuteronomist und Jahwist*, 42–44, sees Exod. 16:35 as dependent on this Joshua text and evidence of a redactional horizon that encompasses both. Noth divides this verse between P (v. 35a) and J (v. 35b), *Exodus: A Commentary*, OTL, Philadelphia, 1962, 131–32.

that became coordinated with passover and prompted the MT textual expansions. It is a literary and rhetorical sign of Israel's first transition to the agrarian culture of Canaan.[13]

In this unit the land claim of the book of Joshua, usually expressed as a matter of conquest (chaps. 6–12) and geographic lists (chaps. 13–21), is set forth in terms of economy and diet. The change from manna to produce signifies Israel's relocation from wilderness to land. The start of the one entails the cessation of the other, something underscored by the expression "that very day" and the reiteration in v. 12. To eat the yield of the land of Canaan is to claim that land. Israel does not have to wait for the completion of the conquest, for the gifts of the land are already available from the plundered fields. "That year" (v. 12) accentuates the change from the "forty years" of v. 6 and indicates that agricultural life has an annual rhythm quite unlike that of daily manna.

[10–12 MT] The two MT additions noted in brackets in vv. 11 and 12 seek to enhance the orthodoxy of Joshua's passover. The unleavened bread of the transition to an agricultural economy has been interpreted as the start of the festival of unleavened bread. This misreading has lead to a concern for calendrical propriety. In the unrevised text the passover and the cessation of manna happen on the same day, the fourteenth. MT revises this so that unleavened bread is eaten *on the day after* the passover proper, and the cessation of manna also takes place on the "morrow" (*mimmāḥărāt*), the day after the passover. This careful distinction reflects Lev. 23:5–6 and other P texts. The vocabulary *mimmāḥărat happesaḥ* "on the day after passover" seems to have been taken from either Num. 33:3, where it indicates the fifteenth of Nisan, or from the notoriously problematic Lev. 23:11.[14]

[13–15] This stunted, cryptic[15] narrative seems to break off before any real plot has a chance to develop and twists into a jarring ending that connects only ambiguously with the following story. It starts with an excessively generalized temporal circumstance (2 Sam. 3:6; 1 Kings 11:15; contrast vv. 1 and 8) and an unmotivated, puzzling shift in locale. Is "in Jericho" to be taken literally, suggesting that the narrative is chronologically out of place? Certainly in its present context this must be construed as "in the territory of Jericho" (cf. 4:19; for the translation "by" cf. 1 Sam. 29:1). Verses 13–14 describe a tentative plot

13. C. Brekelmans, "Joshua v 10–12: Another Approach," *OTS* 25 (1989): 89–95, supports the notion that unleavened bread in this text is not cultic. Instead, along with roasted grain, it is a mark of transition into the new land.

14. Rose, *Deuteronomist und Jahwist*, 25–45. M. Fishbane, *Biblical Interpretation in Ancient Israel*, Oxford, 1985, 145–151, offers a complex theory of the growth of this text based on competing interpretations of Lev. 23:11.

15. Important studies are F. Abel, "L'apparition du chef de l'armée de Yahveh à Josué (Jos. V, 13–15)," *Miscellanea Biblica et Orientalia*, Rome, 1951, 109–13, and Miller, *The Divine Warrior in Ancient Israel*, 128–31.

movement from unrecognition on Joshua's part (v. 13a) through an exchange of question and answer (vv. 13b-14a) to recognition (v. 14b). Seeming to assume the figure to be a human soldier, Joshua approaches closer to challenge him. By prostrating himself, Joshua shows that he acknowledges the figure's self-disclosure and awaits a command or message. So much is reasonably clear and suggests a commissioning story on the order of Judg. 6:11–24 or a revelatory encounter such as Judg. 2:1–5.

The commander strikes an aggressive pose similar to that of the angel who blocks Balaam's path (Num. 22:23, 31) and of the one who threatens Jerusalem with pestilence (1 Chron. 21:16). The sword, weapon of the elite, designates him as more than an ordinary soldier and seems to indicate imminent conflict, readiness for war, and the issuance of an unavoidable challenge. All this locates the story in the tradition of divine war. It is unlikely to be a sanctuary legend as has sometimes been suggested. The motif of a divine being with brandished sword is known from the literary and iconographic traditions of the ancient Near East. Such figures occur in the context of confidence-building oracles as pledges of victory and signs of military power.[16] The same motif, implying military success, is applied to Joshua himself when he brandishes a different sort of sword in 8:18, 26. The point is to assure Joshua (and the reader) of impending victory and Yahweh's participation in the upcoming battle. Given this context, the reader naturally anticipates words of assurance and instruction from this figure. But such words fail to materialize.

The commander's answer to Joshua's either/or question is an enigmatic "neither one." The angelic commander is part of no human army. Joshua needs to broaden his perspective to include Yahweh's supernatural resources. That Yahweh's heavenly army (Judg. 5:20; 2 Sam. 5:24) should have a commander (*śar*) parallels earthly patterns (1 Sam. 14:50; 2 Sam. 19:14 [13E]; 1 Kings 2:32). After his self-identification, the commander begins with what seems to be a formula for announcing the purpose of his visit: "now I have come [to]. . . . " The expected continuation would be along the lines of 2 Sam. 14:15 or Dan. 9:23. Instead, he abruptly breaks off. The narrative thus jumps from appearance and self-identification to Joshua's reaction, without any intervening communication. This leaves a disconcerting unanswered "why" hanging in midair.

Joshua's response at the end of v. 14, couched in subservient "courtly language," creates a second opportunity for the commander to speak. The reader expects an oracle or instructions according to the pattern of 8:1–2 or Judg. 7:9–11. What actually follows has seemed a *non sequitur* to many interpreters. The explanation for the commander's peculiar response must be sought in the compositional history of Joshua. The beginning of the Jericho story (6:1) must

16. O. Keel, *Wirkmächtige Siegeszeichen im Alten Testament,* OBO 5, Göttingen, 1974, 83–88; Rose *Deuteronomist und Jahwist,* 55–64. A well-known example is the supportive message to Ashurbanipal given by Ishtar with a drawn sword in her hand, *ANET,* 451.

have been perceived as fixed, so that 5:13–15 and 6:1 were simply spliced together. Whatever words of confidence or instruction were originally spoken by
the commander were replaced by the present ending in the shape of v. 15. Perhaps the original announcement was cut out as offensive to theological sensi-
bilities. Perhaps it proclaimed an upcoming role for Yahweh's army that could
not be fitted into the narrative of Jericho's fall which now follows.[17] Perhaps
it was an oracle of divine war assurance that was eliminated because it dupli-
cated 6:2 or instructions that would have contradicted 6:3, 5. In any event, the
literary effect of this unexpected twist is to increase the mystery and numinous
nature of the encounter.

What the commander does say in v. 15 is either a quotation of Yahweh's
words to Moses in Exod. 3:5 or a stereotyped formulaic declaration of holiness. This suggests to some interpreters that this unit was originally a sanctuary legend for a shrine in Jericho, a legend that belongs chronologically after
the events of chapter 6.[18] According to this proposal, this numinous appearance authenticated the Jericho sanctuary as a holy place, and what has dropped
out of vv. 13–14a may have been some material offensive to later Yahwism.
To go barefoot represents the liminal state expected of someone encroaching
on holy space.[19] Although this interpretation may correctly identify the original genre of this story, it makes very little sense in the present context. The city
is under divine curse (6:26), seemingly incompatible with the holiness of a
sanctuary. Moreover, if v. 15a is only an alternate stereotypical ending imported to replace something that has been left out, then there is no compelling
reason to see this unit as a sanctuary legend.

Three more likely interpretive possibilities present themselves. As a quotation of Exod. 3:5, this may be a way of drawing a parallel between Joshua and
Moses. This correlation is a theme elsewhere in Joshua (1:5, 17; 3:7; 4:14).[20]
Or perhaps the reader is intended to hear this assertion of the holiness of the
place (*māqôm*) on which Joshua stands in light of the land promise of 1:3 involving "every place (*māqôm*) on which the sole of your foot will step." What
was once alien land has now become Yahweh's land, holy land (compare
22:19; 1 Sam. 26:19–20; 2 Kings 5:15–19). A third possibility is that cursed
Jericho is holy in a negative sense, analogous to the state of *ḥērem*. One notes
that the metal objects of Jericho will be proclaimed both *ḥērem* and holy (6:19).

17. That an alternate tale about Jericho once existed is indicated by the muted betrayal aspects of the Rahab narrative and Josh. 24:11.

18. For example Noth, *Josua,* 23, 39–40.

19. Nelson, *Raising Up a Faithful Priest,* 17–38. The same behavior is expected in the liminal state of mourning: 2 Sam. 15:30; Ezek. 24:17, 23; Mal. 1:8.

20. An unusual direction is taken by the intertextual reading of L. Hawk, *Every Promise Fulfilled,* 21–24, who sees central significance in the words the angel ominously *fails* to go on to cite
from Exod. 3:8.

Jericho as a "shoes-off place" is off-limits to ordinary human usage, in accord with the curse of 6:26.

In spite of its enigmatic nature, the literary function of this unit remains reasonably clear. The manifestation of Yahweh's heavenly commander serves to introduce the warlike themes of subsequent chapters. It is Joshua's authorization to begin the campaign and a guarantee that it will be successful. Similar heavenly visitations as signs of divine participation in warfare were standard elements in contemporary campaign reports.[21] The appearance of the Divine Warrior's commanding officer brandishing a sword signifies that battle is impending and that Yahweh's heavenly army has been mobilized. In the paradigmatic conflict at Jericho, Israel will not be alone, but will participate as an ally of the superhuman army of the Divine Warrior. That at least part of Jericho's territory is already holy perhaps serves as a proleptic confirmation of a successful outcome. The narrative also authenticates the leadership of Joshua. He is Yahweh's humble servant, properly using the courtly language of the inferior. He is ready to hear and obey the commands that will soon follow.

Capturing Jericho
Joshua 6:1–27

UNREVISED TEXT

MT REVISION

Instructions

1:1 Now Jericho closed up and was closed off.[a] No one went out or came in. 2 Yahweh said to Joshua, "See, I have given into your [sg] power Jericho and its king, valiant warriors.[b] 3 You [pl] shall circle the city, all the warriors.

1:1 Now Jericho closed up and was closed off *because of the Israelites*. No one went out or came in. 2 Yahweh said to Joshua, "See, I have given into your [sg] power Jericho and its king, valiant warriors. 3 You [pl] shall circle the city, all the warriors *going around the city once.*[c] *Do [sg] this for six days. 4 Seven priests will carry seven ram's horn trumpets in front of the ark. On the seventh day circle the city seven times with the priests blowing the trumpets.*[d]

21. J. Van Seters, "Joshua's Campaign of Canaan and Near Eastern Historiography," *SJOT* 4 (1990): 1–12.

5 When they blow long on the ram's horn, the whole people will shout out a loud war cry and the wall of the city will collapse. The people will go up in a frontal attack."

6 So Joshua son of Nun summoned the priests and said to them,

7 "Say to the people, 'Go forward and circle the city. Let the armed soldiers[h] go in front of Yahweh.'"

The First Six Days

8 The seven priests carrying seven ram's horn trumpets in front of Yahweh went along and blew the trumpets with the ark of the covenant of Yahweh following,

9 and the armed soldiers were going before them and the priests were a rear guard after the ark, continuously blowing trumpets.[i]

10 Joshua ordered the people, "Do not shout. Do not let your voice be heard until the day I tell you "Shout!" Then shout!

11 The ark of Yahweh circled the city once. They went back to camp and stayed overnight in the camp.

12 Joshua got up early in the morning, and the priests lifted up the ark of Yahweh.

13 The seven priests carrying the seven trumpets

5 When they blow long on the ram's horn, *as soon as you hear the trumpet blast,*[e] the whole people will shout out a loud war cry and the wall of the city will collapse. The people will go up in a frontal attack."

6 So Joshua son of Nun summoned the priests and said to them, *"Lift up the ark of the covenant and let seven priests carry seven ram's horn trumpets in front of the ark of Yahweh."*[f]

7 He said[g] to the people, "Go forward and circle the city. Let the armed soldiers go in front of *the ark of* Yahweh."

8 *As soon as Joshua had spoken to the people* the seven priests carrying seven ram's horn trumpets in front of Yahweh went along and blew the trumpets with the ark of the covenant of Yahweh following,

9 and the armed soldiers were going before the priests *who were blowing the trumpets and* the rear guard *were coming* after the ark, continuously blowing trumpets.

10 Joshua ordered the people, "Do not shout. Do not let your voice be heard *and do not let a word escape your mouth*[j] until the day I tell you "Shout!" Then shout!

11 He made[k] the ark of Yahweh circle the city, *going around* once. They went back to camp and stayed overnight in the camp.

12 Joshua got up early in the morning, and the priests lifted up the ark of Yahweh.

13 The seven priests carrying the seven *ram's horn* trumpets were

were going in front of Yahweh and the armed soldiers were going in front of them and the rear guard were coming after the ark of Yahweh continuously blowing trumpets.[l]

14 They circled the city at one time[m] and they returned to camp. They did this six days.

The Seventh Day

15 On the seventh day they got up early at dawn and circled the city seven times. It was only on this day that they encircled the city seven times.[o]

going in front of *the ark of* Yahweh *continuously blowing on the trumpets* and the armed soldiers were going in front of them and the rear guard were coming after the ark of Yahweh continuously blowing trumpets.

14 They circled the city *the second day*[n] once and they returned to camp. They did this six days.

15 On the seventh day they got up early at dawn and circled the city *in this way* seven times. It was only on this day that they circled the city seven times.

16 At the seventh time, the priests blew the trumpets, and Joshua said to the people, "Shout, for Yahweh has given you the city! **17** The city and everything in it shall be devoted to Yahweh. Only Rahab the prostitute shall live and everyone with her in the house [because she hid the messengers we sent].[p] **18** As for you, keep away from the devoted things lest you covet[q] and take some of the devoted things and put the camp of Israel into a devoted state and make it taboo.[r] **19** All the silver and gold, the [vessels of] bronze and iron, are holy to Yahweh. They should go as treasure of Yahweh. **20** [The people shouted.][s] They blew the trumpets, and as soon as the people heard the trumpet blast, the people shouted a loud war cry and the wall collapsed. Then the people went up to the city in a frontal attack [and they captured the city]. **21** They devoted to destruction everything in the city—man and woman, young and old, cattle, sheep, and donkeys—with the edge of the sword.

Aftermath

22 But to the two young men[t] who had scouted [the land] Joshua said, "Go to the house of the woman [the prostitute] and bring out the woman from there, along with everyone who belongs to her just as you swore to her."[u] **23** So the young men who had scouted went and brought out Rahab, her father, her mother, her brothers, and everyone who belonged to her, and [they brought out] her entire clan, and let them stay outside the camp of Israel. 24 The city they burned and everything in it, except that they put the silver and gold, the [vessels of] bronze and iron into the treasury of the house of ^{v} Yahweh, 25 but Rahab the prostitute and her family [and everyone who belonged to her] Joshua preserved alive. So she still lives among Israel today, because she hid the messengers ^{w} whom Joshua sent to scout out Jericho. 26 At that time Joshua swore this oath:

"Cursed be the one [before Yahweh] ^{x} who [starts to] ^{y} build this
    city [Jericho].
At the cost of his firstborn he shall lay its foundations.
At the cost of his youngest he shall set up its gates." ^{z}

27 So Yahweh was with Joshua and his fame spread throughout the land.

a. Evidently a fixed expression. The translation attempts to convey the sense of blocking entrance (active qal) while being blocked off for exit (passive pual; Noth, *Josua*, 34). Alternate translations: "shut up inside and out" (NRSV); "shut up tight" (taken as intensive; JPSV).

b. Although evidently a misplaced marginal gloss on v. 3, perhaps on the basis of 1:14 or 10:7, "valiant warriors" is present in both OG and MT.

c. With the addition of the verb *nqp* hiphil "go around" (also in v. 11 MT) and "once," the expanded MT clarifies that the encirclement of Jericho is not to be understood as a static siege, but as a parade around the city. The translation uses "circle" for *sbb* in order to capture the ambiguity of the unrevised text in vv. 3, 7, and 14.

d. MT expansion based on vv. 8 and 13.

e. MT expansion based on v. 20.

f. 4QJosh^a has this MT expansion, in part from 3:6 (compare v. 4).

g. "He said" follows MT Qere, 4QJosh^a (with explicit subject), S, V, T. MT has Joshua promulgate to the priests the additional commands of v. 6. This required a change of the original imperative at the start of v. 7 into an indicative. According to the Qere, it is Joshua who commands the people to advance. According to the Kethib, the priests do so. The imperative plural "say" of the unrevised text is reflected in OG as a conflated doublet (*legōn paraggeilate*) and may be the source of the plural of the MT Kethib.

h. "Armed soldiers" (*ḥālûṣ*) is literally "the girded up (for battle)"; compare 4:13.

i. Tentatively follows OG, uncertainly reconstructed (partially on the basis of v. 13) as *whḥlwṣ hlk lpnyhm whkhnym hm'sp 'ḥry 'rwn hlwk wtqw' bšwprwt*. Thus the unrevised text asserts that the rear guard consisted of priests. This may be the result of a corruption, since in v. 13 the rear guard is not explicitly said to be composed of priests. MT either harmonizes v. 9 with v. 13 by carefully distinguishing between the priests and the rear guard, or alternatively witnesses to an uncorrupted text which it has obscured by expansion. 4QJosh^a supports MT in vv. 7–9. The Greek translator took vv. 8–9 as a continuation of the instructions rather than as the start of the action.

j. MT and 4QJosh[a] conflate doublet readings.

k. The MT pointing as hiphil enlarges the role of Joshua.

l. V. 13 can be reconstructed if we recognize a haplography in OG from *hlk* to *hlk* and then allow for reactions to this loss. The haplography would have been *šprwt lpny yhwh hlkym whḥlwṣ hlk [lpnyhm whm'sp hlk] 'ḥry 'rwn yhwh hlwk wtqw' bšwprwt*. To patch this haplography, OG has inserted as subjects "rest of the people" (twice) and "the priests" (details in Holmes, *Joshua: The Hebrew and Greek Texts*, 34–36). MT expands with a note about trumpet blowing similar to the one added to v. 9. The translation assumes infinitive absolutes for *hlk* and *tq'* (see BHS notes b and d). Alternate translations: "marching and blowing" or "blowing louder and louder"; Waltke and O'Connor, *Hebrew Syntax*, 35.3.2. b, c.

m. The ambiguity of the unrevised text surfaces again with *pa'am 'aḥat*. Although in v. 11 this must mean "one time," in the context of group encirclement it could be understood as "all at once," "at a single moment" (10:42; Isa. 66:8). Again the translation seeks to capture the ambiguity. For another opinion, J. Niehaus, "Pa'am 'Ehat and the Israelite Conquest," *VT* 30 (1980), 236–38.

n. OG has this typical expansion in v. 12 instead.

o. Follows MT. OG lost v. 15b through homoioteleuton (*p'mym* to *p'mym*) and corrected "seven times" in 15a to "six" in light of v. 16.

p. MT expansion from v. 25.

q. Follows OG. MT transposed the letters of *tḥmdw* "covet" into *tḥrymw* "devote to destruction," misreading *r* for *d* (cf. 7:21; Deut. 7:25).

r. The interpretation of *'kr* as a notion analogous to "taboo" is indicated by passages such as Judg. 11:35 and 1 Sam. 14:29.

s. A premature expansion from later in this verse, absent in OG.

t. Follows OG. See verse 23 and the text note to 2:1.

u. The two MT bracketed expansions occur in OG in v. 23 instead, presumably as coincidental examples of the tendency of texts to develop in predictable ways. OG lost "just as you swore to her" through homoioteleuton from *lh* to *lh*.

v. Follows MT. OG omits "house of" here and at 9:23 to avoid anachronism.

w. Follows MT as more difficult; OG corrects to "spies."

x. Not present in OG (= LXX[A]). LXX[B] associates "before Yahweh" with the word "oath." OG is supported by 4QTest in omitting the bracketed MT expansions in this verse.

y. MT *yāqûm ûbānâ* is an inceptive hendiadys denoting "tries to build" (NRSV, NAB; cf. 7:13).

z. "At the cost of" represents the *beth* of price, compare 2 Sam. 23:17. OG adds an explicit reference to the fulfillment of the curse, found in similar form in 1 Kings 16:34 (MT and LXX, but not Lucianic recension). For a complete analysis of the textual evidence for this verse, L. Mazor, "The Origin and Evolution of the Curse upon the Rebuilder of Jericho," *Textus* 14 (1988): 1–26.

Once more OG permits us to recover a shorter text earlier than the obviously expanded MT. The processional aspects of surrounding Jericho are much less explicit in the earliest recoverable text than they are in the more familiar expanded version. A comparison of the two forms of v. 3 illustrates this difference. The verb *sbb* can denote either "surround" in a static sense (Gen. 37:7; Judg. 16:2; 20:5; 2 Kings 3:25; 6:15) or the active "march around" (Ps. 48:13 [12E]). The unrevised text is ambiguous and could be understood as reporting daily sorties out to take positions surrounding the city in a sort of *pro forma* siege. This ambiguity extends to vv. 7a and 14, although in v. 11 the ark itself obviously "goes around" Jericho. It is only on day seven (v. 15) that the reader comes to realize that a procession of the whole people must be intended. The alternative of a sevenfold reconfiguration of a stationary encirclement would be unacceptably awkward. Whether the whole people paraded in a circle around Jericho on the other six days remains unclear in the unrevised text.[1] In contrast, the expanded text explicitly describes circling processions from the start (text note c and v. 4). The procedure for day seven is made unambiguously the same as before by the addition of "in this way" to v. 15.

The story of Jericho exhibits evidence of a complex history of growth, even in its shorter OG form. Although division into written sources has often been suggested,[2] this hypothesis is unlikely because the climactic collapse of the wall is referred to only once. Some of the discrepancies and tensions are:

> the ark disappears from the scene after v. 13 and is absent from the climactic seventh day
> confusion is generated by two sets of trumpeters: the seven priests and the rear guard (vv. 8–9, 13)
> trumpets blow continuously (vv. 8–9, 13), but a single trumpet blast is the signal for attack (vv. 5, 16, 20)
> the constant trumpet din contrasts with the call for vocal silence until the war cry is uttered (vv. 10, 16)
> the trumpet signal is reported twice (vv. 16 and 20)
> vv. 24 and 25 seem to be doublets of vv. 21 and 23
> there are two decisive signals for attack: the trumpet (v. 20) and the command to shout (vv. 10, 16)

Another disturbing feature involves the order of the ark's escort. There seems to be a competition for attention between the armed soldiers in front of the ark (v. 7) and the seven trumpet-blowing priests whose place is also in front of the ark (v. 8). To compound the reader's disorientation, the rear guard also blows

---

1. The Greek translator reflects this ambiguity by using *periïstēmi* with the dative of *kyklos* for v. 3, *perierchomai* for vv. 11 and 15, and *perikykloō* for v. 14. Verse 7 is a paraphrase.

2. For example, Dus, "Die Analyse zweier Ladeerzählungen des Josuabuches," 108; Maier, *Das altisraelitische Ladeheiligtum*, 32–59; Otto, *Das Mazzotfest in Gilgal*, 65–86. H. Seidel, "Der Untergang Jerichos (Jos. 6) — Exegese ohne Kerygma?" *Theologische Versuche* 8 (1977): 11–20, traces five stages of development from a basic ritual narrative. A variation on this is the opinion of Wilcoxen, "Narrative Structure and Cult Legend," 52–53, that three alternative versions of a ritual have been merged.

trumpets (v. 9). Verse 13 eventually clarifies this confusing data: the armed soldiers walk in front of the seven priests who in turn are in front of the ark, with
the rear guard following.[3]

In light of these irregularities, it is likely that a simpler form of the narrative once existed. Since it is absent from the climax, the ark has probably come
late into the story,[4] in order to function as a redactional connection to chapters
3–4. The trumpet-blowing priests seem to add elements of cultic procession to
an earlier divine warrior conquest narrative. Even Joshua, although featured in
vv. 10, 16, 26–27, competes for attention with the signal trumpet and may himself have come into the story at a later stage.[5] It is also sometimes suggested
that the present Jericho narrative has replaced an older story involving betrayal
(chap. 2) and military struggle (24:11). It is methodologically fruitless to pursue these speculations beyond the evidence offered by the text itself.

However, two components of the narrative are obviously redactional because they connect to the larger plot of Joshua. These are unrestricted *ḥērem*
and the fate of Rahab. Jericho's *ḥērem* involves not only people and animals
(v. 21) but also the inanimate booty of the city (vv. 18–19, 24). The devotion
of human beings connects back to the question of Rahab's survival (2:10) and
will be the pattern for *ḥērem* found in the conquest narratives that follow (cf.
8:2, 27; 11:14, etc.). The more rigorous practice of putting all nonliving booty
into a state of *ḥērem* as well prepares for the Achan story (vv. 18–19). Perhaps
this extra severity is also connected with the notion that Jericho represents a
paradigm for the entire enterprise of conquest (8:2; 10:1; 24:11) or seemed appropriate because the conquest of Jericho was so completely the work of Yahweh that all booty should have been a divine possession. As a redactional linkage, then, *ḥērem* relates to the pre-deuteronomistic aggregate of chapters 2–11.
This is not to suggest, however, that DH's interest in *ḥērem* is absent from this
narrative. Although the sweeping form applied to Jericho goes beyond the
ḥērem of Deuteronomy or DH against conquered cities (Deut. 2:34–35; 3:6–7;
20:16–18), it does reflect the *ḥērem* prescription for an apostate Israelite city
(Deut. 13:12–18 [13–19E]). It also echoes the *ḥērem* dedication of the silver

3. By the addition of v. 4 and expansions to v. 6, the MT revision emphasizes the role of the
seven priests and further clarifies that they marched immediately in front of the ark. MT also
stressed their trumpet-blowing responsibilities (v. 8) with expansions to vv. 9 and 13.

4. As suggested by Noth, *Josua*, 41 and Fritz, *Josua*, 68–69, 75–76, who also see the priests
as later accretions. The signal trumpet is sounded in v. 20 without any mention of priests.

5. Noth, *Josua*, 34, 36, 40–43, and Fritz, *Josua*, 65–75, essentially agree on the literary core
as vv. 2a, 3, 4aB–5, 7a, 8a (to *'l-h'm*), 10, 12a, 14 (with Fritz including vv. 1, 15a, 20b and eliminating 8a, 10, and 12a). The most recent critical dissection is that of L. Schwienhorst, *Die Eroberung Jerichos: exegetische Untersuchung zu Josua 6*, SBS 122, Stuttgart, 1986. On the assumption of post-Chronicler redaction (125–29), he pares things down radically so that even the
seven-day pattern is eliminated from the earliest version (39–57; found in parts of vv. 1–2a, 3aA,
5, 14aA, 20b). Schwienhorst uncovers seven successive redactions of this original (23–28).

and gold of pagan images, which are not to be "coveted" (compare v. 18; Deut. 7:25–26). Rahab's reappearance (vv. 22–23, 25) and her exemption from *ḥērem* (v. 17b) is also redactional, pointing backwards and forwards outside the narrative horizon of chapter 6. She functions redactionally at the pre-deuteronomistic level as well, although her residence outside the war camp (v. 23b) reveals the anxieties of DH (Deut. 23:10–15 [9–14E]). The curse of v. 26, with its horizon of fulfillment reaching to 1 Kings 16:34, is most likely the editorial contribution of DH. Joshua's fame in v. 27 would relate to the interests of both the pre-deuteronomistic redactor and DH. The summary that Yahweh was "with" Joshua echoes a repeated DH concern (1:9, 17; 3:7; 4:14).

A ritual background has sometimes been suggested for this story, often in connection with the supposedly cultic nature of chapters 3–5.[6] Such a claim is difficult to evaluate, in part because there is no way to determine whether trumpet-blowing priests or the processional ark were part of the narrative's most primitive configuration. The priests who carry the ark in v. 12 are a continuation of a DH interest carried over from chapters 3–4. Certainly a good deal of the narrative's cultic flavor was contributed by the MT revision. The central thematic core of chapter 6 does not seem to focus on liturgy but on the ideology of the Divine Warrior: victory oracle (v. 2), trumpet signal and war cry (vv. 5, 10, 20), armed soldiers (vv. 7, 9), *ḥērem,* and the ark embodying Yahweh's warlike presence. Etiological concerns certainly played a role in the origin and transmission of this story. It provides an explanation for a substantial city mound near an important Jordan crossing point, perhaps uninhabited at some periods (1 Kings 16:34) and thought to be under some kind of curse (2 Kings 2:19–22). It is most reasonable to think of this as basically a tale of miraculous conquest, but redactionally staged with the trappings of liturgical procession.

From a narratival perspective, chapter 6 is a self-contained plot unit.[7] It starts with background information given in circumstantial sentences (v. 1) and ends with a summary statement (v. 27). Along with chapters 8, 10, and 11, it is the first of four major campaign accounts. Inherent to all four of these are moves from initial situation and confrontation (here vv. 1–2) through military action (vv. 3–21) to Israelite victory and its consequences (vv. 22–27). Like the other three campaign narratives, the Jericho story reflects a double focus on the fate of the city and its king (vv. 2, 24), highlights the role of Joshua (vv. 6, 10, 12, 16, 26–27), stresses the destruction of enemy cities and populations (vv. 21, 24, 26), and concludes with a summarizing statement (v. 27). It also shares with those stories such typical elements as an oracle of assurance (v. 2),

6. Wilcoxen, "Narrative Structure and Cult Legend."

7. For an alternate synchronic reading that understands the repetition as a deliberate literary strategy, see R. Robinson, "The Coherence of the Jericho Narrative: Literary Reading of Joshua 6," *Konsequente Traditionsgeschichte,* OBO 126, Fribourg, 1993, 311–35.

the difficulty of Israel's situation (v. 1), action at dawn (v. 15), punctuation of the narrative action by returns to camp (vv. 11, 14), the disposition of booty (vv. 18–19, 24), and a testimony formula (v. 25). Like the Ai narrative, it focuses on a single city and highlights obedience to instructions from Yahweh and Joshua. As is the case with chapter 10, a miraculous act of Yahweh takes center stage and Joshua utters a bit of poetry.

Jericho is unique, however, because it serves as a paradigm for the entire conquest. Not only is Jericho Israel's first conquest, it is the gateway to Canaan, near a natural crossing point (4:19; 2 Sam. 10:5). The language of the Rahab story has already prepared the reader to equate Jericho with the land as a whole (2:1, 2, 9, 14, 18, 24). A second unusual feature is the secondary and unwarlike part played by Israel's fighters until trumpet and shout trigger the attack and slaughter. Israel engages in a symbolic, ritualistic siege of the city. Trumpets are detached from their battle situation (such as Judg. 7:15–22) and take on a liturgical flavor (as, e.g., Ps. 98:6). The war cry (Jer. 20:16) merges into a shout of cultic joy (1 Sam. 4:5–6). The seven-day timetable is of greater importance than maneuvers on the ground (contrast 8:3–22; 10:9–11; 11:7–8). For this reason the narrative problem is not really the size and extent of the enemy forces (as in 10:3–6; 11:1–5), but that Jericho is tightly closed up behind impregnable walls (v. 1). Spectacular divine intervention resolves this problem when the wall collapses (literally "falls down in its place").

Chapter 6 is closely woven into the fabric of the book and plays a pivotal role in its plot. The obvious redactional links back to the Rahab tale are subtly supplemented by the "closed up" city of v.1 that looks back to 2:5, 7. Connections to the Jordan crossing are provided by the processional ark and the armed men (4:13). The commander of Yahweh's army has appeared at Jericho with his drawn sword to initiate the attack on the city in 5:13–15. Forward references to the Achan incident concentrate in vv. 18–19: "covet" (7:21), "silver and gold" (7:21) and "make taboo" (*'kr*; 7:25–26). News of Jericho's fall will later motivate enemy action (8:2; 9:3; 10:1, 28, 30).

In its unrevised form, the story exhibits skillful plotting. The overall movement is from initial situation (v. 1–2) through action (vv. 3–21) to the consequences of victory (vv. 22–27). The initial situation contrasts the impregnability of Jericho (v. 1) with Yahweh's oracle of assurance (v. 2). The denouement of consequences ties up the loose end of Rahab (vv. 22–23, 25), drives the last nail in Jericho's coffin (vv. 24, 26), and summarizes the implications of victory for Joshua and the morale of Canaan (v. 27). The central action section (vv. 3–21) uses the now-familiar rhythm of command and obedience. Yahweh's commands (vv. 3, 5) and Israel's execution (vv. 8–9, 11–15, 20–21) are bound together by the communicating role of Joshua (vv. 7, 10, 16–19). Yahweh's initial instructions (vv. 3, 5) provide only the most general indication of what is to come, namely encirclement, trumpet and shout, collapse, attack.

Because nothing is said yet about a seven-day period (in contrast to the MT revision), the reader is left to assume that all these events will happen promptly. It only gradually becomes clear that a delay will intervene. Other ambiguities are also evoked and then clarified in the course of the action. For example, the question as to whether the encirclement is a static siege or a moving procession is raised by vv. 3, 7, and 14, and then gradually cleared up by vv. 11 and 15. Confusion about processional order is generated by vv. 7–9 and elucidated by v. 13.

Joshua's instructions (vv. 6–7, 10, 17–19) are interleaved with Israel's obedience to them, thus preserving narrative tension.[8] His initial command to move into position (vv. 6–7) is given through the priests, signaling to the reader that something other than a conventional military maneuver is in the offing. The first action (vv. 8–9) confirms this with a description of an orchestrated procession out to the position of encirclement, one begun and completed by priests and into which the significant number seven is twice introduced. It is only in v. 10 that a note of delay is introduced. Today is not the day to shout after all! Instead the ark circles (whether with or without its entourage is not stated) and a disappointing return to camp follows. The next day begins hopefully with an early morning start, but turns out to be a near-verbatim repeat of the first day and a continuation of the narrative delay (vv. 12–14a). Verse 14 focuses on the troops who surround Jericho (in harmony with v. 3) rather than the ark, which was the focus of v. 11. The plot action begins to move again with the completion of six days (v 14b) and the new auspicious factors introduced in vv. 15–16. These are dawn (see Exod. 14:27; Judg. 9:33 etc.), seven acts of encirclement, a blast on the trumpets, Joshua's command to shout (cf. vv. 5, 10), and his restatement of the promise of v. 2. However, the expected climax still does not materialize, and delay is introduced yet again. Joshua launches into detailed instructions about devoted booty (vv. 17–19). Finally the action is restarted when v. 20 reiterates and resumes the trumpet blowing from v. 16 (*Wiederaufnahme,* see the commentary on 4:10–11). The victorious climax promised by v. 5 is achieved (vv. 20–21). What follows is denouement: Rahab (vv. 22–23, 25), burning and cursing the city (vv. 24, 26), implications and repercussions (v. 27).

Along with the miraculous stoppage of the Jordan, this second supernatural wonder clears the way for the remainder of the conquest. In some ways Jericho's wall serves as a conceptual parallel to the Jordan, as a barrier that must be breached in order for Israel to move forward in acquiring the land. This story is a perfect illustration of the ideology set forth in Deut. 9:3. It is a classic divine war account, in which Yahweh's role is stressed and Israel's is down-

8. According to Culley, "Stories of the Conquest," 36–37, these small movements of instruction, repetition, and execution convey a sense of order and inevitability and display a ritual-like quality.

played. Indeed, this is the most radically theocentric of Joshua's conquest stories. As such it encourages trust in Yahweh's military power and Yahweh's willingness to bring about promised victories. It bolsters national identity and Israel's claim on the land. There would be comfort in retelling such stories when the nation was threatened by outside dangers or in those dark times when faith was limited only to hope that Yahweh's promised deliverance might someday take place. The story of Jericho's fall would become important to later tradition as an illustration of faith and God's power (2 Macc. 12:15; Heb. 11:30).

Coordinated with the theme of Yahweh's military prowess is the subject of obedience and fidelity. Obedience to divine command makes victory possible, just as obedience to Deuteronomy is the key to success. Once victory has been won, Israel is also provided with an opportunity to obey the *ḥērem* command and does so with enthusiasm. Israel is also loyal to its sworn oath to Rahab, while at the same time her survival shows the value of her fidelity and confession of faith. Paradoxically, the Rahab affair also raises a question about Israel's fidelity in regard to Deuteronomy's call for the total liquidation of the enemy (Deut. 7:1–5; 20:16–18). Competing obligations to sworn oath and deuteronomic law collide. This unsettling complication will unfold more pointedly in the story of the Gibeonites (chap. 9).

[1–2] The narrative setting is sketched with two circumstantial sentences. Jericho is prepared for a siege and the daily exits and entrances have been blocked off. Yahweh communicates with the people by speaking to Joshua (as in 1:1; 3:7; 4:1, 15; 5:2, 9), addressing an assurance of victory (compare 8:1, 18; 10:8, 19, etc.) to him directly in the singular. The language is carried over from 2:24. Such oracles of assurance are found in several Joshua narratives (8:1–2, 18; 10:8, 19; 11:6), but are also a feature of Mesopotamian campaign reports.[9]

[3–14] The ring around the enemy, the trumpeting, and the shouting are elements shared with the classic "day of Midian" story of Judg. 7:15–22. The war cry (*tĕrû'â*) is a motif of the divine war tradition (1 Sam. 4:5; 17:20, 52; etc.).[10] The collapse of a city's wall would in itself be equivalent to the defeat of that city (1 Kings 20:30; Jer. 51:44). Each of the surrounding soldiers was to "go up" the mound "straight ahead" (v. 5, lit.). In vv. 7 and 13, Yahweh is flatly identified

9. Weippert, "'Heiliger Krieg' in Israel und Assyrien," 472–74. An easily accessible example is in the Zakir Inscription, *ANET*, 655–56.

10. For these motifs, G. von Rad, *Holy War in Ancient Israel*, Grand Rapids, 1991, 41–51. On the international character of divine war warrior reports, see Kang, *Divine War in the Old Testament and in the Ancient Near East*. It has been suggested that a folk etymology or sound connection between "war cry" and "Jericho" may have played a role in the emergence or this story (C. den Hertog, "Ein Wortspiel in der Jerichoerzählung [Jos 6]?" *ZAW* 104 [1992]: 99–100). In a more rationalistic vein, F. Abel, "Les stratagèmes du livre de Josué," *RB* 56 (1949): 325–28 thinks of the psychological effects of silence followed by a coordinated shout: courage for Israel and terror for the enemy.

with the ark, just as in the earliest recoverable text of 4:5. The use of the verb *'br* in v. 7 provides an echo of the Jordan crossing procession. Priestly trumpet blowing reflects the views of post-exilic texts such as Num. 10:1–9 and 2 Chron. 13:12, 14–15. The careful concern with the order of march (vv. 7–9, 13) echoes the Jordan crossing (3:3–4). The designation for the ark varies as in chapters 3–4. Only in v. 8 does it have its full deuteronomistic title.

[1–14 MT] Much of the narrative tension is eliminated by divulging the seven-day timetable at the outset and clarifying from the start that a circling procession is intended (vv. 3–4). The addition of v. 4 moves the introduction of the ark and the seven priests forward into the initial command of Yahweh, and ark and priests are further accented by additions to v. 6. Supplements to vv. 4, 9, and 13 reiterate and stress the priestly trumpet blowing taken from v. 8. Clarifications added to v. 14 ("the second day") and v. 15 ("in this way") emphasize the similarity of each day's procession.

[15–21] For the compositional pattern of six, then seven, see Exod. 24:16 and 1 Kings 20:29.[11] The *ḥērem* is one center of attention here, the root occurring five times (six in MT) in vv. 17, 18, and 21. It is skillfully used as a redactional link backward to Rahab as an exception to *ḥērem* (17b, 22–23, 25a) and forward to Achan as a violator of the warning (17a, 19, 21, 24b). The paradoxical pattern of using the principle of annihilating foreigners as an opportunity to address the topic of their survival is a pattern that will recur in chapter 9. The narrative motif of *ḥērem* as a test to be failed may also be found in 1 Samuel 15 and 1 Kings 20:42.

Three categories of classification from Israel's culture map interact in vv. 18–19: "devoted" (*ḥērem*), "taboo" (*'ākar*), and "holy" (*qādôš*). Booty is here thought of as both "holy" and "devoted" because it belongs to Yahweh. Because the state of being devoted is contagious, the booty would contaminate Israel's camp and put it into a state of *ḥērem* itself (7:12). This in turn would make the camp "taboo," unable to be used in an ordinary way (cf. 7:25).[12]

[22–27] The narrative ends with a series of wrap-ups concerning Rahab, the execution of *ḥērem*, the curse on Jericho, and Joshua's fame. The directives of vv. 17b–19 are obeyed by vv. 22–25. The parenthetical positioning of vv. 22–23 is required because this action obviously has to take place after the city is taken, but before the burning that completes the *ḥērem* (7:15, 25; 8:28; 11:11, 13). The vocabulary of these two verses is picked up from that of chapter

---

11. For this literary pattern, see S. Loewenstamm, "The Seven-Day Unit in Ugaritic Epic Literature," *IEJ* 13 (1963): 121–33. An easily accessible example is the description of the end of the flood in the Gilgamesh epic (*ANET*, 94).

12. On these categories in Israel's "culture map," see R. Nelson, *Raising Up a Faithful Priest*, 17–38.

2.[13] From the perspective of Deuteronomy, Rahab must be kept outside the clean war camp itself (v. 23; Deut. 23:10–15 [9–14E]), although there is no bar to living "among Israel" (v. 25). Mention of a temple treasury in v. 24 is either anachronistic or proleptic, but the same mode of thought is present in 9:23, 27.

The testimony formula of v. 25 is redactional, used to underscore the reliability of the narrative and the point of Rahab's survival. Thus the genuine etiological concerns that motivated the preservation of the Rahab story resurface here as a later writer's formula.[14] That the spies are here called "messengers" puts the focus on what was really important about their mission, the message gleaned from Rahab and given to Joshua (2:9, 24).[15] The totality of Jericho's destruction and the intensity of its state of *ḥērem* is capped by an open-ended curse (v. 26) suggestive of Deut. 13:16 [17E]. It is not to be rebuilt because it belongs to Yahweh as the spoils of war. A similar literary function is played by sowing salt over Shechem (Judg. 9:45).[16]

Achan's Sin
and Its Consequences
Joshua 7:1–26

Defeat at Ai

7:1 The Israelites committed sacrilege[a] in regard to devoted things. Achan son of Carmi son of Zabdi son of Zerah of the tribe of Judah took some devoted things. Then the anger of Yahweh broke out against the Israelites.

2 Joshua sent men [from Jericho] to Ai, which is near Beth-aven to the east of Bethel.[b] He said to them, "[Go up.] Scout out the land." So the men went up and scouted out Ai. 3 Then they returned to Joshua and said to him, "The whole people need not go up. Two or three thousand men

13. There are also differences in usage between vv. 17, 22–23, 25 and chapter 2, as analyzed by McCarthy, "The Theology of Leadership in Joshua 1–9," 169–70.

14. Here the etiological formula functions rather like the satisfying fairy tale conclusion "and they lived happily ever after," as pointed out by Langlamet, "Josué II et les traditions de l'Hexateuque," 327.

15. That "spy" and "messenger" were not such different functions is suggested by the clandestine message-bearing pair Ahimaaz and Jonathan (2 Sam. 15:27, 36; 17:16–21), whose story in some ways resembles that of Rahab's young men.

16. S. Gevirtz, "Jericho and Shechem: A Religio-Literary Aspect of City Destruction," *VT* 13 (1963): 52–62, who also points out that both salting and cursing can be acts of consecration to a god.

could go up and strike at Ai. Do not give the whole people the trouble of going there, for they are just a few. 4 So there went up [from the people towards there] about three thousand men, but they fled before the men of Ai. 5 The men of Ai struck down about thirty-six of them and pursued them outside the gate as far as Shebarim[c] and struck them down on the slope. Then the hearts of the people melted and turned to water.

The Problem Revealed

6 Joshua tore his clothes and fell flat on his face before [the ark of] Yahweh until evening along with the elders of Israel, and they put dust on their heads. 7 Then Joshua said, "Alas Lord Yahweh. Why indeed have you brought[d] this people across the Jordan? To give us into the power of the Amorites to destroy us? If only we had agreed to live on the other side of the Jordan! 8 Oh Lord,[e] what can I say after Israel has turned its back before its enemies? 9 The Canaanites and the entire population of the land will hear and will surround us and will cut our name off from the earth. What then will you do about your great name?"

10 Yahweh said to Joshua, "Get up! Why have you fallen on your face? 11 Israel[f] has sinned. They have violated my covenant that I imposed on them. They have taken some of the devoted things, they have stolen and they have deceived,[g] and have also put them with their own things. 12 The Israelites cannot prevail against their enemies. They turn their back[h] before their enemies because they themselves have come into a devoted state. I will no longer be with you [pl] unless you destroy the devoted things from among you. 13 Start to sanctify[i] the people and say, "Sanctify yourselves for tomorrow, for thus says Yahweh God of Israel, 'Devoted things are present among you [O Israel]. You will not be able to prevail against your enemies until you remove the devoted things from among you.'[j] 14 In the morning, come near by your tribes and whatever tribe Yahweh selects shall come near by clans, and whatever clan Yahweh selects shall come near by families and whatever family Yahweh selects shall come near by individual warriors.[k] 15 The one selected [with the devoted things][l] will be burned along with everything that belongs to him because he violated the covenant of Yahweh and committed an outrage in Israel.

Discovery and Punishment

16 Joshua got up early [in the morning] and brought Israel near by tribes and the tribe of Judah was selected. 17 He brought the clans[m] of Judah near and he selected the clan of Zerah. He brought the clan of Zerah near

by warriors[n] and Zabdi was selected. 18 He brought near his family by warriors and Achan son of Carmi son of Zabdi son of Zerah [of the tribe of Judah] was selected. 19 Then Joshua said to Achan, "My son, give glory to Yahweh God of Israel and give him thanks and tell me what you have done. Do not hide anything from me. 20 Then Achan answered Joshua, "It is true. I have sinned against Yahweh God of Israel and this is what I have done. 21 I saw among the booty a single beautiful Shinar robe[o] and two hundred shekels of silver and a single gold bar fifty shekels in weight, and I coveted them and took them. They are now hidden in the ground inside my tent, with the silver underneath."[p] 22 Then Joshua sent messengers. They ran to the tent and there it was, hidden in his tent with the silver underneath. 23 They took them from inside the tent and brought them to Joshua and to all the Israelites and emptied them out before Yahweh.

24 Then Joshua took Achan son of Zerah [and the silver and the robe and the gold bar][q] and his sons and his daughters and his cattle, his donkeys, his flocks, his tent, and everything that belonged to him. All Israel was with him. They brought them up to the Achor Valley. 25 Joshua said, "How you have made us taboo! May Yahweh make you taboo today!" Then all Israel stoned him [and burned them with fire and stoned them with stones].[r] 26 They raised over him a great pile of stones [still there today]. Then Yahweh turned from his burning anger. Therefore he called that place Achor Valley as it still is today.

a. For this translation of *m'l* and the concept in Israel's religious thought, see J. Milgrom, *Leviticus 1–16*, AB 3A; New York, 1991, 345–56. Achan committed sacrilege by appropriating (*lqḥ;* compare v. 11) what belonged to Yahweh. "Sacrilege" is what links his sin to the events of chapter 22 (vv. 16, 20, 22, 31). "In regard to" translates a *beth* of specification, Waltke and O'Connor, *Hebrew Syntax*, 11.2.5e.

b. Follows MT. OG lost "Beth-aven east of" by haplography between Beth-aven and Bethel. "Beth-aven" is a polemical vocalization, probably under the influence of Hosea 4:15; 10:5, of a border town between Benjamin and Ephraim (18:12).

c. The Greek translator seems to have taken "as far as Shebarim" as "until they were broken" (as S and T) and combined this with the following verb *nkh* into *synetripsan,* "they destroyed." NAB also takes it as a verbal idea: "until they broke ranks." The name "broken places" may refer to fissured rocks, or, less likely, "quarries" (REV). A historicizing suggestion, supported by Isa. 30:13–14, is "to the broken walls" of the city, on the grounds that it would have been a ruin in the Iron Age (Z. Zevit, "Archaeological and Literary Stratigraphy in Joshua 7–8," *BASOR* 251 [1983]: 31).

d. Follows MT. OG has *h'byr 'bdk* "why has your servant brought over," a theological correction based on a *d* for *r* error.

e. Follows MT on the assumption that the Greek translator omitted this to avoid a near repetition of the start of v. 7.

f. Follows MT. OG has "people" here and in vv. 16, 24 for MT "Israel." It is impossible to decide between these two readings.

g. Follows MT. OG lost "they have stolen and they have deceived" through haplography caused by the repetition of *wĕgam.*

h. 4QJosh[a] expands with "and not their faces" *wl' pnym.*

i. Verbal hendiadys with *qwm* highlighting the beginning of the action; compare 6:26 and NRSV "proceed to sanctify."

j. OG, with mixed support from 4QJosh[a] and T, has the second person plural throughout this verse. This is the preferred reading. The MT insertion "O Israel" (supported by 4QJosh[a]) prompted the conversion of some of these plurals to singulars.

k. Follows MT. OG reads *tqrybw* "bring near" where MT has *yqrb* and *tqrb* "come near." 4QJosh[a] supports OG with hiphil in the first occurrence, suffered a haplography for the second, and supports MT with qal for the third. MT is preferable because it deviates from the practice described in vv. 16–18.

l. Alternate translations for this MT expansion: "in a state of being devoted" (cf. NAB, NJB) or even "caught in the net" (JPSV margin). 4QJosh[a] has *bhm* "with them" for *bhrm.*

m. Construed as plural as suggested by OG and other witnesses.

n. Follows MT as the more difficult reading. S and some Hebrew manuscripts have "families" (i.e., "houses") as the obvious correction. MT "warriors" is supported by 4QJosh[a] and implicitly by the upcoming OG haplography: *lgbrym [wylkd zbdy wyqrb 't-bytw lgbrym].* Once the level of family is reached, Joshua deals with individuals rather than groups. Zabdi the grandfather of Achan comes forward as an individual to represent his family as patriarch. Then his family is screened by individual warriors and his grandson is taken. See D. Barthélemy, *Critique Textuelle de l'Ancien Testament,* OBO 50/1, Göttingen, 1982, 6–8.

o. Shinar is an exotic designation for Babylon (Gen. 10:10). Because it would be peculiar for the construct "robe of Shinar" to signify place of origin, it is better to interpret this as "a robe made of Shinar fabric." For an alternate hypothesis, D. Stec, "The Mantle Hidden by Achan," *VT* 41 (1991): 356–59.

p. The doubly determined form for "my tent" may represent a conflation of alternate readings "my tent" and "the tent," Waltke and O'Connor, *Hebrew Syntax,* 13.6b. OG lost "by weight" because of its similarity to the preceding word (*mšqlw* and *šqlym*) and *b'rṣ* "in the ground" because of its resemblance to the following *btwk* (visual confusion of ' and *t*).

q. MT expands on the basis of v. 21.

r. MT expands with what is expected from v. 15 and duplicates the stoning using a different verb, perhaps in anticipation of the cairn of stones in the next verse. Both expansions are absent in OG, while S and V omit only the stoning doublet. An alternate explanation for the evidence would read with MT and assume an inner Greek haplography from *lithois* to *lithois,* possible only in the word order of LXX[A] (*pas Israel lithois*).

The conquest began in chapter 2 with a positive example story, but now in chapter 7 it is punctuated by a negative one. The stories about Achan (7:1, 14–26) and Ai (7:2–9; 8:1–29) were originally independent tales. They have been joined together into a single plot movement in which the capture of Ai serves as the ultimate narrative goal of the combined whole. The narrative arc of 7:1 finishes at 7:26, but the one that begins at 7:2 is not completed until 8:29. In other words, Achan has been inserted into the Ai plot. The cautionary Achan story has become the primary obstacle to the resolution of the Ai plot line. It seems to have been substituted for a tactical miscalculation or a failure to consult Yahweh as the original cause of Israel's defeat. Conversely, the Ai defeat now serves as the context for the discovery of Achan's sin. The two stories correlate in that both finish with a stone cairn erected at their geographic locus and a testimony formula (7:26; 8:29). The most substantive redactional links, however, occur in Yahweh's response to Joshua's lament (7:10–13), where the themes of defeat and devoted things are brought together. The Achan story, in turn, is editorially linked to the capture of Jericho by the warning of 6:18 (cf. 7:12, 21) and the contrasting parallels between Rahab and Achan (see below). Jericho's booty provides the occasion for Achan's crime, and Jericho's fate is a prototype for his (6:24 and 7:15; 6:21 and 7:24).

Other redactional connections to the larger story are provided by vv. 5b (a reversal of 2:11; 5:1), v. 7 (Jordan crossing), and perhaps v. 13 (compare 3:5). The context of Jericho (v. 2) requires the change in locale reported by v. 24 in order to get the climactic action to the site of the cairn and the name Achor. Because the redactional attachment of Jericho to Achan to Ai shows no deuteronomistic features, it must be taken to be an element of the pre-deuteronomistic act of composition that brought together chapters 2–11 into a literary whole. Although there are some minor indications of successive editorial development (Amorites vs. Canaanites in vv. 7 and 9; differences between burning and stoning in vv. 15 and 25), a detailed reconstruction of the process is impossible. In the story about the altar built by the eastern tribes, Achan will serve as an example of their presumed sacrilege (22:20).

The Achan story is one for which a clear etiological purpose must be admitted.[1] It explains both a grave cairn and the striking name of the place where it was located, "Taboo Valley." The lamely-attached testimony formula of v. 26 is certainly redactional, but recognizing this does not subvert the classification of the story as a cautionary tale with an etiological background. Other examples of grave markers with stories attached are Gen. 35:20, 2 Sam. 18:17, and 2 Kings 23:16–17. The root *'kr* ("make taboo") tied to *ḥērem* violation provides the conceptual link to the site of Achan's grave cairn.[2] A folk etymology linking Achan's name and *'kr* may also have been explicitly present in some

---

1. The role played by etiology in the genesis and transmission of this story is often minimized or denied: Long, *The Problem of Etiological Narrative*, 25–26; B. Childs, "The Etiological Tale Re-examined," *VT* 24 (1974): 392–93. However, the interconnections of *ḥērem* to "taboo" to stoning to a cairn in the Achor Valley link together a substantial portion of this tale.

2. The poetic parallels of Isa. 65:10 and Hos. 2:16–17 [14–15E] suggest that the toponym Achor originally connoted fertility; H. Neef, "Die Ebene-Achor—das 'Tor der Hoffnung.' Ein exegetisch-topographischer Versuch," *ZDPV* 100 (1984): 91–107. The Valley (or Plain) of Achor is usually, but not certainly, identified with el-Buqei'ah.

versions of this tale, although this particular example makes nothing of it. However, this natural association led to the transformation of "Achan" into "Achar" in OG and 1 Chron. 2:7. Because wicked Achan is so clearly identified with a notable family of Judah (v. 1), and because Achor forms part of the border between Judah and Benjamin (15:7), the story of Achan's grave in "Taboo Valley" probably began its life as an anti-Judah polemic by Benjamin. Directed to a larger audience and in its present context, however, it would operate as an example story aiming to discourage misconduct. Its present intention is minatory and parenetic. A similar cautionary tale is that of Jonathan's violation of Saul's battlefield curse in 1 Sam. 14:24–30, 36–46. Saul's vow also involved abstinence from the spoil (v. 30), and an aborted attack resulted from the sin of its violation (vv. 36–37). In both stories the lot identifies the offender and the potential penalty is death. Jonathan is ransomed, but the campaign must be broken off. It is significant that Jonathan judges that his father's curse has put the land in a taboo state (v. 29).

In its present form, the Achan-Ai story is told with the aid of several stock literary genres: spy story (vv. 2–3),[3] community lament (vv. 6–9; cf. Psalms 44 and 74), discovery by means of lot (vv. 14–18; 1 Sam. 14:40–42), and confession as a doxology of judgment (vv. 19–21). The skillfully crafted plot starts with the problem of Achan's sin and Yahweh's anger (v. 1) and the associated problem of the defeat at Ai (vv. 2–5). It moves through lament (vv. 6–9) to two episodes of revelation, first of the cause of the problem in a Yahweh speech (vv. 10–13) and then of the perpetrator of the crime by means of the sacred lot (vv. 14–23). It climaxes with the eradication of the cause of Yahweh's wrath (vv. 24–26). The narrative predicament of v. 1 is expressly overcome in v. 26, while the expectations set up by v. 15 are met in a satisfying manner by vv. 24–25. The Ai story portion of this chapter reflects a close parallel to the plot of Judg. 20:18–48. The preliminary defeat of vv. 2–5 functions in the same way as Judg. 20:19–25, and Joshua's lament nicely parallels Judg. 20:23, 26–27.

Unfolding discovery runs through the plot line to provide character motivation and dramatic interest. Both the (literally) hidden problem and Yahweh's reaction to it are revealed to the reader immediately (v. 1). Joshua's attempts to discover the facts about the military situation lead to information that proves unhelpful (vv. 2–3). Israel's defeat (vv. 4–6) discloses some undefined problem to Joshua, who seeks answers through the rhetorical questions of his lament (vv. 6–9). Yahweh uncovers the facts of the crime (vv. 10–12) and provides a procedure for exposing the perpetrator (vv. 13–15). This procedure is followed in tension-building detail and Achan is identified (vv. 15–18). "Do not hide" says Joshua (v. 19), so Achan reveals the whole hidden truth, validated by the discovery in his tent (vv. 21–23). At the end the narrator discloses the implications concealed within the name Achor (vv. 24–26).

3. Wagner, "Die Kundschaftergeschichten im Alten Testament."

The rhetoric strives to emphasize the heinous nature of Achan's deed. Achan and Israel have "committed sacrilege" (v. 1), "sinned" (vv. 11, 20) and "violated the covenant" (vv. 11, 15). Verse 11 provides a numbing catalogue of negative interpretations of the crime, listed in repetitive formula. Achan is judged to have committed an "outrage in Israel" (v. 15), a technical term for a violation of communal order that endangers the whole community (cf. Judg. 19:23–24; 20:6, 10).[4] The word *lqh* "take, appropriate" first characterizes the misdeed (vv. 1, 11, 21), but then plays a corresponding role in its detection and punishment (vv. 23, 24). However, it is through use of the ritual categories of contagious *ḥērem* and taboo (*'kr*) that the dangerous nature of Achan's deed is most clearly exposed.

Things and people set off as Yahweh's property could fall into the category of *ḥērem*. Although often presumed to be a category connected only with the practice of war, things and people could come into a state of *ḥērem* in other ways as well (Exod. 22:19 [20E]; Lev. 27:21). Nothing or no one in a state of *ḥērem* could be redeemed (Lev. 27:28–29). The categorization of people and booty in warfare as *ḥērem* and thus as subject to destruction could be the result of a vow (as Num. 21:2–3, Mesha Inscription, *ANET* 321). In Joshua, as in Deuteronomy, however, it results from God's command (10:40; 11:12; Deut. 7:2; 20:17). *Ḥērem* implies total destruction as a means of rendering Yahweh's property unavailable for human use and ownership. At least in this sense the incineration of *ḥērem* was a sort of whole burnt offering (Deut. 13:17 [16E]). However, this same end could also be achieved by putting such things into Yahweh's treasury (Josh. 6:19, 24) or turning them to over the priests (Num. 18:14; Ezek. 44:29). On the other hand, human beings in a state of *ḥērem* apparently had to be killed (1 Sam. 15:33; 1 Kings 20:42). *Ḥērem*, as a ritual state of something or someone in Yahweh's possession, correlates with the state of holiness (Lev. 27:21, 28; Josh. 6:19), and like holiness, *ḥērem* was thought to be contagious (Deut. 7:26). Thus Achan's appropriation of *ḥērem* was a most dangerous act because it transformed Israel and its camp into a state of *ḥērem*, subject to destruction (6:18; 7:12).[5]

A coordinate effect of appropriated *ḥērem* seems to have been to put the people into a state of taboo, that is, a state of dangerous ritual disability that excludes one from society. That the verb *'kr* can mean this is almost invariably obscured in translations, but is clear from texts such as Gen. 34:30, Judg. 11:35 (proposed reading), 1 Sam. 14:29 (where it is the result of a curse or vow), and 1 Kings 18:17–18 (where it results from prophetic decree).[6] The link between the ritual

---

4. J. Marböck, *"nabal," ThWAT,* V, 181–84.

5. N. Lohfink, *"ḥāram," TDOT* V, 180–99.

6. The same participle is used for Achan/Achar in 1 Chron. 2:7. On the definition "taboo," see R. Mosis, "*'akar,*" *ThWAT* VI, 74–75. For a denial that it means "taboo," see J. Stamm, "Das hebräische Verbum *'akar," Or* 47 (1978): 339–350.

states of *ḥērem* and taboo provided the traditional etiological connection between Achan's deed and the name of the valley where his grave marker was identified.

The contribution of DH may be recognized in the language of violating covenant in vv. 11 and 15 (cf. 23:16).[7] The anger of Yahweh is a classic deuteronomic cause for disaster (Deut. 6:15; 7:4; 11:17; 29:26) and an important structural pattern of DH (again 23:16; Judg. 2:14, 20; 3:8, etc.).[8] Thus DH was able to utilize this inherited combination of stories to serve its own theological purpose. The catastrophe at Ai perfectly illustrates the deuteronomistic axiom that defeat is caused by sin (1 Kings 8:33). Achan serves as a exemplary demonstration of Deut. 7:25–26 and 13:18 [17E], just as Deut. 13:13–18 [12–17E] seems to have served as a general model for the fate of Jericho. Achan is one of several examples in DH of the ideological pattern that sin brings defeat and removal of sin leads to restoration (Judg. 2:11–18; 6:1–7:23; 10:6–11:33; 1 Sam. 7:3–11). The configuration of Deut. 1:19–3:11 (DH) is remarkably close to that of Joshua chapters 7–8: spies (Deut. 1:22–25), "melted" hearts (v. 28), acknowledgment of sin (v. 41), defeat (vv. 43–46), removal of the faithless (Deut. 2:14–16), victory oracle (Deut. 2:24–25; cf. Josh. 8:1–2), and subsequent triumph (Deut. 2:31–3:10). In both narratives the anger of Yahweh (Deut. 1:34, 37; Josh. 7:1, 26) and the loss of the divine presence (Deut. 1:42; Josh. 7:12) play a controlling role.[9]

The intercession by Moses in the context of Israel's disobedience and divine wrath (Deuteronomy 9 and 10) may have provided a model for Joshua's lament (vv. 6–9). Contacts include prostration before Yahweh (Deut. 9:25), the verb "destroy" (*šmd* hiphil, Deut. 9:8; 10:10), the twin issues of Israel's name and Yahweh's reputation (Deut. 9:14, 28), destruction of the problem by fire (9:21), and moving forward to victory (10:11). There are also similarities to Josiah's actions in 2 Kings 22–23: tearing clothing (2 Kings 22:11, 19) and purging by fire (23:4, 6, etc.). DH seems to be drawing a parallel in proper leadership between Moses, Joshua, and Josiah.

The tales of Rahab and Achan are also parallel in some ways. Both function as example stories. They serve as foils to each other, contrasting models of fidelity and infidelity. Rahab is a positive example of faith and the benefits of seizing the opportunities offered by Yahweh's action. Achan, in contrast, is an example of infidelity and of making improper use of opportunity. Both hide (by burying, *ṭmn:* 2:6; 7:21; other verbs: 2:4; 6:25; 7:19), but for very different reasons. Rahab hides the "messengers" sent by Joshua (6:25); the messengers sent to Achan's tent find what he had hidden (7:22). Her fidelity and her understanding of the implications of *ḥērem* (2:10) mean that she and all asso-

---

7. Weinfeld, *Deuteronomy and the Deuteronomic School,* 340.

8. D. McCarthy, "The Wrath of Yahweh and the Structural Unity of The Deuteronomistic History," *Essays in Old Testament Ethics,* New York, 1974, 99–110.

9. C. Begg, "The Function of Josh 7:1–8:29 in the Deuteronomistic History," *Bib* 67 (1986): 320–34.

ciated with her (2:13; 6:23) live; those associated with Achan the violator of *ḥērem* perish (7:15, 24). A special edge is given to these comparisons by the shocking and ironic difference in background between Rahab the foreign prostitute (6:17, 25) and the Judahite whose proper genealogy is rehearsed three times. The ritually unclean Rahab is prudently kept outside the war camp (6:23), but it is Achan the pedigreed Judahite who contaminates the camp with *ḥērem* (6:18).[10]

The tale of Achan dampens the triumphalism of chapters 1–6. It would serve as an admonition and a caution to a succession of audiences faced by the challenge of obedience in times of temptation and the discouragement of political impotence of the sort reflected in the communal lament psalms. The failure to meet the test of devoted things is a motif in other stories in the national tradition (1 Samuel 15; 2 Kings 20:42). It functions to raise larger issues of disloyalty. For Israel to permit any individual to commit apostasy is to share in a collective sin and risk collective disaster. Israel's claim on Yahweh's victorious presence is not absolute or automatic. Thus the logic of cause and effect permeates the text. Transgression leads to the inability to prevail, to retreat, and ultimately to death. Readers are to realize that Yahweh will not be with them and they will not prevail unless they vigorously destroy the causes of apostasy.

For DH the particular crisis of infidelity was one of violating the covenant of Deuteronomy. At the root of the nation's ills lay Yahweh's anger. It is significant that the unrestricted *ḥērem* violated by Achan reflects Deut. 7:25–26 and 13:13–19 [12–18E].[11] In these texts *ḥērem* is the appropriate reaction to perilous paganism and internal apostasy. For DH, the point of *ḥērem* is contemporary religious purity and the reformation of an apostate people, not the technical details of a long-past conquest. The theology of DH calls for lament and confession in the manner of 1 Kings 8:33–50 and reform in the style of Josiah's purge. Restoration of national glory is possible, but perhaps in the last analysis only because of the argument of v. 9, that Yahweh's reputation is bound up with that of the nation (cf. Deut. 9:26–28).

[1] The detailed genealogy of v. 1 prepares for the step-by-step procedure of vv. 14, 16–18 and ties Achan to a notable Judahite family (for Zerah, see Gen. 38:30; 46:12).[12] In a society in which corporate solidarity was the norm, all Israel is implicated in Achan's crime as a matter of course (vv. 1 and 15).[13] In addition, appropriated goods in a state of *ḥērem* are contagious, putting the camp

---

10. For the ideological implications of these parallels against the background of *ḥērem*, see Rowlett, "Inclusion, Exclusion and Marginality in the Book of Joshua."

11. *Ḥērem* is usually limited to people and animals (Deut. 20:16–18; 1 Sam. 15:3, etc.).

12. However, the clan of Carmi was also associated with Reuben (Gen. 46:9; Num 26:5–6).

13. For a discussion of how corporate responsibility influenced by the concept of *ḥērem* is reflected in this story, see J. Porter, "The Legal Aspects or the Concept of 'Corporate Personality' in the Old Testament," *VT* 15 (1965): 361–80, and J. Kaminsky, *Corporate Responsibility in the Hebrew Bible*, JSOTSup 196, Sheffield, 1995, 67–95.

and nation into that same perilous state (6:18; 7:12). The reader knows that some disaster is imminent, but Joshua and the spies operate in ironic ignorance.

[2–5] The dispatch of spies parallels the auspicious start of the Jericho campaign (compare the wording of v. 2 with 2:1). This creates dramatic tension with the negative outlook of v. 1. It also invites the reader to make comparisons between the contrasting experiences of effortless, miraculous victory at Jericho and the setbacks and stratagems involved with Ai, as well as between Rahab's fidelity and Achan's perfidy. The geographic precision of v. 2 echoes the genealogical precision of v. 1.

The spies' report of only a few defenders and Joshua's dispatch of three thousand troops turns out to be inadequate in light of the figures later given in 8:3, 12, 25. The usual ideological function of an inadequate Israelite army is to glorify the victory of Yahweh (Deut. 20:1–8; Judg. 5:8; 7:2). This narrative reverses the pattern. Overconfidence and tactical misjudgment were probably the causes of Israel's defeat when the Ai story stood alone, but now the incorporation of the Achan story means that the anger of Yahweh has become the causative factor. Although Israel's flight in v. 4b is no real surprise to the alerted reader, it is striking how fully Israel and the enemy have swapped expected roles in v. 5. Now it is the enemy who "strikes down" and "pursues," verbs used elsewhere of Israel (for example 10:10; 11:8). The formula for the extent of pursuit (10:10–11, 41; 11:8) traditionally emphasized Israel's victory, not its rout. Israel now experiences the enemy's fear, and the language of 2:11 and 5:1 is reversed. The "about thirty-six" deaths provide an ironic, comic opera flavor. Such great terror resulting from so few casualties emphasizes the extent of the panic and the abject state of Israel's morale.

[6–9] Joshua falls on his face a second time, but for a very different reason than in 5:14. He laments along with Israel's elders, who are apparently originally at home in the Ai story (8:10). In the present form of the narrative, their presence expands the horizon of the lament to the whole nation. The ark is not present in the earliest recoverable text of v. 6 or in v. 23. Joshua's prayer moves from a description of Israel's plight (vv. 7–8) to motivation for Yahweh to act (v. 9), but it lacks any specific request or petition. It is similar to the laments found in the book of Psalms in vocabulary and in its questioning of Yahweh's ultimate purposes, but was obviously composed specifically for this particular literary context. Joshua questions the objectives and benefits of the spectacular Jordan crossing. The standard notion of Yahweh giving the enemy into Israel's power ("hand;" 2:24; 6:2; etc.) is shockingly reversed. The usual effect of what the enemy hears about Israel (2:10; 5:1; etc.) is turned on its head in v. 9, and the pattern of "surrounding" set up at the siege of Jericho (6:3 etc.) is inverted. From a deuteronomistic perspective, the promises of Deut. 12:29 and 19:1 seem to have been undone, and the tremendously significant reputation of Yahweh's name (1 Sam. 12:22; 2 Sam. 7:23; 1 Kings 8:41–42) has been endangered.

[**10–15**] Verse 10 marks the end of what Joshua's prostration began in v. 6 and counters Joshua's queries with Yahweh's own rhetorical question. In vv. 11–12 Yahweh divulges the cause of Israel's defeat, in vv. 13–14 orders what must be done, and in v. 15 announces judgment on the offender. As in v. 1, Yahweh in v. 11 insists on corporate responsibility for the act of the individual. Word choice emphasizes that this is criminal behavior worthy of severe punishment: sin, theft, and deceit (*kḥš* denotes both hiding and deception). The violated covenant (vv. 11, 15) may refer narrowly to the command to devote Jericho's booty (6:17–19) or, in the larger deuteronomistic context, to the book of Deuteronomy (23:16; Deut. 17:2; Judg. 2:20; 2 Kings 18:12, etc.) The use of the verb *'br* in the expression "violate the covenant" elicits from the reader an ironic comparison with the crossing of the Jordan (v. 7). Fulfillment of the threat that Yahweh would no longer be "with" the people (v. 12) would erase the reiterated promise of 1:5, 9; 3:7, 10; 6:27. The foundational cause of this potential catastrophe is stressed by using the root *ḥrm* five times in vv. 11–13.

Sanctification is commanded (v. 13) to prepare for firsthand contact with Yahweh's activity (3:5; Exod. 19:10–11) and perhaps also to counter the effects of contagious *ḥērem.* Yahweh's command is backed up by what sounds like prophetic speech in v. 13b: messenger formula, accusation, threat. The people are to "come near" (*qrb*), that is, approach the locus of Yahweh's presence (cf. vv. 6 and 23) for divine judgment (Exod. 22:7–8 [8–9E]). Although the sacred lot is not actually mentioned in the selection process (v. 14), the use of the verb *lkd* (cf. 1 Sam. 10:20–21; 14:41–42) and the step-by-step procedure clearly implies its use.[14] Yahweh in v. 15a employs the juridical form of an apodictic judgment expressed as a participle ("whoever is selected") followed by the consequent punishment. Burning was thought appropriate for the gravest sexual offenses (Gen. 38:24; Lev. 20:14; 21:9) and seems to have been intended to extinguish the offender's personhood by reducing him or her to the most infinitesimal form possible. That the culprit's possessions (and family?) are to be burned may indicate the effect of contagious *ḥērem;* they must be treated as Jericho's booty was (6:24).

[**16–23**] Verses 16–18 unfold the divine judgment procedure prepared for by the genealogy of v. 1 and the instructions of v. 14.[15] The somewhat obscure grammatical subject of "he selected" in v. 17 must be Yahweh. Achan's confession follows his selection in order to confirm the lot's verdict, to locate clearly the blame for Israel's military failure, and to satisfy reader curiosity about the crime's sordid details. Joshua triggers this confession by calling for a "doxology of judgment," praise for and acknowledgment of Yahweh's glory and equitable

14. On the lot see J. Lindblom, "Lot-Casting in the Old Testament," *VT* 12 (1962): 164–178 and R. Wilson, "Israel's Judicial System in the Preexilic Period," *JQR* 74 (1983) 229–48.

15. For Israel's tribe, clan, and family structure, see N. Gottwald, *The Tribes of Yahweh,* Maryknoll, N.Y., 1979, 245–92.

justice (v. 19).[16] With the self-accusation formula "I have sinned" (v. 20; 1 Sam. 15:23–24; 2 Sam. 12:13; 19:21 [20E]; 24:17), Achan acknowledges his own responsibility, while distancing the people as a whole from collective culpability. The "thus and so" (*wĕkāz'ōt wĕkāz'ōt;* in this translation: "this is what") communicates that Achan gave a more extensive explanation, but what follow are the core details needed to advance the story and satisfy the reader (2 Sam. 17:15; 2 Kings 5:4; 9:12). Verse 21 points directly back to the warning of 6:18. Cloth, silver, and gold represent traditional items of plunder (2 Kings 7:8). Achan's use of the word "booty" cannot be intended to exculpate him, for at Jericho all the booty fell into a state of *ḥērem* and was not subject to division among the troops. Achan's detailed information makes the discovery of the devoted things possible, which in turn corroborates his story, verifies his guilt, and makes it possible to turn the contraband over to its legitimate owner by emptying it out "before Yahweh" (v. 23; cf. vv. 6:19, 24). That the silver was "underneath" (v. 22), just as predicted, is a satisfying detail of confirmation. That the devoted things were confined to his tent and buried there might be a comforting suggestion that the danger of *ḥērem* contagion was actually limited.

[24–26] Yahweh's sentence from v. 15 is carried out. Things and people affected by *ḥērem* contagion are brought up (from the lower Gilgal/Jericho location of the larger context) to the execution site. Presumably Achan's tent receives special mention as an obviously contaminated item. Israel's explicit participation is critical in order to demarcate the line of guilt between Achan who dies and the nation which goes on to victory. The MT expansion to v. 24 clarifies that the devoted goods were also destroyed. Joshua interprets Achan's crime as laying a taboo state on the nation (v. 25), a taboo that had to be properly redirected back upon Achan and confined to him. Again an MT expansion (v. 25) seeks to clarify that Achan's children and animals were also destroyed ("them") and that fire was indeed employed in accordance with v. 15. The pre-MT text was unclear as to whether the sentence of v. 15 included Achan's family as well as his possessions. However, their death is certainly intended by use of the list form often found in *ḥērem* texts (v. 24; cf. 6:21; 1 Sam. 15:3). There can have been no other reason to bring them up to Achor.[17] That Achan's children, but not his wife, are mentioned may indicate that they were in some sense viewed as his possessions.[18] The mound of stones presumably was thought of as disempowering the dead and entombing any further potential for damage from them.

---

16. For the classic description of the doxology of judgment, see G. von Rad, *Old Testament Theology*, New York, 1962, I, 357–59. An unexpected example is 1 Sam. 6:5.

17. G. Driver, "Affirmation by Exclamatory Negation," *JANESCU* 5 (1973): 107–13, suggests that the verb used for Achan's family indicates "drive away with stones" and reads 22:20b as asserting that Achan "alone perished."

18. This same pattern is evidenced in the Job folktale.

Capturing Ai
Joshua 8:1–29

The Plan

8:1 Yahweh said to Joshua, "Do not fear or be terrified. Take the whole army with you. Go up now to Ai. See, I have given into your [sg] power the king of Ai and his people and his city[a] and his land. **2** Do [sg] to Ai [and its king] what you did to Jericho and its king. However its booty and cattle you [pl] may plunder for yourselves.[b] Position [sg] your ambush against the city to its rear."

3 So Joshua and the whole army set out[c] to go up to Ai. Joshua chose thirty thousand valiant warriors and sent them out at night. **4** He commanded them, "[See.] You are an ambush [against the city] to the rear of the city. Do not move [very] far from the city, but all of you be ready.[d] **5** I and all the people who are with me will approach the city. When they come out to engage us as before, we will flee before them. **6** They will come out after us until we have drawn them away from the city, for they will think, 'They are fleeing before us as before,' [and we will flee before them].[e] **7** But you will rise out of the ambush and approach[f] the city[g] and Yahweh your God will give it into your power. **8** As soon as you seize the city, set the city on fire. Act according to the word of Yahweh.[h] See, I have commanded you."

Its Execution

9 Joshua sent them off and they went into ambush. They stayed between Bethel and Ai to the west of Ai. [Joshua spent that night among the people.][i] **10** Joshua got up early in the morning and mustered the people. Then he and the elders [of Israel][j] went up in front of the people to Ai. **11** The whole army that was with him went up[k] and approached. They came opposite the city [and camped][l] on the north side of Ai[m] with the valley between them and Ai. **12** He took about five thousand men and positioned them as an ambush between Bethel and Ai on the west side of the city. **13** The people positioned the main camp, which was on the north side of the city, and its rear guard on the west side of Ai. [Joshua went that night into the middle of the valley.][n] **14** As soon as the king of Ai saw this, he[o] hurried out early to engage them [Israel][p] in battle, he and all his people [to the meeting place in front of the Arabah.][q] He did not know that there was an ambush against him behind the city. **15** Joshua and all Israel let themselves be beaten before them[r] and fled in the direction of the wilderness, 16 and all the people who were in the city[s] were called out to pursue them. They pursued Joshua and so let themselves be drawn away from the city. 17 No one was left in Ai [and Bethel] who had not gone out after Israel. They left the city open and pursued Israel.

18 Yahweh said to Joshua, "Extend [the sword in][t] your hand toward Ai, because it is into your hand that I will give it!" So Joshua extended the sword in his hand toward the city. 19 The ambush quickly rose from its place and charged as soon as he extended his hand. They entered the city and captured it. They immediately set the city on fire. 20 Then the men of Ai turned around and looked. There was the smoke of the city rising toward the sky! They had no chance to flee one way or the other. [The people who were fleeing toward the wilderness turned against the pursuit.][u] 21 Joshua and all Israel saw that the ambush had captured the city and that the smoke of the city was rising, so they turned and struck down the men of Ai. 22 Those others came out of the city to engage them, so that they were in the middle of Israel. Some were on one side and some on the other. They struck them down until no one was left who ran away or escaped. 23 But they seized the king of Ai alive and brought him to Joshua.

24 When Israel had finished killing the whole population of Ai in the open country on the slope[v] where they had chased them [and they all fell by the edge of the sword] until they were finished off, all Israel returned to Ai and struck it down with the edge of the sword. 25 All who fell that day—men and women—were twelve thousand, all the men of Ai. 26 Joshua did not pull back his hand with which he had extended his sword until he had devoted to destruction the whole population of Ai.[w] 27 However Israel did plunder for themselves the cattle and the booty[x] of that city, according to the word which Yahweh had commanded Joshua. 28 Then Joshua burned Ai and made it a permanently deserted mound, as it still is today. 29 He hanged the king of Ai on a tree until evening. At sundown Joshua gave the order and they took his body down from the tree, threw it at the opening [of the city gate],[y] and raised over it a [great] pile of stones that is still there today.

a. Follows MT. OG lost "and his people and his city" through haplography from *w't* to *w't*.

b. Alternate translation: "You may plunder only its booty and cattle (cf. v. 27, NJB, NRSV)."

c. Alternate translation maximizing *qwm* as a stress on the beginning of an action and reducing the tension with v. 10: "prepared to go up" (JPSV, REB, NAB).

d. The MT expansions in this verse are generally supported by 4QJosh[a].

e. MT dittography from the end of v. 5.

f. Follows OG *wngštm 'l* as fitting the context better (v. 11) and less theological than MT *whwrštm 't* "and take possession of."

g. Vv. 7–8 follow MT. OG lost "and Yahweh your God . . . with fire" due to an inner-Greek haplography: *polin ka[i dōsei . . . pyri ka]ta to rēma touto* (graphic similarity in uncial letters between *kaid* and *kata*).

h. Follows MT as compatible with v. 27. OG "this word" may have arisen by misreading an abbreviation for the divine name.

i. MT expands to clarify that Joshua remained with the main army. 4QJosh[a] apparently does not have room for this expansion. See v. 13.

j. Both OG and 4QJosh[a] lack this expansion.

k. 4QJosh[a] has "and they turned."

l. MT expansion anticipating v. 13.

m. At this point OG begins a long haplography covering much of vv. 11–13, one triggered by the repetition of "on the north side of Ai/the city" in vv. 11b and 13a. Subsequently OG must have shifted the location of the main body from "the north side" to "the east side" in order to put the two troop contingents on opposite sides of Ai. 4QJosh[a] does not appear to have room for all of MT.

n. Absent in OG and apparently 4QJosh[a]. This expansion may itself have suffered an early corruption. MT, supported by V and hexaplaric Greek, asserts that Joshua reconnoitered between the main camp and the city in the intervening valley (the *gay* of v. 11). Some Hebrew witnesses harmonize to v. 9, adjusting *wayyēlek* to *wayyālen* "and he spent the night." S has *'m* "people" for *'mq* "valley." The MT expansions in vv. 9 and 13 emphasize the timetable by explicitly reporting the nights that preceded the mornings of vv. 10 and 14.

o. Follows OG. The MT gives the subject as "the men of Ai" with attendant plural verbs, anticipating "all his people."

p. Both OG and 4QJosh[a] lack this expansion.

q. MT expansion or gloss to clarify the geographical situation, perhaps indicating a place where various paths joined to head down toward the Jordan valley. Or perhaps this has something to do with the *mô'ēd* (previous "agreement" about battle tactics) of Judg. 20:38. The Arabah in this context would indicate the direction of the Jordan valley (as apparently 11:2, 16; 12:8).

r. OG suffered a long haplography from *lpnykm* in v. 15 to *'ḥrykm* in v. 16. This assumes that the Greek translator did not know what to do with the niphal of *ng'* and paraphrased with two verbs "he saw and retreated." Margolis, *Joshua in Greek,* 131.

s. Kethib "city," Qere "Ai." This unsurprising variation also occurs between MT and OG in vv. 11, 18, 28.

t. MT expansion adds the sword of v. 18b to "your hand." OG conflates the original "your hand" and the expanded reading found in MT into "your hand with the sword in your hand."

u. Either an MT anticipatory expansion or a deliberate OG omission to create a more coherent narrative. Omitted here on the principle of preferring the shorter reading.

v. Partially follows OG; compare 7:5. OG has *bhr bmwrd* "on the mountain, on the slope." The first word must be an expansion or a gloss. MT *bmdbr* "in the wilderness" stems from misreading and transposing the letters of the more difficult original *bmwrd* (Margolis, *Joshua in Greek,* 138).

w. OG lost this entire verse through homoioteleuton from "the population of Ai" (the OG reading at the end of v. 25) to "the population of Ai" (Margolis, *Joshua in Greek*, 140).

x. Alternate translation: "It was only the cattle and the booty that Israel plundered" (compare NJB, NRSV).

y. OG offers just one word *pht* "pit" for MT *pth š'r h'r* "opening of the city gate." "Opening" is more difficult than "pit" and preferable. The short OG reading indicates that "city gate" was a gloss to explain the somewhat cryptic "opening."

The methodological antithesis to the text-critical approach taken here is to assume that a highly dissonant original text, possibly a result of the combination of two different versions, was subsequently abbreviated by the OG to eliminate difficulties.[1] However, a comprehensive comparison of OG and MT in Joshua does not support the contention that OG routinely shortened texts to achieve greater coherence. In this chapter there are creditable mechanical explanations for those OG gaps that are often judged to be deliberate omissions in vv. 7–8, 11–13, 15–16, and 26 (notes g, m, r, w). Conversely, it is possible to trace the "logic" of the MT expansions in 9b, 13b, and 14a (notes i, n, q). It is only at v. 20b that a reasonable case could be made for an OG correction by omission (note u). The text-critical methodology followed here continues to assume that expansions are always more likely than deliberate deletions and that full weight should be given to mechanical explanations for pluses and minuses.

Even without the disruption introduced by later textual developments, this narrative is rough and confused. There is repetition of information on the positioning of the ambush (vv. 9, 12, 13) and of the main force (vv. 11 and 13). An arresting inconsistency is the size of the ambush, thirty thousand in v. 3 over against five thousand in v. 12. Other examples of the jagged unfolding of the story are:

> the movement of the people to Ai is reported twice (vv. 3a and 10)
> Ai is put to the torch by the ambush (vv. 8, 19; vb. *yṣt*), then burned down by Joshua (v. 28; vb. *śrp*)
> Joshua's extended sword is introduced late (v. 18)
> the sword is both a signal to attack (vv. 19–20) and a symbol of victorious power (v. 26)
> v. 20b MT (see note u) prematurely springs the trap[2]

1. Classically J. Wellhausen, *Die Composition des Hexateuchs und der historischen Bücher des Alten Testaments*, Berlin, 1899, 142; See Barthélemy, *Critique*, 10–12.

2. These irregularities have naturally led to theories of redactional growth. According to M. Rösel, "Studien zur Topographie der Kriege in den Büchern Josua und Richter, *ZDPV* 91 (1975): 161–62, the core story was 7:2–5a; 8:10–12, 13b. Boling, *Joshua*, 236, divides between Dtr1 and Dtr2. Fritz, *Josua*, 87–91, identifies the original story as 10–12, 14–15, 19, 21, 23, 29.

The redactional work of DH is visible in vv. 1–2, 22b, and 27, and also in v. 29 where Deut. 21:22–23 is scrupulously obeyed. The deuteronomistic twist given to the plot is revealed by use of language parallel to that describing the defeats of Sihon and Og in Deut. 2:31–35 and 3:1–7. In both texts there is a strong emphasis on divine assurance (8:1b–2a; Deut. 2:31; 3:2) and the execution of *ḥērem* (8:25–26). Cattle and booty are excluded according to the standard DH pattern (v. 27; 11:14; 22:8; Deut. 2:34–35; 3:6–7).

The story of Ai is a classic example of the role played by etiological factors in the development and transmission of a conquest narrative. The identification of Ai with et-Tell, apparently uninhabited after Iron I, is nearly universal. This imposing ruin on the road between Jericho and Bethel would be a natural focus for a Benjaminite conquest tradition once such stories began to develop. That the designation *hāʿāy* (always with the article) almost certainly means "the Ruin"[3] indicates that etiology, and not historical memory, first generated this story. A second point of attachment would seem to be a pile of stones at a (gateway?) opening in the wall that was popularly taken to be the grave cairn of the king of Ai. The testimony notices about these phenomena (vv. 28, 29) are certainly redactional, but this only means that the collectors or authors were aware of the obvious etiological point and used it to bolster the rhetorical power of the story. As in the case of the folk etymological connection between Achan and Achor in chapter 7, this story as written makes no direct mention of the foundational "name means ruin" correlation, but leaves the reader to detect Ai's name covertly implied in the "permanently deserted mound" of v. 28.

The plot that became attached to Ai was a traditional one in which military reverse is remedied by the ruse of simulated retreat and ambush.[4] This same plot motif was used in slightly different form to narrate the attack on Gibeah in Judg. 20:15–48. There too, unexpected defeat provides the narrative problem (Judg. 20:15–25), Israel reacts properly (v. 26), and Yahweh's oracle predicts success (v. 27–28). The forces are arranged, the trap baited by retreat and sprung (vv. 29–36a), leading to an immense slaughter and the burning of the city (vv. 45–48). These two stories also share a substantial amount of vocabulary.[5] This is true in part because they are examples of the same stock plot, but probably also because of intertextual contacts.[6] This particular example of the

---

3. KB³, 771.

4. For classical parallels, A. Malamat, "Die Eroberung Kanaans: Die israelitische Kriegsführung nach der biblischen Tradition," *Das Land Israel im biblischer Zeit: Jerusalem Symposium 1981*, GTA 25, Göttingen, 1983, 24–25.

5. For example "as before" (8:6 and Judg. 20:32), "did not know" (8:14 and Judg. 20:34), "smoke rising" (8:21 and Judg. 20:38, 40), and "direction of the wilderness" (8:15 and Judg. 20:42).

6. W. Roth, "Hinterhalt und Scheinflucht: der stammespolemische Hintergrund von Jos 8," *ZAW* 75 (1963): 296–304, thinks that the Ai narrative was constructed on the basis of the Gibeah battle.

traditional plot strongly emphasizes Joshua's role, in part by the inclusion of his extended sword hand (vv. 18, 26). He is the subject of a large portion of the verbs, the object of Yahweh's address, and the one who fleshes out Yahweh's bare commands with tactical detail. The conventional plot has also been enhanced with local geographic detail. Bethel provides a constant point of reference (7:2; 8:9, 12). One reads of "the Shebarim" or "broken places" (7:5), the "direction of the wilderness" (8:15), "in the open country on the slope" (v. 24; 7:5), and "the opening" (v. 29). The MT tradition supplements this with "the meeting place in front of the Arabah" (v. 14). The general picture of an ambush hidden to the west, a conspicuous parade of the main body in from the east or northeast, and its positioning to the city's north across a valley are all compatible with a location at et-Tell.[7]

The plot begins with the defeat reported in 7:2–5. The genuine flight of this setback and its humiliation (7:4, 8) are countered by emphasizing that the second retreat is merely a ruse (8:5–6, 15). The modest numbers of chapter 7 are rebutted by the large ones of 8:3, 25. Because so much of the unfolding plot is revealed ahead of time by Joshua (8:4–8), there is little dramatic tension or suspense. Verse 4 prepares for the disposition of troops in vv. 11–13, v. 5 for the action of vv. 14–15, v. 6 for vv. 16–17, v. 7 for v. 19a, and v. 8 for v. 19b. Joshua's preview, however, prepares the reader for the action only up through setting the city on fire. Thus from v. 20 on, closing the trap and slaughtering the enemy dramatically unfold without reader foreknowledge.

Although the narrative chronology is not presented either explicitly or clearly, it is the path of least interpretive resistance to read vv. 3–9 (instructions, setting the ambush) as happening on the night before the main action. The main action starts the next morning (vv. 10–13) with the intentionally conspicuous march and the encampment of the main body. It continues early that same day when the king of Ai observes Israel's conspicuous activity (v. 14). The resultant combat, slaughter, and devastation continue until evening (v. 29). The two additions in MT (vv. 9b and 13b) restructured this earlier chronology into one involving a first night (vv. 3–9) and a first day (vv. 10–13a), then a second night (v. 13b) followed by a second day (vv. 14–29).

Overall, the plot is structured according to the now familiar pattern of command and obedience. Yahweh's speech (cf. 3:7–8; 6:2–5; 7:10–15) offers renewed reassurance and promise, introduces the double objectives of king and city, establishes the *ḥērem* pattern, and introduces the tactical factor of ambush. The destruction of the king of Ai is as important as that of the city (vv. 14, 23), and these two parallel themes culminate together in the testimony formulas of vv. 28 and 29. The narrative is framed in a chiastic way by vv. 1–2 and 27–29. The themes of the introduction (king, city, booty) return at the

---

7. Z. Zevit, "Archaeology and Literary Stratigraphy in Joshua 7–8, *BASOR* 251 (1983): 23–35.

finale (booty, city, king) to produce a satisfying feeling of completion. There is a similar chiastic frame around the speech of Joshua in vv. 3–10. The movement of the main army (vv. 3a, 10) encloses the ambush (vv. 3b, 9), which in turn encloses the word "command" (in vv. 4a, 8b). In the description of the battle itself, the narrative makes skillful use of the technique of alternating viewpoint. In vv. 14, 16–17, and 20 matters are seen from the Ai perspective, while vv. 15, 18–19, 21 present the action from Israel's standpoint. These two separate perspectives are then brought together in the confusion of v. 22, where the reader has trouble sorting things out. The effect is to create the disorienting impression of a confusing melee. A similar approach to the problem of telling simultaneous stories can be found in 1 Kings 20:16–21. The narrative then takes up the objects of Israel's violence in turn (vv. 24–29): the inhabitants on the field of battle, the population remaining in the city, the city itself, and the king. The symbolic sword, which opened the frame in v. 18 on the victory phase of the plot, now closes it in concert with a notice of *ḥērem* (v. 26). This in turn provides an opportunity to nail down the question of booty (v. 27).

Every conquest story in Joshua is a territorial claim and an assertion of national identity. If one were to risk correlating archaeology with literary history, the emergence of a conquest narrative connected to Ai could be dated to a time after the Iron I settlement phase had concluded[8] and Ai was a nameless deserted ruin. One could speculate that Philistine pressure on the central highlands would lead to the development of such stories in order to strengthen claims to those territories. In the case of Jericho one might postulate a similar effect produced by incursions from Moab (Judg. 3:13). In any case, the emerging tradition that Israel had entered the land through a violent invasion would naturally tend to attach tales of conquest to conspicuous ruins such as Jericho and Ai.

One must also read this story in light of its correlation with the Achan episode. Just as the defeat at Ai was interpreted in terms of Achan's disobedience and Yahweh's anger, so victory at Ai serves as a paradigm of the relationship between obedience and success. This is the reason for the emphasis on divine instructions (vv. 1–2, 18) and careful obedience to them (vv. 26–29). For a series of audiences over time, this text would evoke obedience ("act according to the word of Yahweh;" v. 8), while at the same time producing hope and confidence that national success is certain as long as Yahweh and Yahweh's promise stand behind the endeavor. It is significant that the tension between divine promise and the need for human planning and action is not dissolved. From Yahweh's perspective success may be guaranteed; from the

8. On the interplay between the archaeology of Ai and the Bible, J. Callaway, Ai (et-Tell): Problem Site for Biblical Archaeologists," in *Archaeology and Biblical Interpretation*, Atlanta, 1987, 87–99.

human standpoint it requires tactics and subterfuge. These two perspectives are brought together by the sword brandished by Joshua, as both human signal and medium of divinely assisted victory (cf. Exod. 17:11).[9]

[1–2] Yahweh's introductory words signal that the situation has returned to what it had been before the Achan incident. Yahweh is again "with" Israel (reversing 7:12; cf. 1:5, 9; Deut. 31:8), and Yahweh's encouraging promises remain in effect (1:2–3; 2:24; 6:2). These verses also telegraph much of what is to follow: use of the whole army (3a, 11); ambush (vv. 4, 12); victory over both the king (v. 14, 23, 29) and his people/city (vv. 22, 24–26, 28); taking booty (v. 27). However, readers are not prepared for Joshua's sword (vv. 18–19, 26). As a redactional connector, Yahweh's speech links back to Jericho and, by its emphasis on "the whole army," to the previous defeat at Ai, especially to 7:3.

[3–9] In a carefully framed speech, Joshua previews the upcoming action. This time there are clear tokens of success in the shape of "the whole army" (as in 10:7; 11:7) and "valiant warriors" (1:14; 10:7). The word for ambush in vv. 4, 7, 12, 14, 19, 21 (*'ôrēb*) stresses the participants; the word in v. 9 (*ma'rāb*) refers to their place of concealment (Judg. 9:5; Ps. 10:8). "Behind" in v. 4 is "west" both as the opposite of the eastern approach side and as a compass direction.[10]

[10–13] The main action begins with the usual cliche in v. 10 (3:1; 6:12; 7:16). The presence of elders links back to the initial setback (7:6). Verse 11 foregrounds "the whole army" with a subject-first sentence and contrasts it to the ambush of v. 9. Unlike the ambush, it advances in an obvious manner as it comes "opposite" or "over against" (*neged*) the city. Then v. 12 restates the position of the ambush, and v. 13 clarifies the relationship of two contingents, the ambush being the "heel" or rear guard (Gen. 49:19) of the main army.

[14–17] Israel's visibility on the opposite ridge triggers the king's reaction. There is emphasis on how completely the enemy is fooled: "did not know," "no one was left," "left the city open." The "openness" of the city will be significantly echoed by the "opening" of v. 29. A description of flight is usually the narrative signal for the decisive end of a battle (1 Sam. 4:10; 2 Sam. 18:17; 19:9 [8E]), but here it serves as a prelude for the victory phase of vv. 18–26.

[18] Verse 19 will interpret Joshua's unsheathed weapon as a signal to attack, but here it sounds like a sign of effective power that guarantees victory, similar to Moses' upraised arms (Exod. 17:8–15) or the arrows of 2 Kings 13:14–19. The traditional translation of *kîdôn* as "javelin" is still followed by NAB, but it should properly be understood as a curved or crescent-shaped

---

9. Culley, "Stories of the Conquest," 39–41, who speaks of a "shimmering effect" created by the interplay of the divine and human perspectives.
10. KB[3], 35.

sword.[11] Such weapons appear in ancient Near Eastern iconography, brandished as symbols of victorious sovereignty.[12]

[19–26] A subject-first sentence refocuses attention on the ambush group. The attack is coordinated by Joshua's raised sword, a dramatic picture remembered by Sir. 46:2. The expression *yādayim lānûs* in v. 20 (the dual of "hand" as "power" or "opportunity" with the infinitive construct) captures the desperate situation neatly, indicating that there was no escape on either side. Verse 22 is complicated and obscure. A subject-first sentence shifts attention to a new group, most likely intending to say that the Israelite ambush left Ai and attacked the enemy from the rear.[13] The deuteronomistic formula of total destruction at the end of v. 22 (cf. Deut. 2:34; 3:3; 2 Kings 10:11) will be repeated with brutal regularity in the chapters to follow (10:28, 30, 33, 37, 39, 40; 11:8). With an object-first sentence, v. 23 introduces the conventional motif of seizing living prisoners (10:26–27; 1 Sam. 15:8; 1 Kings 20:18; 2 Kings 7:12; 10:14) in order to indicate absolute victory. To display the enemy leader's body was a manifest insult (1 Sam. 31:10). Attempts to emphasize the totality of the massacre create some logical confusion in vv. 24–25. A subject-first sentence (v. 26) highlights Joshua's role and concludes the climactic slaughter with a reference to the symbolic sword that initiated it in v. 18.

[27–29] The conclusion completes the themes introduced by vv. 1–2: booty, destruction like that of Jericho, and the king's fate. The theme of burning the conquered city (6:24) will be repeated for Hazor (11:11, 13). Ideologically this could relate to Deut. 13:17 [16E] or etiologically to visible traces of conflagration in the ruins of Ai. Possibly a word play is intended between *tēl* "mound" and the hanging (verb *tlh*) of the king in v. 29. It is left to the reader to make the implicit connection between "permanently deserted mound" (reflecting Deut. 13:17 [16E]) and the name Ai.

Reading the Law
Joshua 8:30–35

8:30 Then Joshua built an altar to Yahweh God of Israel on Mt. Ebal. **31** Just as Moses servant of Yahweh had commanded the Israelites, as it

---

11. KB[3], 450; NJB translates as "sabre."

12. Keel, *Wirkmächtige Siegeszeichen im Alten Testament*, 77–82. For the lance of Zimri-Lim in one of the Mari documents as a suggested parallel, see M. Anbar, "La Critique biblique à la lumière des Archives royales de Mari," *Bib* 75 (1994), 70–74.

13. REB understands the subject to be soldiers of Ai: "Those who had come out to contend with the Israelites were now hemmed in by the Israelites."

is written in [the book of] the law of Moses: "an altar of unworked stones against which iron has not swung." They offered burnt offerings to Yahweh upon it and sacrificed peace offerings.

32 He wrote there on the stones the copy of the law of Moses that he had written,[a] in the presence of the Israelites. 33 All Israel and its elders and officers and its judges were standing on either side of the ark facing the levitical priests who carry the ark of the covenant of Yahweh—both resident alien and full citizen—half in front of Mt. Gerizim and half[b] in front of Mt. Ebal,[c] just as Moses the servant of Yahweh commanded at first[d] to bless the people [Israel].

34 And afterwards he read aloud all the words of the law, the blessing and the curse, according to all that is written in [the book of][e] the law. 35 There was not a word of all that Moses commanded[f] which Joshua did not read aloud in the presence of the whole assembly of Israel and the women and the dependents and the resident aliens who lived among them.[g]

a. Follows MT. "Which he had written," is lacking in LXX[B] but probably not in OG proper (see Rahlfs, *Septuaginta,* Württemberg, 1935; Barthélemy, *Critique,* 13). The reference to Joshua's obedience to Deut. 17:18 was not understood and dropped as awkward (Margolis, *Joshua in Greek,* 146).

b. The doubly determined form preserves merged alternate readings: *wĕhaḥăṣî* "and half" and *wĕḥesyô* "and half of him [= them]."

c. Since the people are to hear the reading of the law, one assumes they would face inward. Alternate translation: "half facing Mt. Gerizim and half facing Mt. Ebal" (cf. JPSV, REB, NAB).

d. Alternate translations: "commanded to bless the people the first time" (cf. NAB) or "to bless first," that is before cursing (cf. REB).

e. MT expands "law" with "the book of" (see also v. 31), while OG expands with "of Moses."

f. Follows MT. OG and 4QJosh[a] add "Joshua" after "Moses commanded."

g. 4QJosh[a] positions the Ebal ceremony closely after the Jordan crossing and immediately before 5:2. A different form of the end of v. 35 connects this pericope with the Jordan crossing, along with an editorial transition leading into 5:2–7. This extra material uses the verb *ntq* "touched" as in 4:18 and refers to those "carrying the ark."

This section is isolated from its context and clearly the product of deuteronomistic redaction. It begins abruptly with *'az* and the imperfect, used to indicate a tenuous and approximate chronological connection: "about this time" (cf. 10:12; 22:1).[1] In the textual tradition it is a "floating pericope," known to occur in three different locations. In MT it comes immediately after the victory at Ai and before the notice in 9:1–2 about the kings' reaction to certain unspecified events. OG positions this unit after 9:1–2 instead. Some have taken this as evidence that it was

1. I. Rabinowitz, "*'az* Followed by Imperfect Verb-Form in Preterite Contexts: A Redactional Device in Biblical Hebrew," *VT* 34 (1984): 53–62.

an addition later than the divergence of the OG and MT text forms, so that it was subsequently slotted into slightly different places.[2] A third and more divergent location is offered by 4QJosh[a], which places the pericope closely after the Jordan crossing and immediately before the circumcision, that is, just before 5:2. Certainly the OG location is plausible, connecting the kings' reaction immediately to the story of Ai (cf. the position of 5:1; 6:27; 10:1–2; and 11:1) and taking 9:3 alone as an appropriate introduction to the Gibeonite incident. However, the MT location better fits the deuteronomistic need to push fulfillment of Moses' directive of Deut. 27:2–8 as early in the overall story as tactically possible and lets 9:1–2 and 3–4 serve together as narrative preparation for the Gibeon story: the kings did one thing, but the Gibeonites did another. This structural correlation between vv. 1–2 and 3–4 is a forceful argument in favor of the MT order. The Qumran text location is the least likely to be original. For one thing, it perfectly matches the demand of Deut. 27:2–3 to set up the stones and write on them on the very day of crossing the Jordan. It is hard to see why anyone would later move the pericope away from this position, but easy to understand how it might have been later transferred there to show that Deuteronomy was obeyed precisely. Moreover, the placement in 4QJosh[a] relies on suspect pluses to the text of 8:35 and a transitional bridge (note g). Either MT or OG are preferable to the longer and suspiciously easier Qumran text.

The fact remains that this unit is manifestly disconnected from its context whichever of the three possible locations one chooses.[3] In MT it breaks the easy flow between 8:28–29 and 9:1. In OG it violates the structural unity of 9:1–2 and 3–4. In the Qumran position there is a difficult geographical contradiction between Gilgal (4:19–20; 5:9) and Ebal and Gerizim.[4] Yet there are geographic problems with the MT/OG position as well, for the people will still be at Gilgal in 9:6. Apparently DH broke into the sequence of the pre-deuteronomistic source material in order to insert Joshua's obedience to Deut. 11:29 and 27:2–13 precisely at this point. Presumably the idea was that it was only the conquest of Ai that gave Israel its first access to Shechem. Although Deuteronomy commands that the Ebal/Gerizim event happen on the very day of the Jordan crossing (Deut. 27:2), the pre-deuteronomistic structure inherited by DH permitted nothing more than an

2. E. Tov, "Some Sequence Differences between the MT and the LXX and Their Ramifications for the Literary Criticism of the Bible," *JNSL* 13 (1987): 152–54.

3. So much so that J. Soggin, *Joshua: A Commentary,* OTL, Philadelphia, 1972, 220–31, felt justified in moving the pericope to a point in the final assembly at Shechem, between 24:27 and 28.

4. However, a tradition that connects the Ebal/Gerizim ceremony closely to the Jordan crossing seems to lie behind the peculiar geographical coordination of these mountains with Gilgal in Deut. 11:30. There are rabbinic traditions that reflect the same sequence of events as the Qumran text and probably reflect the same motivation to harmonize Joshua with Deuteronomy: *y. Soṭa* 7:3, *t. Soṭa* 8:7–8. Josephus *Ant.* 5.1.4 has Joshua erect an altar and sacrifice on it immediately after crossing the Jordan, but in *Ant.* 5.1.19 positions the Ebal/Gerizim ceremony after Joshua's last battle. See A. Rofé, "The Editing of the Book of Joshua in the Light of 4QJosh[a]," *New Qumran Texts and Studies,* STDJ 15, Leiden, 1994, 89–104.

erection of stones at that stage of the narrative (chap. 4). The actual name Shechem is not used here, just as it is completely missing from Deuteronomy itself.

This unit was constructed by DH in order to report Joshua's obedience to the command of Moses given in Deut. 11:26–28; 27:2–13. Written in deuteronomistic vocabulary, it transforms the imperatives of Deuteronomy into obedient indicatives. A comparison of parallel texts shows that the author utilized Deut. 11:26–29 (blessing and curse at the two mountains) and 17:18 (the royal copy of the law) in order to portray Joshua's obedience to what is commanded in 27:2–13. However, DH also characteristically understood the whole event in terms of the public reading of the law in Deut. 31:9–12 (DH).

> v. 30 is based on Deut. 27:4–5
> v. 31 is based on Deut. 27:5–7a
> v. 32 is based on Deut. 27:2–3, 4, 8 as well as 17:18
> v. 33 is based on Deut. 27:12–13 as well as 11:29 and
> 29:9–10 [10–11E]
> vv. 34–35 are based on Deut. 31:11–12 as well as 11:26–28

Everything here goes back to Deut. 27:2–13 and the other supporting texts: the altar and its construction, its location, the two sorts of sacrifice, writing on the stones, blessing and curse, the participants. There is nothing left over to represent any sort of earlier tradition of altar foundation or liturgical etiology. The narrative is the product of creative writing based on a string of revered texts.[5]

DH has added some idiosyncratic twists. There are three explicit "footnotes" to the commands of Moses (vv. 31a, 33b, 35a) and two notices of the comprehensive character of the audience (vv. 33a, 35b). The staging has been altered so that location of the people is defined as being on either side of the ark and "in front of" (or perhaps "facing," see text note c) the two opposing mountains, rather than on them as in Deut. 27:12–13. The twelve tribes no longer play any role, and the levitical priests have been separated out from the mass of tribal Levites of Deut. 27:12 and associated with the ark.[6] The ark has been picked up from chapters 3–4, 6, and written into the scene to become a focus for the staging of the ceremony. Blessing dominates here (v. 33b) rather than cursing as in Deuteronomy 27. The generalized "blessing and curse" of Deut. 11:26–29 are here concretized into precisely those contained within the written law, that is, Deuteronomy 28.

---

5. Interpretation of the Iron I installation found on Mt. Ebal by A. Zertal remains open. See A. Mazar, *Archaeology of the Land of the Bible,* New York, 1990, 348–50. It must be stressed that this particular text relates exclusively to Deuteronomy and not directly to any tradition about any actual sanctuary.

6. They are not explicitly connected with the sacrifices of v. 31, but come on stage as carriers of the ark as in chapters 3–4. For the DH ideology of priesthood, see R. Nelson, "The Role of the Priesthood in the Deuteronomistic History," *Congress Volume Leuven 1989,* VTSup 43, Leiden, 1991, 132–47.

There is some confusion about the stones that receive the written law. In the source text the law is written on stelae clearly different from the unhewn stones of the altar (Deut. 27:2–4, 8). However, 8:32, in reporting seriatim Joshua's obedience to Deut. 27:5–8, could be understood to state that Joshua wrote on the altar stones. This may represent a lack of concern for detail or a misunderstanding of Deut. 27:8. However, it is more likely that the writer simply assumes that readers are perfectly familiar with the cited text and will understand that the stones of v. 32 are different from the stones of v. 31.[7]

Joshua is here portrayed as a royal figure leading a ceremony of covenant renewal, taking what would be the king's role in the time of the monarchy. One particular detail of this royal description of Joshua is his fulfillment of the king's obligation to write for himself a copy of the law for personal use. This is noted in v. 32. Understood against the background of Deut. 17:18 (the only other occurrence of the phrase "copy of the law"), Joshua is here pictured as reproducing his own personal copy of the law on the stones: "the copy of the law of Moses that he [Joshua] had written." Read as part of the comprehensive DH story, Joshua performs a royal act of covenant mediation parallel to that of Josiah (2 Kings 23:1–3).[8] This redactional goal has been achieved by DH's conceptual unification of Deuteronomy's command for the rite at Ebal/Gerizim with the program of public law reading (Deut. 31:9–13; 2 Kings 23:2–3).

It is often observed that Joshua preserves no conquest story for Shechem. Nevertheless, to report the building of an altar is to make a land claim in another way. This same motivation lies behind the stories of altars built by the patriarchs (Gen. 12:7, etc.) and the one rebuilt by Elijah on Mt. Carmel (1 Kings 18:30–32). The central heartland belongs to Israel, not because of battle, but as part of Yahweh's promise of effortless occupation (1:3). It has also been noticed that this narrative parallels Greek traditions of foundation ceremonies for new colonial settlements. These involved the erection of stelae inscribed with precepts, altar building, and sacrifice. Tales of these foundation ceremonies share with this text the socially important purpose of building community identity.[9]

The Ebal/Gerizim ritual is placed at a critical juncture in the overall plot of Joshua, dividing the conquest drama into two acts. As a powerful and effective act of blessing, it completes Israel's return from the deviation of the Achan episode and the violation of the covenant (7:11, 15). As a reminder of the written law of Deuteronomy, it prepares the reader for the legal dilemmas to be presented by the upcoming Gibeonite episode, where the concept of a human

---

7. For a different analysis of the situation: M. Anbar, "The Story about the Building of an Altar on Mount Ebal: The History of Its Composition and the Question of the Centralization of the Cult," *Das Deuteronomium*, BETL 68, Leuven, 1985, 304–309, who postulates influence from the Joshua text on the redactional development of Deut. 27:2–8.

8. Nelson, "Josiah in the Book of Joshua," 535–36.

9. These parallels are explored by Weinfeld, "The Pattern of the Israelite Settlement in Canaan."

covenant plays a central role. Most importantly, this text underscores the validity and importance of the law, which is written and displayed publicly, then read out to absolutely everybody in Israel's social structure (vv. 33, 35). Every word is read (v. 34; cf. Deut. 4:2). In doing this Joshua provides a parenetic model, for he himself is scrupulously obeying the very law that he is proclaiming. Readers of many different generations could be expected to see themselves in their ancestors' situation at Ebal and Gerizim. Looking back to past infidelity and forward to the challenge of living out the law in new situations, they would be urged by this text to renewed allegiance to the law and rejuvenated hope in the power of Yahweh's blessing.

[30–31] The first of Joshua's three obedient acts is altar building. Perhaps the use of the title "Yahweh God of Israel," although not unusual in Joshua, is used to cross-reference this story to the Achan incident (7:13, 19, 20). Constructing altars from materials in a natural state was part of Israel's early ethos (Exod. 20:24–25). Stressing this reflects the text's aim of repristinating foundational loyalties.

[32–33] Joshua's second act is to transcribe his own copy of the law onto stones. Public display of legal texts was practiced in the ancient world in order to underscore their authority and validity. Details of the precursor Deuteronomy text, such as the erection and plastering of the stones (27:2, 4) and exactly how the blessing of the people took place (27:12) are glossed over. In contrast, an exhaustive list of participants (cf. 23:2; 24:1) stresses the theme of undivided obedience. A typical deuteronomistic touch includes the marginalized "resident alien" (*gēr;* traditionally "sojourner") in the audience both here and in v. 35.

[34–35] Joshua's third act is to read the law. In doing this, he moves beyond what was commanded in Deuteronomy 27 into the DH agenda set forth in Deut. 31:10–13. It is emphasized that this law is a written one (cf. 1:8; 23:6; 2 Kings 22:13; 23:3, 24). The audience is not just the *qāhāl,* the assembly of Israel's free male citizens (defined in Deut. 23:2–9 [1–8E], but also includes the subordinate members of the social system. The entire community is responsible for keeping the law.

The Gibeonite Trick
Joshua 9:1–27

Deception

9:1 When [all] the kings who were across the Jordan in the hill country and in the lowlands and on the whole coast of the Great Sea opposite Lebanon—the Hittites and the Amorites, the Canaanites, the Perizites, the Hivites and the Jebusites—heard, 2 they formed a unified alliance to fight Joshua and Israel.

3 But when the population of Gibeon heard what Joshua had done to Jericho and Ai, 4 they for their part acted with cunning. They set out pretending to be messengers.[a] They took worn out sacks for their donkeys and worn out wine skins, split and mended, 5 with worn out, patched sandals on their feet and wearing worn out clothes. [All] the bread of their provisions was dry and crumbly.[b]

6 They went to Joshua at the Gilgal camp and said to him and Israel,[c] "We have come from a distant country. So now make a covenant with us." 7 Israel said to the Hivites, "Perhaps you live among us. So how could we make a covenant with you?" 8 Then they said to Joshua, "We are your servants." Joshua said to them, "Who are you and from where have you come?" 9 They said [to him], "Your servants have came from a very distant country because of the name of Yahweh your God. For we have heard a report[d] about him and everything he did in Egypt 10 and everything he did to the two[e] kings of the Amorites who were across the Jordan, to Sihon king of Heshbon and to Og king of Bashan who was in Ashtaroth. 11 So our elders and the whole population of our land said to us, 'Take provisions in your hand for the journey and go to meet them and say to them, "We are your servants. So now make a covenant with us."' 12 This is our bread. We took it as provisions warm [from our houses] on the day we left to come to you, but now here it has dried up and become crumbly. 13 And these wineskins were new when we filled them, but now they have split. And [these] our clothes and our sandals have worn out from the very long journey." 14 The men took some of their provisions, but they did not ask for the decision of[f] Yahweh. 15 Joshua made peace with them and made with them a covenant protecting their lives. The leaders of the community swore an oath to them.

Discovery and Dilemma

16 At the end of three days after they had made a covenant with them, they heard that they were their neighbors and were living among them. 17 So the Israelites marched out and came to their cities [on the third day]. Now their cities were Gibeon, Chephirah, Beeroth, and Kiriath-jearim. 18 But the Israelites did not strike at them because the leaders of the community had sworn an oath to them by Yahweh the God of Israel. The whole community grumbled against the leaders. 19 Then [all] the leaders said to the whole community, "We have sworn an oath to them by Yahweh the God of Israel, so now we cannot touch them. 20 We will do this with them and let them live,[g] so that wrath will not come against us because of the oath

which we swore to them. 21 [The leaders said to them] Let them live." So
they were woodcutters and water haulers for the whole community, just
as the leaders had declared concerning them.[h]

Confrontation and Consequences

22 Joshua summoned them and spoke to them, "Why have you deceived
us, saying 'We are very distant from you' when you live among us?
23 So now you are cursed. One of you shall always be a slave, a woodcutter[i] for the house of my God."[j] 24 They answered Joshua, "It was
forcefully told to your servants that Yahweh your God had commanded
Moses his servant to give you the [whole] land and to destroy the whole
population of the land before you. So we were very afraid for our lives
because of you and did this thing. 25 Now here we are in your power. Do
whatever is good and proper in your opinion to do to us."

26 So he treated them in this manner.[k] He delivered them from the power
of the Israelites and they did not kill them. 27 On that day Joshua designated
them as woodcutters and water haulers for the community and for the altar
of Yahweh[l] (as they still are today) at the place which he should choose.

a. Follows MT in reading the otherwise unattested hithpael of *ṣyr* and taking the
force of the hithpael as "to pass oneself off as" (2 Sam. 13:5; 1 Kings 14:5). The versions
(OG, V, S, T) suggest the hithpael of *ṣyd* "gathered provisions," an easier reading assimilated to vv. 5 and 12. The confusion of *d* and *r* lies at the root of this problem.

b. Follows MT. The Greek has a translational doublet for "sandals." The authentic
OG offers no doublet for "crumbly," contrary to the assertion of most commentators;
see Greenspoon, *Textual Studies in the Book of Joshua*, 65–68 and Margolis, *Joshua in
Greek*, 153–54. "Moldy" may be intended instead of "crumbly." The root *nqd* is associated with speckled animals (Gen. 30:32) as well as granulated jewelry (Cant. 1:11)
and decorated cakes (1 Kings 14:3).

c. Here and in v. 7 the Hebrew uses the singular form *'îš yiśrā'ēl* collectively. Textual witnesses exhibit several alterations intended to smooth out this situation, including the kethib/qere at the start of v. 7. For the assembled nation portrayed as an
individual, compare Deut. 27:14; Judg. 8:22; 20:11; 21:1; 1 Sam. 11:8. Often this expression indicates Israel as a military organization.

d. Taken as a suffixed infinitive construct used as a noun.

e. Follows MT. In OG the letter *beta* as an abbreviation for "two" dropped out before *basileusin*, "kings."

f. Follows MT. OG deleted "the decision of" ("the mouth of") as an anthropomor-
phism.

g. Infinitive absolute with *waw* continuing the force of a finite verb (Waltke and
O'Connor, *Hebrew Syntax*, 35.5d).

h. The bracketed MT expansion is lacking in OG and V. The rest of this verse follows MT and understands the past tense of v. 21b as an anticipatory summary of vv. 23

and 27. Another possibility is to revocalize the *waw*-consecutive verb as a jussive, "and let them be," so that the leaders' speech continues as far as "whole community" (cf. NJB). The Greek translator took this verb as a future and likewise extended the quoted speech. Because the final phrase of the verse is awkward in the genuine OG, some Greek manuscripts fill out the verse with "and the whole community did" before "as the leaders said to them" (adopted by REB and NAB). S has a conflate reading. See Barthélemy, *Critique*, 15–17.

i. Follows OG, literally "there will not be cut off from you a slave, that is (*oude* representing an explicative *waw*) a woodcutter." MT reads the plural and fills out the formula from vv. 21 and 27: "and woodcutters and water haulers."

j. Follows MT. OG replaces the anachronistic reference to the temple with "for me and my God" (cf. 6:24).

k. The *kēn* ("this manner") may point back to Joshua's curse of v. 23 or to v. 25b (JPSV), or it may look forward to vv. 26b-27 (NRSV).

l. Follows MT. OG continues with "therefore the population of Gibeon have been woodcutters and water haulers for the altar of God (= Yahweh)." Although this could have been lost by MT through homoioteleuton from "altar of Yahweh" to "altar of Yahweh," it has the character of an expansion intended to fill out and relieve the awkwardly compacted phraseology (Margolis, *Joshua in Greek*, 167).

The uneven state of the narrative reflects a complicated history of composition.[1] The transitions between Joshua and Israel (literally "the man of Israel") in vv. 6, 7, and 8 are jolting. Then a third group of players materializes suddenly in v. 15, "the leaders of the community," a phrase characteristic of priestly material. The decision to permit the Gibeonites to live, albeit as servants, seems to be taken twice, first by these "leaders" (vv. 20–21) and then by Joshua (vv. 23, 26–27). Although only the Gibeonites have a role in the story, four foreign towns are mentioned (v. 17b). Another confusion involves the question of culpability. Israel is the only actor to raise any hesitation (v. 7), but is also the first group to fall for the Gibeonite ruse (v. 14). Yet grumbling is directed at the "leaders" because of their inconvenient oath (v. 18b). Joshua as spokesperson and decision-maker can hardly be held blameless either (vv. 6, 7, 15a, 26–27). Some have thought that successive redactions have sought to reapportion blame.

Probably a completely satisfying explanation for these irregularities is impossible, but the story does seem to fall rather clearly into two phases in terms

1. Möhlenbrink traces two parallel stories, a Gilgal "Israel" version and a Shiloh "Joshua" version, "Die Landnahmesagen des Buches Josua," 241–45. G. Schmitt, *Du sollst keinen Frieden schliessen mit den Bewohnern des Landes*, BWANT 91, Stuttgart: 1970, 30–37, also thinks of parallel sources. Hertzberg, *Josua, Richter, Ruth*, 66–69, opts for vv. 16–21a as the basic narrative, as does P. Kearney, "The Role of the Gibeonites in the Deuteronomistic History," *CBQ* 35 (1973): 1–19. R. Sutherland, "Israelite Political Theories in Joshua 9," *JSOT* 53 (1992): 65–74, postulates the earliest story as the "man of Israel" version (vv. 4–7, 11–14, 16) linked to the politics of pre-monarchic democracy. A later "Joshua" stratum (vv. 3, 8–10, 15a, 22–27) advances the structures of monarchy. Finally a post-exilic P-like addition (vv. 15b, 17–21) gives authority to the elite priestly "leaders of the community."

of a double thread of etiology. One etiology explains the Gibeonites' alliance with Israel and another their diminished status as cult servants. That is to say, their deceit first explains the alliance (vv. 3–15), but subsequently justifies their demotion (vv. 16–17, 22–27). Thus the narrative begins as a generally non-partisan tale explaining the presence of ethnic enclaves (up to v. 15), but then continues with a more hostile sequel rationalizing the demotion of the Gibeonites into servants (from v. 16 on). Supporting a break at v. 15 is a change in the references to Israel at that point. Israel is called "man of Israel" in vv. 6, 7, and 14 ("Israel" in the translation), but referred to as the "sons of Israel" in vv. 17, 18, and 26 ("Israelites" in the translation).

Beyond this observation, the critical reader can also recognize the contributions of DH, revealed by characteristic language and theological interests. For example Israel's problem with the Gibeonite alliance is set forth in terms of the principles of Deut. 20:10–18: "peace" (v. 15; Deut. 20:10–11) for towns very distant, annihilation for the peoples of the land of inheritance. The claim to be from a "(very) distant country" (variations on $r\bar{a}h\hat{o}q$; vv. 6, 9, similarly v. 22) reflects the language of Deut. 20:15. It is significant that the six-nation list of v. 1 is precisely and distinctively that of Deut. 20:17. The mere question of a "covenant" would also recall Deut. 7:1–4 for readers sensitive to Deuteronomy. The language of vv. 9–10 is mostly deuteronomistic (see 2:10 and 1 Kings 8:41), as is that of v. 24 and the last words of v. 27 (centralization). Although the story in its basic form does not require the presuppositions of Deut. 20:10–18 to work, the dilemma faced by Israel has been sharpened by the inclusion of allusions to Deuteronomy in its present shape.[2]

A good case can also be made that vv. 15b, 18–21 represent a P-like correction involving distaste over the idea of foreign temple servants. Joshua temporarily disappears after v. 15a and the "leaders" take his place, only to disappear themselves after v. 21. The language of $n\check{e}s\hat{i}'\hat{i}m$ "leaders" and $'\bar{e}d\hat{a}$ "community" (vv. 15, 18, 19, 21, 27) is characteristic of the Priestly Writing. These "leaders of the community" do essentially the same thing as Joshua will do again in vv. 22–27. Moreover, grumbling (root lwn; traditionally "murmuring") against authority is a common P theme. This P-like section presents the problem as one of unbreakable oath rather than covenant and focuses on the question of the Gibeonites' continued "living" (vv. 20a, 21a). The addition

2. C. Schäfer-Lichtenberger, "Das gibeonistische Bündnis im Lichte deuteronomischer Kriegsgebote: zum Verhältnis von Tradition und Interpretation in Jos 9," *BN* 34 (1986): 58–81, sees the entire chapter as a narrative exposition of Deuteronomy chapter 20, and Rose, *Deuteronomist und Jahwist,* 173–92, holds a similar opinion. Kearney, "Role of the Gibeonites," 1–8, insists that the ruse can only be understood on the basis of Deuteronomy chapter 20. However, the concepts of Deuteronomy are not required to make this story work. Violence against the local population is obviously part of the pre-deuteronomistic plot of Joshua. It is to this that the kings are reacting in 5:1 and 9:1–2. The Gibeonites are simply countering the threat with cunning rather than belligerence, claiming to live outside the territory that Israel is attacking.

seeks to preempt how readers will understand v. 23. By emphasizing that these foreigners are to be servants *of the community* (v. 21), it seeks to temper the statement of v. 23 that they will serve the sanctuary, in order to prevent any thought that alien people might compromise the Temple. Ezekiel 44:7–9 reveals this as a priestly concern. The divergent notions of v. 21 (community) and v. 23 (temple) are put together by the summary v. 27 (community and altar).[3] Introduced by the leaders' oath in v. 15b, this P-like material serves as a excursus on the theme of internal conflict, the authority of elite "leaders," and protection for the Temple's holiness.

In what remains after the deuteronomistic and P-like elements are subtracted, two stages of growth are visible: an initial plot in vv. 3–15 and a further unfolding of matters in vv. 16–17, 22–27.[4] The plot of vv. 3–15 is self-contained so that nothing really points outside its more narrow framework. The preparations of vv. 4–5 lead directly to the demonstration of the Gibeonite claim in vv. 12–13. Their initial claim of distance and their request for a covenant in v. 6 leads on to the repetition of their request in v. 11. Israel's hesitation in v. 7 is answered by the Gibeonite assertion of v. 9. Their crafty plan comes to fruition in v. 14 when the stale provisions "prove" their false story. Israel carelessly fails to consult Yahweh, so that the very group that raised the objection of v. 7 becomes the first to succumb to the trick. Joshua's offer of peace in v. 15a closes the frame. This is precisely the opposite of what he had done to Jericho and Ai, the factor that first launched the plot in v. 3. Thus vv. 3–15 constitute a self-contained narrative.

In this core plot the threat to the Gibeonites and their trick work together to set up the narrative tension. Will the trick work? Will they survive? Narrative tension builds through the description of their preparations, the alarming objection of v. 7, and the unfolding of their prevarication. It is finally relieved by their success and survival in v. 15. Joshua and the collective "man of Israel" play coordinated roles. Joshua is spokesperson and decision-maker. Israel provides an ironic twist by raising the essential objection and then heedlessly falling for the trick anyway.[5] The tale of the Gibeonite trick is etiological in the

---

3. The presence of a P-like redaction is asserted by Fritz, *Josua,* 101–107; J. Halbe, "Gibeon und Israel: Art, Veranlassung und Ort der Deutung ihres Verhältnisses in Jos IX," *VT* 25 (1975): 613–15; A. Mayes, "Deuteronomy 29, Joshua 9, and the Place of the Gibeonites in Israel," *Das Deuteronomium,* BETL 68, Leuven, 1985, 321–25; and Sutherland, "Israelite Political Theories." Others counter that the terms *nāśî* "leader" and *'ēdâ* "community" are also used to refer to pre-exilic realities, for example Exod. 22:27 [E28]; 1 Kings 12:20. Noth, *Josua,* 55–57, and J. Liver, "The Literary History of Joshua IX," *JSS* 8 (1963): 236, reflect this opinion. P-like language is also found in Josh. 22:10–34.

4. The case for this is made by Halbe, "Gideon und Israel," 613–71, and Fritz, *Josua,* 101–107.

5. Möhlenbrink, "Landnahmensagen des Buches Josua," 241–45, and G. Schmitt, *Du sollst keinen Frieden schliessen,* 30–34, divide the chapter into Joshua material and Israel material. It is often proposed that motives of blame or exculpation lie behind the successive redactions of this

sense that it answers the question prompted by v. 7. Why does the enclave of the Gibeonites exist "among us"? Why do they enjoy a treaty understanding with us when we have been forbidden to make covenants with our alien neighbors? By the time v. 15 is reached, the answers to these questions have been provided. The narrative understands that the resulting situation is problematic (v. 14b), but provides only an explanation for its origin, not a polemic or a call for change. One need not look to Deuteronomy as the source of the uneasiness that provides the basic horizon of the story, for the prohibition of such agreements is a feature of pre-deuteronomic law (Exod. 23:32; 34:12)[6] and non-association with the inhabitants of the land is implicit in the basic plot of Joshua (chap. 2; 5:1; 9:1–2, etc.).

Full appreciation of this tale requires the reader to take on, at least in part, the perspective of the Gibeonites. Other examples of this sort of thing in Israel's narrative art can be found in the Rahab story, in the Ark Story where the perspective of the Philistines is described (1 Sam. 4:6–9; 5:1–6:12), and in the war with Ben-hadad (1 Kings 20:16–18, 23–25, 30b–34). More generally, appreciation for an underdog's cleverness is universally part of the folktale world. Another group of Hivites at Shechem are involved with Israel in a similar tale in Genesis 34. There, however, it is Israel who plays the successful trick (v. 13), and the foreigners' eagerness for an alliance leads to their destruction rather than to deliverance.

In the core story of vv. 3–15, the Gibeonite ruse remains undiscovered.[7] The report of its unmasking (v. 16) is the precipitating event in what seems to be a secondary unfolding of the original tale. Now the problematic consequences of the successful ruse are explored. In this sequel the etiological focus moves away from the question of how the Gibeonites achieved a treaty relationship to the further question of how they (or some of them) fell into the demoted status of cultic slaves. Now their trick, which is viewed neutrally or even with wry appreciation in vv. 3–15, becomes the justification for their degradation into an underclass (v. 23). This secondary unfolding increases the scope of Israel's predicament by revealing that four towns are involved, not just one (v. 17b). The tone becomes disapproving and juridical. In fact, the examination and submission of the Gibeonites follows the same condemnatory pattern as Gen. 4:10–12. To sum up, vv. 16–17, 22–27 seek a supplementary solution to the

---

chapter. Both of these suggestions are obviated by a recognition of the division between vv. 3–15 and 16–17, 22–27. Joshua and Israel play essential and complementary roles both in the core story and in its later unfolding.

6. J. Halbe, *Das Privilegrecht Jahwehs: Ex 34:10–26*, FRLANT 114, Göttingen, 1975, 230–55.

7. Liver, "The Literary History of Joshua IX," 227–33, reads the story as suggesting that Joshua and Israel were quite willing to be deceived. After all, why would a "far off" people even need a covenant? For this reason, he postulates an earlier story in which deception played no part.

story line. The death of the Gibeonites at the hands of hostile Israel (v. 17) is prevented by Joshua (v. 26), but their deceit is suitably punished by Joshua's curse (vv. 23, 27). That vv. 16–17, 22–27 could never have constituted an independent story is shown by their reliance on vv. 3–15 to provide background and narrative tension. The key notion of "living among" (*yāšāb běqereb*) Israel (vv. 16, 22) is repeated from v. 6.

One objection to this neat two-part division presents itself. Although the unmasking of the ruse by v. 16 is not absolutely required by the presentation of vv. 3–15, it also comes as no particular surprise. A ruse or trick continues to generate narrative tension until it is "discovered." Disguises and pretenses are usually meant to be revealed, as the examples of 1 Sam. 28:8, 12; 2 Sam. 14:3–20; 1 Kings 14:2–6; 20:38–41 make clear. It is hard to imagine that the core story could really have been told without some sort of discovery of the masquerade. Perhaps the original unmasking was so underdeveloped that the tale had a narrative instability, which encouraged the addition of further material.

It is possible to coordinate these two stages of the narrative roughly with what we know or can guess about the history of the Gibeonite enclave from 2 Sam. 4:2–3; 21:1–6 and Solomon's subsequent policy toward non-Israelite ethnic groups in 1 Kings 9:20–22.[8] The Gibeonites once enjoyed the status of a divinely protected ethnic minority, although without the full right to take blood vengeance. These two circumstances are indicated by the report that a nationwide famine resulted from their slaughter by Saul and that royal intervention was required to hand over Saul's sons for execution by them (2 Sam. 21:1–9). The evacuation of Beeroth and the hostility of the assassins of Ishbaal may also point to Saul's hostile policy (2 Sam. 4:2–3). These narratives indicate that a special association existed between Gibeon and Israel, while 2 Sam. 21:2 implies that something was felt to be irregular about it in certain circles. This is precisely the situation that vv. 3–15 seek to explain, affiliation in the light of some disapproval. It may be significant that the predominance of the "man of Israel" in this core narrative reflects a sort of tribal democracy appropriate to an early period.

In a similar way, the later unfolding of the story (vv. 16–17, 22–27) seems to reflect Gibeon's situation after Solomon's move to assimilate foreign enclaves

---

8. For explorations of historical connections, see J. Blenkinsopp, *Gibeon and Israel,* Cambridge, 1972, 28–40; J. Briend, "Israël et les Gabaonites," *La Protohistoire d'Israël,* Paris, 1990, 121–82; F. Fensham, "The Treaty Between Israel and the Gibeonites," *BA* 27 (1964): 96–100; J. Grintz, "The Treaty of Joshua with the Gibeonites," *JAOS* 86 (1966): 113–126; Halbe, "Gibeon und Israel," 630–41; B. Halpern, "Gibeon: Israelite Diplomacy in the Conquest Era," *CBQ* 37 (1975): 303–16; M. Haran, "The Gibeonites, the Nethinim and the Sons of Solomon's Servants," *VT* 11 (1961): 159–69; Mayes, "Deuteronomy, Joshua 9, and the Place of the Gibeonites in Israel," 321–25. In contrast, H. Rösel, "Anmerkungen zur Erzählung vom Bundesschluss mit den Gibeoniten," *BN* 28 (1985): 30–35, properly urges caution in drawing sweeping historical conclusions from material such as this.

into a system of geographic districts (1 Kings 4:7–19) and his imposition of state slavery upon them (1 Kings 9:20–21). This situation fits the intent of the supplementary sequel, that is, to justify the demotion of a protected group to the status of temple slavery. Perhaps Solomon's early use of the Gibeon high place (1 Kings 3:4–5), his temple-building, and the later designation of subordinate temple staff as the "servants of Solomon" (Ezra 2:55–58), provide evidence that it was Solomon himself who designated some Gibeonites as temple slaves in Jerusalem. It must remain open as to how late in the monarchy a justification for this policy might have been felt necessary. The information preserved about the four alien towns (v. 17b) points to a relatively early date. On the other hand, the notice about state slavery in 1 Kings 9:20–21 is cast in deuteronomistic terms and thus reveals an interest in this topic at least into the late monarchy. Perhaps the secondary unfolding of vv. 16–17, 22–27 was the work of DH. It is wise to avoid dogmatism on such matters. It seems, however, that the political situation assumed in these supplementary verses reflects the monarchy period and sees Joshua as a reforming royal figure.

Although the successive redactional stages of the end product remain visible to the eye of the critic, the final form of the text works surprisingly well as a narrative. Overall there are two major successive movements from action through dialogue to decision. There is also an abbreviated subsidiary movement from dialogue to decision imbedded within the second movement:

> first movement, vv. 1–15
>   action, vv. 1–5
>   dialogue, vv. 6–13
>   decision, vv. 14–15
> second movement, vv. 16–27
>   action, vv. 16–17
>   ancillary movement (dispute), vv. 18–21
>   dialogue, vv. 18–19
>   decision, vv. 20–21
>   dialogue, vv. 22–25
>   decision, vv. 26–27

The reader naturally takes these movements in chronological order. The first movement reports the actions of the enemy kings and the Gibeonites, a dialogue between the Gibeonites and Israel/Joshua, and a problematic and hasty decision. It focuses on the success of the ruse and ends with the unstable situation of undiscovered deception and inappropriate covenant and oath. The second movement reports an aggressive action by Israel, a confrontational dialogue between Gibeon and Joshua, and a second decision which ameliorates the consequences of the first foolish one. It focuses on Gibeonite perfidy and the curse of diminished status. However, there is a pause in this second movement between the action of vv. 16–17 and the following dialogue and decision of vv. 22–27. Verses 18–21 report on an internal controversy (grumbling about the oath) and decision (to let the foreigners live). This deliberation within the ranks of Israel appropriately takes place before Joshua goes on to confront the Gibeonites publicly in v. 22. This interrupting subsidiary movement concentrates on the dilemma of unbreakable oath. In contrast with the unstable situation of v. 15, the decision of vv. 26–27 achieves narrative rest and balance with a state of affairs that preserves the oath and covenant while punishing the duplicity. This stable situation endures up to the reader's own day. One might think of a melody that halfway through hangs suspended on the dominant note (v. 15), then returns to the settled place of the satisfying tonic at its close (vv. 26–27). Let us follow this narrative structure in more detail.

First movement—Action
(vv. 1–5)

Against the backdrop of the belligerent coalition of the kings who have heard the news (vv. 1–2), the population of Gibeon, whom we will discover have no king, react completely differently when they hear (vv. 3–4). They choose to counter Israel's ruse at Ai with cunning of their own. The narrative problem from the Gibeonite perspective is survival. Their preparations to be deceptive messengers are described in detail, with special end-stress emphasis on their dry and crumbly bread (v. 5) to prepare for vv. 12 and 14a. But for now the reader is left to wonder what all this is about.

Dialogue (vv. 6–13)

Verse 6 explains what they have been up to. They base their request on their assertion of being "distant." Israel and Joshua play correlated roles. First Israel sets forth the narrative problem from the reader's perspective by picking up the word "covenant" and by opposing the possibility of "among us" (*bĕqirbî*) to the claim of "distant" (v. 7). The mention of Hivites underscores the peril by pointing back to the list of v. 1, which in turn points directly back to the Deut. 20:17 roster of those nations to be annihilated. The Gibeonites' request is restated to Joshua, but now in terms that reveal that they envision covenant status as subordinate vassals (v. 8). Their polite, courtly language of being "servants" will later turn out to have a sharply ironic edge (v. 23). Joshua's request in v. 8b gives them the opportunity to tell their story. They state their case with convincing rhetoric in vv. 9–11, then turn in vv. 12–13 to the physical evidence of their supposed journey. As liars often do, they tell partial truths: they really have heard a report (vv. 3 and 9) and they did take provisions (vv. 4–5 and 11). Their story is cast into convincing, devout deuteronomistic language that seeks to indicate that their motives are of the highest (cf. v. 9 with 1 Kings 8:41–42). Of course the forewarned reader enjoys the irony of their pious claptrap. The two stages of their argument are punctuated by v. 11, which restates the core of their request from vv. 6 and 8: "servants," "covenant." By highlighting the provisions in v. 11 the narrative prepares for the upcoming "proof" that will clinch Israel's decision (v. 14a). In vv. 12–13 the Gibeonites use the rhetoric of contrast (then warm and new, now dried up, crumbly, split) and end decisively with the concept they are trying to sell: "very long journey."

Decision (vv. 14–15)

All three Israelite participants agree in turn. Israel, who raised the proper objection, turns out to be the first to yield. The reader gets the signal that Yahweh would have disapproved if asked. The manufactured evidence of vv. 12–13 "proves" the lie of vv. 6, 9–11. Perhaps there is a implied double meaning to their taking provisions. On the one hand by this act they "prove" the Gibeonite claim, but at the same time they may be participating in a covenant-making meal or taking on a responsibility to protect those with whom they have eaten. Joshua as decision-maker and spokesperson makes peace and a protective covenant. The leaders back it up with an oath. This threefold decision (by Israel, Joshua, and the leaders) seems to secure the covenant beyond question. The reader has received an answer to the question of how such a relationship came to be. The story seems to draw to a close, only to be reactivated by Israel's unsettling discovery.

Second movement—Action
(vv. 16–17)

Once more an act of hearing pushes the story forward (v. 16 and vv. 1, 3, 9). What Israel hears is exactly what was feared in v. 7, that Gibeon *is* "living among them." The problem that was only implicit in the first movement now surfaces, and the narrative question changes from how Gibeon obtained a covenant to how they came to be punished for their deception. The direction of travel is now reversed. Israel's reaction is to march forth to confront those who, by the standards accepted by the ancient reader, should die. Verse 17b is a delayed exposition that exacerbates the problem. Before this movement continues and the question of a proper response can be completely resolved, however, an intra-Israel debate ensues.

Ancillary movement
(vv. 18–21)

This internal debate settles the question of death and the future of the Gibeonites, at least as far as the authority of the leaders is concerned, but leaves in suspension the decisive verdict of Joshua and the response of the malefactors. The two parties to the dialogue are introduced as grammatical subjects in v. 18a. Israel is blocked in its justifiable retaliation by the common motif of the inopportune but unbreakable oath (Num. 30:2; Judg. 11:36; 21:7). The leaders restate the dilemma (v. 19) and go on to lay out a double-track solution. Potential "wrath" (cf. 22:20) is avoided by letting these foreigners live, but demoting them to an underclass status (cf. Deut. 29:10 [11E]) punishes a duplicity that has endangered the community.

Second movement (continued)— Dialogue (vv. 22–25)

As the narrative refocuses from internal debate back to external relations with Gibeon, Joshua appropriately returns as spokesperson. With an accusatory question (v. 22) he concentrates the issue by laying out side by side the lie of "distant" (vv. 6, 9) and the reality of "among us" (vv. 7, 16). The resolution (v. 23) is a formulaic curse: representatives of the Gibeonites would always be temple slaves. The announcement of curse leads to a confession (vv. 24–25), highly satisfying to the Israelite reader, in which truth replaces lie and the Gibeonites themselves acknowledge the suitability of their punishment.

Decision (vv. 26–27)

Verses 26–27 assure the reader that the verdicts of vv. 21 and 23 were carried out and the threat against the Gibeonites was removed. Nothing really new is added here, but the threads are tied up. The Gibeonites serve both community (v. 21) and cult (v. 23), and the twin realities of their continued existence and their humble status persist into the reader's own time.

Reading this chapter in the larger context of the book of Joshua highlights parallels with Rahab. In both stories a threatened foreign element outwits Israel through cleverness, extracting an oath insuring life (2:12–14; 9:15, 20). Each speaks with appreciative knowledge of Yahweh's mighty acts (2:9–10; 9:9–10), although the Gibeonites do so dishonestly. As a result, the descendants of each still "live among" Israel (6:25; 9:16). The most significant difference is that the problematic issue of skirting the *ḥērem* and violating the law is downplayed in regard to Rahab, but highlighted in regard to Gibeon. Rahab remains a positive figure as the savior of her family, but the Gibeonites slide from the status of successful tricksters to unmasked and enslaved deceivers.

This difference correlates with the relationship of the Gibeonite story to the Achan incident. There is a contextual rhythm here. Chapter 9 provides a problematic prelude to the victory of chapter 10 just as chapter 7 (Achan) did for chapter 8 (Ai). Just as Achan and Ai are redactionally interlinked (Achan being a narrative obstacle to success at Ai), so the Gibeonite alliance is presented as the trigger for the following conflict (10:1–5). The danger of the Gibeonite story is that of foreigners "living among us" (*bĕqereb;* vv. 7, 16, 22; cf. 10:1 MT). This peril coordinates with that of the Achan story, *ḥērem* present "among" Israel (again *bĕqereb;* 6:25; 7:12–13). The shadow of possible disobedience to the law and the problematic presence of unconquered peoples left in the land (15:63; 16:10; 17:12–13; 23:4, 7, 12–13) has started to loom over the book of Joshua, in spite of protestations to the contrary (11:23).

This story functions to bolster national identity in relation to the land, but in a way different from the heroic tales of successful conquest[9] or the divinely authorized division of the land. Here the reader is confronted with the ideological challenge of the non-Israelite neighbor. For readers of successive periods, these Gibeonites could epitomize continuing Canaanite populations, potential or actual foreign allies, conquerors and captors, and eventually those non-Jewish elements who shared the land after the return from exile. In each situation the question arose as to what sorts of relationships with or attitudes toward the "nations" would be faithful to an identity as Yahweh's people. This tale warns of the duplicity of outsiders and justifies repressive measures against them. By negative example, it encourages Israel to obey deuteronomic law about foreign entanglements and to seek the will of God about them. Yet it also encourages acceptance of the troublesome status quo, for the Gibeonites are permitted to live and given a place in the social system. In the next chapter, even Yahweh will fight to protect them. The continued existence of the nations may be a matter of failure and disobedience, but here the combined authority of Joshua and the leaders of the community support a sort of toleration, albeit one that sounds suspiciously colonialist and oppressive to modern ears. In the last analysis, the presence of foreign elements cannot undermine Israel's identity nor its claim to the land. As the Gibeonites themselves are made to declare, these realities are assured by the acts and promises of Yahweh (vv. 9–10, 24).

[1–2] These verses are a deuteronomistic redactional introduction to the second conquest phase, chapters 9–11. They are the first part of a bracket that closes with 11:17 ("all their kings"; also v. 18 MT). The simple fear of 5:1 has now progressed into enemy activity spread over the entire land west of the Jordan. More narrowly, these verses prepare for the enemy alliance of chapter 10 and correspond to the summary of 10:40 ("hill country," "lowland"). The Gibeonite story represents the change in conditions between 9:1–2 and 10:1–2, advancing the plot from the generalities of 9:1–2 to the specifics of 10:1–5.

---

9. On the other hand, submission of the enemy was a rhetorical feature in ancient Near Eastern campaign accounts. For some striking examples, see K. Younger, *Ancient Conquest Accounts: A Study in Ancient Near Eastern and Biblical History Writing,* JSOTSup 98, Sheffield, 1990, 201–204.

That Israel's hostile enemies are kings, whereas the Gibeonites are governed by elders (v. 11; cf. 10:2), continues the book's characteristic belligerence towards Canaanite monarchy (e.g., 6:2; 8:1–2, 29; chap. 12) and echoes the social polemic implicit in the Rahab story.

[3–5] A subject-first sentence in v. 3 shifts attention to the Gibeonites. Their response is both differentiated from the aggression of the kings and compared to the Israelite ruse at Ai with "for their part" (*gam-hēmmâ*). "Cunning" (*'ormâ*) has both positive (Prov. 1:4) and negative (Exod. 21:14) implications, and both are exploited in this chapter. The deliberately detailed description of their preparations slows the action down and underscores the shrewd artifice of their ruse.

[6–13] "Distant land" is put in emphatic first position in the Gibeonite request (v. 6). That a vassal treaty is envisioned by the phrase "make a covenant with us (*lānû;* vv. 6, 11)" is suggested by the parallels 1 Sam. 11:1; 2 Sam. 3:12; 1 Kings 20:34. The recital of victories against enemies outside of Canaan (vv. 9–10) cleverly fits with the Gibeonite claim to be outsiders themselves. Their insincere "confession of faith" repeats language from Rahab's testimony in 2:9–11, prodding the reader into making comparisons.

[14–15] The object-first word order of v. 14b emphasizes Israel's rash carelessness. The three principals act in turn with *waw*-consecutive verbs: the men took, Joshua made, the leaders swore. No one is more to blame than the other, and the agreement is certified in triplicate.

[16–17] The discovery is reported without embellishment, for how it happens is not of interest to the narrative. These towns are located in Benjamin (18:25, 26, 28 LXX; also 1 Sam. 4:2) and remained a matter of interest after the exile (Ezra 2:25).

[18–21] The matter of sworn oath and the preservation of life invites the reader to draw comparisons with Rahab's story (2:12–13). The famine of 2 Sam. 21:1 would be an example of the sort of wrath feared.

[22–27] The curse of v. 23 sounds proverbial and follows the formula found in 1 Sam. 2:33; 2 Sam. 3:29; 1 Kings 2:4 and parallels; Jer. 33:17–18; 35:19. Its nature as an aphorism explains its telegraphic language (especially in the corrected text) and perhaps the somewhat odd expression "house of *my* God." Stereotypical ethnic curses are also preserved for the Kenites and Canaanites (Gen. 4:11–12; 9:25). The wording indicates that temple service would always be the lot of some Gibeonites, but perhaps not the whole ethnic group as suggested in vv. 21 and 26. If it is correct that this portion of the story reflects post-Solomonic developments, their service would have been for the Jerusalem temple. An honest dread of Yahweh (v. 24) replaces their false confession of vv. 9–10 and provides a satisfying return to the start of the story (v. 3). Readers sensitized to Deuteronomy would recall at this point that nations with whom Israel makes peace are to be put to forced labor (Deut. 20:11).

Triumphant
Campaign in the South
Joshua 10:1–43

Victory at Gibeon

10:1 When Adoni-zedek king of Jerusalem heard that Joshua had captured
Ai and had devoted it to destruction—he did to Ai and its king just as he
had done to Jericho and to its king—and that the population of Gibeon
had made peace with Israel [and were among them],[a] **2** they were very
afraid, because Gibeon was a large city, like one of the royal cities [and
because it was larger than Ai], and all its men were warriors. **3** So Adoni-
zedek sent word to Hoham king of Hebron, Piram king of Jarmuth,
Japhia king of Lachish, and Debir king of Eglon: **4** "Come up and help
me that we may strike at Gibeon, because it has made peace with Joshua
and with the Israelites."[b] **5** Then the five kings of the Amorites [gathered
and] went up—the king of Jerusalem, the king of Hebron, the king of Jarmuth, the king of Lachish, and the king of Eglon, they and all their encampments, and camped against Gibeon and attacked it.

6 The men of Gibeon sent word to Joshua at the Gilgal camp: "Do not
abandon[c] your servants! Come up to us quickly, rescue us, and help us,
because all the kings of the Amorites, the population of the hill country,
have gathered together against us." **7** So Joshua went up from Gilgal, he
and the entire army with him, all valiant warriors.[d] **8** Then Yahweh said
to Joshua, "Do not be afraid of them, for I have given them into your
power. Not one of them can stand against you." **9** Joshua came upon them
suddenly, having come up overnight from Gilgal.[e]

10 Then Yahweh demoralized them before Israel. He struck a mighty
blow against them at Gibeon. He[f] pursued them by way of the Beth-
horon ascent and struck them down as far as Azekah and Makkedah.
11 When they were fleeing from Israel and while on the slope of Beth-
horon, Yahweh threw down stones[g] from the sky as far as Azekah. So
they died.[h] More died from the hailstones than the Israelites killed by the
sword.

12 Then Joshua spoke to Yahweh on the day Yahweh gave the Amorites into the power of Israel, when he had struck them down at Gibeon
and they were struck down before Israel.[i] He said [in the sight of Israel]:[j]

"O Sun, stand still at Gibeon!
And Moon, at the valley of Aijalon!

13 The sun stood still and the moon stood motionless
Until a nation took revenge on its enemies."k

[Is this not written in the Book of Jashar?]l So the sun stood motionless
in the middle of the sky and was in no hurry to go down for an entire day.
14 There has not been a day like it before or since when Yahweh obeyed
a human voice, for Yahweh fought for Israel. [15 Then Joshua and all Israel with him returned to the camp at Gilgal.]m

Execution of the
Five Kings

16 These five kings fled and hid in the cave atn Makkedah. 17 Then it
was reported to Joshua, "The five kings have been found, hidden in the
cave at Makkedah!" 18 Joshua said, "Roll [large] stones against the
mouth of the cave and station some men by it to guard them. 19 But do
not stand there yourself. Pursue your enemies and attack them from the
rear. Do not let them enter their cities, for Yahweh your God has given
them into your power." 20 As soon as Joshua and the Israelites had finished striking them such a very mighty blow that they were annihilated
—although there were survivors among them and they entered the fortified cities—21 then the whole people returned safely [to the camp] to
Joshua at Makkedah. Not even one person threatened the Israelites.o
22 Joshua said, "Open up the mouth of the cave and bring these five
kings out of the cave to me." 23 [They did so.] They brought [these] the five
kings out of the cave to him: the king of Jerusalem, the king of Hebron, the
king of Jarmuth, the king of Lachish, the king of Eglon. 24 When they
brought them [these kings] out to Joshua, Joshua summoned all Israelp and
said to the commanders of [the men of] war who had gone outq with him,
"Come forward and put your feet on the necks of these [kings]." So they
came forward and put their feet on their necks. 25 Then Joshua said to them,
"Do not fear or be terrified. Be brave and strong, for Yahweh will deal in
this manner with all your enemies whom you will be fighting." 26 Afterwards Joshua struck them down and put them to deathr and hanged them
on five trees. They were hanging on the trees until evening. 27 At sundown
Joshua gave the command and they took them down from the trees and
threw them into the cave where they had hidden themselves. They set
[large] stones over the mouth of the cave that are still there to this very day.

Conquests in the South

28 On that day he [Joshua] captured Makkedah and struck it [and its king]
with the edge of the sword. He devoted its to destruction and everyone in it.

He left no survivors. He dealt with the king of Makkedah just as he had dealt with the king of Jericho.

29 Joshua and all Israel with him passed on from Makkedah to Libnah and fought with Libnah. 30 Yahweh gave it [also] and its king into the power of Israel. He struck it and everyone in it with the edge of the sword. He left no survivors in it. He dealt with its king just as he had dealt with the king of Jericho.

31 Joshua and all Israel with him passed on from Libnah to Lachish and encamped against it and fought against it. 32 Yahweh gave Lachish into the power of Israel and he captured it on the second day. He struck it [and everyone in it][t] with the edge of the sword, just [exactly] as he had dealt with Libnah. 33 Then Horam king of Gezer came up to help Lachish, but Joshua struck him and his people down, until he left him no survivors.

34 Joshua and all Israel with him passed on from Lachish to Eglon and encamped against it and fought against it. 35 They captured it on that day. They struck it with the edge of the sword. He devoted to destruction everyone in it [on that day],[u] just [exactly] as he had dealt with Lachish.

36 Joshua and all Israel with him went up [from Eglon] to Hebron and fought against it. 37 [They captured it.] They struck it with the edge of the sword [and its king and all its cities] and everyone in it.[v] He left no survivors, just [exactly] as he had dealt with Eglon. He devoted it to destruction and everyone in it.

38 Joshua and all Israel with him turned back to Debir and fought against it. 39 He captured it and its king and all its cities.[w] They struck it with the edge of the sword and devoted to destruction everyone in it. He left no survivors. Just as he had dealt with Hebron, so he dealt with Debir and its king—and just as he had dealt with Libnah and its king.[x]

40 So Joshua struck the whole land, the hill country, the Negeb, the lowlands, the slopes, and [all] their kings. He left no survivors. He devoted to destruction everything that breathed, just as Yahweh God of Israel had commanded, 41 [Joshua struck][y] from Kadesh-barnea to Gaza and the whole land of Goshen as far as Gibeon. 42 All these kings and their land Joshua captured at one time, for Yahweh the God of Israel fought for Israel. [43 Then Joshua and all Israel with him returned to the camp at Gilgal.][z]

a. MT expansion from chapter 9. OG offers "with Joshua and with Israel" as the object of the Gibeonites' peacemaking. This is probably an expansion from 10:4, but the possibility of an MT haplography cannot be excluded: '*t-y[hwš' w't-y]śr'l*.

b. 4QJosh[a] lacks *bny* before "Israel."

c. Literally "do not withdraw your hand from."

d. Taking the *waw* before "all" as explicative. Alternate translation: "and all the valiant warriors" (cf. NAB).

e. Verse 9b is an adverbial noun clause, Waltke and O'Connor, *Hebrew Syntax*, 38.8d. 4QJosh[a] has *hlk* "marched" for "came up," probably reflected in the Greek *[eis]eporeuthē*.

f. Yahweh can hardly be intended as the subject of "pursued" and "struck down" as understood by NJB. JPSV and REB take Joshua as the implied subject. It is also possible to vocalize the last three verbs as plurals, with Israel as the implied subject (NRSV, NAB, S, OG in part).

g. Follows 4QJosh[a]. This was expanded in MT by "large" and in OG with "hail."

h. Follows MT. For "and they died" OG reads *wyhyw* "and there were."

i. Follows OG. MT lost by homoioteleuton something like *byd yśr'l ky hkm bgb'wn wykw* ("into the power of Israel, when he had struck them down at Gibeon and they were struck down") because of the similarity of *byd yśr'l* and *lpny yśr'l*. MT expanded *lpny yśr'l* with *bny* (compare OG [here LXX[A]], S).

j. Probably a misplaced gloss caught up into MT.

k. Alternate translation, assuming haplography of the preposition usually required by this verb (*yqm [m]gwy*): "until he took revenge on the nation of his enemies." The OG subject *theos* is an inner Greek corruption from *ethnos*.

l. MT expansion, probably on the basis of 2 Sam. 1:18.

m. Verse 15 and 43 are MT expansions to reinforce the connection to Gilgal (cf. v. 21), Margolis, *Joshua in Greek*, 181, 205.

n. Understanding the preposition *b* as "in the vicinity of" as in 5:13.

o. Literally "no man sharpened his tongue against." Although it is usually assumed that dittography of the *l* in "Israel" generated *l'yš*, here it taken as an emphatic *lamed*. See Waltke and O'Connor, *Hebrew Syntax*, 11.2.10i. Exod. 11:7 has the same idiom with "dog" as the subject.

p. Follows OG. MT "every man of Israel" is probably intended as the same collective expression for the troops used in 9:6–7.

q. Masoretic *hehālĕkû'* is striking. The definite article is used with the verb to form a relative clause, Waltke and O'Connor, *Hebrew Syntax*, 13.5.2d. The final *aleph* may be a dittograph of the following letter or a double vowel letter as found at Qumran, Waltke and O'Connor, *Hebrew Syntax*, 19.7c n. 31.

r. Follows MT. OG lacks *'hry-kn wymytm* "afterwards and he put them to death," probably due to an inner-Greek haplography: *Ies[ous meta touto kai ethanatōsen aut]ous*.

s. "It" follows Hebrew and Targum evidence along with the Lucianic recension. See Margolis, *Joshua in Greek*, 190. MT offers "them" in agreement with its expansion of this verse with "and its king." In vv. 28–38 both MT and OG have a large number of secondary readings intended to harmonize the repeated formulas, making textual reconstruction of these verses uncertain.

t. MT ("and everyone in it") and OG ("and devoted it to destruction") each represent harmonizing additions.

u. Absent in both OG and S.

v. "They captured it" and "and its king and all its cities" are MT expansions from v. 39.

w. Follows MT. OG apparently witnesses the less problematic "its precincts," (the noun *ḥāṣēr*, "enclosure" or "village"), perhaps in harmony with 15:48–51.

x. Follows MT. This last clause is absent in LXX[B] but present in LXX[A]. It seems too awkward for a harmonizing addition or an expansion, and its loss is best explained as a haplography caused by the repetition of "and its king."

y. Not present in OG and V. Thus v. 41 is a direct continuation of v. 40b.

z. Not present in OG and S. MT has been expanded to reinforce a connection to Gilgal (cf. v. 15).

Chapter 10 divides neatly into the battle at Gibeon (vv. 1–14), the episode of the five kings (vv. 16–27), brief stereotypical reports of victories in the south (vv. 28–39), and a summation of southern conquests (vv. 40–42). Verses 16–27 are attached to the narrative movement of vv. 1–14 by means of a chronological backtrack and overlap represented by vv. 18–20. This shows that these two stories were originally independent, even though in their present form they deal with the same group of kings. A similar conclusion must be drawn about vv. 28–39. This highly formulaic series of battle reports grows out of the Makkedah episode, but there is only a partial congruence of the cities involved with those of vv. 1–27.

Deuteronomistic language is visible in v. 25 (Deut. 1:21; 3:28; 31:6–8, 23), v. 40 ("everything that breathed," Deut. 20:16), and the phrase "left no survivors" throughout vv. 28–40. Deuteronomistic orthodoxy is reflected in vv. 13b–14 and 27. Beyond this, however, it is difficult to sort out authorial and redactional matters. It is highly likely that the names of the five cities (vv. 5, 23) and the poetic fragment with its frame (vv. 12–14) represent material added by DH from other sources (see below). Presumably the three interconnected basic narratives (vv. 1–11, 16–27, 28–39) were all part of the pre-deuteronomistic book of Joshua. They are tightly secured into chapters 2–11 by the enemy's fear (v. 2; cf. 2:9; 5:1), Ai and Jericho (vv. 1, 28, 30), the Gibeonite alliance (vv. 1–2, 4, 6), Gilgal (vv. 7, 9), and *ḥērem* (vv. 1, 28, 35, 37, 39). The language of 10:1–12 closely parallels that of 11:1–9 (cf. 10:1 with 11:1; 10:5b with 11:5b; 10:8a with 11:6a; and 10:9a with 11:7a).[1]

The three accounts of vv. 1–39 were put together in order to be read as a single narrative movement to describe conquest in the south. In the story of the battle of Gibeon (vv. 1–14), a compositional technique of backtrack and overlap provides three successive perspectives on the victory, with the overlap to

---

1. For a detailed historical-critical analysis of the chapter, see P. Weimar, "Die Jahwekriegserzählungen in Exodus 14, Josue 10, Richter 4, und 1 Samuel 7," *Bib* 57 (1976): 51–62. He proposes a combination of a Gibeon story and a Makkedah story by the pre-deuteronomistic "collector," to which DH added the campaign of vv. 28–42. DH created this on the basis of an earlier three-part narrative involving only Libnah, Lachish, and Eglon. Viewed broadly, this hypothesis is a plausible explanation of the present text. Weimar also believes that the original Gibeon story told of a battle between Gibeon and Israel (55) and that it reflected in some way the Davidic victory reported in 2 Sam. 5:17–25. Recently B. Margalit, "The Day the Sun Did Not Stand Still: A New Look at Joshua x 8–15," *VT* 42 (1992): 466–91, traces a "hero saga" (vv. 1–7, 9, 10b, 16–27) and a "Yahweh war" story (vv. 8, 10a, 11) containing the misunderstood poem (vv. 12–14).

the story of the five kings in the cave providing yet a fourth. Verse 10 follows the slaughter and pursuit to Azekah. Then v. 11 retraces the enemy flight again to Azekah, adding hailstones to the divinely induced panic. Verses 12–14 relate yet a third aspect of the victory at Gibeon, the miracle of extended daylight described by a poetic couplet and its interpretive frame. Then the bridge section vv. 16–21 goes over the last part of the slaughter and pursues it to the finish. One literary effect of all this overlapping is to communicate a long and extended pursuit. After this, the triumphant chase from Gibeon to Azekah and on to Makkedah easily unfolds into the second story of the five kings at Makkedah (vv. 21–27). This in turn leads into the serial attacks against Makkedah and the other southern cities (vv. 28–39) that make up the third major story. Makkedah was integral to the second and third stories and was put into the first to create a common thread running from vv. 10 through 21 to 28. The summary of vv. 40–42 looks back at the implications of the whole chapter and brings the three stories together by reiterating their common themes: battle success, elimination of survivors, defeated kings, and Yahweh's combat for Israel.

This chapter parallels at many points the ideological tradition of ancient Near Eastern campaign reports. In these propagandistic documents one finds enemy coalitions, astronomical phenomena, emphasis on victory in a single day, the incomparability of the triumph, successful pursuit, the escape and hiding of enemies, and especially divine intervention.[2] These similarities reflect analogous literary aims. Both Joshua and these campaign reports seek to increase the wonder of the accomplishments they report and to promote a certain religious and political ideology. For Israel the ideology being advanced was not the power of the king as in the texts from Assyria or Egypt, but their own national identity as the people of a powerful God and as the legitimate masters of Canaan. These conquest accounts insist that "Yahweh fought for Israel," in accordance with divine war ideology (23:3, 10; Exod. 14:14, 25b; Deut. 1:30; 3:22; 20:4). The vanquished kings and cities are representative of all hostile forces that might undermine Israel's national identity and claim to the land. The pointed reference to Deut. 20:16 in v. 40 reminds readers that elimination of the indigenous population was a critical (if unfulfilled) necessity. Verses 40 and 42 make it clear that Israel's title to the land is the ideological issue at the core of all three of these conquest accounts.

[1–11] The narrative of vv. 1–14 divides into the threat of vv. 1–5 and the repulse of vv. 6–14. The language of the threat is nicely balanced by the language of the repulse: "sent word" (vv. 3, 6), "come up . . . help . . . because" (vv. 4, 6), "went up" (vv. 5, 7). The narrative problem of the hostile and imposing coalition is answered by Yahweh's decisive participation as Divine Warrior. This is further underscored by a fragment of traditional poetry (vv.

2. Weinfeld, "Divine Intervention," 121–47. Also see Younger, *Ancient Conquest Accounts,* 204–225, and for hanging up enemy corpses and placing feet on necks consult 223, 317 n. 86.

12b–13a) surrounded by editorial interpretation (vv. 12a, 13b). The catchword "at Gibeon," (vv. 10 and 12) connects the poem to its context. The section ends with the provisional interpretive summary of v. 14, which will be echoed in the final summary of v. 42. The MT expansion of v. 15 further witnesses to the summary nature of v. 14.

From a strategic standpoint it would be natural for Jerusalem to be apprehensive about the defection of the four Gibeonite towns to its north and west and to seek an alliance with towns farther to the south. Yet the motif of a coalition of enemy kings is also a way of describing the intensity of the peril in order to emphasize the wonder of Yahweh's deliverance (cf. 11:1–5; Judg. 5:19; 1 Kings 20:16; and mythopoetically, Pss. 2:1–3; 48:5 [4E]). The kings with exotic names who gather for attack in Gen. 14:1–3 provide another parallel. The narrative mechanism of a coalition also permits a single story of victory to cover a large geographic area. The names of these cities reappear in the same order in 12:10–12a, but the direction of literary dependence is unclear. It is likely, though, that chapter 12 served as the source for these towns, which would make them the redactional contribution of DH. The earlier designation for the coalition would have been, "the five kings of the Amorites" (v. 5; cf. 5:1). These same city names recur in vv. 5 and 23, first to underscore the threat, then to emphasize how totally the threat was eliminated. The number five may also be a folkloristic touch (13:21; Gen. 14:2; 47:2; 1 Sam. 17:40). The tradition that Adoni-zedek was a pre-Israelite king of Jerusalem connects to the similar tradition about Melchizedek. These may be interchangeable names for the same fabled character. There must also be some oblique correlation to the Adoni-bezek of Judg. 1:5–7, who was said to have died in Jerusalem. Since "Debir" is elsewhere the name of a city, what looks like its conversion into a personal name may indicate a mistransmission of the tradition or the author's creative invention of names to add color to the narrative. The peculiar names Hoham and Piram may represent the same process.[3]

The "they" in v. 2 presumably refers to the people of Jerusalem. There is an ironic reversal. The apparent folly of Israel's alliance with Gibeon has turned out to be a strategic advantage (according to v. 2) and an opportunity for a decisive Israelite victory. The "help" requested by Adoni-zedek (v. 4) is undone by the "help" provided by Israel (v. 6), a motif partially repeated in v. 33. In v. 6 the Gibeonites address their request in the courtly language of vassals ("your servants"; cf. 9:9) and with overstated rhetoric ("all the kings of the Amorites"). Yahweh's oracle of assurance in v. 8 comes directly to Joshua as in 8:1; 11:6, to be passed on to the whole nation in v. 25 (cf. 8:7). Its precise formulation is deuteronomistic (1:5; Deut. 7:24; 11:25). An impressive night march leads to the surprise and rout motif common to divine war narratives (as in

3. J. Barr, "Mythical Monarch Unmasked? Mysterious Doings of Debir King of Eglon," *JSOT* 48 (1990): 55–68.

11:7–8; note the shared language of v. 9a with 11:7a). Panic is Yahweh's characteristic weapon (Exod. 14:24; Judg. 4:15; 1 Sam. 7:10; etc.), resulting in a "mighty blow" (v. 20; Judg. 11:33; 1 Sam. 19:8; etc.). The addition of "and Makkedah" to the pursuit formula (v. 10) is a redactional preparation for the upcoming story of the kings in the cave. Pursuit from Gibeon via the Beth-horon pass to Azekah makes perfect geographic sense, the remarkable distance (30 km) indicating the magnitude of Israel's victory.

Verse 11 overlaps with v. 10 in reporting an incident during the enemy's retreat from Beth-horon to Azekah (note the telling absence of Makkedah at this point). Hailstones are a weapon of the divine warrior (Exod. 9:18–26; Job 38:22–23; Isa. 30:30).[4] Isaiah 28:21 probably refers to the tradition of this incident. Yet another chronological flashback occurs with vv. 12–14 in order to furnish a third perspective on the victory at Gibeon.

[12–14] The intended sense of this section is plain enough in the final form of the text. It glorifies Joshua as the leader whose extraordinary request for extended daylight was uniquely heeded by Yahweh (v. 14). It celebrates Israel's conviction that Yahweh fought for them. This was the incident that most impressed later generations about Joshua (Sir. 46:4; Josephus, *Ant.* 5.1.17). It stresses themes repeatedly emphasized in Joshua, namely Yahweh's support for Joshua (1:5–9, 17; 3:7; 4:14) and the Divine Warrior's spectacular engagement in Israel's battles (23:3, 10).

The opening syntax (*'az* followed by the imperfect) indicates that this incident is intended as a flashback, an event which took place before the completion of the previously reported Israelite victory.[5] This may be translated "it was at this time that" or "this is when." This syntax often seems to indicate the addition of supplementary material to a established narrative (Exod. 15:1; Num. 21:17; 1 Kings 8:12). The redactional connection provided by v. 12a is anxiously repetitive (see text note i), alluding to what has already taken place with "Amorites" (to vv. 5, 6), "the power of Israel" (to v. 8), "struck down before Israel" and "at Gibeon" (both to v. 10a). Suggestions that the poetic citation properly begins with v. 12a overlook the completely redactional makeup of this half verse. In some ways this sounds like the historicizing superscriptions prefaced to certain psalms. The subject of "he said" is most naturally taken to be Joshua, not Yahweh.

Following Joshua's poetic lines, the narrator guides the reader to interpret them as denoting extended noontime daylight (v. 13b) in harmony with that biblical view which sees sun and moon as mere chronological markers rather than as supernatural beings (Gen 1:16). The precise positioning of this incident in the sequence of the previous narrative remains indefinite. However, the natural way

---

4. For a Hittite parallel, see Younger, *Ancient Conquest Accounts,* 208–209. For stones as a divine weapon in a Sumerian poem, *ANET,* 578.

5. Waltke and O'Connor, *Hebrew Syntax,* 31.6.3b.

to read the text is to associate the extended daylight with Israel's prolonged pursuit and slaughter of the enemy (v. 10b). Verse 14 comments on the significance of the marvel, linking back both to the first part of v. 12 ("Joshua spoke") and to the previous narrative of combat (vv. 8, 10–11). This somewhat autonomous unit ends with the abrupt re-introduction of the five kings in v. 16, v. 15 being an MT expansion.

There are clear indications that the poem of vv. 12b–13a was not originally part of its present context. Although Joshua is supposedly speaking to Yahweh, the poem itself addresses the sun and moon. Moreover, the prose explanation disregards the moon and concentrates only on the sun, while assigning to the sun (v. 13b) the verb that the poem itself uses of the moon (*'md*; "stand motionless, come to a standstill"). The verb used by the poem for the sun (*dmm*), is open to a number of translations. It normally means "cease," and could be taken to imply "be silent," "remain dark," "hold military position," "be stunned into immobility or silence." However, the prose context forces the reader to understand *dmm* as "stand still, become set, freeze," by collapsing it into the moon's verb *'md*. Another anomaly is that the valley of Aijalon has played no role in the preceding narrative. Furthermore, the position of the sun over Gibeon to the east (from the perspective of Beth-horon) and the moon over Aijalon in the west means that it would still be morning, not a likely time to request further daylight and totally at odds with the sun's position in the "middle of the sky" in v. 13b. Thus this couplet is a fragment of a larger work (in that it refers to unmentioned events) and was not originally joined to its present context. This anomaly seems to have been sensed by whoever added the notice that this is a quotation from the Book of Jashar (see text note 1).

It follows that the poetic fragment originally described something very different from what v. 13b interprets it to report, the sun standing still at midday. There have been three general critical approaches to discovering what the poem signified in its original context: a natural phenomenon misinterpreted miraculously, an astrological oracle understood incorrectly, or a mythic statement taken literally. Here a fourth approach is suggested, one which seeks to discover how the poetic fragment would have functioned in its original literary context.

Naturalistic explanations often begin from understanding the verb *dmm* as "remain dark, do not shine." The parallel second verb *'md* could then have a similar meaning based on one understanding of Hab. 3:11.[6] Thus the couplet has been taken as a call either for the heavenly bodies to darken or for the sun not to rise and the moon to stay in place, so that predawn darkness might be preserved for the early morning attack reported in v. 9. Some have linked this assumed darkening with the hailstones of vv. 10–11 and see it as a description

6. For the text-critical reconstruction of Hab. 3:11, see Margalit, "The Day the Sun Did Not Stand Still," 490–91.

of the sun hiding in the clouds before a hailstorm. Another suggestion has been a rain of meteorites with diffused light. Others have thought of a solar eclipse. The poem has also been taken as a prayer that the sun not dissipate the morning mist so that surprise could be preserved.[7] In order to avoid the pitfalls of historicizing, it would be better to link the supposed darkening of the heavenly bodies to the daytime darkness of the Day of the Lord tradition (Amos 5:8, 18; 8:9). This ominous celestial blackout is an act of the Divine Warrior that motivates the enemy's panicked flight.[8] The editor who utilized this poetic fragment is thought to have prosaically misunderstood both verbs as "stand still" and thus constructed a miracle of extended daylight from a natural or mythopoetic darkening of the heavenly bodies.

A second hypothesis looks to the ancient practice of reading heavenly omens. It has been suggested that Joshua was originally asking for a good omen involving the sun and moon as portents. Translating the key verb *dmm* as "be silent" leads to the notion that he is appealing to the heavenly bodies to be quiet and not give any oracle favorable to the enemy.[9] Another suggestion is that the poem may have originally entailed the omen of a eclipse.[10] Others, noting that the simultaneous appearance of both sun and moon on the proper day of the month was considered to be a good omen in Assyria, have suggested that this was a prayer of incantation asking that the sun and moon "stand" in opposition over Gibeon, thus making a favorable day.[11]

A third group of hypotheses about the original meaning for the couplet begins from the ancient perception that the sun and moon were gods. It has been suggested that the sun was the protective deity of Gibeon and that perhaps sun and moon are reflected in the names of Beth-horon and Aijalon. Some have taken this to mean that the couplet was not originally connected to a battle at all but was an old cultic incantation against the sun and moon gods to silence them or check their power.[12] Or perhaps the protective deities of the cities involved are being directed not to intervene. This last interpretation rests on understanding the verbs *dmm* and *'md* (on the basis of 1 Sam. 14:9) as "stay put, hold position" in the sense of non-

7. For these various opinions see W. Phythian-Adams, "A Meteorite of the Fourteenth Century B.C.," *PEQ* 78 (1946): 116–24; R. Scott, "Meteorological Phenomena and Terminology in the Old Testament," *ZAW* 64 (1952): 19–20; J. Sawyer, "Joshua 10:12–14 and the Solar Eclipse of 30 September 1131 B.C.," *PEQ* 104 (1972): 139–46; J. Bright, "Joshua," *IB* II, 605.

8. Margalit, "The Day the Sun Did Not Stand Still," 481–82.

9. J. Heller, "Die schweigende Sonne," *Communio Viatorum* 9 (1966): 73–78.

10. R. Wilson, "Understanding 'the Sun Stood Still,'" *Princeton Theological Review* 16 (1918): 46–54.

11. J. Holladay, "The Day(s) the Moon Stood Still," *JBL* 87 (1968): 166–78; Younger, *Ancient Conquest Accounts,* 212–20. For a variation see J. Walton, "Joshua 10:12–15 and Mesopotamian Celestial Omen Texts," *Faith, Tradition, and History,* Winona Lake, Ind., 1994, 181–90.

12. J. Dus, "Gibeon—ein Kultstätte des Šmš und die Stadt des benjaministischen Schicksals," *VT* 10 (1960): 353–74; Heller, "Die schweigende Sonne," 73–78. Alternatively this could be seen as a polemic against Judah's own flirtation with the cult of the sun (Ezek. 8:16; 2 Kings 23:11).

participation in battle.[13] However, an explanation based on the ideology of the Divine Warrior would seem to be more compatible with Israelite culture. The poem is connected to its prose context by geography ("at Gibeon") and the idea that Yahweh does battle using heavenly auxiliaries. Habakkuk 3:11 suggests that the sun and moon were understood as part of Yahweh's heavenly host, who engage in battle as cosmic powers (Judg. 5:20). From this perspective the contribution of sun and moon would not be extended daylight, but active participation in the battle. Psalm 121:6 discloses the potential destructive potency of these two heavenly powers. Such aid from heavenly bodies is a theme present in contemporary battle reports and other comparative sources.[14] Thinking of a warlike context then, *dmm* and *'md* could connote "hold position" or "stand to fight" (1 Sam. 14:9; 2 Sam. 2:28). Perhaps sun and moon aid Israel by remaining in their given positions, east and west of the battle theater centered on Beth-horon. Perhaps the sun rising in the east over Gibeon and the moon setting over the Aijalon valley to the west are seen as blocking the escape routes. Or perhaps they are asked to "stand still" in sense of a portentous act symbolizing and inducing victory, similar to Moses holding out his arms (Exod. 17:11–12) or Joshua his sword (Josh. 8:18). In any case, they have a beneficial and auspicious effect, for their participation helps decide the outcome of the battle as a victory for Israel.

However, an even more likely approach is a fourth one that takes seriously the poetic rhetoric of the fragment. The original speaker was neither Joshua entreating sun and moon nor Yahweh commanding them, but the *poet* apostrophizing or addressing the heavenly bodies. If this fragment were part of a poem like Exodus 15, Deuteronomy 32, Judges 5, or Habakkuk 3, how would the verbs *dmm* and *'md* most likely have been understood when addressed to sun and moon in the context of divine war victory? The verb *dmm* and its associated roots often indicate a stunned reaction in the face of a startling catastrophe or astonishing revelation: "be speechless with terror, be stunned into motionless rigidity."[15] Thus in Exod. 15:16, the nations are as immobile or as silent as a stone at the terrifying passage of Yahweh's people. Similarly, the moon's verb *'md* is to be understood on the basis of Hab. 3:11, where the moon (and sun?) stand still in the face of the dazzling manifestations of Yahweh's theophany. A human example of this verb used for a stunned pause is 2 Sam. 20:12, where passing soldiers shocked at Amasa's murder stop still. Using different vocabulary, Joel 4:15–16 [3:15–16E] and Isa. 24:21–23 also describe

13. Blenkinsopp, *Gibeon and Israel*, 41–52.
14. Iliad 2. 412–15; Miller, *The Divine Warrior in Early Israel*, 123–28. For other examples and the ideological importance of victories won within a single day, see Younger, *Ancient Conquest Accounts*, 212–20.
15. A. Baumann, "*dāmāh* II," *TDOT*, III, 260–65, who suggests "silence in the face of an impending catastrophe or one that has already struck, or in preparation for a revelation" (261). Compare Amos 5:13; Lev. 10:3; Ps. 31:18 [17E]; Isa. 23:2; Jer. 48:2; Lam. 2:10; 3:28. For associated roots *dwm, dmh* II see Isa. 6:5; Hos. 4:5–6.

sun and moon reacting to Yahweh's deeds according to the same mythopoetic concept. Envisioning the Joshua fragment in such a poetic context, one realizes that originally these two heavenly entities were being called upon to stand frozen or fixed, or perhaps silent, in stunned reaction to an awe-inspiring victory. The poet is making a dramatic appeal to the heavenly luminaries to react to Israel's astonishing triumph with astonished immobility (v. 12b), and then goes on to report that they indeed stood frozen in shock and amazement "until a nation took revenge on its enemies" (v. 13a).[16]

This mythopoetic rhetoric was converted by the redactor's prosaic restatement. Yet this was not so much a misunderstanding as an act of demythologizing, of making orthodox a problematic bit of tradition.[17] Because calling upon heavenly beings falls considerably outside the horizon of deuteronomistic orthodoxy (23:7, 16; Deut. 17:3; 2 Kings 23:5, 11), the redactor (presumably DH) has directed Joshua's speech *away* from sun and moon and toward Yahweh. This was intended to deflect the reader from any sub-orthodox understanding of the poetic couplet as an address to two gods or autonomous astral beings. For this redactor, the sun and moon were not involved as powers or deities or even as shocked witnesses, but only as time markers, providing a longer day. The text as we now have it points decisively away from astral powers and directly to Israel's God, who listened to Joshua's request addressed, as was proper, to Yahweh. The mythopoetic notion that sun and moon stood frozen in amazement has been converted into an orthodox assertion that Yahweh caused the sun to stop moving. Thus Yahweh "obeyed a human voice" and "fought for Israel" (v. 14).

[16–27] A new narrative movement begins with the reintroduction of the five kings in v. 16 and ends with their fate in vv. 26–27. Verses 18–20 connect this to what has come before by describing events simultaneous to vv. 10, 11, and 12–13. The role of the cave and the heap of stones in the story points to an etiological origin or transmission,[18] but their function in the present form of the

16. The poetic apostrophe of Deut. 32:43 is similar. It is a summons to praise directed to the heavens and gods at the occasion of Yahweh's vengeance on his enemies:

Praise, O heavens, his people,
   worship him, all you gods!
For he will avenge the blood of his children,
   and take vengeance on his adversaries. (NRSV)

This is restored according to the Greek and 4QDeut^q; see A. van der Kooij, "The Ending of the Song of Moses: On the Pre-Masoretic Version of Deut 32:43," *Studies in Deuteronomy*, VTSup 53, Leiden, 1994, 93–100.

17. As already suggested by Fritz, *Josua*, 112.

18. The testimony formula of v. 27 is redactional; Childs, "A Study of the Formula 'Until this day,'" 288. Yet it remains plausible that supposed gravesites served as points of fixation for Israel's traditions (7:26; 8:29; Gen. chapter 23; 2 Sam. 18:17, etc.). The identification of Makkedah, part of Judah's Lachish district (15:41), remains controversial, although the suggestion of Kh. el-Qôm (146104; name preserved by nearby Kh. Beit Maqdûm) is growing in acceptance and makes geographic sense in the context of vv. 28–39.

narrative is to emphasize the utter finality and totality of Israel's victory. What might look like a double etiological tradition involving vv. 16–18 (hiding, immuration) and 26–27 (hanging, burial) is actually a narrative necessity resulting from the way this story has been attached to the one that precedes it. As it has already done twice (vv. 11 and 12), the narrative backtracks once more to the panic and rout of v. 10. Now the "and Makkedah" of that verse is picked up, and the special fate of the kings becomes the focus. Trapping them in their refuge is a narrative strategy to permit the rest of the battle to run its course towards unopposed total victory (v. 21). The literary effect is to increase dramatic tension and to integrate the tale of the five kings into the movement of the first story. Verse 20 reports only on the last stage of the rout and slaughter. The parenthetic qualification that some escaped serves both to enhance dramatic tension and to link this section to the coming attacks on Hebron, Lachish, and Eglon. The plot can not come to full completion until these survivors have been dealt with in some way. Conversely, the kings who are executed in vv. 16–27 are carefully passed over in the following section (vv. 32, 35, 37 [restored text]).

The execution of the kings is preceded by a double movement of command and obedience in which the language of Joshua's two directives is impeccably echoed by Israel's obedience. Verse 22 is obeyed by v. 23a, then the last part of v. 24a is complied with in v. 24b. This rhythm of obedience has the effect of inducing the reader to expect that the comforting imperatives of v. 25 will also be heeded. Placing feet on the necks of the vanquished (v. 24) is a symbol of unconditional surrender and makes Israel's victory public and certain. The psychological impact of this symbolic act was appreciated in the iconography of the ancient world (*ANEP*, 351, 355, 393; cf. Deut. 33:29; 1 Kings 5:17 [3E]; Ps. 110:1). Here what is usually a royal symbol is democratized, for it is the military commanders (*qāṣîn;* Judg. 11:6, 11) who perform it in sight of "all Israel." The assurance formula of v. 25 links back to 1:7, 9 and 8:1 and points forward to the rest of this chapter and chapter 11.

Hanging up bodies (v. 26) is a demonstrative act of contempt (1 Sam. 31:10; 2 Sam. 4:12). DH makes sure that the law of Deut. 21:22–23 is obeyed (cf. 8:29). The story concludes in an satisfying manner by returning to the "stones into/over the mouth of the cave" that launched the action in v. 18. The testimony formula points to these stones as visible signs of Israel's territorial claims by insisting that they be remembered as marking the graves of the land's previous claimants. Israel's title of ownership is based on the victories of its heroic ancestors, and these are certified by the witness of these stones. It was important that each generation be told that they "are still there to this very day."

[28–39] These six victories are described in a stereotyped and purely formulaic way using divine war vocabulary (compare 8:22, 24). They are connected together by conventional itinerary links. The formulas freely vary from report to report in no discernable pattern. "Joshua and all Israel with him" are the grammatical subjects of each report after Makkedah. Each city is "struck with the edge of the sword" and all seven reports carefully make the deuteronomistic point that "he left no survivors" (cf. 8:22; 11:8, 11, 14, 22; Deut. 2:34; 3:3). Aside from v. 33, once these formulas are removed, nothing really remains but a bare list of cities. Makkedah, highlighted by an object-first sentence, comes first as the location of vv. 16–27. Three of the cities go back to the five of vv. 1–17: Lachish, Eglon, Hebron. They are enclosed by two new cities, Libnah and Debir. Gezer (v. 33) comes at the center of the catalog (three before, three after) and is atypical. As Lachish's distant ally its capture is not reported. Instead the "help" provided by King Horam serves as a contrasting foil to Israel's successful "help" of Gibeon (v. 6). The text respects what author and reader would know of historical reality in reporting no capture of Gezer and not picking Jerusalem up from the initial group of five cities (16:10; 1 Kings 9:16). Jarmuth is not picked up either, probably because it was too far away from the circle of cities surrounding Makkedah (see the appendix).

It is almost certain that this conquest itinerary is a literary construction rather than an authentic vestige of popular tradition.[19] The parallel stories told about these towns in 14:6–15; 15:13–17; Judg. 1:9–15 are much more likely to represent genuine traditions. The author inherited Makkedah from the previous story. The other five localities seem to have been chosen because they closely surround Makkedah. The three appropriate ones from the previous list, supplemented by two others, trace a pattern around Makkedah from northwest to southwest and then east to southeast.[20] This is not to deny that there is a certain tactical logic to controlling the approaches to Jerusalem from the west and south (just as the Gibeonite alliance would have cut off the west and north) or that this reiterated sequence of reports has much in common with ancient Near Eastern battle accounts.[21] Debir (v. 39) is unique in having associate towns (or "precincts" in OG). Because Debir still had a king to kill, unlike Hebron, the comparison to Hebron was supplemented by a comparison with Libnah, the last city in the list to have a living king. The MT additions to v. 37 obscure the logic behind this com-

19. In contrast with R. David, "Jos 10,28–39, temoin d'une conquête de la Palestine par sud?" *Science et esprit* 42 (1990): 209–229, who traces in these verses an alternate southern conquest tradition that began and ended at Debir.

20. This assumes Makkedah as Kh. el-Qom 146104, Libnah as T. Bornât 138115, and Eglon as T. 'Aitun 143099, all disputed identifications. Libnah as T. es-Safi 135123 and Eglon as T. Beit Mirsim 141096 would also fit the hypothesis. Lachish as T. ed-Duweir 135108, Hebron as el-Khalîl 160103, and Debir as Kh. er-Rabûd 151093 are generally accepted. LXX reads "Adullam" for "Eglon" throughout this chapter (and LXX[B] at 15:39), but the original OG reading was "Eglon." See Greenspoon, *Textual Studies in the Book of Joshua*, 170–71.

21. Similarities include the tracing of an itinerary, redundant repetition, total destruction, and summary statements. See Younger, *Ancient Conquest Accounts*, 226–28, 251–53 and "The Conquest of the South (Jos 10, 28–39)," *BZ* 39 (1995): 255–64. Perhaps the author is imitating such accounts. More likely, the construction of ideologically motivated campaign reports by either Assyrian kings or biblical authors would tend to utilize the same rhetorical features.

positional maneuver. The whole conquest enterprise is of a single piece, linked together by external and internal equations: Makkedah and Libnah are like Jericho; Lachish and the others are like the city before them on the list. The intended effect of this incessant reiteration is to impress readers with the speed (one or two days per city; vv. 32, 35) and totality of Israel's success.

[40–42] A summary explains that the momentous effect of these victories was the capture of the entire south. In this way, a limited number of individual conquest reports are expanded to cover "the whole land." The generalizing language of listing topographic zones is similar to that of 12:8 and Judg. 1:9 and aims to produce an all-inclusive description. It is uncertain whether "slopes" (v. 40) refer to the descents down to the west or to the east, but perhaps both are intended. The totality of the massacre is emphasized by a deuteronomistic formula in v. 40 ("devoted to destruction everything that breathed"), significantly taken from Deut. 20:16 (cf. Josh. 11:11, 14). The language of "survivors" and *ḥērem* echoes the catalog of vv. 28–39. In v. 41 a generalized geographic description of the "from . . . to" pattern (cf. 11:17; 12:7; 13:3–6) traces the southern limit of conquest as the line between Kadesh-barnea and Gaza. To the north the territory conquered is the unidentifiable "land of Goshen" (15:51) up to Gibeon as the northernmost point. This reference back to Gibeon skillfully takes the reader back to the start of the narrative, thus creating a satisfying compositional design. The ideological goal of the entire chapter is reached in v. 42. All our land was captured because Yahweh fought for us against the kings who opposed us. This land is our land and we are Yahweh's people.

Triumphant
Campaign in the North
Joshua 11:1–23

Defeat of the
Northern Coalition

11:1 When Jabin king of Hazor heard, he sent word to Jobab king of Maron,[a] to the king of Shim'on,[b] and to the king of Achshaph, 2 and to the kings who were from the north part of the hill country,[c] in the Arabah south[d] of Chinneroth, in the lowlands, and in Naphoth-dor on the west— 3 the Canaanites from east and west, the Amorites, the Hittites, the Perizzites, the Jebusites in the hill country, and the Hivites below Hermon in the land of Mizpah. 4 They went out with [all] their encampments [a great people], like the sand of the seashore in number, with very many horses and chariots. 5 All these kings converged and came and camped together at the waters of Merom in order to fight with Israel.

6 Yahweh said to Joshua, "Do not be afraid of them, for tomorrow at this time I am going to set [all of]ᵉ them out before Israel as dead bodies. You are to cripple their horses and burn their chariots. 7 So Joshua and the entire army [with him]ᶠ came against them suddenly by the waters of Merom and attacked them. 8 Yahweh gave them into Israel's power. They struck them down and pursued them as far as Great Sidon and Misrephoth-maim, and to the east as far as the valley of Mizpeh. They struck them down until he left them no survivors. 9 Joshua dealt with them just as Yahweh had told him. He crippled their horses and burned their chariots.

Capture of Hazor
and Other Cities

10 Joshua turned back at that time and captured Hazor and struck down its king with the sword.ᵍ Hazor was formerly the head of all those kingdoms. 11 They struck down everyone in it with the edge of the sword, devoting them to destruction.ʰ Nothing that breathed was left, and he burned Hazor. 12 Joshua captured all the cities of these kings and all their kings. He struck them down with the edge of the sword. He devoted them to destruction, just as Moses the servant of Yahweh had commanded. 13 However Israel did not burn any of the cities which stoodⁱ on their mounds, except that Joshua burned Hazor alone. 14 The Israelites plundered for themselves all the booty [of those cities and the cattle],ʲ but they struck down every person with the edge of the sword until they destroyed them. They did not let anything that breathed survive. 15 Just as Yahweh had commanded Moses his servant, so Moses commanded Joshua and so Joshua did. He did not set aside anything of all that Moses had commanded him.ᵏ

Summary

16 So Joshua took the [this] whole land, the hill country, the whole Negeb, the whole land of Goshen, the lowlands, the Arabah, the hill country of Israel and its lowlands, 17 from Mount Halak which ascends towards Seir as far as Baal-gad in the valley of Lebanon below Mount Hermon. He captured all their kings, struck them down, and killed them. 18 For a long time Joshua waged war against [all] these kings. 19 No city made peace with the Israelites [except the Hivites who lived in Gibeon].ˡ They captured every one in battle. 20 The hardening of their hearts was from Yahweh, so that they engaged Israel in battle, in order to devote them to destruction without there being any mercy for them, but rather to destroy them, just as Yahweh had commanded Moses.ᵐ

21 At that time Joshua went and cut off the Anakim from the hill country, from Hebron, from Debir, from Anab—from the whole hill country

of Judah and the whole hill country of Israel.[n] Joshua devoted them to destruction along with their cities. 22 The Anakim were no longer left among [the land of] the Israelites. The only survived in Gaza, Gath,[o] and in Ashdod. 23 So Joshua took the entire land according to all Yahweh spoke to Moses. Joshua gave it as hereditary property to Israel according to their allotments by their tribes. And the land had rest from war.

a. The Greek tradition preserves the original place names. MT "Madon" is unattested in any source outside of Joshua (12:19 MT). It is given in LXX[B] as "Maron" (*Marrōn;* visual confusion of *d* and *r*) and thus identified in this version with Merom, vv. 5, 7. Maron is known from Egyptian and Assyrian sources. See H. Rösel, "Studien zur Topgraphie der Kriege in den Büchern Josua und Richter," *ZDPV* 91 (1975): 171–83; N. Na'aman, *Borders and Districts in Biblical Historiography,* Jerusalem Biblical Studies 4, Jerusalem, 1986, 119–43.

b. For "Shimron" (Zebulun, 19:15) LXX[B] consistently has "*Symoōn,*" that is "*Shim'on,*" a town known from multiple Egyptian sources. MT must have assimilated the original Shim'on to "Samaria" (MT consonants, LXX[A] and V), with the Masoretic vocalization intending to differentiate this town from the northern capital. For details, Barthélemy, *Critique,* 18–20. See the text note on 12:20.

c. Follows the Masoretic vocalization. Alternate translation: "from the north, in the hill country" (compare REB, NAB, JPSV).

d. Follows MT. OG offers *[m]ngd* "opposite," adopted by REB and NAB. The traditional list of Deut. 1:7; Josh. 11:16; 12:8 supports MT.

e. Either an expansion by MT or a mangled partial dittography of the following *ḥllym* "dead bodies."

f. MT offers a conflated doublet. "With him" '*mw* is not present in OG. When revocalized as "his people" this is seen to be an alternate reading for '*m hmlḥmh* "people of war" ("army" in the translation).

g. Follows MT. OG lacks "he struck down with the sword," but there is no obvious explanation for this minus. The phrase does not have the character of a scribal expansion.

h. Understanding the infinite absolute as adverbial to "struck down," Waltke and O'Connor, *Hebrew Syntax,* 35.4a.

i. Alternate translation: "which still stand" (compare REB, JPSV).

j. Tendentious MT specification of the difference between that which was devoted to destruction and allowable plunder.

k. Follows OG. MT "all that Yahweh had commanded Moses" is a theologizing improvement.

l. MT supplement for clarification. For various Greek readings that attempt to "correct" this verse, see Greenspoon, *Textual Studies in the Book of Joshua,* 134–36.

m. For the translation of this complex sentence, see Waltke and O'Connor, *Hebrew Syntax,* 38.8b (constituent noun clause) and 39:3.5d (restrictive use of *kî;* cf. Gen. 17:15; Amos 7:14).

n. Follows MT. OG has "the entire people of Israel and the entire hill country of Judah." There is no obvious explanation for this reading.

o. Follows MT. The loss of "and in Gath" by LXX[B] is an inner-Greek haplography according to Margolis, *Joshua in Greek,* 225–26.

Temporal markers divide this chapter neatly into three sections: vv. 1–9, 10–20, and 21–23. The use of the vague expression "at that time" in vv. 10 and 21 suggests that the reader is intended to take these three reports as coordinated or overlapping in time rather than as purely sequential. Chapter 11 is a literary mirror of chapter 10. Now a northern coalition assembles and is destroyed just as handily as the southern alliance was, leading to Israel's control of the rest of the land. The general structure of chapter 10 is repeated. Battle in the field (10:1–14; 11:1–9) is followed by the capture of cities (10:28–39; 11:10–15), followed in turn by a generalizing summary (10:40–42; 11:16–20, 23). The vocabulary also follows the pattern of chapter 10. Compare 10:1 with 11:1, 10:5b with 11:5b, 10:8a with 11:6a, 10:9 with 11:7, and 10:40–41 with 11:16–17. The rest of the language in chapter 11 is equally stereotypical, and the geographic information is highly generalized. The basic form of the chapter goes back to the pre-deuteronomistic book of Joshua, as is clear from the parallel of v. 1 to 5:1, 9:1, and 10:1. The language and interests of DH are visible in vv. 3, 8, 9, 11, 12, 14, 23, and especially in v. 15.

For these reasons, little in this chapter can be attributed to genuine early tradition. It is largely a literary composition. If there is any traditional core at all, it would seem to be limited to the incident of a battle at the "Waters of Merom" (v. 7) and the association of the name Jabin with Hazor.[1] The imposing remains of Bronze Age Hazor, visible amid and around the Israelite city reputedly refounded by Solomon (1 Kings 9:15), would naturally have given rise to tales of its conquest by Israel.[2] Such a majestic mound (v. 13) would be a silent witness that Hazor was the "head of all those kingdoms" (v. 10).[3]

In addition to the chronological links at vv. 10 and 21, the chapter is held together by a rough narrative logic. A problem (the mighty coalition, vv. 1–5) is overcome by divinely promised victory (v. 6), first in the field (vv. 7–9) and then against the cities (vv. 10–15). This is followed by the consequences of victory (vv. 16–20). This same plot movement is then repeated in a minor way with reference to the Anakim in vv. 21–22. Finally, v. 23 summarizes the entire conquest. A general thematic and ideological unity is also provided by the stereotypical

---

1. Y. Yadin, *Hazor, with a Chapter on Israelite Megiddo,* London, 1972, 5–6, argues on the basis of Mari texts that Jabin was a dynastic name for Hazor's kings.

2. This was also the case with the ruins of Jericho and Ai. The relation of this narrative to that of Judges chapters 4–5 is a matter of controversy. O. Eissfeldt, "Die Eroberung Palästinas durch Altisrael," Kleine Schriften, III, Tübingen, 1966, 367–83, is the classical exponent of the notion that the two narratives go back to the same tradition. The respective locations of the supposed battles are totally different, however, and the only real link is Jabin, who significantly does not appear in Judges chapter 5. On the relation of the two Hazor stories and their origin as a reflection of the impressive ruins of Hazor, see V. Fritz, "Das Ende der Spätbronzezeitlichen Stadt Hazor Stratum XIII und die biblische Überlieferung in Josua 11 und Richter 4," *UF* 5 (1973): 123–39. Fritz attributes the destruction of Hazor to the Sea Peoples. For a review of other positions, Kang, *Divine War,* 161–64.

3. The Mari letters reveal the prominence of Hazor in an earlier period. See A. Malamat, "Hazor 'the Head of All Those Kingdoms,'" *JBL* 79 (1960): 12–19.

language of holy war violence which permeates vv. 8–14, 16–17, 19–21 (strike down, capture, take, devote to destruction, burn, destroy, the sword). Yahweh is less directly involved here than at Jericho or Gibeon. Yahweh's role is limited to giving assurance (v. 6), claiming responsibility for the final result (v. 8), and issuing commands to be obeyed (vv. 9, 12, 15, 20). The narrator eventually reveals that Yahweh had a hidden role in the enemy's decision to fight (v. 20) and a strategic goal for the entire conquest struggle (v. 23).

Once again Israel's national identity and ownership of the land provides the ideological focus. The extent of the land that Israel claims is fully set forth (vv. 16–17). Yahweh is responsible for victory even when there is no obvious miracle (v. 8). In accordance with the theology of DH, possession of the land is coordinated with obedience to the law of Moses as set forth in Deuteronomy (vv. 11–12, 14). With Yahweh's backing, an obedient Israel can be totally successful (v. 23), even in the face of great odds and superior weaponry (vv. 1–4) or against dreadful ogres like the Anakim (vv. 21–22). Whatever current crises they may face, readers are urged not be afraid (v. 6) but to be obedient (vv. 9, 12, 15).

As a theology of history, vv. 18–20 are especially arresting. Yahweh's plan to destroy them leads to divine intervention in the choices made by the enemy. Their choices may not necessarily be to their advantage, but are to the advantage of Yahweh's scheme. Seemingly negative realities such as incessant enemy attacks and the protracted struggle were actually opportunities for Israel to obey the law faithfully. At the same time, Israel's faithful obedience in destroying the enemy turned out to be the very mechanism by which Yahweh kept the promise to them. Thus the gracious action of Yahweh, hidden behind human choices, and the fidelity of Israel worked together to bring the divine will to fruition.

[1–4] Jabin is motivated by what he has heard, but the content of this report is unstated. The reader must fill in the gap from 10:1–2. The narrative seeks to make the coalition formidable and to build dramatic tension. Three other kings of named cities join the alliance, along with a vague company of unspecified northern kings. The name Jobab occurs as an exotic foreign name in Gen. 10:29; 36:33–34 (but also in Benjaminite genealogies in 1 Chronicles). Verse 2 throws a wide geographic net, encompassing a territory oddly created by taking geographic terms appropriate for Judah (hill country, Arabah, Negeb, lowlands [Shephelah], cf. 10:40) and awkwardly converting them into northern areas. The hybrid result describes an "Arabah" of the Jordan valley (as in 12:3) "south" (as a reflection of "Negeb") of Lake Chinneroth and an otherwise unknown northern "Shephelah" (see below on v. 16 and 12:8). This shows that the authorial perspective is thoroughly Judahite. Naphoth-dor seems to mean the region under the administrative control of Dor (12:23; 1 Kings 4:11; the gloss at 17:11 suggests an individual city). Verse 3 continues the elaboration of Jabin's forces with a modified traditional list of nations, including a wide range of Canaanites (broadly located as in Num. 13:29), Jebusites beyond those defeated in chapter 10, and Hivites in addition to those in the Gibeonite alliance (Judg. 3:3; 2 Sam.

24:7). Verse 4 makes the coalition even more awesome. They are innumerable as sand (Judg. 7:12; 1 Sam. 13:5) and have dreaded horses and chariots, traditionally the enemy's decisive weapon (17:16–18; Judg. 1:19; 4:13; 5:22). They are unified and their force is concentrated (v. 5).

Apparently Madon/Maron, Shim'on/Shimron, Achshaph, and perhaps even Hazor, have been culled from the list in 12:10–24, making their role in any genuine tradition even more problematic. The "Waters of Merom" locale is impossible to locate, although the direction of the escape routes suggests a site in southern Upper Galilee.[4]

[6–9] Yahweh's oracle of assurance precedes victory as in 8:1 and 10:8. It is strengthened by a formulaic "tomorrow" (Judg. 20:28; 1 Sam. 9:16; 2 Kings 7:1). "Dead bodies (root *ḥll,* literally "pierced ones") is a technical term for those slain in battle. The directive to cripple the chariot horses (by cutting a tendon of a rear leg) is not guidance on battle tactics[5] but a way of making them useless for future battles (2 Sam. 8:4). This, along with burning the chariots, may be an expression of premonarchic Israel's low level of military technology, but it also represents a sort of *ḥērem* by making the devoted animals and military equipment (Ps. 46:10 [9E]) useless for military purposes. This action would also be in line with the ideology of Deut. 17:16.

Israel's move from south to north is assumed but not described. The "sudden" attack (v. 7), modeled after 10:9, implies that Yahweh provided victory (v. 8, cf. 6:2) in the shape of an unreported panic as in 10:10. The usual pursuit formula follows with the directions of flight given as northwest towards Sidon, towards the unknown locale of Misrephoth-maim, and northeast towards the unidentifiable valley of Mizpeh, no doubt to be associated with the land of Mizpah below Mt. Hermon (v. 3). Elsewhere Great Sidon is the border limit of Asher (19:29). Misrephoth-maim (perhaps "burning places of waters") is also a border point in 13:6, where it seems to indicate the south boundary of the Sidon area.[6] Thus the enemy is driven to the edges of Israel's claimed territory. In accordance with the expected formula (8:22; 10:33, etc.), there are

---

4. A favorite candidate for Merom is T. el Khirbeh 190275 with the name preserved at nearby Marun er-Ras 192278. The town is mentioned in Egyptian and Assyrian sources. Another is T. Qarn Hattin 193245, advocated by N. Na'aman, *Borders and Districts in Biblical Historiography,* Jerusalem Biblical Studies 4, Jerusalem, 1986, 119–43. But perhaps *mrwm* simply indicates "a height" rather than a proper name, as suggested by Rösel, "Studien zur Topographie," 179–180.

5. Kang, *Divine War in the Old Testament and in the Ancient Near East,* 164, and others suggest that laming the horses was the first stage in the attack, thereby permitting a successful assault on the chariots. This interpretation violates the plain sense of the text. The two parts of the command of v. 6 and of the indicative report of v. 9 are presented as coordinated actions and in both cases follow an indication of victory.

6. The last part of the name could be revocalized as *miyyam* to indicate "of the sea" or "western." A similarity of names suggests Kh. Musheirefeh 161276, west from the battle area, but the suggestion of the Litani River is also attractive. See Aharoni, *Land of the Bible,* 238; Na'aman, *Borders and Districts,* 49.

no survivors. Obedience to Yahweh's command in v. 9 provides a tentative conclusion and brings the first battle report to a close.

[10–15] The second report begins with a vague temporal connection and Joshua's turning away from the pursuit in order to obliterate Hazor (vv. 10–11). Hazor's political domination (v. 10b) echoes its initiation of the conspiracy at the start of the narrative. An object-first sentence turns attention to the other cities (vv. 12–14). Total annihilation of the population is emphasized for both Hazor and the other cities using the formulaic language of destruction, including a significant deuteronomistic reference to the *ḥērem* law of Deut. 20:16 in vv. 11 and 14 ("nothing that breathed"; also 10:40). This is the sort of *ḥērem* practiced against Ai (8:2, 27) and the kings east of the Jordan (Deut. 2:35; 3:7), but not the extraordinary devotion of all booty that was specially commanded for Jericho. The twin focus on enemy cities and enemy kings continues a theme from earlier chapters (e.g., 2:2–3; 6:2; 8:1–2). Like Jericho and Ai, Hazor was burned, but according to v. 13 there was no wholesale destruction of cities by fire. The point seems to be that other visible ruin mounds, either deserted or now occupied by Israelite towns, did not result from Israelite destruction, but already existed as such at the time of conquest. Israel did not destroy captured towns, but appropriated them, thus realizing the principle of Deut. 6:10–11 and Josh. 24:13. A second narrative conclusion is reached with v. 15, which picks up the assertion of v. 12b and emphasizes Joshua's scrupulous obedience. Joshua has now fully accomplished what Yahweh required of him in 1:7.

[16–20] This geographic summary of Joshua's achievements parallels that of 10:40–41, but extends to a description of all the conquered land. Verse 16 begins with a reprise of southern territory using the classic four divisions (hill country, Negeb, lowlands [Shephelah], Arabah; 12:8; Deut. 1:7), to which the enigmatic "land of Goshen" of 10:41 has been added. The territorial extension to the north follows the procedure of v. 2 and provides the "hill country of Israel" with an otherwise unattested "Shephelah" or "lowlands," again indicating a Judahite perspective. The designation "hill country of Israel" is found only here and in v. 21 and would seem to be an imitation of the genuine toponym "hill country of Judah" (15:48; 18:12; 20:7; 21:11). If "Shephelah of Israel" is to be taken seriously, it could indicate the area between the mountains of Samaria and the coastal plain of Sharon, or perhaps the less elevated portions of Galilee in eastern Asher. Verse 17 uses a different tactic and describes the land by its border points in a "from . . . to" pattern. An east to west line was already drawn in 10:41; here it is south to north. In both form and content, this resembles 12:7 and 13:5–6. The southern limit is Mt. Halak (probably Jebel Halaq), bordering on Seir, the territory of Edom. The north terminus is an unidentified Baal-gad at the south (that is, Mt. Hermon) end of the Beqaʻ Valley in Lebanon. Judges 3:3 refers to this locale as Mount Baal-Hermon.

Verse 18, which might seem to undermine the miraculous character of holy war, intends to communicate what great effort went into the overthrow of these enemy kings. This verse has the effect of converting the limited number of stories actually related into representative examples of a larger unreported campaign. It also may be a reference to the expectation of a gradual conquest as reflected in Deut. 7:22. In any case, v. 18 serves as the first logical term in the complicated theological syllogism of vv. 18–20:

> Conquest took a long time
> Furthermore, no enemy cities made peace
> These two circumstances happened because Yahweh hardened enemy hearts
> This hardening meant that they kept on attacking Israel
> This in turn resulted in maximum destruction without mercy
> In doing this, Israel followed Yahweh's command

The command referred to is Deuteronomy's law of *ḥērem*, given through Moses. This line of reasoning is generally similar to the plot of the DH report of the victory over Sihon, in which Israel's peaceful request was met by a stubborn defiance of spirit and heart inculcated by Yahweh (Deut. 2:30) that eventually resulted in the enemy's destruction. However, the precise formulation of Yahweh's act here is often assumed to reflect P-like language (*ḥzq* piel), the expression used to describe the hardening of Pharaoh's heart in Exodus.

[21–22] Abruptly attention returns to the south with a second vague temporal marker. The Anakim (perhaps "necklace people") were located by tradition in and around Hebron/Kiriath-arba (15:13; 21:11). Possibly they are mentioned in the Execration Texts (*ANET,* 328). Israelite folklore credited them with impressive height and associated them with the mythic Nephilim and Rephaim (Num. 13:32–33; Deut. 1:28; 2:10–11; 9:2). Their great size was apparently inferred from their megalithic building remains (compare Og's bed, Deut. 3:11). Certainly tales about gigantic previous inhabitants are common to many peoples. A Judahite perspective again shows in v. 21, where the designation "hill country" by itself is used for the south first, and then only subsequently enlarged and split into "hill country of Judah and hill country of Israel." This report answers the question of why a group traditionally associated with the Hebron/Debir/Anab area was also connected with Philistia. The opinion that they persisted in Philistia is reflected in Jer. 47:5 LXX and fabled encounters with huge and peculiar descendants of the Rephaim at Gath (2 Sam. 21:16–22). These verses are in some tension with 10:36–39, according to which Hebron and Debir have already been conquered. They also conflict with 14:12–15; 15:13–14. However, DH or some other deuteronomistic redactor may have felt a need to mention their destruction and expulsion at this particular point in the story in order to fulfill Deut. 9:1–3. That 14:15b echoes 11:23b seems to be evidence of some sort of redactional relationship between

11:21–23 and 14:6–15, but no credible conclusions can be drawn about transpositions or insertions based on this limited evidence.[7]

[23] The armed conflict is decisively over. This summary directs the reader's attention first backwards, then ahead. Yahweh has kept the promise of 1:3–5. The task assigned to Joshua in 1:6 and Deut. 31:7 has been thoroughly and obediently completed by taking "the entire land according to all Yahweh spoke to Moses." The verb *lqḥ* "take" (vv. 16, 19, 23) with the land as its object is used in this chapter along with the verb *lkd* "capture" (v. 10) commonly employed in earlier chapters, especially in the summary of 10:42. The role of Moses is emphasized (as in vv. 12, 15, 20), indicating that Joshua has also fulfilled 1:7–8. The land is quiet and at peace (cf. 2 Kings 11:20), the situation that results when Israel remains loyal to Yahweh according to DH (cf. Judg. 3:11, 30; 5:31; 8:28). The conquest is portrayed as total, reflecting the DH ideology of passages such as 12:7–8; 21:43–45. In the final form of the book, however, the totality of the conquest is held in tension with the concept that some land and peoples remained unconquered (13:2–6; 15:63; 16:10; 17:12–13, 16, 18). This is even true to some extent within DH itself (23:4–5, 7, 12–13).

With the capture of the land now behind him, Joshua turns to the second task given him in 1:6: "put the people in possession of the land" (*nḥl* hiphil). The root *nḥl* reflects the language of passages like Deut. 4:21; 15:4; 19:10. Although the theme of "allotment" remained underdeveloped in the DH form of Joshua, it is certainly present (1:6; 11:23; 12:7). In the final form of the book, the supplementary chapters 13–21 explore this subject more fully. Thus the noun *naḥălâ* in 11:23 forges an important link to what follows (13:6; 14:3, 13; 17:4, 6, 14; 19:49), as does the word "allotments" (12:7; 18:10).

List of Defeated Kings
Joshua 12:1–24

Two Kings East
of the Jordan

12:1 These are the kings of the land whom the Israelites struck down and whose land they took over across the Jordan toward the east, from the Wadi Arnon as far as Mount Hermon, and the entire Arabah eastward: 2 Sihon king of the Amorites who lived in Heshbon ruling from Aroer

---

7. Noth, *Josua*, 71, suggests that 14:6–15a is DH and was once attached directly to 11:21–23a.

(which is by the rim of Wadi Arnon) and the middle of the wadi, half of Gilead, as far as the Wadi Jabbok, the border of the Ammonites, 3 and the Arabah as far as the Sea of Chinneroth on the eastern side, and as far as the sea of the Arabah (the Salt Sea) on the eastern side by the way of Beth-jeshimoth, and southward below the slopes of Pisgah and the adjacent area.[a] 4 Og king of Bashan, one of the remainder of the Rephaim, who lived in Ashtaroth and Edrei, 5 and ruling in Mount Hermon and in Salecah and in all Bashan as far as the border of the Geshurites and the Maacathites and half of Gilead,[b] the territory of Sihon king of Heshbon. 6 Moses the servant of Yahweh and the Israelites struck them down and Moses [the servant of Yahweh] gave it as property to the Reubenites, Gadites, and the half-tribe of Manasseh.

Kings West of the Jordan

7 These are the kings of the land whom Joshua and the Israelites struck down from the Jordan westward, from Baal-gad in the valley of Lebanon as far as Mount Halak which ascends toward Seir. Joshua gave it to the tribes of Israel as property according to their allotments, 8 in the hill country, in the lowlands, in the Arabah, in the slopes, in the wilderness, and in the Negeb—the Hittites, Amorites, and Canaanites, the Perizzites, Hivites, and Jebusites:

9	the king of Jericho	[one]
	the king of Ai (which is near Bethel)	[one]
10	the king of Jerusalem	[one]
	the king of Hebron	[one]
11	the king of Jarmuth	[one]
	the king of Lachish	[one]
12	the king of Eglon	[one]
	the king of Gezer	[one]
13	the king of Debir	[one]
	the king of Geder	[one]
14	the king of Hormah	[one]
	the king of Arad	[one]
15	the king of Libnah	[one]
	the king of Adullam	[one]
16	the king of Makkedah	[one]
	the king of Bethel[c]	[one]
17	the king of Tappuah	[one]
	the king of Hepher	[one]
18	the king of Aphek of Sharon[d]	[one]

19 . . . . [e]

the king of Hazor	[one]
20 the king of Shim'on	[one]
the king of Maron[f]	[one]
the king of Achshaph	[one]
21 the king of Taanach	[one]
the king of Megiddo	[one]
22 the king of Kedesh[g]	[one]
the king of Jokneam of Carmel	[one]
23 the king of Dor of Naphath-dor	[one]
the king of Goiim of Galilee[h]	[one]
24 the king of Tirzah	[one]
Total of all kings: thirty.[i]	

a. This translation attaches the first word of v. 4 (*ûgĕbûl*) to the end of v. 3, based on the usage of 13:23, 27; 15:12, 47; Num. 34:6; Deut. 3:17, where similar translations seem warranted. MT puts this word into construct with Og: "the boundary of Og." The Greek translator failed to understand this word and omitted it, followed by NRSV, REB. See Barthélemy, *Critique,* 21–22.

b. This translation reflects the equivocal nature of MT without emendation. Hexaplaric Greek witnesses add the preposition *'d* through dittography after *hgl'd* "Gilead," but the more difficult MT should be followed. REB and some commentators err in attributing this plus to the Lucianic LXX. For details, see Barthélemy, *Critique,* 22. Almost all translators include this "half of Gilead" as part of Og's kingdom. Thus NRSV: "and over half of Gilead to the boundary of King Sihon." The alternative is to understand this "half of Gilead" as a designation for Sihon's kingdom (cf. v. 2): "as far as the border of the Geshurites and Maacathites and [as far as] the half of Gilead, [that is] the territory of Sihon." In other words, Og's dominion reached southward down to the boundary of Sihon's half of Gilead. It is not always easy to decide between "border" and "territory" as a translation for *gĕbûl*. For help, M. Ottosson, "*gĕbhûl,*" *TDOT* II, 361–66.

c. OG lacks Bethel, perhaps excised because of its presence in v. 9 (Margolis, *Joshua in Greek,* 238–39) or on the basis of Judg. 1:22–26.

d. Follows OG. Behind LXX[B] is an original "Aphek of Sharon" (Rahlfs, *Septuaginta;* Margolis, *Joshua in Greek,* 239–40). Since there were at least three Apheks, it would be reasonable to add this specification (cf. vv. 22 and 23). MT separates into "Lasharon," an otherwise unknown place name.

e. At this point MT adds "the king of Madon" to harmonize with 11:1–5, where MT "Madon" replaced the preferable "Maron" of OG. Madon would have been missed by copyists familiar with the MT of 11:1: Hazor, Shim'on/Shimron, Madon, Achshaph.

f. Follows OG. MT's curious "Shimron-meron" is a false combination of Shim'on (Greek *Symoōn*, MT *Shimron*) and Maron (Greek *Marrōn*), perhaps facilitated by assonance.

g. The OG order is Kedesh, Taanach, Megiddo.

h. Follows LXX[B], compare Isa. 8:23 [9:1E] and perhaps Judg. 4:13, 16. MT has "Gilgal."

i. In this critical reconstruction there are thirty kings, a conventional number (2 Samuel 23, Prov. 22:20). MT totals thirty-one and OG twenty-nine.

Lists of names are notoriously prone to scribal error and variation both in order and spelling. Probably the form of the list which preceded the MT and OG versions lacked the repeated numeral "one" since this is absent from OG. Moreover the division of compound names (Aphek and Lasharon, v. 18) together with the combination of discrete names (Shimron-meron, v. 20) indicates that the dividing term "king" was originally absent as well.[1]

A twofold enumeration of vanquished kings provides a summary of the conquest. Stories previously told in Deuteronomy 1–3 and Joshua are evoked by the verbs "struck down" (*nkh;* from chaps. 7–11) and "took over" (*yrš;* from chap. 1). Parallel language links together the work of Moses with that of his successor Joshua (vv. 1, 6–7). Thus the first list of two kings (vv. 1–6) summarizes the career of Moses and provides generalized geographic descriptions of the land he acquired. The second list (vv. 7–24) outlines Joshua's accomplishments without further geographic detail. Similar summarizing lists of defeated nations are known from Assyrian and Egyptian royal inscriptions.[2] The two sections of vv. 1–6 and 7–24 differ in character and origin. The first is a purely literary recapitulation in deuteronomistic style of material from Deut. 2:26–3:7. The second is a topographic list from an unidentifiable source (vv. 10–24) that has been provided with a deuteronomistic introduction (vv. 7–8) and the appropriate addition of Jericho and Ai (v. 9).

This summary chapter stresses the decisive result of the leadership of Moses and Joshua. The whole land on both sides of the Jordan unquestionably belongs to Israel. The previous political organization of petty kingships was decisively shattered, king by king. Present national identity is reinforced by reference back to a golden age when all Israel together, south, north, and east of the Jordan, properly organized into its foundational tribes, enjoyed possession of the land under the unified leadership of Moses, servant of Yahweh, and Joshua his successor. Both Moses and Joshua give the land "as property" (*yĕruššâ;* vv. 6, 7; cf. 1:15; Deut. 3:20). Thematic threads from the whole book of Joshua are gathered together here: Moses and Joshua (1:1–2, 5, 17), divine war, the eastern tribes (1:12–17; 4:12; 22:1–34), land distribution (1:6; 11:23; chaps. 13–21), conflict with alien kingship (2:10; 5:1; 9:1–2; 10:1–5, 42; 11:1–2, 17–18), and catalogs of enemy groups (3:10; 9:1; 11:3; 24:11).

In the final form of Joshua this chapter marks a turning point. Between chapters 1–11 and 13–21 the book's strategy for bolstering national identity and land ownership changes, and attention shifts from capture in war to land distribution.

---

1. For the textual problems presented by vv. 16–20, see Barthélemy, *Critique*, 23–27. For geographical issues see Aharoni, *Land of the Bible*, 230–32.

2. For examples see Younger, *Ancient Conquest Accounts*, 230–32.

From now on, instead of the battle reports to which this chapter looks back by naming the names of defeated towns, the focus will be on Israel's claim to the land expressed in acts of apportionment and further lists of toponyms. Thus chapter 12 points backward to previous victories in its content and forward to geographic lists by its form.

[1–6] The overall south to north extent of the east Jordan territory is sketched by v. 1, "from Arnon to Hermon."[3] Then its two divisions are taken up in turn by vv. 2–3 and 4–5. These territorial descriptions share language and conceptions with Deut. 2:36–37; 3:8–17, and to some extent with Josh. 13:8–33. Thus v. 1b is almost exactly equivalent to Deut. 3:8b, while vv. 2–3 reflect portions of Deut. 1:4a; 3:12b, 16–17. Verses 4 and 5 parallel elements of Deut. 1:4b; 3:10–11, 13–14. Some puzzling features in these descriptions can be cleared up by comparison with the Deuteronomy parallels. For example, the odd "and the middle of the wadi" in v. 2 (and Deut. 3:16) is clarified by the fuller formula "and the city in the middle of the wadi" found in Deut. 2:36 (and Josh. 13:9, 16).

These descriptions are hard to translate, but the general picture is clear. Verse 1 outlines the whole territory under discussion, with careful attention paid to the Jordan Valley ("the entire Arabah eastward"), which will be picked up in v. 3. For Sihon and Og, their traditional cities of residence are given first. The ancient connection between Heshbon and Sihon is supported by the song preserved in Num. 21:27–30. For Sihon (vv. 2–3) a line of extent is traced south (Aroer) to north (to where the upper Jabbok forms the Ammonite border). Then attention turns to the Arabah, that is the eastern portion of the Jordan valley. Here two directional lines are drawn. The first runs towards Lake Chinneroth (Chinnereth) on the north. Then a second one points southward to the Dead Sea via Beth-jeshimoth and then further on south to the slopes going down to the Dead Sea from Mt. Pisgah. "The way of Beth-jeshimoth" presumably refers to the road running from the Jordan through this town to Heshbon.[4]

For the dominion of Og (vv. 4–5), the description starts with three generalized statements: in Mt. Hermon, in Salecah,[5] and in Bashan. The first two are the northwestern and northeastern extremes of Israel's territory east of the Jordan. Bashan is the usual regional designation for Og's territory, generally embracing the area north of the Yarmuk. Then directional lines run vaguely northwest to the territory of Geshur and Maacah (southern and northern Golan Heights respectively) and south to Sihon's territory. An aside based on Deut. 3:11 reminds the reader that Og was one of the towering Rephaim (2 Sam. 21:16–22), so his defeat was all the more wonderful.

---

3. For territorial descriptions in this form see Aharoni, *Land of the Bible,* 86–87, and Num. 13:21; 2 Sam. 24:2.

4. Aharoni, *Land of The Bible,* 62.

5. This was probably a regional name, preserved at the location Salkhad 311212.

It is not entirely clear whether "half of Gilead" in v. 5 refers to territory ruled by Og or to Sihon's territory forming Og's southern border (see text note b). Deuteronomy 3:8–17 defines the kingdoms of Sihon and Og on the basis of the land assigned to Reuben and Gad (Sihon) and Manasseh (Og). The phrase "half of Gilead" in Josh. 12:2, 5 seems to connect to its use in Deut. 3:12–13, where "half of the hill country of Gilead" is assigned to Reuben and Gad and "the rest of Gilead and all of Bashan" to Manasseh. The north and west extent of the Reuben/Gad half in Deut. 3:16–17 is almost precisely that of Sihon's kingdom in Josh. 12:2–3: "as far as the Wadi Jabbok, the border of the Ammonites, and the Arabah . . . from Chinnereth a far as the sea of the Arabah." Thus the Jabbok forms the boundary between Sihon's "half of Gilead" and Og's territory, except that the Jordan plain (Arabah) up to the Sea of Galilee belongs to Sihon (and Gad, 13:26–27). This close relationship to Deut. 3:8–17 indicates that one should understand "half of Gilead" in 12:5 as Sihon's territory. In 13:31 the expression is applied to the territory of Og.[6]

[7–8] Again Joshua follows the pattern of Moses. The word "allotments" reflects 11:23 and prepares for the coming land division. The geographic and ethnic descriptions of vv. 7–8 mirror 11:16–17 and also reflect the generalized land divisions of 9:1 and 10:40 and the catalog of Deut. 7:1. The "Baal-gad to Mt. Halak" line is a north-to-south parallel to the south-to-north line given for the territory east of the Jordan in v. 2. A six-part territorial description in v. 8a is balanced by a nation-list of six names in v. 8b. This makes the point that all the land was conquered and all was distributed.

[9–24] For the reader prepared by chapters 2–11, three segments of this list stand out as familiar. The paradigmatic conquests of Jericho and Ai come first (v. 9). The five cities of 10:3 are listed in the same order with Jerusalem at their head in vv. 10–12a. The four cities of the 11:1 coalition are given with Hazor at their head in vv. 19b–20. Moreover, the four "extra" names of cities that were defeated in the southern campaign, but whose kings were not trapped in the cave (Makkedah, Libnah, Gezer, Debir), are scattered around in vv. 12b–16a. In a very general way the listed cities range from south to north: vv. 10–16a in the south, vv. 16b–18 in the center, and vv. 19–24 in the north. Thus the south section includes the cities of chapter 10 and four others, while the north section includes the cities of chapter 11 and seven others, one of which is [Naphath-]Dor, mentioned as a region in 11:2. The central section of vv. 16b–18 has no contacts with the previous narratives. One literary effect of listing cities unmentioned in

---

6. Biblical descriptions of the Transjordan raise convoluted issues beyond the scope of this commentary. Consult M. Ottosson, *Gilead: Tradition and History*, ConBOT 3, Lund, 1969, 53–116; J. Bartlett, "Sihon and Og, Kings of the Amorites," *VT* 20 (1970): 257–77; M. Wüst, *Untersuchungen zu den siedlungsgeographischen Texten des Alten Testaments. I. Ostjordanland*, Wiesbaden, 1975, 12–24, 28–57. For the relationship of Num. 21:21–35 to Deut. 2:31–3:3, see Noth, *Numbers*, 160–66.

previous narratives is to communicate that the stories told represent only an illustrative sample of a larger struggle (cf. 11:18). The incessant repetition "king of" nails down the total defeat of the system of Canaanite city-states.

The literary history of this list remains clouded. Because it is not merely a rehash of the book's narratives, it clearly reflects to some degree a genuine source with a previous history of its own. Yet at the same time, its present form has been modified to fit it for its new role as a summary, most clearly by appending Jericho and Ai to its beginning. It is likely, but not certain, that this list served as the source for the names of the Jerusalem and Hazor coalitions (vv. 10–12a for 10:3, 5, 23; vv. 19b–20 for 11:1). The cities of the campaign launched from Makkedah in 10:28–39 could also have derived from this list if the author eliminated from the 10:3 coalition Jerusalem (as not yet conquered) and Jarmuth (perhaps as too far from Makkedah) and then chose Makkedah, Libnah, Gezer, and Debir from 12:12b–16a to construct a stereotyped campaign report.[7] The original purpose of a city-list starting from Jerusalem and covering south, central, and north Palestine remains an enigma. It seems to lack any discernable political or geographic rationale. Perhaps it was compiled for educational purposes or created as an imitation of Egyptian or Assyrian lists of conquered places. The MT addition of "one" after each item recalls the custom known from the Arad ostraca of following names with tally marks or numbers.[8]

See the appendix for site identifications. Geder ("wall") is too common a toponym to be identified, although it could be the Gedor of 15:58. According to 1 Kings 4:10, Hepher is to be sought for in the third district of Solomon in the Sharon, but the Zelophehad material in 17:2–3 may suggest a location nearer Shechem.[9] "Goiim ('nations') in Galilee" can hardly be a city name by itself, but relates to the ethnic diversity of that region (Isa. 8:23 [9:1E]). It may be a shortened form of something like Harosheth-haggoyim (Judg. 4:2).

---

7. On the prehistory of this list and its role in the composition of chapters 10–11, see V. Fritz, "Die sogenannte Liste der besiegten Könige in Josua 12," *ZDPV* 85 (1969): 136–61; and *Josua*, 132–37. For the opposite opinion that the list derives from narratives in Joshua and elsewhere, see Schmitt, *Du sollst keinen Frieden schliessen*, 116–20.

8. Y. Aharoni, *Arad Inscriptions*, Jerusalem, 1981, nos. 38, 49, and others.

9. On this problem see A. Lemaire, "Le 'Pays de Hépher' et les 'filles de Zelophehad' à la lumière des ostraca de Samarie," *Sem* 22 (1972): 13–20; Na'aman, *Borders and Districts*, 158–62. A likely location is T. el-Muhaffar 170205.

The Command
to Divide the Land
Joshua 13:1–7

13:1 Now Joshua had reached old age. Yahweh said to him, "You have reached old age, but very much of the land remains to be taken over. **2** This is the land that remains: [all] the districts of the Philistines and of [all] the Geshurites[a] — **3** (From the Shihor, which is near[b] Egypt, northward as far as the territory of Ekron is considered to be Canaanite. There are five rulers of the Philistines, for Gaza, Ashdod, Ashkelon, Gath, and Ekron) — and of the Avvites **4** in the south; the whole land of the Canaanites from Arah[c] which belongs to the Sidonians, to Aphek, to the border of the Amorites; **5** and the land of the Gebalites,[d] and the whole Lebanon eastward, from Baal-gad below Mount Hermon to Lebo-hamath. **6** The whole population of the hill country from Lebanon to Misrephoth-maim, all the Sidonians, I will dispossess before Israel.[e] Simply[f] allot it to Israel as hereditary property just as I commanded you. **7** So now divide up this land as hereditary property for the nine tribes and the half-tribe of Manasseh.[g] From the Jordan to the Great Sea in the west you shall give it, the Great Sea being the border.[h]

a. These are the southern Geshurites of 1 Sam. 27:8, not the northern Geshurites of Josh. 13:11, 13.

b. Although *'al pĕnê* is often translated "east of," the more general "in the vicinity of, near" takes less for granted. See J. Drinkard, " '*al penê* as 'East of,' " *JBL* 98 (1979): 285–86.

c. Taken as an unknown place name *'rh* with the preposition *min,* which seems to be required by the grammar and is suggested by OG "from Gaza." Pointed as the MT this would be an unknown place name "Mearah" or the word for "cave."

d. Gebal is Byblos (1 Kings 5:32 [18E]).

e. Follows OG. MT expands to "children of Israel."

f. The restrictive adverb *raq* implies: "in spite of the situation just described, nevertheless your task is to divide." See Waltke and O'Connor, *Hebrew Syntax,* 39.3.5.

g. The unexpected definite article with Manasseh may be the result of the following textual disturbance or may indicate an adjectival force, "the Manassehite half-tribe."

h. Follows OG in restoring "from the Jordan" in v. 7 to "half tribe of Manasseh" in v. 8. Compare note a at 13:8. MT suffered a long haplography between the two occurrences of "the half-tribe of Manasseh." See Margolis, *Joshua in Greek,* 248; Barthélemy, *Critique,* 28–30; A. G. Auld, "Textual and Literary Studies in the Book of Joshua," *ZAW* 90 (1978): 413–14.

A major turning point in the book is signaled by a renewed command of Yahweh. Just as the command of 1:2–9 initiated chapters 2–12, so the directive of 13:1–7 launches chapters 14–21. The notice of Joshua's advanced age (v. 1a) leads one to expect a farewell situation in which the aged leader will deliver a testament or final words of advice before death. The use of this expression in 23:1b introduces just such a scenario. Yet the reader discovers that before there can be a farewell, the task of dividing the land must be completed. What is more, before this land division actually gets under way in chapter 14, there are two diversions or detours: the land that remains (vv. 2–6) and the territory of the eastern tribes (vv. 8–32).

The repetition of 23:1b by 13:1a is evidence that the division of the land was inserted into the DH form of Joshua at a later date. Joshua's old age is an appropriate motive for his final words of chapter 23, but less germane to the context of land division. The presence of two scenes motivated by the pressure of Joshua's advanced age are implausible in a plot constructed from a single authorial perspective. Moreover DH has already given the command for allotment in 11:23.[1]

Joshua 13:1–7 shows evidence of internal literary development. The discontinuity between the line of thought of vv. 1 and 7 and that of vv. 2–6 is apparent.[2] The logic of v. 1 (the land that remains to be taken over or possessed) leads directly to v. 7 in which Joshua is commanded to divide up "this land" (so that it can be fully possessed). Verses 2–6 represent an excursus, exploring the extent of territory that remained outside the area of Israelite settlement and control. In v. 1 the reader encounters what one might call the "primary problem," which is resolved by the command of v. 7 to divide up the land so it can be taken over. However, in the intervening vv. 2–6, the reader is also led to explore a "secondary problem," the notion of "the land that remains." This refers to an idealized inheritance that will not be allotted and settled within the context of the book of Joshua. This secondary problem is resolved by the promise of 6a that Yahweh will eventually dispossess them. These primary and secondary problems are in turn held together by v. 6b: even though some land remains, Joshua is to get on with his task of allotment.

The description of the "land that remains" in vv. 2–6 is coterminous with neither the following tribal allotments nor the deuteronomistic conception of idealized borders.[3] It reflects instead a tradition of expansive borders over

---

1. Noth, *Josua,* 10, and *The Deuteronomistic History,* 40–41.

2. Both Noth, *Josua,* 73–74, and Smend, "Das Gesetz und die Völker," 497–500, agree that vv. 2–6 represent an interpolation.

3. The notion that the land of promise is entirely on the Canaan side of the Jordan is utterly undeuteronomistic, as pointed out by M. Weinfeld, "The Extent of the Promised Land—the Status of Transjordan," 67–68. The notion that Lebo-Hamath (the Entrance of Hammath) is the idealized northern extremity is also at odds with the deuteronomistic alternative of the Euphrates (Deut. 1:7; 11:24; Josh. 1:4).

much of Syria-Palestine also found in Num. 34:1–12 and Judg. 3:3. The "land that remains" is essentially "Canaan" as defined by the area of former Egyptian control minus the tribal allotments, that is, Philistia and territory in the north.[4] Verses 2–5 also contain later geographical expansions that are not easy to sort out, but which reveal the interest of later readers in the details of this theological geography. The notion of "land that remains" also accents the tension within the final form of Joshua concerning the extent of Israel's initial victory. Yahweh fulfilled completely the promise of a totally successful conquest (1:3–6; 11:23; 21:43–45; 23:1); however, some peoples remained unconquered (13:13; 15:63; 16:10; 17:12–13; 19:47). From the perspective of literary criticism, one might choose to read these contrasting evaluations as irony on the part of the narrator, undercutting the triumphalistic claims of total conquest.[5] Yet this is not the only place where the Hebrew Bible witnesses to the tension between lavish promise and restricted fulfillment or resorts to an "already, but not yet" paradigm to describe the paradoxical nature of God's good gifts.

Verses 1–7 follow a conceptual pattern already introduced by chapter 12, one which will provide the theological infrastructure for the chapters to follow. In this pattern, static geographic data is converted into active "salvation history" celebrating Yahweh's faithful gift of the land. In the case of 13:1–7, the theme of land which yet remains to be granted would have been particularly powerful in exilic and post-exilic times, when possession of the full extent of the land of promise was only a memory and a hope. Thus old bits of traditional geographic data were transformed into claims on the future. In such a context, these verses would call readers to faithful obedience, even while they had to wait for complete possession of the promise. Divide up what you have now and wait in faith for what remains, they are told (v. 6b).

[1] A subject-first sentence introduces a new topic. Yahweh's speech initiates the second movement of the book, marking the transition between conquest and colonization and raising the narrative problem that the following allotment will resolve. Joshua's age precipitates the problem. Although a transition in leadership is at hand, the land remains to be possessed. The syntax is emphatic: *you* are old, but *the land* remains to be taken over. Here the verb *yrš* has the force found in 18:3 or Judg. 2:6, not "seize" so much as "colonize." This leads to the imperative "divide up" of v. 7, but first a tangential subject follows, brought forward by a second understanding of *š'r* "remain." Verses 1 and 7 speak of land yet to be divided and settled. Verses 2–6 describe land not yet conquered.

[2–6]. Yahweh's speech veers away from the imperative that the reader expects after v. 1 to an intervening statement of geography. The description of

4. Aharoni, *Land of the Bible,* 67–77, 263–39; Na'aman, *Borders and Districts,* 39–73.
5. For example Eslinger, *Into the Hands of the Living God,* 25–54; Polzin, *Moses and the Deuteronomist,* 126–34.

"the land that remains," in the sense of "remains to be conquered," partially follows the form of a "from . . . to" line of extent. This formula fixes terminal points in order to define the territory that extends between them.[6]

The description focuses on three successive zones: a southern area of Philistines, Geshurites, and Avvites (vv. 2–3), a second area of uncertain location with its inland border in common with some group of Amorites (v. 4), and a northern region consisting of Lebanon (v. 5). Subsequent additions have somewhat obscured this three-part structure:

> in the south, a list: the districts of the Philistines, Geshurites, and Avvites (v. 2, the last word of v. 3)
> > a supplement, what is considered Canaanite: from the Shihor to the border of Ekron (v. 3a)
> > a supplement listing the five rulers of the Philistines (v. 3b)
> all the Canaanite land: from Arah to Aphek to the border of the Amorites (v. 4)
> all Lebanon from Baal-gad to Lebo-hamath (v. 5)
> > a supplement: the Gebalites (first words of v. 5)

The south zone is reasonably clear (see text note a). These Avvites are also mentioned in Deut. 2:23 as living near Gaza, that is, between Egypt and Philistia. The second, "Canaanite" zone cannot be located with confidence. The restored place name Arah is unknown. If either the Aphek in the Sharon (12:18) or the one near Acco (19:30; Judg. 1:31) is intended, this would be coastal Palestine. However, since the intended area is likely to be farther north, this would be the Aphek northeast of Beruit (T. Afqa 231382). The third zone, Lebanon, follows traditional formulas for this region (compare Judg. 3:3; 2 Kings 14:25; Ezek. 47:15–16; Amos 6:14) and relates to the north border of the "land of Canaan" in Num. 34:7–8. Baal-gad marks the northern limit of Israelite conquest in the Lebanon in 11:17 and 12:7, so here it is seen as the southern point from which the line of extent runs north.[7]

Yahweh indicates an idealized and expanded vision of promised territory that stretches far north of Palestine. This corresponds ideologically to other visionary descriptions such as Deut. 1:7 and Josh. 1:4, as well as to the fabled expanse of the hegemony of David and Solomon (1 Kings 8:65; 1 Chron. 13:5). If "the Shihor" of v. 3 is to be understood as an eastern arm of the Nile, the southern limit would be pushed even beyond the traditional "Brook of

---

6. See Aharoni, *Land of the Bible,* 86–87. Compare 12:1–3; 13:16, 26; Num. 13:21; Deut. 11:24. For a nonbiblical example, see the treaty text from Sefire, I B, lines 9–10, in W. Beyerlin, *Near Eastern Religious Texts Relating to the Old Testament,* OTL, Philadelphia, 1978, 260.

7. For Lebo-hamath see B. Mazar, "Lebo-hamath and the Northern Border of Canaan," *The Early Biblical Period: Historical Essays,* Jerusalem, 1986, 189–202, and Aharoni, *Land of the Bible,* 71–72.

Egypt."[8] From a pedestrian historical standpoint, this territorial sweep represents almost pure promise, never matched by reality.

In v. 6a, Yahweh's promise, stressed by a first-person pronoun, solves the problems raised by this geography lesson. A description that approximately parallels the northern third zone serves as the direct object of Yahweh's promise. This summary, again in a north-to-south "from . . . to" format, apparently depends on the narrative of 11:8. It understands Misrephoth-maim to be the northernmost extent of Joshua's conquest and thus the southernmost point of the remaining territory. The object-subject-verb word order strongly highlights the topic of these unconquered peoples. Taking the certainty of promise as a given (see text note f), Joshua's present task in v. 6b is simply to cast the lots (niphal of *npl*) for Israel's inherited property. The problem of the land that remains and Yahweh's promise will take care of itself. The current responsibility of Israel's leader is merely to obey. This echoes the spirit of Deut. 29:28 [29E].

[7] With *we'attâ* the text returns to the resolution of the situation set forth in v. 1 and recasts the imperative of v. 6. Joshua is to divide "this land," that is the land of v. 1. This partition will commence in chapter 14. First, however, mention of the nine and one-half tribes triggers yet another detour in the shape of a review of what took place under Moses (vv. 8–33).

The Tribes
East of the Jordan
Joshua 13:8–33

Introduction

13:8 As for the other half tribe of Manasseh,[a] together with it the Reubenites and Gadites had taken their hereditary property which Moses had given them across the Jordan to the east, just as Moses the servant of Yahweh had given them: **9** from Aroer which is on the rim of the Wadi Arnon and the town which is in the middle of the wadi, and the entire plateau of Medebah to Dibon; **10** and all the cities of Sihon king of the Amorites who ruled in Heshbon, to the border of the Ammonites; **11** and Gilead and the territory of the Geshurites and Maacathites, and all Mount Hermon, and all Bashan to Salecah; **12** the entire kingdom of Og in Bashan, who ruled in Ashtaroth and in Edrei. (He survived from the remainder of the Rephaim.)

---

8. See N. Na'aman, "The Shihor of Egypt and Shur That Is before Egypt," *TA* 7 (1980): 95–110.

Moses had struck down and dispossessed them. 13 But the Israelites did not dispossess the Geshurites or the Maacathites, so Geshur and Maacath still live among Israel to this day. 14 It was only to the tribe of Levi that he did not give hereditary property. [The offerings by fire of][b] Yahweh the God of Israel is their hereditary property, just as he promised to them.[c]

For Reuben

15 Moses provided[d] for the tribe of [the children of] Reuben for their clans. 16 Their territory[e] extended from Aroer which is on the rim of the Wadi Arnon and the town which is in the middle of the wadi, and the entire plateau to[f] 17 Heshbon, and all its cities which are on the plateau: Dibon, Bamoth-baal, Beth-baal-meon, 18 Jahaz, Kedemoth, Mephaath, 19 Kiriathaim, Sibmah, Zereth-shahar on the hill of the valley, 20 Beth-peor, Ashdoth-pisgah,[g] and Beth-jeshimoth—21 that is[h] all the cities of the plateau and the entire kingdom of Sihon king of the Amorites who ruled in Heshbon,[i] whom Moses struck down with the leaders of Midian, Evi, Rekem, Zur, Hur, and Reba, princes[j] of Sihon who lived in the land.

22They [the Israelites] killed with the sword Balaam son of Beor the fortuneteller in addition to those slain.[k] 23 The border of [the children of] Reuben was the Jordan and its adjacent territory.[l] This was the hereditary property of Reuben for their clans, the cities and their precincts.[m]

For Gad

24 Moses provided [to the tribe of Gad][n] for the children of Gad for their clans. 25 Their territory was Jazer and all the cities of Gilead and half the land of the Ammonites to Aroer which is near Rabbah; 26 and from Heshbon to Ramath-mizpeh and Betonim, and from Mahanaim to the territory of Lidebir;[o] 27 and in the valley Beth-haram, Beth-nimrah, Succoth, and Zaphon, the rest of the kingdom of Sihon king of Heshbon, the Jordan and its adjacent territory to the end of the Sea of Chinnereth on the other side of the Jordan eastward. 28 This was the hereditary property of the children of Gad for their clans, the cities and their precincts.

For Manasseh

29 Moses provided for the half-tribe of Manasseh [and it was for the half-tribe of the children of Manasseh][p] for their clans. 30 Their territory was from Mahanaim, all Bashan, the entire kingdom of Og king of Bashan, and all the tent villages of Jair that are in Bashan, sixty cities. 31 Half of Gilead, and Ashtaroth and Edrei, the cities of the kingdom of Og in Bashan

belonged to the children of Machir son of Manasseh, to half of the children of Machir for their clans.

32 These are what Moses apportioned in the plains of Moab on the other side of the Jordan east of Jericho. [33 But to the tribe of Levi Moses did not give hereditary property. Yahweh the God of Israel is their hereditary property, just as he promised to them.][q]

a. Follows a shortened form of OG (compare NJB). MT lost this phrase along with a piece of v. 7 by homoioteleuton (see text note h on 13:7). The reconstruction of what was lost is uncertain. Although the Greek is expansive: "As for the two tribes and the half tribe of Manasseh," LXX^B fails to reflect "with it." See Barthélemy, *Critique,* 28–30.

b. Not present in OG or v. 33 MT. MT expanded and changed the original plural pronouns (see OG and v. 33) to singular to harmonize with Deut. 18:1–2. See text note q.

c. At this point OG adds a summarizing statement similar to v. 32: "And this is the hereditary property which Moses apportioned to the Israelites in the plains of Moab on the other side of the Jordan opposite Jericho." There is no mechanism to explain its loss, so the shorter MT is preferable. The text behind OG seems to have felt a need for a formal heading to vv. 15–31 similar to that provided for the west Jordan tribes at 14:1.

d. Translating *ntn* without a direct object.

e. In this context *gĕbûl* must indicate "territory" rather than "border" (as in Josh. 1:4). These lines of territorial extent do not make sense as boundaries.

f. Follows OG in omitting "Medeba." MT may be explained as a slightly misplaced gloss on "plateau" influenced by v. 9. The translation also follows OG and other witnesses in reading the preposition "up to" *'d* for MT *'l.* Beyond this, it is difficult to determine the text behind the Greek translation; Margolis, *Joshua in Greek,* 254.

g. Given the context, this seems be a town name here, although "slopes of Pisgah" is a more general geographic designation elsewhere (Deut. 3:17; Josh. 12:3).

h. Taking the *waw* as explanatory or explicative.

i. Follows MT. OG lost "who ruled in Heshbon" by haplography from *'ăšer* to *'ăšer*. To untangle the Greek witnesses for the rest of the verse, see Margolis, *Joshua in Greek,* 257–58, and Greenspoon, *Textual Studies in the Book of Joshua,* 138–40.

j. Alternate translation: "vassals."

k. Follows MT. For "slain," OG apparently had the noun *tropē* "rout," translating the root *ḥwl/ḥyl*. See Margolis, *Joshua in Greek,* 259, and Holmes, *Joshua, the Hebrew and Greek Texts,* 57.

l. The translation here and in v. 27 takes the *gĕbûl* of the Jordan to mean its associated territory. See also 12:3–4 and 15:12, 47.

m. This translation for *ḥāṣēr* tries to encompass both "enclosed space" and "suburban settlement." The word probably has the second meaning in chapters 15–19, but stone sheep enclosures may be intended here.

n. MT conflates "the tribe of Gad" given by S and "the children of Gad" found in OG, the latter reading being preferable as less expected.

o. Follows MT instead of the better-known "Debir" given by OG, S, and V. The versions may have taken the initial *lamed* as a preposition without translating it or it may have dropped out because of the final *lamed* of the previous word. This would be the same place as Lo-debar (2 Sam. 9:4, etc.).

p. MT adds a conflate doublet with a different word for "tribe."

q. MT repetitive expansion. In this expansion MT reflects the original (that is, OG) text of v. 14, without "offerings by fire" and with the plural pronoun suffixes.

Because the book of Joshua is concerned with the entire nation, land distribution includes all the tribes. The logic of chronology means that the eastern tribes have to be dealt with first. These tribes were significant both to DH and to the redactor who added chapters 13–19. DH introduced them immediately following the opening commands (1:12–18), again at the Jordan crossing (4:12), and in the conquest summary (12:1–6). DH returns to them again as a focus of interest just before Joshua's farewell (22:1–6). In the final form of the book they continue to punctuate the main (western) story line: 13:8–33; 20:8; 21:36–39; 22:7–34. This preoccupation was more ideological than practical. By the time of the DH, much of the territory described had been lost for generations. Reuben's allotment north of the Arnon had been Moabite since the mid-ninth century and Gilead was an Assyrian province after 732. Although one may suppose some sort of interest in the east bank region in the time of Josiah, these geographic notices remain utopian and idealistic. The notion of Reuben as an substantive reality would have long since been only a memory, and the territory assigned to it here is as much the result of editorial schematization as genuine tradition. It is significant that Reuben is conspicuously missing from both David's census (2 Sam. 24:5–6) and the Mesha Inscription.

Several forms of territorial data[1] are combined here: the kingdoms of Sihon and Og, the traditional Aroer/Arnon boundary, generalized lines of extent, and city-lists for Reuben and Gad. Lines of extent in the "from . . . to" pattern are found in vv. 9, 16, and 26. These were used to represent territories in an imprecise way: Exod. 23:31; Num. 21:24; 2 Sam. 24:2. City-lists, in contrast, are thought to have had an administrative purpose. The city-lists for Reuben and Gad (vv. 17–20, 27) seem to be related in some way to the Solomonic districts VII and XII.[2]

Verses 9–12 form a prelude to the more detailed presentation of vv. 15–32, summarizing generally what the rest of the chapter surveys by individual tribe. Both sections have the same overall movement: from the Arnon border (vv. 9, 16) to Gilead (vv. 11, 25, 31) to Bashan (vv. 11, 30), as well as from Sihon (vv. 10, 21, 27) to Og (vv. 12, 30). The predominant direction of movement is from south to north. This initial summary is connected to what follows by a network of repeated proper names: Aroer, Sihon, Gilead, Bashan, Og, Ashtaroth and

---

1. Detailed topographic studies are offered by S. Mitmann, *Beiträge zur Siedlungs- und Territorialgeschichte des Nördlichen Ostjordanlandes*, Wiesbaden, 1970, 231–46, Ottoson, *Gilead: Tradition and History*, 118–35, and Wüst, *Untersuchungen zu den siedlungsgeographischen Texten*.

2. 1 Kings 4:14, 19. See Aharoni, *Land of the Bible*, 314; Kallai, *Historical Geography*, 65, 69–72.

Edrei, Heshbon, Mahanaim. This gives the reader the impression of solidarity and common heritage.

Fixed introductions ("Moses provided," "their territory was" vv. 15–16, 24–25, 29–30) and conclusions ("this was the hereditary property" vv. 23, 29) give unity and structure to vv. 15–32. Manasseh lacks its own conclusion. Instead v. 32 serves as the conclusion for the whole, forming with v. 8 an envelope for the larger unit. The phrases "for their clans" in the introductions and "cities and precincts" in the conclusions forge links to the west Jordan tribes in chapters 15–19, where these expressions are common. Repetition connects the eastern tribes together:

> "the entire kingdom of Sihon," Reuben (v. 21)
> "all the cities of Gilead," Gad (v. 25)
> "the rest of the kingdom of Sihon," Gad (v. 27)
> "half of Gilead," Manasseh (v. 31)

and

> "from Aroer . . . to Heshbon," Reuben (vv. 16–17)
> "from Heshbon . . . and from Mahanaim," Gad (v. 26)
> "from Mahanaim . . . , " Manasseh (v. 30)

The three territories are described with decreasing attention to detail. For Reuben there is an overall description of extent in the "from . . . to" format (v. 16), followed by a twelve-item city-list, (vv. 17–20), followed by a catalog of enemies (vv. 21b–22). For Gad there is a generalized area description (v. 25) followed by a four-item city-list (v. 27a) embedded in a complex "from . . . to" description of extent (vv. 26, 27b). The report for Manasseh is the least detailed.

Joshua 13:9–32 apparently derived some of its content from Deut. 3:8–17 and Josh. 12:2–6. Thus 13:9–11 reflects expressions from Deut. 3:10a, 12, and Josh. 12:2, 5, while 13:12 echoes Deut. 3:10b–11a and Josh. 12:4, 6. Another example of literary dependence is v. 30, which collapses the "tent cities of Jair" from Deut. 3:14 into Og's sixty cities (Deut. 3:4). This is followed by the somewhat startling topic of Machir (v. 31), apparently triggered by Deut. 3:15.[3] Numbers 32:34–38 offers parallel city-lists for Reuben and Gad, but describes a different distribution of settlement, one probably closer to the facts. There Reuben centers around Heshbon, while Gad is settled throughout the area.

Here traditions of geography support territorial claims and undergird national identity. Judges 11:13–27 provides a literary reflection of how geographic traditions could have functioned as land claims in actual life. There Jephthah uses Israel's conquest of Sihon and its consequent claim to the territory north of the Arnon against the Ammonites. Songs containing geographic

---

3. For the literary growth of this section, see Noth, *Josua*, 73–79, and Wüst, *Untersuchungen zu den siedlungsgeographischen Texten*, 40, 221–39.

and conquest traditions are used to make similar claims in Num. 21:13–15, 26–30. Perhaps comparable songs preserved some of the items of traditional geography reported here. Recopied school texts or a literary work like the "Book of the Acts of Solomon" could have preserved administrative city-lists.

[8] Once again Moses provides Joshua with a model for obedience. Mention of the western half-tribe of Manasseh in v. 7 provides the opening for a somewhat awkward transition to a flashback about the eastern half-tribe and its neighbors. A subject-first word order foregrounds Reuben and Gad as a new topic. Verse 8 reiterates the act of Moses, underscoring his fundamental role in allocating their territory (compare 1:14–15; 22:4).

[9–12] This summary section piles up traditional geography, but without the precision found in vv. 15–32. The geographic skeleton of vv. 9 and 11 has been enriched by history in vv. 10 and 12. However, a degree of organization is provided by describing three large areas. The first of these is a line of extent from the Arnon northward around the Medeba plateau, continuing back around south to Dibon (v. 9). The Aroer/Arnon boundary was significant as Israel's disputed frontier with Moab and thus is often cited (12:2; 13:16; Deut. 3:16; 2 Sam. 24:5). The "town in the middle of the wadi" may refer to some location halfway along the valley toward the Dead Sea, or perhaps to an otherwise unknown suburb of Aroer in the canyon itself. In this latter case, the formula intends to say that the center of the canyon was the border (as apparently in Deut. 3:16 and Josh. 12:2).[4] The second area is north of the first, consisting of all Sihon's former cities eastward to the Ammonite border (v. 10). The third area is further north again, a wide expanse of several territories (Gilead, Geshurites and Maacathites, Hermon, Bashan) eastward to Salecah (v. 11). In describing this last area (v. 12), the text makes reference to Og's former kingdom, offers an excursus about Og, and reminds the reader that it was Moses who defeated "them" (that is Sihon and Og).

[13–14] The text digresses to specify the first of two exceptions to this general picture. Triggered by a mention of the territory of the Geshurites and Maacathites in v. 11, v. 13 carefully excludes these two groups, in harmony with Deut. 3:14 and Josh. 12:5. For Israel's relations with them in the Davidic monarchy, see 2 Sam. 3:3; 10:6. Levi, in an emphatic grammatical position, constitutes the second exception, and the circumstances of Levi's special case are set forth (v. 14).

[15–23] The following descriptions are more concrete than the preceding condensed summary. The reader is not to understand each bit of geographic data as a distinct item, for the text piles up parallel descriptions for the same areas, creating an impression of completeness and amplitude. The statements

---

4. 2 Sam. 24:5 (read with LXX^L representing OG) shows that this phrase eventually become little more than a conventionalized complement to Aroer.

that these allocations were "for their clans" is more than just rote formula. Clans, as endogamous kinship units, had as one of their chief functions the preservation of land tenure. For example, it was the clan's duty to redeem and restore land for its constituent families.[5]

For Reuben a line of extent is drawn northward from the Arnon line to Heshbon (v. 16). Then a city-list (vv. 17–20) follows. This list first covers the west of the region, then skips to the east (v. 18), and ends in the northwest (vv. 19–20). A title and inclusio for the list is provided by the repeated identification of these places as cities on or of "the plateau" (vv. 17 and 21).[6] Many of these locations are mentioned in the Mesha Inscription for the very same reason that they occur here, to strengthen a land claim. Because this territory was certainly Moabite after the ninth century,[7] by the time of this chapter's composition its claims would have been more utopian than realistic. Moreover the territory here assigned exclusively to Reuben was also inhabited by Gad.[8] Therefore the tidy split of this territory between Reuben and Gad is also artificial. Perhaps this partition was based on the old Solomonic districts. Reuben was simply assigned what had been the twelfth district and Gad the seventh (1 Kings 4:14, 19).

There is a deviation from geographical description to conquest tradition in v. 21b–22, triggered by the reference to Sihon's kingdom in v. 21a. The text amalgamates Sihon with material about the five kings of Midian and Balaam taken up from Num. 31:8.

[24–28] Gad's territory consists of two lines of extent and a city-list, supplemented by more generalized references. Verse 25 begins by vaguely cataloging three zones: Jazer, Gilead, and half of the Ammonite territory up to Aroer (a different Aroer from that of vv. 9, 16). Here "Gilead" denotes only the territory south of the Jabbok, in contrast to v. 31; 12:2, 5; and Deut. 3:12–13.[9] In v. 26a the first line of extent runs from Heshbon (thus coupling with Reuben's line, vv. 16–17) to Ramath-mizpeh and Betonim. The second (v. 26b) runs north of the

---

5. Lev. 25:23–28, 41, 49; Num. 36:6–12. See C. de Geus, *The Tribes of Israel*, Amsterdam, 1976, 133–56; Gottwald, *The Tribes of Yahweh*, 257–337.

6. Originally "on the plateau" and "on the hill of the [Jordan] valley" (now attached to Zereth-shahar in v. 19) were probably district names in an administrative city list. A third district from the same list apparently continues in v. 27 under the rubric "in the valley." See the discussion in Fritz, *Josua*, 143–44. A similar list of Moabite place names, also identified with the term "plateau," was available to the editors of Jeremiah (Jer. 48:21–24). In addition, Jer. 45:8 may refer to the districts "valley" and "plateau."

7. Mesha Inscription; Isa. 15:2, 4, 9; 16:8–9; Jer. 48:1–2, 19, 21–24, 32, 34; Ezek. 25:9.

8. Mesha Inscription, lines 10–11. Dibon is Dibon-gad in Num. 33:45, and Heshbon is a levitical city of Gad in Josh. 21:39.

9. This discrepancy, along with that of Gad's possession of half of Ammon, which contradicts v. 10 and Deut. 2:16, is solved with a conjectural emendation by B. Oded, "A Note on Josh xiii 25." *VT* 21 (1971): 239–41. Probably successive expansions have created this muddle. See Fritz, *Josua*, 145 and Wüst, *Untersuchungen zu den siedlungsgeographischen Texten*, 145–74.

first from Mahanaim to Lidebir/Lodebar. In addition a west border extends northward along the Jordan to the Sea of Galilee (v. 27b). Verse 27 also adds "the rest of the kingdom of Sihon" as a parallel designation for areas already covered in v. 25. The city-list (v. 27a) has only four items, running south to north in the Jordan Valley. This list seems to be titled "in the valley," apparently the designation for some sort of administrative district in the Jordan Valley. This provides a parallel to the apparent district names "on the plateau" and perhaps "on the hill of the valley" that occur in Reuben's city-list (vv. 17, 19). Zaphon is recorded as a clan of Gad in Gen. 46:16 and Num. 26:15.

[29–31] Manasseh's territory is described vaguely, without either a complete line of extent or a city-list, and in no discernable order. The delineation begins "from Mahanaim" as does the second line of extent for Gad, but tends northwestward from there to embrace Bashan and the zone of Jair. This generally corresponds to Solomon's sixth district (1 Kings 4:13). There is no terminus for this line. "Half of Gilead" (v. 31) refers to the portion of Gilead north of the Jabbok. This is in harmony with the usage of 12:2, 5, but contrasts to v. 25 where the term Gilead is restricted to Gad's territory.

After mention of Og's capital cities, attention abruptly narrows to the clans of Machir east of the Jordan. This transition is awkward, bridged in modern translations with phrases like "these were allotted" (NRSV) or "in other words."[10] The expression "half of the children of Machir" indicates that elements of this major clan were also present west of the Jordan (as perhaps indicated by Judg. 5:14). This interest in the details of Manassehite clan structure is picked up again in 17:1–3.

Prelude to the Distribution
Joshua 14:1–15

Introduction to the Allocation of Canaan

14:1 These are the inheritances the Israelites received in the land of Canaan, which Eleazar the priest and Joshua son of Nun and the heads of the families of the tribes of the Israelites apportioned to them. 2 Their hereditary property was by lot[a] just as Yahweh had commanded through Moses to the nine and one-half tribes. 3 Indeed[b] Moses had given the hereditary property of the two and one-half tribes[c] on the other side of

10. Boling, *Joshua*, 333.

the Jordan, but he did not give any hereditary property among them to the Levites. 4 It was because the descendants of Joseph were two tribes, Manasseh and Ephraim, that they[d] did not give the Levites a section in the land, except cities to live in and their pasture land for their cattle and their flocks. 5 The Israelites did just exactly what Yahweh had commanded Moses and divided up the land.

Caleb and Hebron

6 The children of Judah approached Joshua in Gilgal and Caleb son of Jephunneh the Kenizzite said to him, "You know the word Yahweh spoke to Moses the man of God in Kadesh-barnea about you and me. 7 I was forty years old when Moses the servant of Yahweh sent me from Kadesh-barnea to scout out the land. I brought him back a report of what I really thought.[e] 8 My companions who went up with me made the people's heart melt, but I remained loyal to Yahweh my God. 9 So Moses swore on that day, 'Surely the land on which your foot has stepped shall be hereditary property for you and your children forever, because you remained loyal to Yahweh my God.' 10 So now, here Yahweh has let me live, just as he promised. It is forty-five years since Yahweh spoke this word to Moses while Israel journeyed in the wilderness. So now, here I am today eighty-five years old. 11 I am just as strong today as I was the day Moses sent me out. My strength for war then was as my strength is now for going out and coming back.[f] 12 So now, give me this hill country, which Yahweh promised me that day, for[g] you yourself heard that day that the Anakim are there with large fortified cities. Perhaps[h] Yahweh will be with me[i] and I shall dispossess them, just as Yahweh promised."

13 So Joshua blessed him and gave Hebron to Caleb son of Jephunneh as hereditary property. 14 Therefore Hebron still belongs to Caleb son of Jephunneh the Kenizzite as hereditary property today, because he remained loyal to Yahweh the God of Israel. 15 Formerly the name of Hebron was Kiriath-arba. He was the greatest man[j] of the Anakim. And the land had rest from war.

a. Repointing the first word to start a new sentence. The Masoretic pointing as a construct ("by the lot of their inheritance") takes this as the conclusion of the previous sentence (compare NAB, JPSV).

b. Construes *kî* as emphatic adverb, Waltke and O'Connor, *Hebrew Syntax*, 39.3.4e.

c. Follows MT. OG suffered a haplography at the start of this verse from "half-tribe" to "half-tribe."

d. Indefinite "they," equivalent of the passive.

e. Literally "I brought him back a word just as was with my heart."

f. This idiom implies vigor in both military and ordinary pursuits (1 Sam. 29:6 or 2 Kings 11:8). Compare JPSV: "for battle and for activity."

g. There are several ways to construe this verse. Here (as NRSV) the first *kî* is understood as causal. The Anakim menace motivates Caleb's request. Another possibility is to take this first *kî* as concessive and connect the thought to Caleb's intention to attack them: "Though you too heard on that day that the Anakim are there . . . , if only the LORD is with me, I will dispossess them" (cf. JPSV). NAB attaches the first *kî* to Yahweh's promise in v. 12a, then understands the second *kî* as emphatic: ". . . as you yourself heard. True, the Anakim are there . . . , but if the Lord is with me I shall be able to drive them out."

h. This is intended to be a hopeful, expectant statement (Gen. 16:2).

i. Correcting the problematic object pronoun *'ôtî* to the preposition with pronoun suffix *'ittî*.

j. Follows MT, referring to the one for whom the city was named. OG "metropolis" translates *h'm hgdwlh*, "the great mother [city]" (cf. OG at 15:13; 21:11). The designation "mother" for an important city is found in 2 Sam. 20:19 and perhaps is reflected in Metheg-ammah (2 Sam. 8:1).

Verses 1–2, 5 seem ready to begin the land distribution that the reader has been expecting since 13:7. Yet there are two more digressions to cover before the main act can begin, the Levites (vv. 3–4) and Caleb (vv. 6–15).

[1–5] Verse 1a functions as the heading for the apportionment that follows in chapters 15–19: "These are . . . in the land of Canaan." The repetition of much of v. 1 by 19:51 brackets the entire distribution process within an envelope structure. To this core sentence are attached all sorts of supplementary data intended to clarify and explain, so that the result is a rather baroque accumulation of details.[1] Verse 1b specifies that those who executed the distribution were precisely those set forth in Num. 32:28 (cf. Num. 34:16–29). The participation of Eleazar (also 19:51; 21:1; 24:33) reflects priestly interests. Verse 2 defines the lot as the method for apportionment, as commanded in Num. 26:55 (cf. 33:54; 34:13), and specifies the recipients as the nine and one-half tribes. This last reference then triggers a contrastive flashback to Moses and the eastern tribes in v. 3a, highlighting in turn a different agent, different recipients, and a different locality.

In a further digression, the Levites are emphatically excluded from the distributions made by either Moses or Joshua and Eleazar (vv. 3b-4). In v. 4 the causal clause comes first in the sentence, followed by what is being explained: because Joseph gave rise to two tribes, no territory was given to Levi. This somewhat peculiar logic is more mathematical than theological, in contrast to other places where Levi's lack of inheritance is mentioned (e.g. 13:14). Here because twelve is assumed to be the fixed number of possible inheritances, Levi's exclusion rests on its thirteenth position. Interest in the cities and pastures of the Levites is paralleled by Num. 35:1–8 and points forward to chapter

---

1. On the literary growth of these verses, see Auld, "Textual and Literary Studies in the Book of Joshua," 415–17; Wüst, *Untersuchungen zu den siedlungsgeographischen Texten*, 202–205.

21. Verse 5 returns to the main topic, orienting the reader to the coming action and underscoring the theme of obedience. Now the focus is not exclusively on the obedience of Joshua (contrast 13:7), but on that of the entire nation. The text presses the theme of legitimate inheritance, using the root *nḥl* five times. A second theme is obedience, stressed by repetition of the "obedience formula" in vv. 2b and 5a.[2] Israel follows precisely what was laid down in Num. 32:28–32. Any apparent deviations, such as the upcoming endowment to Caleb, in no way compromise Israel's obedience to the divine plan. The lot, which will figure prominently in coming chapters, is likewise a token of obedience. It too was a feature of Yahweh's command (Num. 26:55–56) and, as is proper, is attended to by the priest Eleazar. The traditional tribal borders are therefore not optional or due to historical contingency, but the result of Yahweh's gracious guidance.

[6–15] This account follows a pattern repeated several times in Joshua (Achsah, 15:18–19; the daughters of Zelophehad, 17:3–6; Joseph, 17:14–18; Levi, 21:1–3). These five narratives move from a *confrontation* to a statement of a *case and request* to a *grant of land,* and usually conclude with a *summary* of the results. The genre label "land grant narrative" has been chosen here to order to describe their content without presuming too much about their origin and transmission. All four elements of the pattern appear in four of the five stories:

confrontation: 14:6a; 17:3–4aA; 17:14a; 21:1
case and request: 14:6b–12; 17:4aB; 17:14b–16; 21:2
    flashback to Moses: 14:6a–9; 17:4aB; 21:2
land grant: 14:13; 17:4b; 17:17–18a; 21:3
    reference to Yahweh's command: 17:4b; 21:3
summary of results: 14:14–15; 17:5–6; 17:18b; 21:41–43[3]

These stories are intended to justify land tenure by pointing back to an endowment by an authorized figure (such as Joshua or Caleb) to an ancestor and by setting forth a case that legitimates the claim to ownership. Such narratives would also build group identity around the figure of the ancestor making the claim (Caleb, Achsah/Othniel, Mahlah and her sisters) or the territory possessed (Hebron, springs, wooded hill country). Such land grant narratives would likely have had their social setting in the practice of storytelling on the

2. This formula is frequent in Joshua: 1:7, 13; 4:10; 7:11; 8:27, 31, 33, 35; 10:40; 11:12, 15, 20; 21:8.

3. Although the tale of Caleb's grant to Achsah is only two verses long (15:18–19), it still contains the first three elements: confrontation (v. 18), request and case (v. 19a), and land grant (v. 19b). Dialogue plays a central narrative role in that example, and in 17:14–18 as well. Numbers chapter 32 is also a land grant narrative. It reflects the same outline, but is filled out with even more dialogue: confrontation (vv. 1–2), case and request (vv. 3–5), land grant (v. 33), summary of results (vv. 34–38).

clan and village level. Two examples operate on the tribal level (Joseph, Levi), but the second, at least, seems to be a literary imitation of the traditional genre. This land grant narrative provides an etiology for why Caleb's descendants control Hebron. Because Kenaz is sometimes associated with Edom (Gen. 36:11, 15, 42) and the Kenizzites are once listed among non-Israelite nations (Gen 15:19), Caleb's identification as one may indicate that the background of his clan was foreign to mainstream Judah. If so, the need for such an etiology would be all the more pressing. Yet the tale as told also participates in the genre of legend or example story in that Caleb is presented as a model of straight talk and fidelity to Yahweh. This is underscored by the threefold repetition of a special loyalty formula (vv. 8, 9, 14), apparently firmly attached in tradition to the figure of Caleb (Num. 14:24; 32:12; Deut. 1:36). There is also some evidence that Caleb's name "dog" would have suggested fidelity and self-abasement to one's god or overlord.[4]

The fabled semidivine (Num. 13:33) Anakim giants must have played a role similar to such figures in other cultures. They functioned as hairraising characters in folktales (Goliath) and as explanations for megalithic artifacts (compare the "bed" of Og of the Rephaim, Deut. 3:11). Their mention here provides a delicious irony for the alert reader, for it was the fear of these very Anakim that had originally terrified Israel's previous generation into disobedience (Num. 13:28; Deut. 1:28).

Verse 6a (*confrontation*) establishes the setting and characters. Although the children of Judah play no further role in the narrative, their presence is a redactional indicator that Caleb's story is intended to be the first part of the larger Judah allotment. The Gilgal setting, which is also soon forgotten (since "this hill country" in v. 12 implies a location near Hebron), performs much the same function.

The narrative emphasis rests on Caleb's rhetorical statement of the *case* (vv. 6b–12). Caleb's argumentation centers on the story of his loyalty. The distinctive loyalty formula, literally "to follow Yahweh fully," is first asserted by Caleb (v. 8), then confirmed in turn by Moses (v. 9) and the narrator (v. 14).[5] Caleb's noble act of fidelity led Moses to promise what Joshua ought now to fulfill. Caleb refers to himself repeatedly (vv. 7–8, 10–11), because his own straightforward character and loyal behavior make up the core of his argument. Supporting ar-

---

4. D. Thomas, "Kelebh 'Dog': Its Origin and Some Usages of It in the Old Testament," *VT* 10 (1960): 410–27; G. Botterweck, "*keleb*," *TDOT* VII, 146–57. The issue continues to be discussed: G. Brunet, "L'Hébreu Kèlèb," *VT* 35 (1985): 485–88; O. Margalith, "KELEB: Homonym or Metaphor?" *VT* (1983): 491–95.

5. Or "fulfill [something] in obedience to Yahweh." According to Rose, *Deuteronomist und Yahwist*, 264–66, who sees Caleb as originally a non-Israelite military hero, this phrase was originally connected to holy war. He points out that there is a progression of usage here from loyalty to Caleb's God (v. 8b) to Moses' God (v. 9b) to Israel's God (v. 14b).

guments are his great age (surely after forty-five years[6] I should get what is coming to me!), his abiding vigor and military competence, and the troublesome presence of the Anakim. Rhetorical skill is portrayed in Caleb's care to include Joshua into his story ("about you and me," v. 6; "you yourself heard," v. 12), the sharp contrast drawn between Caleb and his fainthearted companions (v. 8), and his appealing, hopeful modesty ("perhaps Yahweh will be with me," v. 12). The prestige of Moses' oath is bolstered by the prophetic title "man of God" (v. 6). Verse 11 works to overcome any possible flaw in Caleb's case introduced by mention of his great age. Word order stresses that Caleb is still as strong as ever.[7] That his capacities now are just what they once were is emphasized by balanced repetition: "today/the day . . . then/now." As his argument moves from retelling the past (vv. 6b–9) to describing present conditions (vv. 10–12), Caleb increases the urgency of his case by repeating "so now, look" (v. 10) and then turns to his request with a third "so now" (v. 12). At times his speech becomes overloaded and uncoordinated, communicating urgency and passion to the reader.

The story reaches its *resolution* in Joshua's response of blessing and bestowal (v. 13). Blessing in the Hebrew Bible effects a powerful transfer of continuing success and material prosperity. In fact, the word "blessing" is the the lexical equivalent of a land grant in the Achsah story (15:19). Here Joshua's power-laden blessing provides a positive answer to Caleb's hopeful "perhaps" of the previous verse. Verses 14–15 explore some of the *results* of this climax. The loyalty formula is repeated once more. Further information of interest about Hebron is supplied. The redactional "to this day" formula[8] underscores the purpose of this tale, to assert Israel's claim to this town. The repetition of the formula "the land had rest from war" from 11:23 has the effect of a cross-reference, directing attention back to the wider topic of the successful conquest reported in earlier chapters in preparation for the upcoming allocation of the land.

Somewhat at odds with the pro-Caleb tone of this narrative, however, is a curious counter-movement. There is an increasing restriction of the territory under discussion from "the land on which your foot has stepped" promised by Moses (v. 9; quoted from Deut. 1:36) to "this hill country" with its "cities" requested by Caleb (v. 12) down to the single city of Hebron granted by Joshua (v. 13). The reader senses a certain polemic flavor in this, as though the narrator wishes to modify Caleb's wild claims, while still affirming his legitimate prerogatives. This would be expected in a story once peculiar to one clan, but transmitted later by a more inclusive group. Within the fabric of the story itself are internal tensions between the notions of conquest (vv. 12, 15b) and of land division (vv.

6. Allowing for forty years in the wilderness, this yields a five-year period for the conquest.

7. Caleb was remembered for this in Sir. 46:9–10.

8. Its redactional character is clear, as shown by Childs, "A Study of the Formula 'Until this Day,' " 287. However, this observation does not undercut the etiological purpose of the land grant narrative.

13–14), reflecting its awkward redactional placement. On the one hand the conquest of Hebron has already been reported (10:36–37) and the Anakim wiped out (11:21–22; contrast 14:12). On the other hand, Caleb's conquest of Hebron will be reported again in 15:13–14, making 14:13–14 sound premature.

This narrative has a close relationship to 11:21–23, probably indicating its literary dependence on that passage. The topic of Anakim, the locale of Gilgal, and the repetition of 11:23 in v. 15, all suggest this. There are other contacts with the larger story of Joshua. Verse 9 echoes the promise of success given to Joshua in 1:3. Joshua 21:11 will remind the reader of this story when reporting about the levitical cities. The mention of Gilgal provides the reader with the only notice of a locale for the upcoming land division until the scene shifts to Shiloh in chapter 18. There are also contacts to the larger canonical story, especially to Caleb's mission and promise (Numbers 13–14), and verbal ties to Deut. 1:22–36.

The Caleb story reflects theological themes common to Joshua. Like Caleb, Israel's ancestors followed Yahweh's plan obediently and faithfully and thus gained title to the land. Even if now the shadow of loss and disobedience has fallen over the gift of the land, the people's renewed fidelity could still lead to the fulfillment of divine promise. Caleb's loyalty to Yahweh serves as a stirring example, which if followed might lead to Yahweh's renewed presence (v. 12), blessing (v. 13), and the land's rest from war (v. 15). After the Babylonian conquest, Hebron and the territory around it fell prey to the encroaching Edomites and became part of Idumea (1 Macc. 5:65; 14:33), although some Jews apparently still lived there as well (Neh. 11:25). The loss of this city, so intimately associated with the patriarchs and David, may explain the special attention given to it in the book of Joshua. Hebron belonged to Yahweh's people, and they did not intend to forget it.

Judah
Joshua 15:1–63

The Border of Judah

15:1 The lot[a] for the tribe of [the children of] Judah for their clans extended southward to the border of Edom, the wilderness of Zin being the southern limit.[b] 2 Their south border extended from the end of the Salt Sea, from the bay which faces south.[c] 3 It goes south from the ascent of Akrabbim, crosses to Zin, goes up south of Kadesh-barnea, crosses by Hezron, goes up to Addar, and turns toward Karka. 4 It crosses to Azmon and goes by the Wadi of Egypt. The border ends at the sea. This will be your[d] south border.

5 The east border is the Salt Sea as far as the mouth of the Jordan.

The border on the north side extends from the bay of the sea at the mouth of the Jordan. 6 The border goes up to Beth-hoglah and crosses north of Beth-arabah. The border goes up to the Stone of Bohan the son of Reuben. 7 The border goes up to Debir^e from the Valley of Achor northward, turning to Gilgal,^f which is opposite the ascent of Adummim, which is south of the wadi. The border crosses to the waters of En-shemesh and ends at En-rogel. 8 The border goes up by the valley of the son of Hinnom to the slope of the Jebusite on the south (that is, Jerusalem). The border goes up to the top of the mountain that is opposite the valley of Hinnom on the west, which is at the north end of the valley of Rephaim. 9 The border turns from the top of the mountain to the Waters of Nephtoah spring and goes to the ruins of^g Mount Ephron. The border turns toward Baalah (that is, Kiriath-jearim). 10 The border turns westward from Baalah to Mount Seir, crosses to the slope of Mount Jearim on the north (that is, Chesalon), goes down to Beth-shemesh, and crosses by Timnah. 11 The border goes to the slope of Ekron on the north. The border turns toward Shikkeron, crosses Mount Baalah, and goes to Jabneel. The border ends at the sea.

12 The west border is the Great Sea^h and its shoreline. This is the border of the Judahites surrounding their clans.

Caleb's Section

13 He gave a section among the children of Judah to Caleb son of Jephunneh according to Yahweh's command to Joshua: Kiriath-arba (who was father of Anak), that is, Hebron.^i 14 Caleb dispossessed from there the three sons of Anak: Sheshai, Ahiman, and Talmai [the offspring of Anak].^j 15 Then he went up from there against the inhabitants of Debir (formerly the name of Debir was Kiriath-sepher). 16 Caleb said, "Whoever strikes Kiriath-sepher and captures it, I will give him Achsah my daughter as wife." 17 So Othniel son of Kenaz, Caleb's brother, captured it, and he gave him Achsah his daughter as wife. 18 Now it happened that when she arrived she prodded him into asking for a field from her father.^k When she got down off her donkey, Caleb asked her, "What do you want?" 19 She said, "Give me a blessing because you have given me arid land,^l so give me pools of water." So he gave her the upper pools and the lower pools.

The Cities of Judah
in Districts

20 This is the hereditary property of the tribe of the children of Judah [for their clans].^m 21 The outlying cities of the tribe of the children of Judah were up to the border of Edom.

In the Negeb:
Kabzeel, Arad,[n] Jagur,
22 Kinah, Dimonah, Ararah,[o]
23 Qedesh, Hazor-ithnan,[p]
24 Ziph, Telem, Bealoth,
25 Hazor-hadattah, Kerioth-hezron (that is, Hazor),
26 Amam, Shema, Moladah,
27 Hazar-gaddah, Heshmon, Beth-pelet,
28 Hazar-shual, Beersheba and its daughter towns,[q]
29 Baalah, Iim, Ezem,
30 Eltolad, Chesil,[r] Hormah,
31 Ziklag, Madmannah, Sansannah,
32 Lebaoth, Shilhim, En-rimmon.[s]
[In all,] twenty-nine cities and their precincts.[t]
33 *In the lowlands:*
Eshtaol, Zorah, Ashnah,
34 Zanoah, En-gannim, Tappuah, Enam,
35 Jarmuth, Adullam, Socoh, Azekah,
36 Shaaraim, Adithaim, Gederah, and Gederothaim.[u]
Fourteen cities and their precincts.
37 Zenan, Hadashah, Migdal-gad,
38 Dilan, Mizpeh, Jokthe-el,
39 Lachish, Bozkath, Eglon,
40 Cabbon, Lahmas, Chitlish,
41 Gederoth, Beth-dagon, Naamah, and Makkedah.
Sixteen cities and their precincts.
42 Libnah, Ether, Ashan,
43 Iphtah, Ashnah, Nezib,
44 Keilah, Achzib, and Mareshah.
Nine cities and their precincts.
45 Ekron, its daughter towns and precincts.
46 From Ekron toward the sea—everything which was near Ashdod
and its precincts.
47 Ashdod, its daughter towns and precincts. Gaza, its daughter towns
and precincts as far as the wadi of Egypt and the Great Sea and its
shoreline.
48 *In the hill country:*
Shamir, Jattir, Socoh,
49 Dannah, Kiriath-sannah[v] (that is, Debir),
50 Anab, Eshtemoh, Anim,
51 Goshen, Holon, and Giloh.

Eleven cities and their precincts.
52 Arab, Dumah, Eshan,
53 Janum,ʷ Beth-tappuah, Aphekah,
54 Humtah, Kiriath-arba (that is, Hebron), and Zior.
Nine cities and their precincts.
55 Maon, Carmel, Ziph, Juttah,
56 Jezreel, Jokdeam,ˣ Zanoah,
57 Kain, Gibeah, and Timnah.
Ten cities and their precincts.
58 Halhul, Beth-zur, Gedor,
59 Maarath, Beth-anoth, and Eltekon.
Six cities and their precincts.
59A Tekoah, Ephrathah (that is, Bethlehem), Peor,
Etam, Koulon, Tatam, Sores,
Karem, Gallim, Bether, and Manahath.
Eleven cities and their precincts.ʸ
60 Kiriath-baal (that is, Kiriath-jearim) and Rabbah.
Two cities and their precincts.
61 *In the wilderness:*
Beth-arabah, Middin, Secacah,
62 Nisbhan, the City of Salt, and En-gedi.
Six cities and their precincts.
63 However, the children of Judah were not able to dispossess the Jebusites, the inhabitants of Jerusalem.ᶻ So the Jebusites still live [with the children of Judah] in Jerusalem today.

a. Follows MT. OG here and at 16:1; 17:1 has *gbwl* "border," apparently to harmonize with 18:5–10, which seems to indicate that lots were not actually cast until then. The same variation occurs in 21:20, 40. For the opinion that OG is the better text in these passages, see Auld, "Textual and Literary Studies," 416–17.

b. Follows MT. OG ("from the wilderness of Zin to Kadesh southward") may have used Num. 20:16 and perhaps Num. 34:3–5 to clarify a confused text. Alternate translation: "the Wilderness of Zin toward the south, from the limit of Teman" (Fritz, *Josua,* 154).

c. Perhaps this is not a "tongue of water" or "bay" as here, but a tongue of land as JPSV: "the tongue that projects south," presumably referring to the Lishan peninsula.

d. Follows MT as the more difficult reading. OG harmonizes the awkward pronoun into "their."

e. Follows MT. OG ("upon the fourth of the valley") reflects a confusion in letters between *dbrh* "Debir" and *rb'h* "four."

f. Follows MT. OG lacks "northward" and reads "went down" for the unique use of "turn." Although MT is presumably corrupt, involving a dittography in *ṣpwnh pnh* "northward turning," the textual evidence is not clear enough to permit correction. The name of the border point is uncertain because 18:17 has "Geliloth" ("districts") rather than the enigmatic "Gilgal," which in any case cannot represent the better-known crossing point. Alternate translation: "Achor, and then turns northward to Gilgal" (cf. REB, JPSV).

g. Follows OG, represented here by the Lucianic recension and Theodotion which have *ga(e)i*, a witness to '*yy* "ruins of" instead of the less likely MT '*ry* "cities of." See Greenspoon, *Textual Studies in the Book of Joshua*, 76–78 and Barthélemy, *Critique*, 34–35. Compare the note on 18:15 below. BHS is misleading in asserting that OG omits "cities of," because LXX^B represents a corruption of OG at this point.

h. Correcting MT *ym hymh hgdwl* to *ymh hym hgdwl* as implied by T.

i. Follows MT. OG corrects by eliminating Joshua as the recipient of Yahweh's command and by specifying Joshua as the explicit subject of the verb "gave." Where MT has "father" OG has "mother" in the sense of chief city, an error caused by the graphic similarity of *b* and *m* and perhaps bolstered by the OG reading of 14:15.

j. MT doublet or expansion from Num. 13:22.

k. The narrative of MT creates some perplexity in that Achsah urges her husband to a task that she herself goes on to perform. LXX^AB reduces the tension by reading, "She prodded him saying, 'I shall ask my father for a field.'" The Lucianic recension (and OG and V of Judg. 1:14) read "he prodded her to ask," which alleviates the problem in another way (adopted by REB and NJB). MT is preferable as difficult but not impossible. See Barthélemy, *Critique*, 35–36.

l. Literally "land of the Negeb." This translation assumes that the verb is taking a double object: a direct object ("arid land") and a "datival" object ("me"). See Waltke and O'Connor, *Hebrew Syntax*, 10.2.3b. Other translations construe only "me" as the object: "you have set me in the land of the Negeb" (NRSV), or, assuming a word play concerning marriage, "you have given me away as Negeb-land," that is, without a dowry (JPSV).

m. MT expansion from 15:1, 12.

n. Follows OG. MT has transposed the letters to the otherwise unknown "Eder" ('*dr*).

o. That is, '*r'rh* (Kh. 'Ar'arah) as suggested by OG. MT has "Adadah."

p. MT has two separate names here.

q. That is, *wbnwtyh* based on OG and Neh. 11:27. MT has "Biziothiah."

r. Because this name is displaced by "Bethul" in 19:4 MT (cf. 1 Chron. 4:30), the OG reading "Baithel" here is best explained as a harmonization.

s. In agreement with OG and Neh. 11:29 (cf. Josh. 19:7). MT has two names, "Ain and Rimmon."

t. MT and OG both give the figure twenty-nine, but list thirty-six and thirty cities respectively. The reconstructed text totals thirty-three, from which one might choose to remove the four compound toponyms with "Hazor/Hazar" ("enclosure of . . .") to achieve twenty-nine actual cities.

u. OG *wgdrtyh* "and its sheepfolds" reduces the number of cities from the fifteen towns of MT to the total of fourteen specified in this verse. The Greek may be an interpretive translation based on the same text as MT.

v. Follows MT as preferable, although perhaps incorrectly glossed as Debir (Noth, *Josua*, 92). The more expected alternate name for Debir, Kiriath-sepher (cf. 15:15), is given by OG and S. Against MT it could be argued that Kiriath-sannah is a corruption caused by the preceding name Dannah.

w. Follows the MT Qere, LXX^A, V, T. The Kethib is "Janim."

x. Alternately "Jorkeam" as LXX[B] and 1 Chron. 2:44. There has been metathesis and confusion of *r* and *d*.

y. Follows OG. These eleven names were lost in MT due to homoioteleuton. The Hebrew forms are in some cases conjectural.

z. Follows MT and Judg. 1:21. OG offers a smoother text without the introductory direct object marker: "The Jebusites dwelt in Jerusalem and the children of Judah were not able to dispossess them," which A. G. Auld, "Judges I and History: A Reconsideration," *VT* 25 (1975): 274–75, considers original.

Owing to the author's southern perspective, Judah naturally comes first and has far more space devoted to it than to any other tribe. Its idealized land claims are based on three sorts of data: a tribal boundary description (vv. 1–12),[1] an etiological narrative involving the clans of Caleb and Othniel (vv. 13–19), and a list of towns grouped by royal administrative provinces (vv. 20–62).[2] From a form-critical perspective, boundaries delineate between administrative units or tribal claims. They are intended to foster good relations and reduce tensions. Sequences of border points can be found only in Joshua and Num. 34:1–12 ("the land of Canaan"). In distinction, town lists organize administrative units for taxation or conscription. In origin and function they are similar to the register of Solomonic district officials found in 1 Kings 4:7–19.

What one might call "boundary Judah" represents a reality somewhat different from "town-list Judah." "Boundary Judah" lacks Danite Eshtaol and Zorah, which are part of "town-list Judah" (v. 33), yet includes the Benjaminite town of Beth-arabah (v. 6; and perhaps Beth-hoglah, see 18:21), Philistia, and cities assigned in another town list to Simeon (19:2–7). "Boundary Judah" represents traditional tribal concerns, but it probably does not actually represent any genuine historical situation. For example, the boundary description carefully excludes Jerusalem from Judah, but does not really provide enough territory on the south for either the pre-Davidic

1. Literature on the boundaries is extensive. The most important references are A. Alt, "Das System der Stämmesgrenzen im Buche Josua," *Kleine Schriften* I, Munich, 1953, 193–202: Aharoni, *Land of the Bible*, 248–60; Kallai, *Historical Geography*, 99–312; Na'aman, *Borders and Districts*, 75–117; M. Noth, "Studien zu den historisch-geographischen Dokumenten des Josuabuches," *Aufsätze zur biblischen Landes- und Altertumskunde* I, Neukirchen-Vluyn, 1971, 229–80, and "Überlieferungsgeschichtliches zur zweiten Hälfte des Josuabuches," *Festschrift F. Nötscher*, BBB 1, 1950, 152–67.

2. On the Judahite district system see A. Alt, "Bemerkungen zu einigen *judäischen* Ortslisten des Alten Testaments," *Kleine Schriften* II, Munich, 1953, 289–305, and "Judas Gaue unter Josia," 1925, *Kleine Schriften* II, 276–88; Aharoni, *Land of the Bible*, 347–56; F. Cross and G. Wright, "The Boundary and Province Lists of the Kingdom of Judah," *JBL* 75 (1956): 202–26; Kallai, *Historical Geography*, 372–404; N. Na'aman, "The Kingdom of Judah under Josiah," *TA* 18 (1991): 3–71; Noth, "Studien zu den historisch-geographischen Dokumenten des Josuabuches," 229–80; J. Svensson, *Towns and Toponyms in the Old Testament*, ConBOT 38, Stockholm, 1994, 29–59.

city-state nor the urban territory of the monarchic pair "Judah and Jerusalem." Moreover, we know of no pre-monarchic structure to which such a system of boundaries could credibly be ascribed. Only the United Monarchy could provide a need for a boundary system that encompasses both south and north, and such a date is often advanced. Similar border descriptions are found in 16:1–8; 17:7–10; 18:12–20; 19:10–14, 22, 25–29, 33–34, and scholars often assume that they all come from the same administrative system. Such a system would presumably have to predate the districts established by Solomon (1 Kings 4:7–19). However, one must seriously question whether the survival of such ancient inventories of border points is more likely than their later construction as a learned scribal enterprise.[3]

In contrast, the town list is clearly taken from an older source that goes back to an actual administrative situation. "Town-list" Judah goes beyond the traditional tribal borders to include Dan and part of Benjamin. It is generally agreed that Judah's town list is part of the same system as the two Benjamin districts preserved in 18:21–28. Scholars have suggested various periods in the history of Judah for this structure, but the expansionistic reign of Josiah seems most likely. The boundary description and town list may have been transmitted to later generations as list texts for educational purposes or in a literary work analogous to the "Book of the Acts of Solomon" (1 Kings 11:41).

[1–12] This may have once been a static list of border points,[4] but verbs descriptive of the border's course have turned it into a "quasi-narrative": goes, crosses, goes up, turns, goes down. Although the appearance of an actual narrative is suggested at first by the lot and the consecutive verbs of vv. 1 and 2, the sentences soon dissolve into a timeless delineation by means of simple *waw* perfects and verbless sentences. Directional modifiers are included to indicate either the course of the running line or its position in relation to some locality. It is not always easy to tell which option is intended, so that some boundary sections remain in dispute.

First the south border is described in an east to west direction (vv. 1–4). Then the east border is quickly taken care of by v. 5a with a subject-first verbless sentence. Another subject-first sentence begins the most critical border, the one with Benjamin on the north (vv. 5b–11). This is described in the greatest detail, again from east to west. The same data, with omissions and variant verbs, will be used to delineate Benjamin's southern border in the opposite direction in 18:15–19. The west border is briefly dealt with by

---

3. See Na'aman, *Borders and Districts*, 91–92.

4. The secondary nature of the verbs is made clear by a comparison of parallel texts, for example, vv. 1–4 with Num. 34:3–6 and vv. 5–10 with 18:15–20. This was strongly emphasized by Noth, "Überlieferungsgeschichtliches zur zweiten Hälfte des Josuabuches," 161–64.

v. 12a in a way parallel to v. 5a. Verse 12b provides a concluding statement (cf. 18:20).

The south border (vv. 1–4) is parallel to the border of "the land of Canaan" presented in Num. 34:3–6 and the north border of "the land that remains" in 13:4–5. Coordinating v. 2 with Num. 34:3 indicates that "the bay which faces south" was on the east side of Dead Sea, so that the border curves around the south end of the sea before heading west. The south border points can be identified with strong probability. The "Wadi of Egypt" is certainly the Wadi el-'Arish. There is controversy as to whether the delineation set forth in Numbers was derived from Joshua chapter 15 or whether both go back to a pre-Israelite conception of the land of Canaan.[5] However, in either case this border represents an ideological rather than an administrative description.

The north border (vv. 5b–11) parallels much of the south border of Benjamin. Some sort of presence for Reuben west of the Jordan is suggested by the Stone of Bohan (or "Thumb Stone") in v. 6. Debir in v. 7 and Timnah in v. 10 should not be confused with their namesakes further south (15:15, 49, 57). Border points are given in greatest density around Jerusalem (v. 8) because this part of the line was naturally of greatest interest. The designation of Jerusalem as "the Jebusite" may be a learned scribal flourish rather than the preservation of an ancient name.[6] Jerusalem is carefully excluded from Judah, but the line runs very tightly around the south of the city. "The Waters of Nephtoah spring" is usually thought to be the Spring of Merneptah mentioned in *ANET,* 258. The extension of this border all the way to the sea (v. 11), so that it includes Philistia, adds a note of idealism (compare vv. 45–47).

[13–19] This narrative occurs in parallel transmission at Judg. 1:10–15, where dispossessing the three sons of Anak is expanded to become the deed of all Judah. In Joshua, the story exists in redactional tension with 10:38–39, where Debir has already been conquered.

Although the overall action of this story is clear, there are substantial difficulties with translation. The grammatical subject of v. 13 is apparently supposed to be Joshua, but it could conceivably be the "lot" of v. 1 (that is, "it gave") or an impersonal pseudo-passive: "a section was given." In v. 18 the verb *swt* presumably denotes "seduce," "tempt," or "prod," although it seems peculiar that Achsah herself will go on to make the very request she

5. Noth, *Numbers,* 247–50, considers the material in Joshua to be primary. Aharoni, *Land of the Bible,* 69–77, and Na'aman, *Borders and Districts,* 62–65, think of the extent of the Egyptian province of Canaan.

6. The use of this gentilic form in various places as an alternate name for Jerusalem has generated much discussion. See Kallai, *Historical Geography,* 136–37, 396–97; J. Miller, "Jebus and Jerusalem: A Case of Mistaken Identity," *ZDPV* 90 (1974): 115–27.

here induces her new husband to make (see text note k).[7] It is also not clear whether "land of the Negeb" in v. 19 is to be taken as a literal geographical designation or metaphorically as "arid land" generally (see text note l). "Pools of water" is literally "bowls of water," taken by the Greek translator as a place name. Most problematic of all is the verb *ṣnḥ* in verse 18 and the parallel Judg. 1:14. Generally translated almost solely on the basis of context as "get down,"[8] the verb has also been taken as "clap hands" in order to make a noise to get attention.[9] Either of these proposed translations could fit the only other use of this verb in Judg. 4:21 ("bang down" or "go down"). The notion of making a sound seems to be supported by the Greek translation, but the OG may simply be following a different text (from *ṣwḥ* "shout" or *ṣrḥ* "yell") or guessing at an unknown word. The traditional translation "get down" adopted here fits the narratival situation as reflected in Gen. 24:64 and 1 Sam. 25:23.[10] In any case, Achsah's action simply provides the narrative opportunity for Caleb's inquiry, so that one can still understand the story even without fully grasping this verb's meaning.

The narrative of vv. 12–19 makes a land claim involving two related Kenizzite clans. Through it the Othniel clan laid claim to Debir and to two springs. The narrative originally explained why those springs, which were associated in some way with Caleb's town Hebron, instead belonged to Othniel. These claims are first set forth as distribution and conquest reports for Hebron and Debir (vv. 13–17). Verse 13 seems to assume the reader has already encountered 14:13 and the narrative of Joshua's grant to Caleb. The archaic place names and the three Anakim giants (compare a similar expression in 2 Sam. 21:16, 18) add an exotic and heroic touch. The details of v. 14 seem to be taken from Num. 13:22, 28.

The reward of a wife for Othniel (vv. 16–17) leads into a little land grant narrative plot in vv. 18–19. On this form-critical category, see the exposition of 14:6–15. The plot breaks down into *confrontation* (v. 18), *case and request* (v. 19a), and *grant* (v. 19b). Achsah, whose name echoes the provocative sound of anklets (Isa. 3:16, 18), entices her new husband into asking for a field in addition to what he has captured. This may refer to some lost element in the traditional story that receives no follow-up in the present

7. Noth, *Josua*, 86, and Soggin, *Joshua*, 161, delete the suffix to get "she decided to ask her father," which adds nothing to the story line. P. Mosca, "Who Seduced Whom? A Note on Joshua 15:18; Judges 1:14," *CBQ* 46 (1984): 18–22 follows the grammar of 2 Sam. 24:1 and suggests yet another solution: "she beguiled him [Caleb] by asking from her father." B. Lindars, *Judges 1–5*, Edinburgh, 1995, 28–29, proposes the translation "she plotted with him to ask."

8. KB³ 972.

9. This is based on an Aramaic cognate and an interpretation found in *b. Tem.* 16a.

10. On this problem see A. Gibson, "*ṣnḥ* in Judges I 14: NEB and AV Translations," *VT* 26 (1976): 275–83; Lindars, *Judges 1–5*, 29–31; E. Nicholson, "The Problem of *ṣnḥ*," *ZAW* 89 (1977): 259–65.

form of the story, for she goes on to ask for pools, not a field. Perhaps v. 18a is simply a preliminary scene intended to reveal to the reader her generally acquisitive mood. Upon arrival, she dismounts from her animal as is appropriate for interacting with her male social superior (Gen. 24:64 and 1 Sam. 25:23). Her act provides Caleb with the opportunity to question her. Her case and request is based on a need for water and is set out in balanced poetic form (v. 19a):

> Give to me a blessing,
> for an arid land you gave me,
> so give to me pools of water.

Later generations would base their claim to territory lost to the Edomites after the destruction of Judah upon these traditions of the conquest of Hebron and Debir and of Caleb's wedding gift to Achsah. This tale shares several themes with the other land grant narratives in Joshua. For one thing, it illustrates that the ancestors obediently carried out what Moses and Yahweh had commanded (vv. 13–19; 14:6, 9; 17:4). A more subtle theme rests on the narrative circumstance that such land grants often resulted from attempts to solve problems and disputes (v. 19; 17:3, 14–18). This indicates that even in the foundational period, Yahweh's gift of the land was to some degree provisional and required a continuing struggle on the part of the people to realize it completely (v. 16; 17:18).

[20–63]. Verses 20–21a and 63 frame a town list from the kingdom of Judah. The heading of v. 20 connects Judah to a web of similar formulas for the other tribes: 13:23, 28; 16:8; 18:20, 28; 19:8, 16, 23, 31, 39, 48. A similar set of headings and a summary encompasses the land division for the whole people: 13:32; 14:1; 19:51. These formulas reflect editorial efforts to unify material from various sources (districts east of the Jordan, districts of the kingdom of Judah, northern tribe town lists, and so forth) into a single story with a national horizon. Verse 21a provides an explanatory introduction to the Negeb district. Although for the readers of the final form of Joshua this territory was no longer part of Judah, it is explained that in past generations Judah's domain ran south right up to Edom's previous border.

Verse 63 concludes with a sobering notice and etiological formula which shows continuing awareness of Jerusalem's distinctive history and ethnic makeup (cf. Ezek. 16:3, 45). Here, as in 16:10 and 17:12, total success is blocked. The object-first syntax emphasizes that non-Israelites remained at strategic locations. What is seen here as Judah's responsibility is laid upon Benjamin in Judg. 1:21, which contrasts Benjamin's failure with Judah's achievement in Judg. 1:8. The assignment of Jerusalem to Judah here contradicts both the boundary descriptions (15:8; 18:16) and the Benjaminite town list (18:28).

In its present form, the list of Judahite towns is organized into twelve units. These units are summarized by summary totals of "cities and their precincts."[11] The exception is vv. 45–47 (Philistia), which also differs stylistically in being an expansive description rather than a list. For this reason, vv. 45–47 must be seen as an artificial construction and not part of the source catalog of Judah's administrative districts. This artificial district was probably added to round out the list to a total of twelve after the Benjaminite data was transferred to 18:21–28. Thus the Philistia district should be seen as a result of the editorial process that converted material about the *kingdom* of Judah into a description of the *tribe* of Judah. Ekron, Ashdod, and Gaza are listed, but surprisingly not Ashkelon, a circumstance which, if one knew what to make of it, might help date the addition. The twelve district units are distributed among four larger geographical headings: "in the Negeb" (one district), "in the lowlands" or Shephelah (four districts including the Philistia district), "in the hill country" (six districts), and "in the wilderness" (one district). These groupings also go back to the original monarchical administrative system.[12]

A full discussion of this district system is beyond the scope of this commentary, but a few comments are in order. The question of possible overlap between Benjaminite and Judahite districts is raised by the presence of shared place names and the tiny size of the district described in v. 60. One problem centers on the presence of "Kiriath-baal (that is, Kiriath-jearim)" in Judah district X (v. 60) and "Kiriath-jearim" in the southwest Benjamin district (18:28, restored text). Rather than joining these two districts into one, it is better to understand Kirath-baal and Kiriath-jearim as two separate but nearby places. Kiriath-baal (18:14; Baalah, 15:9; Baale-judah, 2 Sam. 6:2) was in Judah, and Kiriath-jearim (9:17; 1 Sam. 7:1–2) was in Ben-

---

11. The translation "precincts" attempts to hold together the two senses "enclosure" and "surrounding area" for the noun *ḥāṣēr*.

12. In assigning numbers to these districts one must first decide whether vv. 45–47 (Philistia) made up one of the original districts. Noth asserted that at least Ekron represents a district, as a sort of place marker for the Danite towns which were saved for later (19:41–46). However, his enumeration, which counts vv. 45–47 as district V, is usually rejected, as in Alt's suggestion to include the Danite towns of 19:41–46 as a district in its own right. There is general agreement on the enumeration and extent for districts I through IX (vv. 21b–59A), and the number (but not the extent) assigned to district X (v. 60). For the remaining Benjaminite districts (18:21–24 and 25–28) problems are created by the question of how to coordinate them into the system. The southwest Benjamin district (18:25–28) was jointed to district X by Alt, Noth, and Cross and Wright, but considered a separate district by Aharoni and Fritz, *Josua*, 162–68 (who sees the v. 60 district as artificial). The northeast Benjamin district (18:21–24) was joined to the wilderness district (15:61–62) by Alt and Noth, but considered a separate district by Cross and Wright, Aharoni (who leaves it outside the system), and Fritz. Kallai is unique in proposing three separate Benjaminite districts, one of which has been lost.

jamin.[13] A second problem is created by Beth-arabah, which occurs both in the northeast Benjamin district (18:22) and in Judah's wilderness district (district XI; 15:61). This led Alt and Noth to propose that 15:61–62 and 18:21–24 originally made up a single district. This, however, is completely unlikely from a geographic standpoint. A better explanation for this overlap is that the northeast Benjamin district (18:21–24) was added to the system at a later stage, leading to a revision of the previous extent of the wilderness district. All the data is explained in the simplest way by postulating that a twelve-district system limited to the kingdom of Judah (15:21b–62 as eleven districts and 18:25–28 as one district) was later expanded by a thirteenth district in Benjamin (18:21–24) at the time of Josiah's expansion into the Assyrian province of Samaria. This new expansion district significantly included Bethel and Geba (2 Kings 23:8, 15) and absorbed Betharabah from the north edge of the former wilderness district. Thus in addition to the eleven districts enumerated below, one should consider 18:25–28 as district XII and 18:21–24 as an expansion district XIII. Consult the appendix for generally accepted site identifications.

I. Negeb district
(vv. 21b–32)

There is an overlap with the Simeon town list (19:2–7): Moladah, Beer-sheba, Hormah, and En-rimmon. Madmannah and Sansannah are probably the same as Beth-markeboth and Hazar-susah in the Simeon list at 19:5. Shilhim (v. 32) is usually taken to be a variant of the Simeonite Sharuhen of 19:6.

II. North lowlands district
(vv. 33–36)[14]

Zorah and Eshtaol are north of the Judah border and part of the Dan list in 19:41.

III. South lowlands district
(vv. 37–41)

Solid (although not undisputed) identifications are Lachish and Eglon. The

---

13. This assumes that the Judahite town was incorrectly glossed as Kirath-jearim at 15:9 and 18:14.

14. Many towns from districts I and II appear in the list found in Neh. 11:25–30, but the nature of this intertextual relationship is unclear. For the hypothesis that the Nehemiah material is dependent in some way on Joshua, see J. Blenkinsopp, *Ezra-Nehemiah. A Commentary*, OTL, Philadelphia, 1988, 328–32. On the three lowlands districts, see A. Rainey, "The Biblical Shephelah of Judah," *BASOR* 251 (1983): 6–11.

precise delineation of this district and district IV depends on several disputed identifications, especially for Makkedah and Libnah. It is unclear whether district III was south of district IV (Aharoni) or west of it (Kallai). Zenan (Zaanan) and Lachish from district III and (Beth-)achzib and Mareshah from district IV are mentioned in the catalog of Micah 1:10–16.

IV. Central lowlands district
(vv. 42–44)

Ether and Ashan also appear in the Simeon list (19:7). These are the only two Simeonite towns that lie outside of district I.

V. South hill country district
(vv. 48–51)

Districts V to X "in the hill country" move generally south to north. Arad Ostracon 25 indicates that Anim represents twin towns, an upper and lower one.

VI. Hebron hill country district
(vv. 52–54)

VII. Ziph hill country district
(vv. 55–57)

District VII continues VI to the east of the central watershed. Perhaps Zanoah and Kain should be taken as "Zanoah of Kain," thus differentiated from the Zanoah of v. 34. "Kain" is not present in OG.

VIII. Beth-zur hill country district
(vv. 58–59)

Beth-anoth was apparently the locale of a temple to the goddess Anath at some period.[15]

IX. Bethlehem hill country district
(v. 59A LXX)

This district is directly north of VIII. The Hebrew forms behind Koulon,

15. See A. G. Auld, "A Judean Sanctuary of 'Anat (Josh 15:59)." *TA* 4 (1977): 85–86. Compare Beth-anath in Naphtali and Anathoth.

Tatam, Sores, and Gallim are uncertain. Manahath is proposed on the basis of the Calebite clan in 1 Chron. 2:52, 54; 8:6. Bether, although not mentioned elsewhere in the Bible, is to be identified with the capital of Bar-Kochba.

X. Kiriath-baal hill
country district (v. 60)

This district is smaller than the others, but perhaps contained more towns than the two named.

XI. Wilderness district
(vv. 61–62)

This covers the Dead Sea area from En-gedi north to Beth-arabah.[16]

Although scholarship has tended to focus on the historical origin of this geographical material, its function in the final shape of the book of Joshua should not be ignored. Judah's district system has been transferred from the realm of bureaucracy to that of theology and from pre-exilic reality to post-exilic aspiration. The large number of toponymic glosses demonstrates that later readers took a continuing interest in this text (vv. 8–10, 13, 15, 49, 54, 60). The quantity of space granted to Judah supports the central role of that tribe's heirs in Yahweh's plan. The mind-numbing detail of the list hammers home their legitimate title to the land, concretized in location after location. The point is that Yahweh gave these territories to the readers' ancestors. The naming of each town serves as a claim on the land, especially on those areas that had fallen into Edomite or other hands. The people's hope in the future is focused on the land of promise described in its most minute detail.

Ephraim
Joshua 16:1–10

16:1 The lot for the children of Joseph went out from the Jordan near Jericho eastward to the waters of Jericho, going up by the wilderness from Jericho to the hill country of Bethel.[a] 2 It goes from Bethel to Luz and crosses to the border of the Archites at Ataroth. 3 It goes down westward

16. On the evidence of the Copper Scroll (3Q15), Qumran is likely to be the site of Secacah rather than of the City of Salt, as is sometimes suggested. See H. Eshel, "A Note on Joshua 15:61–62 and the Identification of the City of Salt," *IEJ* 45 (1995): 37–40.

to the border of the Japhletites as far as the border of Lower Beth-horon and as far as Gezer.[b] It ends at the sea. 4 The children of Joseph, Manasseh and Ephraim, received their hereditary property.

5 This was the territory of the children of Ephraim for their clans. The border of their hereditary property extended from Ataroth-adar[c] on the east as far as Upper Beth-horon. 6 The border goes to the sea. Michmethath is on the north.[d] The border turns east of Taanath-shiloh and crosses by it[e] east of Janoah.[f] 7 It goes down from Janoah to Ataroth and to Naarah, touches Jericho, and goes to the Jordan. 8 From Tappuah the border goes westward by the Wadi Kanah. It ends at the sea. This is the hereditary property of the tribe of [the children of] Ephraim for its clan, 9 along with cities set apart for the children of Ephraim within the hereditary property of the children of Manasseh, all the cities and their precincts. 10 But they did not dispossess the Canaanites who lived in Gezer, so the Canaanites still live within Ephraim today. They were used for forced labor.[g]

a. This verse follows MT. OG lost "to the waters of Jericho" through haplography from "Jericho" to "Jericho." At several points in vv. 1–6, OG represents a text "improved" by omissions and rearrangements. In this verse OG has "desert" in a less troublesome place and moves *lwzh* "to Luz" forward from v. 2 to serve as a synonym for Bethel. These differences may go back to a Hebrew text or may represent translational maneuvers. In either case, the awkward MT remains preferable. Alternate translations are possible. The border may go "east of the waters of Jericho" or "to the waters of Jericho east of the wilderness," and further on, "from Jericho through the hill country to Bethel" or "through the hill country of Bethel."

b. Follows MT. OG lacks "as far as Gezer" here, but adds "and Gezer" at the end of v. 5.

c. Follows MT. OG has Ataroth-orek, "Ataroth of the Archites" here and at 18:13, presumably an assimilation to v. 2. Alternate translation: "their hereditary property on the east was Ataroth-adar." In any case, the sentence refers to a section of the border running from the east point Ataroth westward to Beth-horon.

d. Follows MT. LXX[B] adds "Therma" as another border point, which Margolis, *Joshua in Greek,* 324–35, related to Tormah of Judg. 9:31. Alternate translation: "and the border goes out westward to the north of Michmethath."

e. The masculine object pronoun in reference to a town is problematic. Perhaps the territory of the town is intended. Or perhaps either "the Michmethath" (note the definite article) or "Taanath-shiloh" ("the fig tree of Shiloh") was a geographical landmark rather than a town.

f. This translation is based on the usual reconstruction of the course of the boundary. Running eastward, it curves north around the east side of Taanath-shiloh (Kh. Ta'na el-Foqa), then backtracks southwestward past the domain of Taanath-shiloh to reach east of Janoah (Kh. el-Yanun). Alternate translation following Na'aman, *Borders and Districts,* 152–57: "then the border turns eastward toward Taanath-shiloh and passes it on the east toward Janoah."

g. Follows MT. OG appends material about Pharaoh's capture of Gezer from 1 Kings 9:16. OG lacks the notice about forced labor, either because it was displaced by the OG addition or because the phrase is a MT expansion. It is also absent from Judg. 1:29.

This border description is hard to translate due to the disconnected list nature of the original source and the fragmentary manner in which it was utilized. It is often difficult to decide if a given directional word is intended to refer to the bearing of the line or to its relation to one of the fixed border points. Because of this and because so many of the site identifications are uncertain, only the overall outlines of these boundaries are intelligible.[1] Verses 1–3 correspond to the description of the same border in vv. 18:12–13, as do vv. 6–8 to 17:7–9, which clarifies matters to some extent. As in chapter 15, the verbal structure begins with *waw*-consecutive narrative tenses (vv. 1, 2, and a new beginning at v. 5), then moves into more timeless verbal patterns translated here with the present tense.

This chapter forms a single unit with chapter 17, held together by the common topic of Joseph as a tribal grouping.[2] This pan-Joseph perspective is set forth in the description of the south border in vv. 1–4 and picked up again in 17:14–18. The two chapters portray the situations of Ephraim and Manasseh in parallel configurations. Each border description (16:5–8; 17:7, 9–10) is followed by territorial exceptions or technicalities (16:9; 17:8, 11), then by an observation about persisting Canaanite populations (16:10; 17:12–13). Land grant narratives (see commentary on 14:6–15) for certain Manasseh clans (17:3–6) and then for the Joseph group as a whole (17:14–18) complete the pattern. It is striking that the sequence given in 16:4 is first Manasseh and then Ephraim. This, along with the remark about Manasseh's first-born status in 17:1, has sometimes been taken as evidence that this text originally described Manasseh's inheritance first (in the sequence 16:1–4; 17:1–13; 16:5–10) and then was subsequently reversed into its present arrangement. The existing order seems to reflect the traditional relationship of these "brother" tribes narrated in Genesis 48. It may also be a result of Ephraim's greater political importance and proximity to Judah.

[1–4] The southern border of Joseph is traced by vv. 1–3. It parallels the north boundary of Benjamin in 18:12–13 and the fragment of Ephraim's south border given in 16:5. Although a process of abbreviation has taken place, understandable from a Judah-centered perspective, taken together these verses

1. These boundaries have generated a substantial literature, some of the most recent being Na'aman, *Borders and Districts*, 145–58; E. Campbell, "The Boundary Between Ephraim and Manasseh," *The Answers Lie Below: Essays in Honor of Lawrence Edward Toombs*, Lanham, Md., 1984, 67–74; and H. Seebass, "Zur Exegese der Grenzbeschreibungen von Jos. 16,1–17,13," *ZDPV* 100 (1984): 70–93. See also Aharoni, *Land of the Bible*, 255–57, and Kallai, *Historical Geography*, 138–66.

2. According to Noth, "Studien zu den historisch-geographischen Dokumenten des Josuabuches," 243–46, the original system of fixed border points treated Ephraim and Manasseh as a unity and was only subsequently divided.

offer enough data to reconstruct the route. The line is traced westward from the Jordan to the Mediterranean.

The first verb of v. 1 introduces a sort of "double vision" in that the lot "came out" (presumably out of the container in which it was shaken, cf. 19:1) but at the same time "went out" as the line of the border which is moving away from the Jordan. NAB captures this with "the lot that fell to the Josephites extended." Compare 15:1 and 18:11 for similar ambiguities. Readers would most naturally understand the "waters of Jericho" as the well-known perennial spring on the east side of the city ('Ain es-Sultan). The border thus carefully excludes Benjaminite Jericho, but runs very close to it (cf. 18:12). "The wilderness" is here intended as the route by which the border runs, but it may be a reflection of the border point "wilderness of Beth-aven" found in 18:12. The separation of Bethel from Luz in v. 2 requires explanation since the two place names are elsewhere equated (18:13; Gen. 28:19; Judg. 1:23). Perhaps a compound name "Bethel-Luzah" is intended,[3] or the two cities were separate but very close together.[4] It has also been suggested that this refers to the second Luz reportedly built by a former inhabitant (Judg. 1:26).[5] Most likely, the writer has simply misinterpreted the source material, erroneously treating these two names taken from 18:13 as distinct border points. The Archites and Japhletites (vv. 2–3) were either alien ethnic groups, or, more likely, clans that had not yet fully integrated into the tribal system.[6] This Ataroth is the same as the one in v. 5 and 18:13, but different from the northern Ataroth mentioned in 16:7. Presumably it is identified with its longer name Ataroth-adar ("the Grand") in v. 5 to clarify this distinction. Both Beth-horons lie to the north of the border and thus are in Ephraim (18:13–14; 21:22). Verse 4 provides a transition from the topic of Joseph to its two constituent tribes, first Ephraim (vv. 5–10) and then Manasseh (17:1–13). It serves as a parallel formula to 13:8 and 14:1.

[5–9] The border enclosing Ephraim is introduced by v. 5a and summarized by v. 8b. The south border is represented by v. 5 plus "the border goes to the sea" at the start of v. 6. This boundary fragment describes only the western part of the line and parallels vv. 1–3 and 18:12–13. The north border of Ephraim is drawn first from the center to the east (vv. 6–7), then again from the center to the west (v. 8).[7] The eastern section starts from the pivotal northernmost point of Michmethath and slants southeast to the Jordan (vv. 6–7). The identifica-

3. Kallai, *Historical Geography*, 129–31, 143.

4. Noth, *Josua*, 101, 106, 109.

5. Gottwald, *The Tribes of Yahweh*, 559–560.

6. David's advisor Hushai was an Archite (2 Sam. 5:32), while Japhlet is cataloged as one of several Asher clans located in southern Ephraim rather than Galilee (1 Chron. 7:30–40). See Aharoni, *Land of the Bible*, 244.

7. In 1 Chron. 7:29 the *south* border of Ephraim is described in this same segmented manner, from Bethel east to Naaran (Naarah) and then west to Gezer.

tions of Michmethath, Taanath-shiloh, northern Ataroth, and Naarah are all problematic. This east segment runs from just south of Shechem (17:7), apparently bends clockwise around Taanath-shiloh, and backtracks west slightly to Janoah. Then it runs southeast to include the hill country and exclude the Jordan valley, "touching" but not including Jericho. In v. 8 the descriptive focus returns to the central starting point, this time from Tappuah, the next border point after Michmethath (17:7). In doing this, the description abruptly jumps nine kilometers southward from Michmethath to Tappuah (17:7). After this gap, the west segment goes westward along the Wadi Kanah (17:9). The localization of Tappuah depends on the customary text emendation of 17:7 to read there Jashub, known from the Samaria Ostraca.[8] Verse 9 describes a special circumstance[9] connected with the border delineation. This situation is the same as that described for Manasseh in 17:11, that is, urban islands belonging to one tribe within the general territory of another.

This border delineation includes Shechem as part of Manasseh (as does 17:2 and 1 Chron. 7:19), although other texts assign it to Ephraim (21:21; 1 Chron. 7:28). This inconsistency, along with the exceptions noted in v. 9 and at 17:8–9, may have resulted from Ephraim's subsequent expansion at the expense of Manasseh and shifts over time in clan allegiance.[10] At the same time, the tribal system should also be recognized as an idealized simplification which was ideologically superimposed over a much more complex reality of kinship structures and political arrangements.

[10] An exception focuses on Gezer, reflecting a concern about Canaanite survivals already raised by 15:63 and to be picked up again in 17:12–13, 16, 18. Triggered by mention of Gezer as a border point in v. 3, this notice seems to be acquainted with the information that it was only under Solomon that this city lost its independence and that Solomon was famous for his forced labor policies (1 Kings 9:15–16, 20–21). This verse stands in tension with the assertion of Josh. 10:33. It is paralleled by Judg. 1:29, which may have been its source.[11]

Readers of the book of Joshua in its final form, for whom possession of the land was precarious, would have found the theme of Israel's incomplete conquest significant. Even in the foundational period, they are told, Israel's land tenure remained incomplete. Readers should not fear that their only partial control of the land of promise or the troubling presence of alien populations might void Yahweh's ancient promises or negate their future as Yahweh's people in the land. Even Joshua had to concede some political realities, but only in the

---

8. See for example Kallai, *Historical Geography*, 151–53.

9. *Waw* plus subject plus verbless clause, Waltke and O'Connor, *Hebrew Syntax*, 39.2.3b.

10. Aharoni *Land of the Bible*, 243–48, Kallai, *Historical Geography*, 154–55. The assignment of Shechem to Ephraim in 21:21 is probably an error created in the course of literary composition.

11. See B. Lindars, *Judges 1–5*, 60–61.

short term. Imposed forced labor (v. 10), Israel's increasing strength (17:13), and the forecast that Israel would eventually dispossess the Canaanites (17:18) point readers beyond their present ambiguous situation to faith in the ultimate success of Yahweh's people.

Manasseh
Joshua 17:1–18

The Ten Clans of Manasseh

17:1 The lot took place for the tribe of Manasseh. In fact[a] he was Joseph's first born. It was to Machir, Manasseh's first born, father of Gilead, that Gilead and Bashan belonged, because he had been a warrior. 2 So it took place for the rest of the children of Manasseh for their clans—for the children of Abiezer, Helek, Asriel, Shechem, Hepher, and Shemida. These were [the sons of Manasseh the son of Joseph][b] the males by their clans.

3 Now Zelophehad the son of Hepher [the son of Gilead the son of Machir the son of Manasseh] had no sons, only daughters. These are the names of his daughters: Mahlah, Noah, Hoglah, Milcah, and Tirzah. 4 They approached Eleazar the priest, Joshua [son of Nun], and the leaders saying, "Yahweh commanded Moses[c] to give us hereditary property along with our kinsmen." So according to Yahweh's command he gave them hereditary property along with their father's kinsmen. 5 Manasseh's tracts fell as ten, besides the land of Gilead [and Bashan] across the Jordan, 6 because the daughters of Manasseh received hereditary property along with his sons. The land of Gilead belonged to the rest of the children of Manasseh.

The Border of Manasseh

7 The border of Manasseh extended from Asher to Michmethath which is opposite Shechem. The border goes south to Jashub,[d] En-tappuah. 8 The land of Tappuah belonged to Manasseh, but Tappuah itself, on the border of Manasseh, belonged to the children of Ephraim. 9 The border goes down by the Wadi Kanah. South of the wadi are those cities[e] belonging to Ephraim, although among the cities of Manasseh. The border of Manasseh is on the north side of the wadi. It ends at the sea. 10 Southward belongs to Ephraim and northward belongs to Manasseh.

The sea is its border. They touch Asher on the north and Issachar on the east.

11 In Issachar and in Asher there belonged to Manasseh: Beth-shean and its daughter towns, Ibleam and its daughter towns, En-dor and its daughter towns, Taanach and its daughter towns, and Megiddo and its daughter towns. (The third one is Naphath.)[f] 12 The children of Manasseh were not able to take over these cities and the Canaanites persisted in living in this land. 13 When the Israelites grew strong they set the Canaanites to forced labor, but certainly did not dispossess them.

Expansion of the House of Joseph

14 The children of Joseph spoke to Joshua: "Why have you given me hereditary property by a single lot as a single tract, although I am a numerous people whom until now[g] Yahweh has blessed?" 15 Then Joshua said, "Since you are a numerous people, go up to the forest and clear ground for yourselves there [in the land of the Perizzites and Rephaim],[h] because the hill country of Ephraim is too narrow for you. 16 They [the children of Joseph][i] said, "The hill country is not enough for us, but there are iron chariots among all the Canaanites who live in the valley region, both those in Beth-shean and its daughter towns and those in the Jezreel Valley." 17 Joshua said to the house of Joseph [to Ephraim and to Manasseh],[j] "You are a numerous people and have great strength. You will not have only a single lot, 18 for the hill country will belong to you because it is a forest and you will clear it[k] and its extremities[l] will be yours. For you will indeed dispossess the Canaanites even though they have iron chariots and are strong.[m]

a. Taking *kî* as an emphatic adverb.

b. The MT expansions in vv. 2b and 3a are present in 4QJosh[b].

c. Follows BHS. A number of Hebrew witnesses and versions read "by means of Moses," that is, *byd* instead of the direct object marker.

d. Follows OG *yšyb*, taking it as Yashub (Yasuf) near Tappuah (Sheikh Abu Zarad), a place known from the Samaria Ostraca and midrashic literature. See Kallai, *Historical Geography*, 151–53. MT's unlikely *yšby* "population of" is a result of metathesis.

e. Follows the grammatically awkward MT. Alternate translation: "The border goes down by the Wadi Kanah to the south of the wadi. These cities belonged to Ephraim. . . ." (cf. REB). LXX[B] *iariēl* (LXX[A] *iaeir*) *tereminthos* might represent *y'rym h'lh*, giving "to the wadi of forests; the terebinth belonged to Ephraim," or *'ry 'l h'lh*, "the cities of El of the Terebinth," but these retroversions are uncertain and cannot be used to produce a preferable text.

f. Follows S to a large extent. The textual situation is too complicated to permit the definite recovery of an "original" text. The reading adopted here accounts for the textual evidence in the following way: 1) The last two words ("the third one is Naphath") represent an early gloss, erroneously indicating that the third city on the list (originally En-dor) was to be identified with Naphath[-dor] (11:2; 12:23). 2) Of the doublet Dor and En-dor, Dor (absent from S) is secondary. It was inserted from Judg. 1:27, complete with a superfluous direct object marker and the words "population of," both appropriate to the Judges context but out of place in Joshua. 3) Several of the other cities were also supplemented by the words "the population of" from Judg. 1:27. These supplements are lacking in S. 4) The ancestor of OG misunderstood the gloss about Naphath to mean that there were to be only three cities on the list. It therefore dropped Ibleam, En-dor, and Taanach and kept Beth-shean, Dor, and Megiddo. Homoioteleuton may also have played a role in this shortening process in OG. 5) OG supplemented Naphath with "and its daughter towns." The resulting MT text:

> Beth-shean and its daughter towns,
> and Ibleam and its daughter towns,
> and [direct object marker] the population of Dor and its daughter towns,
> and the population of En-dor and its daughter towns,
> and the population of Taanach and its daughter towns
> and the population of Megiddo and its daughter towns (the third is Naphath).

See G. Dahl, "The 'Three Heights' of Joshua 17:11," *JBL* 53 (1934): 381–83; Barthélemy, *Critique*, 47–48. 4QJoshb witnesses to MT but in the order En-dor, Ibleam, Dor, Taanach, Megiddo.

g. Follows MT, which is obscure. Alternate translation: "to such a degree." OG and V lack these problematic words.

h. The motive for this MT expansion is unclear. "Rephaim" could have originated as a dittography for "hill country of Ephraim," *hrp'ym* from *hr'prym*.

i. MT expands with an explicit subject. The other OG divergences from MT in this verse are secondary: specification of "Ephraim" added to "the hill country," a corruption of "iron" and its reinsertion as a doublet, and the unexplained absence of "valley region."

j. Probably an MT expansion, although a mechanism for an OG haplography does exist: *l'[prym wlmnšh l']mr*.

k. Alternate translation: "because it is forest you can clear it."

l. Follows MT as preferable. Although OG lacks "extremities," this does not have the character of a scribal expansion.

m. Follows MT as preferable. OG reads the more facile and thus presumably secondary "you are stronger than they are." The long-standing proposal to alleviate the difficulty of MT by inserting a "not" before the verb in 18b is methodologically indefensible, although still advocated by Fritz, *Josua*, 170 and *BHS*. In accord with most modern versions, this translation takes the first *kî* in v. 18b as causal, in parallel with the *kî* that begins v. 18, and the last two occurrences as concessive. On concessive *kî*, see A. Schoors, "The Particle *kî*," *OTS* 21 (1981): 271–73.

Chapter 17 forms a unit with chapter 16, held together by a bracketing pattern which encloses the two individual tribes within the larger category of Joseph:

Joseph 16:1–4
Ephraim 16:5–10
Manasseh 17:1–13
Joseph 17:14–18

As in 16:1–4, the inclusive entity of Joseph exists in unresolved tension with the concept of two individual tribes, a tension visible in vv. 1 ("first born"), 10 ("they"), 14 ("single lot"), and the MT supplement to v. 17. The chapter deals first with the ten west bank clans (vv. 2–6), including a short land grant narrative (vv. 3–6a; see commentary on 14:6–15). It moves on to delineate the border for Manasseh (vv. 7–13), and concludes with another land grant narrative for Joseph as a whole (vv. 14–18). Manasseh shares a pattern set up already for Ephraim in chapter 16. Border description (17:7, 9–10) is followed by territorial exceptions and technicalities (vv. 8, 11), followed in turn by a note about remaining Canaanite populations (vv. 12–13).

[1–6] The obscure syntax of vv. 1–2 has driven translators to a variety of paraphrases. In v. 1 and the first part of v. 2, there are three parallel sentences with the preposition *l* expressing a datival or possessive idea. These deal first with the entire tribe of Manasseh (v. 1a), then with Machir (v. 1b; foregrounded by word order), and finally focus in on the actual topic of what follows, "the rest of the children of Manasseh" (v. 2a). The subject of Gilead forms a bracket with the end of v. 6. Mention of the "rest of Manasseh" in v. 2 turns our attention to the west bank, but then in v. 6 the very same phrase reverses its reference and briefly returns the spotlight to the eastern group.

The "rest" are specified in v. 2 as six sons (that is, clans; Num. 26:30–32; 1 Chron. 7:14–19), explicitly specified as "male" in preparation for the narrative to follow. Of these clan names, Shechem is of course well-known, and Helek, Abiezer, Shemida, and perhaps Asriel occur in the Samaria Ostraca.[1] All of these can be located in the central hill country. However, Hepher (12:17; 1 Kings 4:10) seems to be "off the map," perhaps located to the west in the Sharon. The following story indicates Hepher was also "off the map" genealogically, its position displaced by five "granddaughter" clans.[2] As in the case of the land grants to Caleb (14:6–15) and Achsah (15:13–19), land possession given by conquest and lot is underscored and supplemented by a third sort of claim, endowment by Yahweh through Moses and Joshua.

1. These represent administrative records from the Jehu dynasty. *ANET*, 321; Aharoni, *Land of the Bible*, 356–68.
2. 1 Kings 4:10 suggests a location in the Sharon, although Na'aman, *Borders and Districts*, 158–62, proposes a large territory reaching far inland. On the issue of Hepher and the Zelophehad clans, see Lemaire, "Le 'Pays de Hépher' et les 'filles de Zelophedad' "; K. Sakenfeld, "Zelophehad's Daughters," *Perspectives in Religious Studies* 15 (1988): 37–47; H. Seebass, "Machir in Ostjordanland," *VT* 32 (1982): 496–503; Wüst, *Untersuchungen zu den siedlungsgeographischen Texten*, 64–70.

This land grant narrative (vv. 3–6a) relates in some way to the Pentateuchal material in Num. 27:1–11, to which v. 4 seems to refer. As in 14:1 and 21:1, the priest Eleazar and the leaders take part along with Joshua. Contradictory MT textual supplements in vv. 2 and 3 reflect differing genealogical traditions about the relation of Hepher to Manasseh. This gender-based genealogical systemization of clan relationships was apparently based on a linguistic foundation. The five clan names with feminine terminations are taken to be "daughters" in contrast to the six "male" clans.[3] Hoglah and Noah occur in the Samaria Ostraca, and with Tirzah may be located generally north of Samaria. The political relationship of the five "female" clans to the other five clans of Manasseh is conceived as a genealogical link through Hepher, a sixth son of Manasseh. In a male-only inheritance system, however, it was apparently felt that the land tenure of the "female" clans required etiological support in the form of a special command of Yahweh through Moses. Whereas the Pentateuchal texts Num. 27:1–11 and 36:1–12 are concerned to establish a fixed law or custom,[4] the Joshua narrative is intended to validate possession of the land and confirm a traditional clan structure. The linguistic feature of feminine names thus does not undercut, but rather bolsters the territorial rights of these five clans. It is remarkable that in making this land claim Israel's patriarchal culture, usually so preoccupied with perpetuating the names and inheritances of fathers and sons, here preserves a "memory" of mothers and daughters.

[7–10] Instead of a north boundary, the territorial delineation begins with an imprecise line of extent "from Asher to Michmethath."[5] Michmethath represents the first of three border markers for the western part of Manasseh's south border. It then heads south from Michmethath to Jashub and goes on to run west along the Wadi Kanah. This is a fragmentary restatement of Ephraim's north boundary (16:6b–8) that does not report on the east section from Michmethath to the Jordan (16:6–7). The anomaly described by v. 8 may offer evidence for Israel's differential occupation of territory, the rural areas being settled before the cities were absorbed. Manasseh's boundary goes only "to" Jashub and En-tappuah (spring of Tappuah), but does not actually encompass Ephraimite Tappuah. In contrast, the border line of Ephraim is intended to include Tappuah (16:8).

The fractured language of v. 9 makes it difficult to understand the exact role the Wadi Kanah played as a border. While it would be most natural to presume that the wadi simply divided the two tribes north and south for its whole length

---

3. Feminine forms for clan and place names are no surprise. Examples are Tirhanah (1 Chron. 2:48), Zobebah (1 Chron. 4:8), and Ephrathah.

4. M. Weinfeld, "The Case of the Daughters of Zelophehad," *VT* 16 (1966): 518–22.

5. That Manasseh had cities "in Issachar and in Asher" has been the subject of much debate. On the problem of Manasseh's northern frontier and the general extent of its territory, see Kallai, *Historical Geography,* 167–78.

west of Tappuah, there are other possibilities. Perhaps we are to understand that the line "goes down *southward to* the Wadi Kanah" and crosses it (so that there was Manasseh territory south of the valley in which some Ephraimite towns were located), *then* (the *waw* that starts v. 9b) crosses back north so that it runs along the north rim of the wadi. One must also ask whether v. 10a is a repetitive reference to this wadi line, or a more generalized statement about the entire border between the two tribes. The rest of v. 10 quickly surveys the west, north and (north)east limits. The awkward pronoun "they" may refer to both Ephraim and Manasseh, a return to the viewpoint that Joseph as a whole is the topic.

[11–13] Consistent with the absence of any definite north border line (v. 7a) is a wedge of tribal overlap and continued Canaanite control (parallel in Judg. 1:27–28).[6] Beth-shean and En-dor were in Issachar; the other three cities apparently were thought to relate to Asher in some way. The ambivalent textual situation makes the precise geographic circumstances uncertain (text note f). In any case, these verses not only repeat the theme of incomplete possession from 15:63 and 16:10, but also provide an appropriate prologue for the concerns that the Josephites are about to raise.

[14–18] In this short but complex dialogue, Joseph is once more regarded as a unified group. The story as told tends to fall into two somewhat repetitive parts, vv. 14–15 and 16–18.[7] Verse 14 leads to v. 15 and v. 16 leads to vv. 17–18, but the relationship between these two movements is unclear. The problem raised in v. 14 receives an apparent solution in v. 15, but then the Joseph group restates its predicament in v. 16 and Joshua responds once more, offering assurance of a rosy future in vv. 17–18. The solution presented in v. 15 sounds as though Joseph is being directed to be assertive and expand on its core territory by clearing higher forest areas not presently being utilized. The alternative solution of vv. 17–18 seems to counsel patience with what has been assigned in the light of future developments. Therefore it is often suggested that an older version (vv. 16–18) has been supplemented by vv. 14–15 in order to offer an alternate resolution of the question. Verses 14–15 are taken to be chronologically later because they envision the entire land as being under Israel's control, in contrast to vv. 16–18. Perhaps v. 14 was formed on the basis of v. 17b.

6. On the relationship between the Judges and Joshua passages, see Lindars, *Judges 1–5*, 56–60 and A. G. Auld, "Judges 1 and History: A Reconstruction," *VT* 25 (1975): 261–85. Treating Dor as the city south of Carmel and references to the "populations" of these cities fit Judges's purpose of describing a wide-ranging failure to conquer Canaanites. In Joshua the town is En-dor, appropriately located in the area of the border under discussion and hardly a great Canaanite stronghold. Joshua only turns to the issue of alien people in v. 12b. The inclusion of Dor in Joshua would violate the neat east to west line of the other cities.

7. On the literary history of this passage, see Schmitt, *Du sollst keinen Frieden schliessen*, 90–97, who sees vv. 16–18 as a supplement to vv. 14–15.

Be that as it may, it is certain that vv. 16–18, with or without the preliminary material of vv. 14–15, is an example of the genre of a land grant narrative
similar to 14:6–15, 15:13–19, and 17:3–6. Here Joshua grants Joseph future
possession of the forested highlands and further Canaanite territory. The story
displays an etiological interest in illustrating why Joseph was such an expansive and assertive group. Joseph started out with but one lot, the appropriate
share for a single heir. Yet in the end Joseph ended up with more than a single
lot by wresting territory from the forests and the Canaanites.

In the final form of the text, vv. 14–15 and 16–18 can be read together as a
single plot line with two movements. The initial complaint (v. 14) raises the
disparity in size between Joseph's single allotment and their flourishing population. Joshua agrees with their analysis (v. 15). The hill country of Ephraim,
here intended in the geographically restricted sense of "Mt. Ephraim" (1 Kings
4:8), is indeed too narrow. Yes, you are "a numerous people," Joshua agrees,
but advises them to turn that circumstance into an opportunity. Clear the forest up there in the rest of your hereditary property. But this initial solution is
inadequate according to the Joseph group. They go on to restate their case with
additional arguments in v. 16. For one thing, they pick up and distort Joshua's
reference to the narrow Mt. Ephraim highlands (*har 'eprayim*) to assert that the
entire hill country (*hāhār*) of their heritage is inadequate. Moreover, the military superiority of the Canaanites blocks their settlement in the lowlands, particularly to the north. In fact they make explicit reference to the situation of vv.
11–13 by repeating "Beth-shean and its daughter towns" from the list in v. 11.
In this second statement of their complaint, then, the Joseph group has raised
the stakes. Given the menace of "iron chariots," (presumably chariots reinforced with iron components),[8] their constricted inheritance simply cannot be
exploited to a degree sufficient for them.

Joshua's response (vv. 17–18) points to the future and an expanded horizon
of possibilities. As he did in v. 15, Joshua again picks up the language of their
first complaint, "you are a numerous people," and again he turns their own
words around against them. Their large population is actually not a problem,
but the foundation of their expansive future, for with numbers comes strength.
Joseph will make the most of the forested hill country and eventually go on to
dispossess the Canaanites. The hill country in its widest sense (*har* and not just

---

8. Given the resources needed for construction, training, and support, the chariot as a weapons
system signifies superior technological and social organization. Chariots indicate that Canaan is a
more advanced culture. Perhaps the iron in question was used to strengthen the attachment between the pole and the front of the body. R. Drews, "The 'Chariots of Iron' of Joshua and Judges,"
JSOT 45 (1989): 15–23, proposes scythed wheels or iron tires. Nahum 2:3 suggests shiny metal
decoration. In any case iron functions rhetorically as a symbol of invincible strength, aggression,
and brutality, according to J. Sawyer, "The Meaning of *barzel* in the Biblical Expressions 'Chariots of Iron,' 'Yoke of Iron,' etc," *The History and Archaeology of Late Bronze and Iron Age Jordan and North-West Arabia*, JSOTSup 24, Sheffield, 1983, 129–34.

har 'eprayim) will be theirs, the forest cleared to its very edges (v. 18a). More-over, Joseph will go on to "dispossess" (*yrš* hiphil) the Canaanites, no matter what their present strength (v. 18b). This prediction of "dispossession" means that Joseph's control will go beyond the highlands of v. 18a to include even-tual possession of the lowlands referred to in their complaint (v. 16b) as well. Viewed from this perspective, their heritage cannot be construed as only a "sin-gle lot" (v. 17bB), the contention of their original complaint (v. 14).

So far, the heritage of each tribe has been presented as incomplete, marred by foreign holdouts. For Judah it is Jerusalem (15:63), for Ephraim, Gezer (16:10), for Manasseh a list of cities and the valley areas (17:11–13, 16). These notices are paralleled in Judges in a entirely negative context (Judg. 1:21, 27–29). In contrast to the presentation in Judges, however, Joshua leaves the impression that progress was being made. In Jerusalem the Jebusites simply live side by side with Israel. However, forced labor is added to the situation at Gezer (16:10), even though this is not specifically present in the Judges paral-lel. Perhaps this forced labor is as much a theological adjustment to the prob-lem of an incomplete conquest as it is a memory of traditions about Solomon. Again, forced labor is the best Manasseh could do with the five Canaanite cities of their heritage (17:12–13). But Joshua's vision of the future in v. 18 moves beyond mere political domination to eventual total victory.

Division at Shiloh
Joshua 18:1–10

18:1 The entire community of the Israelites gathered at Shiloh and they set up the tent of meeting there. The land was subjugated before them. 2 Among the Israelites seven tribes were left whose hereditary property they had not divided up. 3 Joshua said to the Israelites, "How long are you going to be neglectful about going out to take possession of the land which Yahweh the God of your ancestors[a] has given you? 4 Provide three men per tribe [so I may send them out][b] so they may set out[c] to travel around the land and record it for me as their hereditary property and then come back[d] to me. 5 They shall divide it up among themselves into seven sections. Judah shall stay on its territory to the south and the house of Joseph shall stay on their territory[e] to the north. 6 You shall record the land as seven sections and bring them back to me here so I may cast the lot for you [here][f] before Yah-weh our God. 7 However the Levites do not have a section among you be-cause the priesthood of Yahweh is their hereditary property. Gad, Reuben, and the half-tribe of Manasseh have taken their hereditary property east-ward across the Jordan, which Moses the servant of Yahweh gave them."

8 The men set out to go. Joshua commanded those going to record the land saying, "Go and travel around[g] the land, record it, and return to me. I will cast the lot for you here, before Yahweh in Shiloh." 9 So they [the men] went and passed through the land and recorded it in a document as to cities in seven sections. Then they came back to Joshua [at the camp at Shiloh].[h] 10 Then Joshua cast lots for them in Shiloh before Yahweh. [There Joshua divided up the land for the Israelites according to their allotments.][i]

a. Follows MT. OG has "our God" as in v. 6. There is no way to choose between the readings.

b. MT adds a explanatory detail.

c. Here and at v. 8 a verbal hendiadys with *qwm* emphasizes the beginning of the action (cf. 1:2; 7:13; 8:3).

d. Alternate translation taking the verb as hiphil "bring it back to me." This would also be possible at v. 9.

e. The absence of "on their territory" in OG may be translational.

f. Lacking in OG and S. MT represents a recension emphasizing the Shiloh location here and in vv. 9 and 10.

g. Follows MT. OG lost a verb here through haplography: *l[kw whthl]kw*. In this verse OG uses *chōrobatō* (to explore?) to translate "record" twice and in v. 9 to translate "pass through." According to Greenspoon, *Textual Studies in the Book of Joshua*, 107, 191 n.301, this represents free translation, not a difference in text.

h. MT expands to emphasize the location as Shiloh.

i. MT supplements to stress that not only was the lot cast at Shiloh, but the land was divided there as well. "According to their allotments" reflects 11:23 and 12:7.

Chapters 18–19 form a unit held together by the brackets of 18:1 and 19:51 (Shiloh, tent of meeting) and by the general topic of the seven remaining tribes. At this point the description of land distribution shifts into a third format. The first format (chap. 13) was for the two and one-half east Jordan tribes and involved no lot, only the delineation of their territory. In the second format (chaps. 15–17), the lot "went out" or "was" for each of the largest three tribes without any prior survey of what each allotment might include. Now in chapters 18–19, the setting shifts to a national assembly at Shiloh. The lottery supervised by Joshua is prefaced by a survey and subdivision of the remaining land into seven portions.

These three differing approaches may have been dictated in part by the sort of traditional material available to the authors. However, the changes in format also make a certain narratival sense. Because it had already been determined that Reuben, Gad, and half Manasseh would occupy the east Jordan (1:12–15; 12:6), chapter 13 only needed to report retrospectively their endowment by Moses. The available territory is simply divided into rough thirds south to north. Then the three most powerful tribes with the largest territory become the first to receive their allotment under the direction of Joshua, Eleazar, and the family leaders (14:1–2). It is only when these "big three" have been taken care of (chaps. 15–17) that the narrative turns to the less important seven tribes. Their regions are all smaller than those of the principal three tribes and all of approximately the same size. So it makes narrative sense to report a preliminary division of the remaining land into seven equitable portions to parcel out by lot. For the primary three tribes, whose territories were well-known and obvious to readers (v. 5), the mechanism of allotment could remain unexplained and vague. For the last seven, the process is both clearer and more schematized. In a lottery with seven prizes and seven participants, the lot assigns a predetermined tract to each tribe in turn.

This change in authorial strategy contrasts the three primary tribes with the other seven. The disparity in size and influence of the "big three" is significant for the whole national story. The two competing monarchies were built upon Judah and Joseph respectively. Perhaps for this reason the matter of conquest failures, reported for each of the three large tribes (15:63; 16:10; 17:12–13), is dropped for last seven, even though information about unconquered towns was probably available (cf. Judg. 1:27–36). Whether v. 3 intends a further contrast between three assertive tribes and seven dilatory (or even disobedient) ones is debatable. Certainly Judah is assertive in 14:6, but the matter of tribal initiative plays no real role in the land distribution of chapters 15–17. Joshua's rhetorical address is more a matter of plot motivation than accusation. In chapters 18–19 Joshua becomes more dominant in the allocation process (v. 6), although the presence of the collective leadership of 14:1 will once again be asserted by the closing verse of the section (19:51). Up to now the "lot" has been only a static noun that could easily have been translated by "allotment." Now it takes a more prominent role and is activated into a technique for decision-making, making choices among the seven options.

The order in which these seven are treated makes logical sense from a Judahite perspective. Benjamin comes first as centrally located and closest to Judah; then Simeon, again because of its significance for Judah. The four Galilee tribes follow as more distant in space and Dan as more distant in time in that its town list describes its situation in the distant past. Perhaps there is also some reflection of Pentateuchal tradition behind the circumstance that the sons of wives come first (Rachel: Benjamin; Leah: Simeon, Zebulun, Issachar) followed by the sons of concubines (Asher, Naphtali, Dan).[1]

It is important to note that the narrative sets up an etiology for a document describing tribal allotments "as to cities" (v. 9). The notion of writing is central

---

1. On the various configurations for the tribes, see H. Weippert, "Das geographische System der Stämme Israels," *VT* 23 (1973): 76–89.

to this little story (vv. 4, 6, 8, 9), and what results is precisely the sort of source scholars conjecture was used to provide the geographic data found in the rest of chapters 18–19. Although there are background analogies from Mesopotamia and Greece for written land descriptions used to settle disputes, the purpose here seems to be a purely literary one. It provides a "provenance" for the source utilized by the author.

Although many interpreters have seen this as a traditional oral story connected to Shiloh, it is more likely to be a literary creation intended to introduce the material that follows.[2] It is difficult to imagine what purpose there could have been for a tradition that told only of these particular seven scattered tribes. The narrative only makes sense, as vv. 5 and 7 make clear, in the present redactional shape of Joshua. It was designed precisely and exclusively for its present literary context. Starting from the presupposition that the rest of the land has already been apportioned, it reports Joshua's division of the remainder to the remaining seven tribes. It grows out of a narratival need for a fair division into seven smaller parcels for seven remaining tribes and the author's possession of a source document or documents describing that territory. Although some have taken the survey commission as an earlier mechanism of division later overlaid by the use of the lot,[3] from a narratival perspective this committee answers the need for a fair and equal division, while at the same time providing an etiology for the author's source in the "document" of v. 9. The narrative intends to convince readers that this subsequent division was done in a completely proper manner, that is, by Joshua through the lot in the context of an assembly of the whole nation. Tribal territories were determined fairly by a representative survey committee and parcelled out in Yahweh's approving presence (the tent of meeting in v. 1, "before Yahweh" in v. 10).

This account touches on many of the prevalent themes of the book of Joshua:

> the land was subjugated (11:16, etc.)
> the people's role was to take possession of what Yahweh had
>   given (v. 3 refers to 1:11)
> Joshua as the primary actor (underscored by MT additions
>   to vv. 4 and 10)
> the recurring assembly of the whole nation (chaps. 23 and
>   24; as an *'ēdâ* in 9:15–21; 20:9; 22:12)
> distribution by lot (14:2, etc.)

---

2. Fritz, *Josua*, 177–81, proposes redactional doublets in vv. 4 and 6 and in vv. 8 and 9, but his analysis shows little understanding of narratology. He proposes a core text consisting of vv. 2–3, 6, 9, 10b as a composition of DH.

3. Schmitt, *Du sollst keinen Frieden schliessen*, 106–9.

It also makes deliberate reference to the larger context of land allocation:

Judah and Joseph in v. 5 (chaps. 15–17)
the eastern tribes in v. 7 (chap. 13)
no inheritance for Levi, v. 7 (13:14, 33 MT; 14:3–4; chap. 21)

Certain elements of the text reflect a compositional perspective similar to that of the Priestly Writing ('*ēdâ* "community," "tent of meeting," "subjugate the earth/land" in v. 1 and Gen. 1:28).

Once all elements of literary composition are removed from the picture, there remains no content for any supposed older tradition, except perhaps the location of Shiloh. However, an ideological attachment to Shiloh (rather than the Shechem of 8:30–35 and chap. 24) would be understandable from a Judahite (and priestly) perspective because Shiloh was viewed as the legitimate forerunner to Jerusalem.[4] The choice of Shiloh may also have something to do with its location midway between Jerusalem and Samaria.

The narrative plot begins with v. 1 as exposition, setting out the who, where, and when. Verse 2 establishes the narrative problem. Then in vv. 3–7 Joshua lays out his plan for solving this problem. His speech begins with a motivational introduction (v. 3) followed by a series of imperatival expressions (vv. 4–5a, 6) interspersed with retrospective information (vv. 5b, 7). The action phase begins in v. 8 with a repetition of the basic instructions, which are then carried out in v. 9. The narrative problem is solved in v. 10. This little plot is nicely bracketed by vv. 1 and 10, each of which refer to Shiloh and the presence of Yahweh (tent of meeting, "before Yahweh").

From an ideological standpoint, the story asserts that the geographical shape of Israel in the land was not the result of human will or historical contingency, but of Yahweh's will and of Israel's obedience. Yahweh's will is manifested by the oracular lot (vv. 6, 8, 10) and Yahweh's approving presence (vv. 1, 6, 10). The balance between Yahweh's will and Israel's obedience is nicely set forth by v. 6: *you* (subject-first emphasis) will record, but *I,* Joshua, will then cast the lot in Yahweh's *presence.* The text also intends to convince readers that national identity somehow still encompasses the "all Israel" of past tradition. Archaic geographical and tribal realities still condition the identity of the readers as Yahweh's people. One is reminded of the importance of the twelve tribes in Ezekiel's program of restoration (Ezek. 47:13–48:7). Perhaps the text even implies hopes for the resettlement of the lost territories it conjures up from the past (Simeon in Idumea, Galilee).

[1] The narrative locale is now abruptly Shiloh. Before it had been left vague, although Gilgal was mentioned at one point (14:6). MT expansions (vv. 6, 9, 10) underscore the Shiloh location and identify it as the site of the "camp"

---

4. Consider the presence of the ark at Shiloh; Jer. 7:12; Ps. 78:60; and the textual insertion of the tent of meeting into 1 Sam. 2:22.

so important earlier in the book. The perspective of v. 5 (Judah to the south, Joseph to the north) is of course not from the viewpoint of Shiloh. This is rather the perspective of the overall situation of the tribes, the omniscient perspective of the author and readers.

[2–10] The start of Joshua's speech is more motivational than accusatory. For similar motivational language, compare Exod. 16:28; Num. 14:11; Ps. 13:2–3 [1–2E]. The book's story cannot come to a close until the momentum begun by 1:11 has come to its conclusion, and the final step is now up to the seven tribes. Certainly Yahweh would not be to blame if they never took over their land, for "the land was subjugated before them" (v. 1). There is a bit of word play between "travel around" (hithpael of *hlk*) in v. 4 and "divide up" (hithpael of *ḥlq*) in v. 5. The plan presents a problem from the standpoint of priestly ideology in that it is the layman Joshua who casts the lot (vv. 6, 8, 10). Perhaps the verb of v. 10 is intended as factitive: "Joshua had the lot cast."

Benjamin
Joshua 18:11–28

The Borders of Benjamin

18:11 The lot came up[a] for the tribe of [the children of] Benjamin for their clans. The border of their allotment went out between the [children of] Judah and the children of Joseph. 12 Their border on the north side extended from the Jordan. The border goes up to the slope of Jericho on the north and goes up westward in the hill country, its limits being the wilderness of Beth-aven. 13 The border crosses from there to Luz, to the slope of Luz on the south (that is, Bethel). The border goes down to Ataroth-adar[b] on the mountain that is south of lower Beth-horon. 14 The border turns southward and comes around on the west side from the mountain which is opposite Beth-horon on the south. It ends at Kiriath-baal (that is, Kiriath-jearim), a city of Judah. This is its west side. 15 The south side is from the limits of Kiriath-jearim. The border goes out westward[c] and then goes out to the Waters of Nephtoah spring. 16 The border goes down to the limit of the mountain that is opposite the valley of [the son of] Hinnom, which is in the north of the valley of Rephaim. It goes down by the valley of Hinnom to the slope of the Jebusite[d] on the south and goes down to En-rogel. 17 [It turns northward and][e] it goes to En-shemesh and goes to Geliloth, which is opposite the ascent of Adummim. It goes down to the Stone of Bohan the son of Reuben. 18 It crosses to the slope of Beth-arabah[f] on the north. 19 The border goes down[g] to the slope of Beth-hoglah on the north. The border ends at the north bay of the Salt Sea at the southern mouth of the Jordan. This is the south border. 20 The Jordan borders it on the eastern side. This is the hereditary property of the children of Benjamin for their clans according to its surrounding borders.

The Cities of Benjamin

21 The cities of [the tribe of] the children of Benjamin for their clans are:
Jericho, Beth-hoglah, Emek-keziz,
22 Beth-arabah, Zemaraim, Bethel,
23 Avvim, Parah, Ophrah,
24 Chephar-ammoni, Ophni,[h] and Geba.[i]
Twelve cities and their precincts.
25 Gibeon, Ramah, Beeroth,
26 Mizpeh, Chephirah, Mozah,
27 Rekem, Irpeel, Taralah,
28 Zela, Haeleph,[j] the Jebusite (that is, Jerusalem), Gibeah,[k] and Kiriath-jearim.[l]
Fourteen cities and their precincts.
This is the hereditary property of the children of Benjamin for their clans.

a. Follows MT. OG failed to understand this as a technical term in divination and translated it as "went out" (also at 19:10).

b. Follows MT. OG reads "Ataroth-orech" as at 16:5, reflecting the association of this town with the Archites (16:2).

c. Follows MT, although "westward" might seem out of place since the border will next move eastward. Here as in 15:9 (in the corresponding border description) OG reflects "to the ruins" (LXX[B] *eis gasin*, originally *eis gain* = *'ymh* or *'yymh* "ruin-ward"; Greenspoon, *Textual Studies in the Book of Joshua*, 147–48; Barthélemy, *Critique*, 34–35). This is taken as a place name "Gasin" by NJB. In 15:9 OG "ruins" represents the better text, but here it is apparently a corruption of MT (*'ymh* for *ymh* "westward") under the influence of 15:9 OG. NRSV imports "Mt. Ephron" from 15:9 as a substitute for "westward," compare Noth, *Josua*, 110–11; Na'aman, *Borders and Districts*, 103–104. Other translations simply omit the problematic word (REB, NAB). The preferable text remains "westward."

d. Alternate translation: "of the Jebusites," taking the name of the slope from the ethnic group rather than the city (cf. v. 28).

e. A geographic gloss incorporated into MT, not present in OG.

f. Follows OG and 15:6 in reading "Beth-arabah." MT "opposite the Arabah" arose through graphic similarity.

g. Follows OG, which does not have MT *h'rbth w'br* "the Arabah and it crosses."

This is a dittography of "the Arabah" from the previous verse followed in turn by a scrambled partial dittography of its first letters.

h. Follows MT. OG may have lost this name through homoioteleuton (*h'mny h'pny*), or conversely MT could represent a dittography. Instead of Ophni, LXX[B] and LXX[A] have different names before Chephar-ammoni to make up the total twelve.

i. Geba could refer to the Gibeah of Benjamin and Saul (T. el-Ful 172136). See Gibeah at v. 28 and J. M. Miller, "Geba/Gibeah of Benjamin," *VT* 25 (1975): 145–66.

j. Zela Haeleph may be a single place name as in LXX[AB] (cf. 2 Sam. 21:14, if Zela is really a toponym there). The MT total of fourteen requires that these two names as well as Gibeath and Kiriath-jearim remain separate.

k. In a different district, this Gibeath must be different from the Geba of v. 24. It too could be the Gibeah of Benjamin and Saul. The Masoretic accentuation construes this as the first part of a single toponym ("hill of Kiriath"). This would seem indicate a place near Kiriath-jearim, perhaps the Gibeah or hill where the house of Aminadab was situated (1 Sam. 7:1; 2 Sam. 6:3). Of course it is not the Gibeah of Judah south of Hebron (15:57).

l. Follows OG as represented by LXX[A]. LXX[B] "Gibeath-jearim" reflects an inner-Greek transposition as demonstrated by Margolis, *Joshua in Greek,* 357–58. MT "Gibeath of Kiriath" lost "-jearim" through haplography: *[y'rym] 'rym.*

Benjamin is reported on first because it was of greatest interest from the southern perspective. Benjamin enclosed the border between the two kingdoms and was later included in Persian Judea. As is true for the description of Judah in chapter 15, the boundary of Benjamin is drawn first (vv. 11–20), then its towns are listed (vv. 21–28). The town list is held together by the brackets of vv. 21 and 28. Two districts of towns (vv. 21–24 and 25–28) are presented in the same format as those for Judah and thus presumably come from the same source.[1] As is also the case with Judah, the boundary description represents a somewhat different political situation than the town lists which follow. Thus Bethel/Luz is outside of Benjamin according to the boundary description of v. 13, but is part of the town list in v. 22. The border runs north of Beth-arabah and Beth-hoglah, putting them in Judah (v. 19, see text note f; cf. 15:6), but Benjamin's town list includes them (vv. 21–22).

Traditional and administrative geography has been reutilized in a narrative and theological framework to build and bolster national identity. The communities that produced and read this literature did so in order to hold fast to their claim on the territories of their ancestors.

[11–20] A counter-clockwise border description is introduced by the formula of v. 11b (cf. 19:10) and concluded by the phrase "surrounding borders"

---

1. Besides the literature cited for chapter 15, see K.-D. Schunck, "Bemerkungen zur Ortsliste von Benjamin (Jos 18, 21–28). *ZDPV* 78 (1962): 143–58. A review of studies on the district lists after Alt and Noth is provided by Auld, *Joshua, Moses and the Land,* 35–42.

in v. 20b (cf. 15:12). The north border (vv. 12–13) parallels that of Ephraim (16:1–3a). The west border is traced by v. 14. The south border (vv. 15–19) parallels that of Judah (15:5b–9), but in a reverse direction. The two descriptions are clearly from the same source. The east border is v. 20. Each of the four boundaries is designated as a "side," *pē'â.* This word is used elsewhere in Joshua only in 15:5, perhaps indicating that it was part of the source document shared between Judah and Benjamin.

The north border carefully includes Jericho (v. 12) and runs up west through the highlands to the wilderness of Beth-aven. Use of Beth-aven as a derogatory expression for nearby Bethel (Amos 5:5; Hos. 4:15; 10:5) is reflected in the gloss in 7:2 equating Bethel and Beth-aven. Although it has been suggested that Beth-aven was never anything but a parody name for Bethel,[2] its localization in other texts is consistent with a site between Bethel/Luz and Jericho (1 Sam. 13:5; 14:23).[3] The border runs south of Bethel/Luz and of Beth-horon (v. 13) to exclude them from Benjamin. The western boundary (v. 14) is rather vaguely constructed out of Beth-horon (a border point taken from v. 13) and Kiriath-baal (a point in the border shared with Judah, equivalent to Baalah in 15:9). Thus this west border seems to have been created artificially in order to leave room for Dan,[4] indicating that the boundary source did not reckon with Dan's existence west of Benjamin.

The odd "westward" in the south border (v. 15) could be explained as an erroneous transfer of the east-to-west direction of the boundary line found in chapter 15 to the situation in chapter 18.[5] However, repetition of the verb "goes out" suggests that the border is described as running first westward from "the limits of Kiriath-jearim" and then reversing eastward to Nephtoah.[6] Thus Kiriath-jearim was not the intersection point of the west and south border, but a point along the south border from which the boundary line was drawn successively in two opposite directions. Verse 14 leaves Kiriath-baal clearly in Judah, suggesting that the identification made there with Benjaminite (v. 28) Kiriath-jearim is a misunderstanding.[7] The verb "go down" at the start of v. 16 would appear to be an error for the west-to-east ascent from Nephtoah to the "limit of the mountain." This may indicate that the author reversed an east-to-west source to create Benjamin's border. This border description has

---

2. Noth, *Josua,* 106, 109.

3. Probably T. Maryam 175141. See N. Na'aman, "Beth-Aven, Bethel, and Early Israelite Sanctuaries," *ZDPV* 103 (1987): 13–21; Z. Kallai, "Beth-El—Luz and Beth-Aven," *Prophetie und geschichtliche Wirklichkeit im Alten Testament,* Stuttgart, 1991, 171–88.

4. Noth, *Josua,* 109–110.

5. Noth, *Josua,* 110–11; Na'aman, *Borders and Districts,* 103.

6. Kallai, *Historical Geography,* 133–34.

7. See Noth, *Josua,* 88–89. The connection between 1 Sam. 7:1–2 and 2 Sam. 6:2 does not require the identification of the two nearby sites. However, Judg. 18:12 locates Kiriath-jearim unambiguously in Judah.

"Geliloth" (districts, v. 17) where that for Judah has "Gilgal" (15:7). Both readings are textually solid, though one should probably assume that they reflect the same location in the source document.

[21–24] (District XIII) The towns of this district seem to be located east of the central ridge, in the plains of Jericho, and north into the kingdom of Israel, although more than half of the site identifications are unknown or debatable (see the appendix). Both Ophrah and Bethel are clearly north of the border with Joseph, and if Ophni is to be identified with Jifneh, then it is as well. Avvim, Chephar-ammoni ("village of the Ammonites"), and Ophni appear to be gentilics, like "the Jebusite" of v. 28. Beth-arabah is also listed in Judah's wilderness district (15:61).[8]

Although located in the territory of the kingdom of Israel, this northeast Benjamin district must also have been linked in some way to the kingdom of Judah. This is the only way it could have ended up as part of the same source as the eleven districts of Judah in chapter 15 and the Benjamin district inside the southern kingdom's territory (vv. 25–28). Verses 21–24 thus must describe a supplementary thirteenth district added to this earlier system of twelve. The presence of Beth-arabah in both a Judahite district and this "extra" northeast Benjamin district also suggests a modification of an earlier system. This supplementary district XIII can only stem from some time when Judah controlled northeast Benjamin and southern Ephraim (Bethel, Ophrah). The most reasonable hypothesis is the reign of Josiah, whose reform touched not only Bethel, but included Geba (v. 24).[9] Thus vv. 21–24 represent Benjaminite towns which were once part of the kingdom of Israel and then the Assyrian province of Samaria, but eventually were included into an expanded Judah, presumably at the time of Josiah.

[25–28] (District XII) This district is less problematic, representing territory north and west of Jerusalem, that is, Benjaminite towns which were part of the kingdom of Judah. Along with Gibeon and Kiriath-jearim, Beeroth and Chephirah formed the Gibeonite league in 9:17. Perhaps the flat equation of "the Jebusite" with Jerusalem (v. 28) obscures identification problems we can no longer untangle.[10] Some have joined this southwest Benjamin district to the diminutive Judah district of 15:60 by means of Kiriath-jearim.[11] However, it is likely that the

---

8. For this reason Noth, *Josua*, 111, joined this district together with Judah's wilderness district (15:61–62). However, the resulting district makes little practical sense, joining areas of dissimilar topography and economy.

9. Other suggestions are Jehoshaphat (Cross and Wright, "The Boundary and Province Lists," 209–11), Abijah (Kallai, *Historical Geography*, 334–48, 398–404), and Uzzah (Aharoni, *Land of the Bible*, 350–52). One feature these proposals share is a substantial reliance on the accuracy of the reports in Chronicles.

10. See Miller, "Jebus and Jerusalem: A Case of Mistaken Identity."

11. This is the position of Alt, Noth, *Josua*, 113, and Cross and Wright, "The Boundary and Province Lists."

Kiriath-baal (Judah) of 15:60 (the border point of 15:9; 18:14) is to be kept distinct from Kiriath-jearim, assigned to Benjamin. Thus 15:60 and 18:25–28 describe separate districts.[12] If there is no overlap between 15:60 and 18:25–28, then the eleven (15:45–47 is clearly artificial) districts of chapter 15 and the southwest Benjamin district of 18:25–28 represent twelve divisions of the kingdom of Judah.

The Six Remaining Tribes Joshua 19:1–51

For Simeon

19:1 The lot went out second for Simeon [for the tribe of the children of Simeon][a] [for their clans].[b] Their hereditary property was inside the hereditary property of Judah. **2** They had in their inherited property: Beersheba,[c] Moladah, **3** Hazar-shual, Balah, Ezem, **4** Eltolad, Bethul, Hormah, **5** Ziklag, Beth-marcaboth, Hazar-susah, **6** Beth-lebaoth, and Sharuhen. Thirteen cities and their precincts. **7** En-rimmon, Tochen,[d] Ether, and Ashan. Four cities and their precincts, **8** [all the precincts][e] which surround these cities as far as Baalath-beer, Ramah of the Negeb. This is the hereditary property of the tribe of the children of Simeon for their clans. **9** Some of the section of [the children of] Judah was the hereditary property of the children of Simeon because the section of the children of Judah was too much for them. So the children of Simeon received hereditary property inside their hereditary property.

For Zebulun

10 The lot turned up third for [the children of] Zebulun for their clans. The border of their hereditary property extended as far as Sadud.[f] **11** Their border goes up westward to Maralah, touches Dabbesheth, and touches the wadi which is opposite Jokneam. **12** It reverses from Sadud eastward toward the east to the border of Chisloth-tabor, goes to Daberath, and goes

---

12. Aharoni, *Land of the Bible*, 350–51, 355–56; Kallai, *Historical Geography*, 134–35. An overlap to make a single district out of 15:60 and 18:25–28 would presumably represent a twelve-district system that included the northeast Benjamin district from its inception. This would indicate an origin after the collapse of Assyrian control, rather than the extension and modification of an earlier arrangement.

up to Japhia. 13 From there it crosses on the east eastward to Gath-hepher and Eth-kazin, and goes to Rimmon, bending[g] to Neah. 14 The border turns itself[h] north of Hannathon and it ends at the valley of Iphtah-el. 15 Also Kattath, Nahalal, Shim'on, Idalah,[i] and Bethlehem. [Twelve cities and their precincts.][j] 16 This is the hereditary property of the children of Zebulun for their clans—[these] cities and their precincts.

For Issachar

17 For Issachar the lot went out fourth [for the children of Issachar for their clans].[k] 18 Their border extended toward Jezreel: (Chesulloth, Shunem, 19 Hapharaim, Shion, Anaharath, 20 Daberath,[l] Kishion, Ebez, 21 Remeth, En-gannim, En-haddah, Beth-pazzez). 22 The border touches Tabor, Shahazimah, and Beth-shemesh. Their border ends at the Jordan. [Sixteen cities and their precincts.] 23 This is the hereditary property of the tribe of the children of Issachar for their clans—cities and their precincts.

For Asher

24 The lot went out fifth for [the tribe of the children of] Asher [for their clans]. 25 Their border extended from[m] Helkath (Hali, Beten, Achshaph, 26 Allammelech, Amad, Mishal) and touches Carmel on the west and Shihor-libnath. 27 It reverses eastward to Beth-dagon, touches Zebulun and the valley of Iphtah-el on the north. The border goes northward[n] to Beth-emek and Neiel and goes to Cabul on the north,[o] 28 (Abdon,[p] Rehob, Hammon, Kanah) as far as Great Sidon. 29 The border turns around to Ramah as far as the fortified city Tyre. The border turns around to Hosah and ends at the sea (Mahalab,[q] Achzib, 30 Acco,[r] Aphek, Rehob). [Twenty-two cities and their precincts.] 31 This is the hereditary property of the tribe of the children of Asher for their clans—[these] cities and their precincts.

For Naphtali

32 For [the children of] Naphtali the lot went out sixth [for the children of Naphtali for their clans].[s] 33 Their border extended from Heleph, from the oak in Zaanannim and Adami-nekeb and Jabneel as far as Lakkum. It ended at the Jordan. 34 The border reverses westward to Aznoth-tabor, goes from there to Hukkok, touches Zebulun on the south, touches Asher on the west and Judah.[t] The Jordan is toward the east. 35 Also the fortified cities of Ziddim, Zer,[u] Hammath, Rakkath, Chinnereth, 36 Adamah, Ramah, Hazor, 37 Kedesh, Edrei, En-hazor, 38 Iron, Migdal-el, Horem,

Beth-anath, and Beth-shemesh. [Nineteen cities and their precincts.] 39 This is the hereditary property of the tribe of the children of Naphtali [for their clans—cities and their precincts].ᵛ

For Dan

40 For [the tribe of the children of] Dan [for their clans] the lot went out seventh. 41 The territory of their hereditary property was Zorah, Eshtaol, Ir-shemesh, 42 Shaalabbin, Aijalon, Ithlah, 43 Elon, Timnah, Ekron, 44 El-tekeh, Gibbethon, Baalath, 45 Jehud, Azor,ʷ Bene-berak, Gath-rimmon, 46 and on the west,ˣ Jarkon along with the territory opposite Joppa. 47 Now the territory of the children of Dan was lost to them.ʸ So the children of Dan went up and fought against Leshem and captured it. They struck it with the edge of the sword, took it over, and settled it. Then they called Leshem Dan after the name of Dan their ancestor.ᶻ 48 This is the hereditary property of the tribe of the children of Dan for their clans— [these] cities and their precincts.

For Joshua

49 So they finished apportioning the land according to its borders. Then the Israelites gave hereditary property to Joshua son of Nun among them. 50 By the command of Yahweh they gave him the city for which he asked—Timnath-serah in the hill country of Ephraim. He built a city and lived in it. 51 These are the hereditary properties which Eleazar the priest, Joshua son of Nun, and the heads of the families apportioned to the tribes of the Israelites by lot in Shiloh before Yahweh at the entrance of the Tent of Meeting. So they finished dividing up the land.

a. MT conflates the short reading of OG with a longer alternative found in S and V ("for the tribe of the children of Simeon") into the doublet "for Simeon for the tribe of the children of Simeon." OG is LXXᴬ here; LXXᴮ expands to "for the children of Simeon."

b. MT expands with "for their clans" here and in vv. 17, 24, 32, 39, and 40, to harmonize the formula to that found in this and earlier chapters.

c. Here MT adds a dittography "Sheba," lacking in 1 Chron. 4:28 MT. OG has "Shema" (*šmʻ*) here and at 1 Chron. 4:28, perhaps a contamination from Josh. 15:26. Another suggestion is that the double name reflects two associated Iron Age sites only a few kilometers apart: Tell es-Sebaʻ and Kh. Bir es-Sebaʻ. The city names in vv. 3–6 diverge somewhat from the parallel text in 15:29–32 and these differences should be permitted to stand. 1 Chron. 4:28–32, however, is dependent on Josh. 19:2–7 and may be used as a witness to its text.

d. "Tochen" added from OG (OG: Thachan; LXXᴮ: Talcha) and 1 Chron. 4:32. The Chronicles text enumerates "five" cities, separating "En-rimmon" into "Ain" and "Rimmon" (as does the Masoretic vocalization of Josh. 19:7). The loss of Tochen by MT may have triggered the division of En-rimmon into two cities to make up the total of "four." See text note on 15:32 and Barthélemy, *Critique,* 39–40.

e. MT has a dittography from the end of v. 7, absent in OG.

f. "Sadud" here and in v. 12 follows OG (= LXX^L and OL) and S ("Ashdod"), corresponding to an identification with Tel Shadud (Aharoni, *Land of the Bible,* 117). MT "Sarid" is an error of *r* for *d.* There are, however, some indications of Sarid/Sered as a clan of Zebulun (Gen. 46:14; perhaps Judg. 5:13). See Barthélemy, *Critique,* 52.

g. Redividing *rmwn hmt'r* into *rmwnh mt'r* as Barthélemy, *Critique,* 52–54.

h. Alternate translation: "turns by it [Neah, taken as a landmark rather than a town] north of." Compare 16:6 and Na'aman, *Borders and Districts,* 138.

i. "Shim'on" follows OG for MT "Shimron," see 11:1 and 12:20. "Idalah" could be "Iralah," on the basis of *y. Meg.* 1.77a. See Barthélemy, *Critique,* 54.

j. Here and at vv. 22, 30, and 38, MT follows the format of v. 6 with a summary enumeration. Although several of these represent puzzling totals, the OG pattern elsewhere has been to "correct" the totals rather than eliminate the notice completely. Thus, these are most likely MT expansions.

k. MT fills out the formula from v. 16.

l. Follows OG in harmony with Josh. 19:12; 21:28; 1 Chron. 6:57 [6:72E]. MT corrupted to Rabbith. See Barthélemy, *Critique,* 56–57.

m. Follows OG under the assumption that MT lost a *mem* through haplography: *gbwlm* [*m*]*ḥlqt.* This recovers the sense of the boundary description.

n. On the basis of OG *kai eiseleusetai horia Saphthai.* MT lost "the border goes northward" by haplography: *ṣpwnh* [*whlk hgbwl ṣpwnh*].

o. "On the north" (*mśm'l*) could be taken as a town name "Mishal" (compare NAB; 21:30). Alternate translation: "left of Cabul."

p. Follows OG ("Ebdon" resulting in LXX^B "Elbon"), Josh. 21:30; 1 Chron. 6:59 [74E]; MT reads "Ebron."

q. Suggested by OG, this reading assumes that MT *mḥbl* resulted from a metathesis of a place name known from an Assyrian source as *maḥallibu* (*ANET,* 287). There are two other textual variants of this name in Judg. 1:31: Ahlab and Helbah. Na'aman, *Borders and Districts,* 60, denies this widely accepted identification.

r. Follows Judg. 1:31, LXX^B, and other Greek witnesses. MT 'Ummah resulted from a confusion of *k* and *m* and perhaps a spelling of Acco with an alternate vowel letter as *'kh.*

s. MT reflects a doublet in regard to the position of "the children of Naphtali," conflating the variant word order of OG and S. It also fills out the formula as elsewhere in this chapter.

t. Not in OG, but difficult to explain as an addition to the text. Although possibly a dittography of "Jordan," it is best to retain as an otherwise unknown toponym. Alternate translation: "and Judah at the Jordan on the east."

u. MT "Ziddim, Zer" (*ḥṣdym ṣr*) and OG "of the Tyrians, Tyre" (*hṣrym ṣr*) reflect a corruption which cannot be convincingly unraveled. It may have resulted from something like "from the fortified city of Tyre (*ṣr*) to Sidon (*ṣydwn*)" (compare vv. 28–29) or represent a snowballing dittography of the last two letters of *mbṣr* "fortified."

v. This is the only time OG lacks this particular formula. In MT there is a mechanism for haplography in the first word of v. 40: *lm[śpḥtm . . . lm]th,* but apparently not in the OG exemplar (see brackets in v. 40). Here it is bracketed as an MT harmonization to the standard pattern.

w. OG has "Azor" in place of "Jehud." Azor and Bene-berak occur together in the annals of Sennacherib (*ANET*, 287). Apparently MT lost Azor and OG lost Jehud, each through homoioteleuton (assuming *yhwd* and perhaps *yzwr*).

x. Follows OG *wmym* for MT *wmy* (the start of a supposed toponym Me-jarkon). MT's following *whrqwn* ("and Rakkon") is a dittography of *hyrqwn*.

y. Literally "it went away from them." The assumption of a metathesis of an original *wy's* (hiphil of *'ws*) to *wys'* is unnecessary and cannot really be supported from the Greek.

z. Follows MT. The Greek offers a considerably different text for vv. 47–48. See the discussion below.

As before, boundary information is mixed with town catalogs.[1] However, in contrast to the precise border points given for Joseph, Judah, and Benjamin, the boundaries of the last tribes are more equivocal. They consist largely of frontier towns intended to be included along with their surrounding territories within the tribal area. This implies that the source material used here was a roster of peripheral towns that was subsequently converted into a loose boundary description. Boundary and town list materials are mixed together for Asher, but have been kept distinct for Zebulun, Issachar, and Naphtali. Border lines running along the east/west axis predominate. The boundary descriptions for Zebulun (vv. 10–12), Asher (vv. 24–27) and Naphtali (vv. 33–34) are all of a type in which a border segment is drawn in one direction from a town, then returns to that starting town to run in the opposite direction (cf. the commentary on 18:15). The formula to indicate the return of the perspective to the pivotal town uses the verb *šwb* followed by the new direction eastward or westward (vv. 12, 27, 34). Certain frontiers for Asher and Naphtali are vaguely indicated by junctions with other tribes (vv. 27, 34; cf. 17:10b–11).

Simeon and Dan are described on the basis of town lists alone. There is no compelling reason to think that any of these assorted town lists are connected with the Judah-Benjamin district system of 15:21–62; 18:21–28. The list of Levitical cities duplicates some of these towns for the tribes other than Simeon (21:23–24, 28–32, 34–35) so that for these five tribes every town in chapter 21 finds a reflex in chapter 19. The simplest explanation for this circumstance is that chapter 21 utilized chapter 19 as a source.

1. See Kallai, *Historical Geography*, 179–240, 307–10 on the boundaries and 349–71, 416–38 on the town lists; also Aharoni, *Land of the Bible*, 88–89, 257–62, 311–12. The classic treatment is A. Alt, "Eine galiläische Ortsliste in Jos. 19," *ZAW* 45 (1927). 59–81, who proposed a town list for the Assyrian province of Galilee. Noth insisted that in Galilee the town lists and border descriptions belonged together as a system of fixed border points, "Studien zu den historisch-geographischen Dokumenten des Josuabuches," 229–80. See also Z. Kallai-Kleinmann, "The Town Lists of Judah, Simeon, Benjamin, and Dan," *VT* 8 (1958): 134–60.

These territorial descriptions foster an ideology of land claim and tribal sol-idarity. They evoke long vanished circumstances in order to build group iden-tity and attachment to the land of promise. The atmosphere is that of scribal scholarship. Inherited documents, the nature of which must remain largely un-clear to us, have been restructured into new texts designed to inspire, convince, uplift, and motivate. The incessantly repeated "lot" signals Yahweh's election and gift. The readership's rightful possession of these alienated territories is driven home by the reiterated formula "this is the hereditary property" (vv. 6, 16, 23, 31, 39, 48).

[1–9] Simeon comes next because, like Benjamin, it is of immediate inter-est to Judah.[2] Verse 1 introduces Simeon's situation and v. 8b concludes it. Verse 9 provides an explanation for Simeon's peculiar situation as a result of the oversized lot given Judah. The data consist of two town lists with enumer-ative summaries: vv. 2–6 and 7–8a. An alternate form of this data, with minor scribal differences, occurs as 1 Chron. 4:28–33. Apart from Beersheba and En-rimmon, there is little agreement about the location of these towns (see the ap-pendix). Sharuhen is mentioned in several Egyptian texts (*ANET*, 233), and Hazar-susah, [El]toldah, Ezem, and Ramoth-negeb appear on ostraca from the Negeb area.[3]

The portion of the list in vv. 2–6 along with En-rimmon is related to part of Judah's district I (15:26–32), which is sometimes thought to have provided its source.[4] However, Ether and Ashan (v. 7), presumably in the Shephelah, ap-pear in district IV instead (15:42). The names in the Judah town-list segment and the Simeon list appear in nearly the same order where they overlap (Mo-ladah being an exception). "Biziothiah" from the MT Judah list is not repre-sented because it is a corruption of "daughter cities" (see text note for 15:28). Probably Bethul (19:4) is equivalent to Chesil (15:30) and Sharuhen (19:6) to Shilhim (15:32). Madmannah (15:31) is replaced by "House of Chariots" (Beth-marcaboth, 19:5) and Sansannah by "Horse Corral" (Hazar-susah), as though functional designations have displaced the actual place names.

The division into two districts (vv. 2–6 and 7) suggests an administrative background for this data, although one can only speculate as to date and pur-pose. 1 Chron. 4:31 highlights this division with the assertion that the first dis-trict was Simeon's "until David became king." The association of the Shep-helah towns Ether and Asham with En-rimmon suggests that v. 7 represents a district of northern and western Simeonite towns. Comparable to the town list for Dan (vv. 40–46), the Simeonite list designates special claims within the ter-

2. Literature includes N. Na'aman, "The Inheritance of the Sons of Simeon," *ZDPV* 96 (1980): 136–52, and S. Talmon, "The Town Lists of Simeon," *IEJ* 15 (1965): 235–41.

3. Aharoni, *Arad Inscriptions*, 46–49.

4. Beginning with A. Alt, "Beiträge zur historischen Geographie und Topographie des Negeb III," *Kleine Schriften* III, Munich 409–35.

ritory of "greater Judah." One could postulate various bureaucratic purposes for such a catalog.

Baalath-beer and Ramah of the Negeb (v. 8) indicate the limits of Simeon's territorial extent (presumably southward) out from its assigned towns. It would make more geographical sense for this phrase to apply to all of Simeon's towns rather than to just the last four, and perhaps the MT textual addition intends to clarify this. The reason given in v. 9 for Simeon's atypical situation is clearly from a Judah-centered perspective. The hereditary property (*naḥălâ*) may be Simeon's, but the section (*ḥebel*) itself belongs properly to Judah. In the Second Temple period, all of this territory would lie outside of Jewish control, but this text seeks to assert a historical and theological claim to it.

[10–16] The paragraph for Zebulun consists of a detailed border description (vv. 10b–14) followed by a brief town list (v. 15). These are enclosed by a formulaic envelope (vv. 10a and 16). The border consists of frontier towns that are included with their territory within Zebulun rather than of precise boundary points. The south border is described first (vv. 10b-12), using Sadud as a hinge. First the line is run west from Sadud, apparently along the Kishon River (v. 11), then it goes back (*šwb*) and runs east and northeast from there (v. 12). The east segment running northward is described in v. 13 ("on the east eastward") and the north segment running westward in v. 14.[5] This parallels the pattern used for Asher (vv. 25–29). The turning points are marked at Japhia ("from there") and Rimmon/Neah ("bending," "turns on itself," cf. the expression in 16:6), although site identifications are too uncertain for us to trace the boundary with precision. There is little or no question about the identification of Sadud, Jokneam, Daberath, Rimmon,[6] Bethlehem, and Hannathon. Chisloth-tabor is probably the same as Chesuloth in v. 18 and thus also solidly identified. Japhia's usual identification (Yafa) does not really correspond to a plausible course for the border out of Daberath. The presence of Chesulloth/Chisloth-tabor and Daberath in the Issachar town list indicates that the Zebulun border intends to exclude those towns, as v. 12 implies for Chisloth-tabor ("to the border of").

The boundary description is supplemented by a short town list in v. 15. This circumstance helps us understand the formative process behind the other sections in which these two genres have been mingled. The enumerative summary of MT mysteriously corresponds only to the number of the boundary cities. Kattath and Nahalal occur in slightly different forms in Judg. 1:30.

[17–23] The Issachar section was composed from a town list (vv. 18–21) and a boundary fragment (v. 22). Verse 17 provides a formulaic introduction, and MT adds an enumeration at the end. Solid identifications are limited to

---

5. Z. Gal, "Cabul, Jiphthah-El and the Boundary Between Asher and Zebulun in the Light of Archaeological Evidence," *ZDPV* 101 (1985): 114–27.

6. However, Na'aman, *Borders and Districts*, 137, sees Rimmon as a metathesis of Maron (11:1; 12:20).

Jezreel, Shunem, Daberath, and Chesulloth. The last two of these are part of Zebulun's south border description. Because "Issachar" was the designation for Solomon's tenth district (1 Kings 4:17), there could be some relationship between this data and that administrative unit.[7] Remeth in v. 21 is the same as Jarmuth in 21:29, where it is the OG reading (compare 1 Chron. 6:58 [73E]). This identification is made in part of the basis of the stele of Seti I (*ANET*, 255).

The line of the border fragment (v. 22) could begin with Jezreel in v. 18 if this name has a functioning directive ending ("toward Jezreel"): "toward Jezreel, touches Tabor, Shahazimah, Beth-shemesh, ends at the Jordan." Tabor might be understood as a town name in accordance with 1 Chron. 6:62 [77E] rather than as a reference to the mountain. Shahazimah[8] may be two places accidently run together: Shahaz and Yammah. This seems to be part of Issachar's north border, as suggested by the mention of Tabor and the possible location of Beth-shemesh just southwest of the Sea of Galilee (Kh. Sheikh esh-Shamsawi). This border must correspond in some way to Naphtali's southern border between Aznoth-tabor and the Jordan (v. 33–34), although there are no internal border points in common. The territories of Zebulun, Issachar, and Naphtali all apparently met near Mount Tabor: Chisloth-tabor (v. 12), Tabor (v. 22), Aznoth-tabor (v. 34).

[24–31] The Asher description consists of a boundary delineation into which three portions of a town list have been inserted.[9] Verses 24 and 31 provide a framework. The MT tradition inserts an enumeration based on not counting Tyre and Sidon and counting Rehob only once (v. 30).

Removing the elements of the town list to isolate the boundary description, one may reconstruct:

> south border running west (vv. 25–26): "from Helkath . . .
> and touches Carmel on the west and Shihor-libnath."
> south border running east (v. 27): "it turns around eastward
> to Beth-dagon."
> east border running north (vv. 27–28): "touches Zebulun and
> the valley of Iphtah-el on the north. The border goes
> northward to Beth-emek and Neiel and goes to Cabul on
> the north . . . as far as Great Sidon."

7. Kallai, *Historical Geography*, 315–18. There is also a general correspondence between Naphtali and the eighth district and Benjamin with the eleventh. Joshua's data about the east Jordan tribes largely correlates to Solomon's sixth, seventh, and twelfth districts.

8. Possibly best read as Shahazaimah. The Kethib is Shahazumah.

9. On the territory of Asher see A. Kuschke, "Kleine Beiträge zur Siedlungsgeschichte der Stämme Asser und Juda," *HTR* 64 (1971): 291–313, and E. Lipiński, "The Territory of Tyre and the Tribe of Asher," *Phoenicia and the Bible*, Studia Phoenicia 11, 153–66, who proposes that these toponyms constitute a list divided into six districts and referring to the territory of the kingdom of Tyre.

north border running west (v. 29): "the border turns around
to Ramah as far as . . . Tyre. The border turns around to
Hosah and ends at the sea."

The south border follows the procedure of going out first west from Helkath
(vv. 25–26) and then returning (*šwb*) there to run east (v. 27).[10] The boundary
runs "as far as" Sidon and Tyre but does not include them, just as it "touches"
Zebulun. In general the border may be thought to run along the Kishon on the
south and Zebulun on the east. It then continues on the east side along a long
line running north to include Cabul, turns westward at Sidon's territory to form
a north boundary running somewhere south of the Litani River.[11] Outside Tyre
it bends southwest to hit the coast at Hosah/Usu.

A paucity of identifications makes greater precision difficult. In the boundary description only Cabul may be taken as certain. Hosah is usually but not
universally taken to be Usu, the mainland city by Tyre.[12] Shihor-libnath is
sometimes thought to be two towns. Because the first element is Egyptian
"lake/river," perhaps the lower portion of the Kishon River is intended. Feasi-
ble but uncertain identifications for Beth-emek and Neiel would indicate that
the Beth-emek—Neiel—Cabul segment has been preserved in reverse order,
that is, north to south.

The town-list fragments are placed at what the redactor apparently thought
were appropriate spots in the border description. The first portion of the town
list (Hali, Beten, Achshaph, Allammelech, Amad, Mishal) is inserted into the
south border running west, and Hali and perhaps Beten and Achshaph may be
located near Carmel. The second section (Abdon, Rehob, Hammon, Kanah) is
put into the east border running north via Cabul. Again this makes sense in that
these towns are in the north half of Asher's territory. A miscellaneous third section (Mahalab, Achzib, Acco, Aphek, Rehob) follows at the end. This includes
Mahalab just north of Tyre, but also Acco and Achzib in the midsection on the
coast and Aphek presumably inland. The repetition of Rehob (vv. 28, 30) supports the division of the data into a boundary source and town-list source.[13]
This last group of towns (along with Sidon and with Mahalab in two variant
forms) occur together in the description of unconquered towns in Judg. 1:31.

Asher's inheritance is presented as a kaleidoscopic totality. This indiscrim-

10. The verb *šwb* is also used to indicate two bends in the border in vv. 29. Kallai, *Historical
Geography*, 216–17 offers the alternate view that these verbs in v. 29 describe a reversal in the
border's course from the northernmost border point southward towards fortified Tyre and Hosah.

11. "As far as" suggests that Sidon lay outside Asher's territory according to Aharoni, *Land
of the Bible*, 238, but should have been part of Asher according to Judg. 1:31. In contrast, Kallai,
Historical Geography, 213–15, includes Sidon within Asher's borders.

12. On this question, see Kallai, *Historical Geography*, 217–20.

13. The possibility that there were two towns by this name cannot be excluded. See Aharoni,
Land of the Bible, 144, 162, 441.

inate mingling of two sorts of material reveals a purpose quite different from any sort of archival preservation or geographical research. From the standpoint of the national claim on territory, both boundary cities and interior cities serve the same basic function. The tradition of a past reality, one which reaches back before the formation of the Assyrian provinces (732) or even to Solomon (Cabul, 1 Kings 9:11–13), is kept alive in hope and asserted to have been God's will as expressed through sacred lot. In a similar way the narrative about David's census also preserved this memory of Israel's former northern frontier in that 2 Sam. 24:6–7 corresponds at several points to Josh. 19:28–29.

[32–39] For Naphtali as for Zebulun, the border description (vv. 33–34) and town list (vv. 35–38) have been kept separate. Verses 32 and 39 provide the framework. MT adds a puzzling enumeration (v. 38b).

The border description is difficult to unravel, but clearly comes in two segments corresponding to vv. 33 and 34. The verb *šwb* at the beginning of v. 34 is functioning as it does in vv. 12 and 27 to indicate that a new section of border begins at the original starting point. Thus v. 33 runs east from Heleph to the Jordan. Only Adami-nekeb and Jabneel on this line can be located with any assurance. Then in v. 34 the focus shifts back westward from Heleph to Aznoth-tabor (obviously near Mt. Tabor) and traces a very generalized line from there via Hukkok that follows on the south the edge of Zebulun and then on the west that of Asher.[14] Then follows the eastern border at the end of v. 34, that is, the Jordan. There is no indication of a north border, except perhaps for the mysterious Judah. This deficiency may have resulted from a concern to leave room in the conceptual system for Dan's northern territory.[15] The suggestion that v. 33 represents this missing north border[16] is unconvincing.

In the town list a substantial number of identifications can be made with near certainty. Verse 35 suggests that some or all of these were "fortified towns," although this phrase is associated with textual damage that has occurred at that point. Hammath is probably the Hammoth-dor of 21:32 and Rakkath seems to appear as Kartan (*qrtn* for *rqt*) in that same verse. There is no reason to equate the Beth-shemesh of Naphtali with the town of the same name in the border of Issachar (v. 22).

[40–48] Verses 40 and 48 enclose the data about Dan with standard formulas.[17] Although the language of border is used, what is presented is actually a town list. Therefore the translation construes *gĕbûl* as "territory" rather than

14. The toponym "Judah" in this context is startling if genuine. Kallai, *Historical Geography*, 238, suggests Sayid Hudah.

15. Na'aman, *Borders and Districts*, 46.

16. Noth, *Josua*, 119–21.

17. In addition to literature already cited, see B. Mazar, "The Cities of the Territory of Dan," *IEJ* 10 (1960): 65–77, who sees the list as an expansion of the second Solomonic district made up of four sectors, and J. Strange, "The Inheritance of Dan," *ST* 20 (1966): 120–39, who proposes instead the reign of Josiah.

"border" in v. 41 as well as in vv. 46–47. Verse 47 recounts the special history of Dan in a parenthetical sort of way. The problem here is not explicitly Philistine pressure, but simply the neutral statement that the land "got away from them." The towns that can be located occur to the west of the territory of Benjamin and Ephraim. Eshtaol and Zorah appear also in Judah's district II; Ir-[Beth-]shemesh and Timnah are border points on the Judah/Benjamin boundary. Because Ekron as a Danite city seems implausible, perhaps the two names in v. 43 should be joined together as Timnath-ekron.[18] Even though an actual border is not described, the towns named do form a sort of framing pattern around Danite territory. To the east along the Benjaminite frontier (18:14) are Shaalabbin and Aijalon, then Zorah, Eshtaol, and Ir-shemesh. On the south along Judah's north border (15:11) are Timnah, Ekron, and Baalath. On the north paralleling Ephraim's boundary line (16:3, 5–6a) are Jehud, Azor, and Bene-berak.[19] The west is explicitly marked off by v. 46.

The Danite list has some sort of relationship to the data about Solomon's second administrative district in 1 Kings 4:9. Although Solomon's Makaz has no reflex, one may match Ir-shemesh (v. 41) to Beth-shemesh, Shaalabbin (v. 42) to Shaalbim (cf. Judg. 1:35), and Elon (v. 43) to Elon-beth-hanan. It is often conjectured that the Solomonic district provided the source for the Danite list.[20]

[47–48 LXX] The Greek offers a considerably different and longer text for vv. 47–48:

This is the hereditary property of the tribe of the children of Dan for their clans — their cities and their precincts. The children of Dan did not dispossess the Amorites who pressed them into the hill country. The Amorites did not let them come down into the valley. They narrowed upon them the border of their section. So the children of Judah went up and fought against Leshem [LXX^A; Lachish, LXX^B] and captured it. They struck it with the edge of the sword and settled it. Then they called its name Leshem Dan [LXX^A]. The Amorites continued to live in Elom [Aijalon] and Salamin [Shaalbim], but the hand of Ephraim was heavy on them, and they became forced labor for them.

Although this has sometimes been defended as original,[21] there are strong reasons for believing that this little plot line was secondarily constructed out of Josh.

18. Aharoni, *Land of the Bible*, 312.

19. For this analysis, Na'aman, *Borders and Districts*, 107–12. Compare Cross and Wright, "The Boundary and Province Lists," 208–11. Noth, *Josua*, 77, 109–10, 120–23, suggests that Benjamin had been truncated on the west to make room for Dan.

20. Kallai, *Historical Geography*, 41–45.

21. Holmes, *Joshua: The Hebrew and Greek Texts*, 70; Auld, "Judges 1 and History: A Reconsideration," 277–78, who sees Judg. 1:34–35 as dependent on a text like that of OG. The order of the Greek version represents Josh. 19:46, 48; Judg. 1:34; Josh. 19:47; Judg. 1:35. Lindars, *Judges 1–5*, 69, correctly points out that it is implausible that Josh. 19:47 should have remained in Joshua MT without any telltale trace of Judg. 1:34 and 35 attached, while the same verse should have coincidentally fallen cleanly out of Judges.

19:47 (in a form close to MT) and Judg. 1:34–35. The narrative problem was derived from the hostility of the Amorites in Judg. 1:34 and Dan's problematic circumstances in Josh. 19:47a. A solution in the form of an attack (by Judah!) on
Leshem (or Lachish) was provided by continuing with a version of Josh. 19:47b.
Denouement was offered by Judg. 1:35: the Amorites remained, although put to
forced labor. Certain elements in Josh. 19:47 MT which would not conform to
the conquest of the city by Judah were eliminated: "took it over (as a possession)"; "after the name of Dan their ancestor." The summary formula of v. 48
MT was moved up to follow directly on v. 46 because it would be out of place
after the mastery of the Amorites by Ephraim. This same interest in providing
intertextual connections to the following story of Judges also surfaces in the
Greek textual tradition near the close of Joshua (see Joshua chap. 24).

[**49–51**] Verses 49a and 51 conclude the main business of chapters 18 and
19. The reference to borders in v. 49a reflects the perspective of boundary description, which has provided the overall framework for the available data (except for Simeon and perhaps Dan). Verse 51 concludes in a satisfying fashion
by recapitulating the dramatic setting that was set up by 18:1–10: "Shiloh, tent
of meeting, lot, before Yahweh." A new item of information, that this allotment was also the act of Eleazar and the family heads, points all the way back
to 14:1 and thus provides part of a concluding bracket to the whole process of
west-bank land distribution: "so they finished dividing up the land." In other
words, v. 51 does double duty as a closing bracket for the structural segments
of 14:1–19:51 (nine-and-a-half tribes) and 18:1–19:51 (seven tribes).

Verses 49b–50 report a land grant to Joshua as an individual (compare
Caleb and Othniel/Achsah). This information will reappear as part of a grave
tradition in 24:30, which is probably the source for this notice. The original
form of the name was probably Timnath-heres as in Judg. 2:9 (and LXX^B
here), meaning "portion of the sun." A metathesis, helped by an orthodox urge
to remove the pagan reference, subsequently created Timnath-serah, perhaps
as a word play, "portion of surplus."

Cities of Refuge
Joshua 20:1–9

UNREVISED TEXT	MT REVISION
20:1 Yahweh spoke to Joshua: 2 "Say to the Israelites, 'Set up for yourselves the cities of refuge about which I spoke to you through Moses,	**20:1** Yahweh spoke to Joshua: 2 "Say to the Israelites, 'Set up for yourselves the cities of refuge about which I spoke to you through Moses,

3 so that anyone who kills by striking down a person in error may flee there. They[b] shall be a refuge for you from the blood avenger and the killer shall not be put to death[c]

3 so that anyone who kills by striking down a person in error *inadvertently*[a] may flee there. They shall be a refuge for you from the blood avenger.

4 *He shall flee to one of these cities and stand at the opening of the city gate and declare his case to the elders of that city. They shall admit him into the city and provide him a place. He shall live with them.* 5 *If the blood avenger pursues him, they shall not turn the killer over to his power, because he struck down his neighbor inadvertently and had not previously hated him.* 6 *He shall live in that city* until he can stand before the community for judgment,'"

6 until he can stand before the community for judgment.'"

6 *He shall live in that city* until he can stand before the community for judgment, *until the death of the one who is high priest at that time. Then the killer may return to his own city and his own house—to the city from which he fled.'"*

7 He[d] designated[e] Kedesh in Galilee in the hill country of Naphtali, Shechem in the hill country of Ephraim, and Kiriath-arba (that is, Hebron) in the hill country of Judah. 8 On the other side of the Jordan [east of Jericho] he[d] set up Bezer in the wilderness on the plateau from the tribe of Reuben, Ramoth in Gilead from the tribe of Gad, and Golan in Bashan from the tribe of Manasseh. 9 These were the cities of appointment[f] for the Israelites and for aliens residing among them, so that anyone who strikes down a person in error might flee there and that he might not die at the hand of the blood avenger until he has stood before the community.[g]

a. "Inadvertently" is absent from OG and is a deuteronomistic supplement; compare Deut. 4:42; 19:4.

b. Follows MT. OG and Num. 35:12 add "the cities" as an explicit subject.

c. Follows OG. MT lacks "and the killer shall not be put to death." This along with the OG explicit subject "cities" is reflected exactly by Num. 35:11b–12. These words were probably a casualty of the supplementation process since their content is covered by v. 5.

d. MT has "they" in place of "he" as the grammatical subject in vv. 7 and 8.

e. Follows OG, which reflects *wyqrw* (the verb in Num. 35:11, from *qrh*). This was misread by MT under the influence of the following "Kedesh" as *wyqdšw*.

f. Alternate translation: "of meeting" or "of assembly by appointment."
g. OG and S add "for judgment" from v. 6.

The differences between the short OG and long MT forms of this chapter are best explained as evidence of a further recensional development in the MT tradition. A descriptive narrative that told of Joshua's obedience to Yahweh's command has been supplemented by prescriptive commands detailing how the law is to be carried out. The MT additions are an intertextual development, intended to coordinate Joshua's act with the particulars of Deut. 19:1–13 and Num. 35:25.[1]

The notion of asylum[2] can be found in the covenant code (Exod. 21:12–14) and was originally one of the functions performed by the local sanctuary (1 Kings 1:50–53; 2:28–34). In a case of wrongful death, a "blood avenger" (vv. 3, 5, 9; *gōʾēl haddām*), the victim's son or another male relative, would retaliate based on his status as a family member. The right of asylum helped to limit the social damage of unrestrained blood vengeance. Asylum was probably originally connected to the contagious holiness of the sanctuary altar to which the fugitive clung. As part of Deuteronomy's centralization program, certain elements of cultic life had to be secularized (e.g. tithes, Deut. 14:22–29, and animal slaughter, Deut. 12:15–17). In a similar exercise in secularization, Deuteronomy replaced the sanctuary role of the local altar with a program of regional towns performing the same function. The establishment and function of three such towns (with provision for three more if needed) are set forth in Deut. 19:1–13. A later text (part of the framing introduction for Deuteronomy proper) notes the establishment of three supplementary towns east of the Jordan (Deut. 4:41–43) with toponyms and language shared with Joshua 20 (esp. Deut. 4:43).

[1–3, 6, 7–10] The earliest recoverable text of Joshua 20 describes the appointment of six cities of refuge as a response to the command of Moses (v. 2), but in terms unrelated to the specifics of Deut. 19:1–8.[3] Yahweh explains the concept of asylum cities to Joshua (vv. 1–3, first part of v. 6); then Joshua dutifully carries out the assignment (vv. 7–8). Verse 7 moves from north to south and maps out the cities by three successive geographic regions designated as "the hill country of . . . ." Verse 8 moves from south to north, with the cities designated by tribe as well as geography. Thus all six towns are located with geographic designations ("in the hill country," "in the wilderness," "in Gilead," "in

---

1. See A. Rofé, "Joshua 20: Historico-Literary Criticism Illustrated," *Empirical Models for Biblical Criticism*, Philadelphia, 1985, 131–47, and M. Fishbane, "Biblical Colophons, Textual Criticism and Legal Analogies," *CBQ* 42 (1980): 443–46.

2. See M. Greenberg, "The Biblical Conception of Asylum," *JBL* 78 (1959): 125–32.

3. A. Rofé, "The History of the Cities of Refuge in Biblical Law," *Studies in the Bible*, ScrHier 31, Jerusalem, 1986, 205–39.

Bashan") appropriate to their role as regional centers. Verse 9 summarizes and repeats their purpose in language similar to that of vv. 3 and 6.

The literary relationship of Joshua 20 to the other texts about asylum cities remains problematic. For example, the consonance between v. 8 and Deut. 4:43 is obvious, but the direction of dependence is impossible to determine on internal grounds alone. Obviously, the restriction of Deut. 4:43 to towns east of the Jordan is required by its place in the deuteronomic plot line and cannot be used as evidence one way or the other. Joshua 20 in its pre-MT form seems to follow the general principles of Deut. 19:1–8, but none of its specific details. For example, it ignores the provision for three original and three supplementary cities (Deut. 19:8–9). In the Joshua text, the six cities are appointed all at once by Joshua, and no distinctions are made among them.[4] Moreover, the specific term "city of refuge," that is "of admittance, inclusion" (*miqlāṭ*)[5] is not found in Deuteronomy at all, but is unique to Joshua 20–21 (and Num. 35:9–28; 1 Chron. 6:42, 52 [57, 67E]). The unrevised form of the Joshua text has its closest relationship to Num. 35:9–15. Various patterns of interrelationship among these texts have been suggested, but Noth's conclusion that Num. 33:50–35:29 is generally dependent on Joshua 14–21 and that Num. 35:9–15 depends specifically on Joshua 20 rests on solid critical observations.[6] In fact Num. 35:9–15 depends specifically on the unrevised pre-MT text form of Joshua 20 rather than its MT form. For example, Num. 35:11b–12 is identical with pre-MT vv. 3 and 6 (see text notes b, c, and e). To complicate matters, however, the MT supplement about the death of the high priest in v. 6 closely reflects Num. 35:25. Over time, the process of intertextual harmonization seems to have run both directions. The names and descriptions of these six cities also played a role in the composition process that formed the levitical city-list of Joshua 21 (vv. 1, 11, 27, 32, 36, 38).[7]

The unrevised text is much less deuteronomistic than the revised version. As mentioned, the very term "cities of refuge" never appears in Deuteronomy. Instead of the expression "inadvertently" (*biblî-da'at*), so important to Deut. 19:4–5 and used in the MT revision (vv. 3, 5), the unrevised text simply has the priestly expression "in error" (*bišgāgâ;* vv. 3, 9; Num. 35:11, 15). The extension of asylum rights to the "alien" (*gēr*) in not present in the Deuteronomy

---

4. However, there is a difference in the way they are described. Verse 7 uses a topographic designation that includes a tribal name ("the hill country of Naphtali"), while v. 8 identifies them with a geographical location followed by a tribal name. This may be evidence that some earlier form of the text mentioned only the three western cities.

5. See R. Schmid, *miqlāṭ," TDOT* VIII, 552–56.

6. Noth, *Numbers*, 248–55, and *Josua*, 127.

7. This is the generally accepted theory and involves fewer complications than understanding the literary dependence to have run in the opposite direction, as does A. G. Auld, "Cities of Refuge in Israelite Tradition," *JSOT* 10 (1978): 26–40.

text either. This reflects a priestly concern (Num. 15:15–16). Other expressions of a priestly character found in Joshua 20 are *'ēdâ* "community" and the unique "cities of appointment" in v. 9.

Scholars have sometimes suggested that the national boundaries implied in this chapter might be used to date the institution of the cities of refuge. The state-building situation of the United Kingdom has been proposed, along with expansion under Jeroboam II (2 Kings 14:25, 28) or the ambitions of Josiah.[8] However, one should not necessarily assume an actual historical praxis corresponding to either Deut. 19:1–8 or Joshua 20. The careful distribution of towns in vv. 7–8 leaves the impression of the artificial regularity of a literary construction rather than a genuine political program. Inclusion of territory east of the Jordan in the Joshua text more likely relates to the book's ideological stress on the legitimacy of that region rather than to a given historical period.

This text seeks to anchor the institution of regional asylum cities to Israel's earliest days in the land and justify it as compliance with a command of Yahweh and Moses. With this chapter, the direction of the book of Joshua turns from land apportionment to issues of how life in the land is to lived, the concern of the book's last three chapters. For one thing, life in the land of Yahweh must avoid social injustices such as unrestrained blood vengeance. It is to reflect equitable justice (*mišpāṭ*, v. 6) administered democratically by the "community" and with equality for both full citizen and alien (v. 9). Such fairness is achieved by adherence to divinely instituted governing structures (vv. 1–2).

[4–6 MT] In the MT revision, Yahweh supplements the uncomplicated original command in order to detail administrative procedures for the offender's admission and release. The material not present in OG, principally vv. 4–5 and most of v. 6, revises the original text to bring it closer to Deut. 19:1–8. Deuteronomic characteristics include "inadvertently" in vv. 3 and 5b (Deut. 4:42; 19:4) and the notion of city elders as a juridical body (v. 4, compare Deut. 19:12 and elsewhere in Deuteronomy). The phrasing parallels that of Deut. 19:1–13 (as well as 4:41–43):

> v. 4a: Deut. 4:42b; 19:5b, 11b
> v. 5a: Deut. 19:6, 12
> v. 5b: Deut. 4:42; 19:4, 6

The revision modifies the original notion that the accused shelters in the city until the whole community can make a determination as to culpability. A preliminary hearing before the town elders is added in order to determine whether the killer should even enter the city in the first place. The notion of the death of the high priest is imported from Num. 35:25, although with deuteronomistic coloring (Deut. 17:9; 19:17). This creates an odd second conclusion for the first part

---

8. For a summary of opinions, see Butler, *Joshua*, 214–15.

of v. 6: the offender lives in the city until the trial *and* until the high priest's death. Amnesty at the death of the high priest was a post-exilic ideological development. This was a common royal practice and thus an example of the assumption of the king's functions by the high priest in the Second Temple period.

The singular verbs in the original text of vv. 7 and 8 attribute the selection of all six cities to Joshua alone, which fits the procedure outlined in Num. 35:13–15. In order to harmonize with Deut. 4:41–43 and 19:1–7, however, the revision turned these into plurals (text note d), apparently to allow for Moses to join the action. Thus in the revised text, v. 7 can be understood as something done under Joshua's supervision and v. 8 as a task accomplished while Moses was the leader. This recensional development also created some internal tensions. In v. 6 the killer is in a temporary status before trial by the assembly. With the addition of 4–5, however, the killer's fate has already been decided by the elders without any decision by the whole congregation being in view. Since the elders have already determined that the deed was done "inadvertently" (v. 5), there is no longer any point to the hearing before the community that remains part of the procedure in v. 6. This MT recensional development grew out of a conviction that the Pentateuch (Numbers and Deuteronomy) was canonical and scriptural, in the sense that other texts such as Joshua needed to be adjusted to fit its norms. A similar motive lay behind the MT corrections to 5:10–12.

Levitical Cities
Joshua 21:1–45

Introduction

21:1 The heads of the families of the Levites approached Eleazar the priest, Joshua son of Nun, and the heads of the families of the tribes of [the children of] Israel. 2 They spoke to them at Shiloh in the land of Canaan, "Yahweh commanded through Moses to give us cities to live in and their pasture lands for our cattle." 3 So according to the command of Yahweh the Israelites gave to the Levites from their hereditary property [these] cities and their pasture lands.

4 The lot went out for the clans of the Kohathites. The descendants of Aaron the priest from among the Levites acquired thirteen cities by lot from the tribe of Judah, from the tribe of the Simeonites, and from the tribe of Benjamin. 5 The rest of the descendants of Kohath acquired ten cities by lot from the clans of [a] the tribe of Ephraim, from the tribe of Dan, and from the half-tribe of Manasseh. 6 The descendants of Gershon acquired thirteen cities [by lot] from the clans of the tribe of Issachar, from the tribe of Asher,

from the tribe of Naphtali, and from the half-tribe of Manasseh in Bashan. 7 The descendants of Merari acquired twelve cities for their clans from the tribe of Reuben, from the tribe of Gad, and from the tribe of Zebulun. 8 So the Israelites gave [these] cities and their pasture lands to the Levites by lot, just as Yahweh had commanded through Moses.

For the Aaronic Priests

9 They gave from the tribe of the children of Judah and the tribe of the children of Simeon[b] [these] cities identified here by name.[c] 10 It was for the descendants of Aaron, one of the clans of the Kohathites of the children of Levi, because the lot fell to them [first].[d] 11 They gave them Kiriath-arba (Arba was the father[e] of Anak), that is Hebron in the hill country of Judah, and the pasture lands around it. 12 But the fields of the city and its precincts they had given to Caleb son of Jephunneh as his holding. 13 To the descendants of Aaron [the priest][f] they gave:

Hebron, the city of refuge for the killer, and its pasture lands,
Libnah and its pasture lands,
14 Jattir and its pasture lands,
Eshtemoa and its pasture lands,
15 Holon and its pasture lands,
Debir and its pasture lands,
16 Ashan[g] and its pasture lands,
Juttah and its pasture lands,
and Beth-shemesh[h] and its pasture lands.
Nine cities from these two tribes.

17 From the tribe of Benjamin:

Gibeon and its pasture lands,
Geba and its pasture lands,
18 Anathoth and its pasture lands,
and Almon and its pasture lands.
Four cities.

19 In all the cities of the descendants of Aaron, the priests, were thirteen cities [with their pasture lands].[i]

For the Remaining Kohathites

20 As for the clans of the levitical descendants of Kohath who remained from the descendants of Kohath, their allotted[j] cities were from the tribe of Ephraim. 21 They gave them:

Shechem, the city of refuge for the killer, and its pasture lands in the
hill country of Ephraim,[k]
Gezer and its pasture lands,
22 Kibzaim[l] and its pasture lands,
and Beth-horon and its pasture lands.
Four cities.

23 From the tribe of Dan:

Elteke and its pasture lands,
Gibbethon and its pasture lands,
24 Aijalon and its pasture lands,
Gath-rimmon and its pasture lands.
Four cities.

25 From the half-tribe of Manasseh:

Taanach and its pasture lands,
and Ibleam[m] and its pasture lands.
Two cities.

26 In all there were ten cities with their pasture lands for the clans of the
rest of the descendants of Kohath.

For the Gershonites

27 To the descendants of Gershon, one of the clans of the Levites, from
the half-tribe of Manasseh:

Golan in Bashan, the city of refuge for the killer, and its pasture lands,
and "Beeshterah"[n] and its pasture lands.
Two cities.

28 From the tribe of Issachar:

Kishion and its pasture lands,
Daberath and its pasture lands,
29 Jarmuth and its pasture lands,
En-gannim and its pasture lands.
Four cities.

30 From the tribe of Asher:

Mishal and its pasture lands,
Abdon and its pasture lands,

31 Helkath and its pasture lands,
and Rehob and its pasture lands.
Four cities.

32 From the tribe of Naphtali:

Kedesh in Galilee, the city of refuge for the killer, and its pasture lands,
Hammath[-dor][o] and its pasture lands,
and Kartan and its pasture lands.
Three cities.

33 In all there were thirteen cities of the Gershonites for their clans, with their pasture lands.

For the Merarites

34 To the clans of the descendants of Merari, the rest of the Levites, from the tribe of Zebulun:

Jokneam and its pasture lands,
Kartah[p] and its pasture lands,
35 Rimmon[q] and its pasture lands,
Nahalal and its pasture lands.
Four cities.

36 Across the Jordan opposite Jericho from the tribe of Reuben:

Bezer in the wilderness on the plateau, the city of refuge for the killer, and its pasture lands,
Jahaz and its pasture lands,
37 Kedemoth and its pasture lands,
and Mephaath and its pasture lands.
Four cities.[r]

38 From the tribe of Gad:

Ramoth in Gilead, the city of refuge for the killer, and its pasture lands,
Mahanaim and its pasture lands,
39 Heshbon and its pasture lands,
Jazer and its pasture lands.
In all, four cities.

40 In all, as for the cities of the descendants of Merari for their clans, the rest of the clans of the Levites, their allotment was twelve cities.

41 In all the cities of the Levites within the holdings of the Israelites were forty-eight cities, with their pasture lands. **42** Each of these cities had its pasture lands around it. Thus is was with all these cities.ˢ

Summary of the Conquest

43 So Yahweh gave to Israel all the land he had sworn to give to their ancestors. They took it over and settled there. **44** And Yahweh gave them rest all around, just as [all] he had sworn to their ancestors. Not one of all their enemies withstood them. Yahweh gave all their enemies into their power. **45** Not one of all the good things that Yahweh had promised to the house of Israel failed. Every one was fulfilled.

a. Follows MT. Here and in v. 6 OG and S lack "clans of," perhaps omitted to harmonize with the rest of the chapter.

b. Follows MT. OG and 1 Chron. 6:50 [65E] fill out the pattern with "and from the tribe of the children of Benjamin."

c. Follows MT. What looks like a shorter OG text may be the result of translation difficulties. For conversion from active to passive in translation, see the Greek of 6:24 and 24:33.

d. MT expansion lacking in OG and 1 Chron. 6:39 [54E].

e. Follows MT. As at 15:13, OG has "mother" in the sense of chief city.

f. MT expansion lacking in OG and 1 Chron. 6:42 [57E].

g. Follows OG and 1 Chron. 6:44 [59E]. MT has "Ain."

h. Assigned (as Ir-shemesh) to Dan in 19:41.

i. MT expansion lacking in OG. 1 Chron. 6:45 [60E] expands with a different phrase.

j. Representing MT "cities of their lot." OG and 1 Chron. 6:51 [66E] provide an easier reading "of their territory" here and in v. 40.

k. Follows MT and 1 Chron. 6:52 [67E] in including "in the hill country of Ephraim" (cf. 20:7), which is not present in OG. Perhaps this was removed as a "correction" since Shechem was actually in Manasseh (17:2, 7).

l. 1 Chron. 6:53 [68E] has "Jokmeam" instead. It is common to assume coincidental haplographies and to include both names in the reconstructed list. More probable is the corruption of a single place name caused by confusion of *m* with *b* and *ṣ* with *ʿ*: *qbṣym* and *yqmʿm*. The initial *y* may have resulted from a double form analogous to Kabzeel/Jekabzeel (15:21; Neh. 11:25) and Remeth/Jarmuth (19:21; 21:29; 1 Chron. 6:58 [73E]). Both Jokmeam and Jokneam are known as toponyms (12:22; 19:11; 21:34; 1 Kings 4:12), but neither were in Ephraim.

m. Follows 1 Chron. 6:55 [70E] and OG (Margolis, *Joshua in Greek,* 410). MT wrongly repeats "Gath-rimmon" from the previous verse.

n. Ashtaroth is clearly intended as in 1 Chron. 6:56 [71E]. The MT formation (supported by OG; Margolis, *Joshua in Greek,* 411) apparently was taken thoughtlessly from

Josh. 13:12, where the name appears with the prefixed preposition. This is an important clue to the artificial origin of the levitical city-list as a literary composition rather than as a genuine administrative document.

o. OG, Josh. 19:35, and 1 Chron. 6:61 [76E] indicate that the final syllable is an added element.

p. Represents MT *qrth*, although this name does not occur elsewhere. This is probably a deformation of Kattath (*qtt*) from 19:15, preserved as Kitron (*qtrwn*) in Judg. 1:30. Alternatively, it may be understood as an distorted repetition of Kartan from v. 32 to fill in a haplography (cf. "Gath-rimmon" in v. 25). 1 Chron. 6:62 [77E] seems to have Tabor (= Chisloth-tabor of Josh. 19:12) in its place. However, this town as Chesulloth is really in Issachar (19:18). The complex Greek evidence suggests a form something like the name found in MT (Margolis, *Joshua in Greek*, 416; LXX^B has "Kadesh").

q. Follows OG (Margolis, *Joshua in Greek*, 417) and 1 Chron. 6:62 [77E]. MT "Dimnah" shows confusion of *r* and *d*.

r. The best MT witnesses show an ancient loss of vv. 36–37 through haplography triggered by the repetition of "four cities." The loss was restored in some Hebrew witnesses by taking part of the corresponding text from Chronicles. This is evidenced by the absence of the tag line "city of refuge for the killer," the elimination of which is characteristic of the Chronicles parallel. Verse 36 has been restored on the basis of OG and 1 Chron. 6:63 [78E]. For details, see Barthélemy, *Critique*, 64–67.

s. Follows MT. OG offers a distinctive text for v. 42 and divides the sentence differently. No convincing explanation for this difference presents itself. The Greek also has four additional verses between vv. 42 and 43. Of these, vv. 42A–42C parallel 19:49–50 (the land grant to Joshua). Verse 42D goes on to describe the flint knives of the circumcision: "And Joshua took the stone knives, with which he had circumcised the Israelites who were born on the way in the wilderness, and he put them in Timnath-serah." These knives appear again in the Greek version at 24:31A. Apparently the motive for repeating 19:49–50 here was to provide background for including v. 42D in order to connect these knives to Joshua's home city. The shorter MT is preferable to this folkloristic recensional development in OG.

Form-critically this is a catalog, enumerating or labeling a list of names according to a classification system, in this case according to both the genealogical classification of levitical clans and the geographical one of the twelve tribes.[1] The whole notion of levitical cities stands in some tension with the tenet that Levi possessed no inheritance (13:14 [33 MT]; 18:7; Deut. 10:8–9). Embodying the opinion and language of 14:4, this catalog intends to explain how priests and Levites fit into Israel's settlement in the land. It seeks to anchor idealized levitical demographic patterns into the foundational past and rationalize this as part of a orderly structure. The tribe of Levi has its own special role and status, but is still integrated into the unity of Israel. The rhetorical impact of providing the reader with elaborate details about this purported system is powerful. Indeed, this rhetorical strategy has been so effec-

1. S. De Vries, *1 and 2 Chronicles*, FOTL 11, Grand Rapids, 1989, 68.

tive that it has induced many scholars to accept the historical existence of this artificial system.[2]

Presented in the format of a town list, this has the earmarks of a scholarly imitation rather than an actual archival source. It stresses that Levites have always been an integral part of the national organization as holders of cities and pasture lands, and perhaps wishes to press their contemporary claims on community resources. At the same time, it asserts that the priestly Aaronic branch is more prestigious and significant than the others. This group is listed first and put on par with the three levitical clans, even though genealogically it is only one of the Kohathite families. Moreover, the Aaronic cities all fall within the kingdom of Judah. As a common link between the tribal geographies of chapters 13–19 and the cities of refuge in chapter 20, chapter 21 plays an important role in holding the geographic portions of Joshua together and affirms that Israel legitimately possesses all the promised land, even those areas presently out of its control.

1 Chronicles 6 preserves a parallel form of this list, often reading correctly with the OG of Joshua against MT. Twice Chronicles and the OG of Joshua offer the same inferior reading (vv. 9 and 20), indicating a genetic relationship between the two. The direction of literary dependence between Joshua and Chronicles is disputed. Auld considers Chronicles primary,[3] but the commonly held opinion is that Chronicles depends on a form of Joshua 21 close to the LXX^AB.[4] Whereas Chronicles is consistently shorter, Joshua has a more logical order. It gives an overall review of the distribution of towns within all the tribes first (vv. 4–8), before going on to describe the holdings of each levitical clan tribe by tribe (vv. 9–40). There are numerous indications that the Joshua format is primary to that of Chronicles.[5] Chronicles breaks up the initial summary section of vv. 4–8 by putting the Aaronic priests ahead of the rest of the Kohath clan, so that the Chronicles order is the equivalent of Josh. 21:4 (summary for Aaron), vv. 10–19 (details for Aaron), vv. 5–9 (summary for the rest), vv. 20–39 (details for the rest). A comparison of the way the "by name" formula is used in Josh. 21:9 and 1 Chron. 6:50 [65E] is a conclusive piece of evidence. The Joshua text uses this phrase in a most natural way as an introduction to the list which follows in vv. 13–16 (after the intrusive vv. 10–12). In contrast, Chronicles uses it in an awkward retrospective way because it has changed the original order of presentation. This awkwardness is illustrated by the recourse to parentheses in the REB translation of the Chronicles text and its rearrangement by NAB. Chronicles also picks up narratival elements

2. As E. Ben-Zvi, "The List of the Levitical Cities," *JSOT* 54 (1992): 100 n. 2, points out.

3. A. G. Auld, "The 'Levitical Cities'—Text and History," *ZAW* 91 (1979): 194–206, "The Cities in Joshua 21—The Contribution of Textual Criticism," *Textus* 15 (1990): 141–52, and "Cities of Refuge," 32–37.

4. The classical treatment is that of W. F. Albright, "The List of Levitical Cities," *L. Ginzburg Jubilee Volume*, New York, 1945, 49–73.

5. For more detail see De Vries, *1 and 2 Chronicles*, 64–68.

appropriate to the Joshua context but somewhat out of place in its own presentation: the expression "they gave" (1 Chron. 6:40 [55E], etc.), the Caleb notice (6:41 [56E]), and especially the lot (1 Chron. 6:39 [54E], etc.). Finally, the summary totals correspond to the Joshua version and not to that of Chronicles, which has lost cities by haplography.

Another parallel text, Num. 35:2–8, summarizes the levitical city and city of refuge system and adds a further touch of idealization in v. 8. Much of this chapter depends on Joshua 20–21 just as Numbers chapter 34 depends on Joshua 14–19.[6]

On the assumption that it actually represents some sort of historical reality, much effort has gone into determining a date for this catalog.[7] The eras of the United Monarchy[8] or of Josiah[9] are usually those considered, based on the wide extent of territory involved. However, a Josianic date for the whole list is problematic because the territory covered is too extensive, while a United Monarchy date requires us to propose an excessively early origin for what appear to be later developments in Israel's cultic personnel. Neither hypothesis adequately explains the relationship of the cities named to Joshua 13–20 or the noticeable central gap left in the territory of Ephraim. Because there is no period after Solomon in which a single political structure would have actually controlled all the territory described here,[10] some degree of utopian fancy must enter into a consideration of any later date.[11] In the final analysis there is no way to harmonize the archaeological data that many of these towns were not settled at the time of the United Monarchy with the broad territorial extent of

6. Noth, "Überlieferungsgeschichtliches zur zweiten Hälfte des Josuabuches," 164–67.

7. See R. Boling, "Levitical Cities: Archaeology and Texts," *Biblical and Related Studies Presented to Samuel Iwry*, Winona Lake, Ind., 1985, 23–32 and J. Dearman, "The Levitical Cities of Reuben and Moabite Toponomy," *BASOR* 276 (1989): 55–66. For the history of research on this issue, see Kallai, *Historical Geography*, 447–58, and Auld, "Levitical Cities," 201–204.

8. Classically W. F. Albright, *Archaeology and the Religion of Israel*, Garden City, N.Y., 1969, 117–121. Also see B. Mazar, "The Cities of the Priests and the Levites," *Congress Volume Oxford 1960*, VTSup 7, Leiden, 1960, 193–205, who sees the towns playing a defensive and tax collection role in David's recently conquered territories; T. Mettinger, *Solomonic State Officials*, ConBOT 5; Lund, 1971, 98–101, who ties them to Davidic border fortresses; Kallai, *Historical Geography*, 459–76.

9. Alt connected them to Josiah's removal of local priests in "Bemerkungen zu einigen judäischen Ortslisten des Alten Testaments," and to Josiah's resettlement of south Judah in "Festungen und Levitenorte im Lande Juda," *Kleine Schriften* II, 306–15. The gaps in central Judah and Ephraim are taken to be the areas where Josiah closed local sanctuaries. M. Haran, Studies in the Account of the Levitical Cities," *JBL* 80 (1961): 45–54, 156–65, points out that utopian features are present no matter what date is chosen. Na'aman, *Borders and Districts*, 203–36, considers this list to be a literary production linked to a national perception of restored glory under Josiah.

10. Kallai, *Historical Geography*, 279–93, 313–22.

11. Thus M. Haran, "Studies in the Account of the Levitical Cities," *JBL* 80 (1961): 45–54, 156–65, who sees the list as a utopian composition from the time of Hezekiah, but based on a real institution.

the list. Nor is it possible to adduce a convincing political rationale for such a system. It is best to see the catalog as a largely artificial construction, although erected on the foundation of an inherited source list which covered only the kingdom of Judah (vv. 13–18).[12] That the final product covers the territory of all twelve tribes is a function of its literary purpose, not evidence of an early origin. One might compare the land re-distribution program of Ezekiel 48.

However, the first part of this composition represents a core list covering the kingdom of Judah (vv. 13–18; Judah/Simeon and Benjamin). That this portion of the larger list was inherited by the author as a source is evidenced by its non-idealized total in v. 19 (nine plus four equals thirteen). In fact, this awkward total required a deviation in the remaining idealized system. Only three cities could be assigned in Naphtali (v. 32) in order to reach the ideal total of forty-eight (v. 41; twelve times four). The total of nine for Judah/Simeon was either original to the source list or created when Hebron as a city of refuge was added to a twelve-item catalog (see below). In either case, the author's unwillingness to rectify the number by eliminating a city from vv. 13–16 is the strongest possible evidence that an inherited source has been used. This core list is not entirely in harmony with other lists previously presented in Joshua. For example, Beth-shemesh is a town in Dan in 19:41 (as Ir-Shemesh). Two of the Benjaminite towns, Anathoth and Almon, are not listed elsewhere in Joshua.

Plotting the towns of this core list on a map describes an arc around the heartland of Judah, south and west and then north:

> from Judah's district VII on the west: Juttah
> from district V on the south: Jattir, Eshtmoah, Debir, Holon
> from district IV on the west: Ashan and Libnah
> farther north on the west: Beth-shemesh
> the four Benjaminite towns are in sensitive border areas
> north of Jerusalem

A general resemblance to the list of Rehoboam's fortresses (2 Chron. 11:5–12) suggests a similar origin for the core list as a description of a defensive ring around Judah and Jerusalem.[13] If there is any validity to this suggestion, the territory being defended is restricted so that district I to the south and district II to the west are excluded. Any attempt to date this list also needs to account for Geba (v. 17). A border fortress of Asa (1 Kings 15:22), it later was in that part of Benjamin outside of Judah (18:24), but later still fell within Josiah's

---

12. In agreement with Fritz, *Josua*, 210–12, and Na'aman, *Borders and Districts*, 216–36.

13. Miller, "Rehoboam's Cities of Defense and the Levitical Cities," *Archaeology and Biblical Interpretation*, Atlanta, 1987, 273–86.

sphere of reform (2 Kings 23:8).[14] Perhaps the wording of v. 9 ("identified by name") points to the intervening transmission of this list as a school exercise. The rest of the system was generated artificially to match the core list inherited by the author. This was done by picking up the cities of refuge (along with their geographical situations) from Joshua 20 and then culling cities from the tribal lists of chapters 13, 16–17, and 19.[15] A detailed comparison with the previous chapters from which these names were taken is impossible here[16] but a few significant items may be noted. The telltale *b* in Beeshterah (v. 27) carries over the preposition from "in Ashtaroth" from 13:12 (see text note n). Verses 36–37 reproduce the three names of 13:18 in the same order. This also is true (with a gap) for vv. 28–29 and 19:20–21 (Jarmuth = Remeth). Verses 38–39 reproduce selected items from 13:25–26 in reverse order. Pairs reoccur in the same order between v. 32 and 19:35 (Kartan is generally accepted as a variant of Rakkath[17]) and between v. 23 and 19:44. In fact, except for the enigmatic Kibzaim/Jokmeam (v. 22, see text note l) and perhaps Kartah (v. 34, probably equivalent to Kattath, 19:15, see text note p), every town in vv. 20–40 may be found in chapters 13, 16–17, 19, and 20 (compare text notes m and q).

Each tribe (except Naphtali) provides four towns. That this is true without regard to whether a given tribe has cities of refuge or not indicates that whole artificial structure depends on the previous existence of Joshua 20 and never existed without the cities of refuge as a part of the pattern. Another indication of this is that the irregularity for Naphtali (Kedesh as a city of refuge and two others) was forced by the presence (or addition as a city of refuge) of Hebron in the core list. Mention of the city of refuge always comes first (although for Manasseh it of necessity comes first in its eastern half, v. 27). The order of the cities of refuge is not that of chapter 20 but has been controlled by the tribal order, which must have been an inherited or predetermined item for the compiler. This also means that the division between cities of refuge east and west of the Jordan towns had to be abandoned so that each levitical clan could receive two. The eastern half of Manasseh is thus separated from the other eastern tribes so that Gershom may have Golan, but split off from its western half to give the remainder of the Kohathites a reasonable number of towns (vv. 25–27). The broad geographic designations taken from 20:7 ("hill country of . . .") are treated as tribal territories (cf. 20:7 to 21:21, 32).

14. The core list is dated to the time of Josiah by Na'aman, *Borders and Districts*, 228–30.

15. Na'aman, *Borders and Districts*, 216–27; Ben-Zvi, "The List of the Levitical Cities."

16. This is done by Na'aman, *Borders and Districts*, 220–25, who explores the logic behind the selections and some errors made out of ignorance or confusion. For example, Heshbon was taken out of Gad's boundary description, although it properly belongs to Reuben. Manassehite Ramoth-gilead went to Gad so that each tribe east of the Jordan could have a city of refuge.

17. Noth, *Joshua*, 126, 129.

There are other indications of artificial composition. One is the unambiguous separation of Levites and priests, which was largely a post-exilic development.[18] Another is that Shechem, properly a town of Manasseh (17:2, 7) is located in Ephraim, apparently because Manasseh already had Golan as a city of refuge and because of the way Shechem is designated in 20:7 ("in the hill country of Ephraim"). Heshbon is assigned to Gad and not Reuben (13:17) because of how 13:25–26 was read. Genealogical structures have been overlaid onto geographical structures in an unrealistic way. Thus the Merari group is assigned two widely separated areas (Zebulun and Transjordan), a distribution unlikely to be the result of actual policy. Because only a sketchy border description was available for Ephraim from chapter 16, there is a peculiar hollowness to its territory. In contrast, there is a high density of Levites in the small territories of Zebulun and Issachar and, because of what was available from 17:11, in the "Canaanite" portion of Manasseh. Nevertheless, the connection of Gershon to the north may reflect in some elusive way a memory of that group's presence at the Dan sanctuary (Judg. 18:30).

The tribal order is roughly geographic: first three south and central tribes (vv. 20–27), then central and northern tribes (vv. 28–35), then the eastern tribes (vv. 36–39). However, the divisions of this geographic order have been broken up in an awkward way by the genealogical segments. Transjordanian Manasseh is grouped with Issachar and the two Galilee tribes while Zebulun has been put with Reuben and Gad. The levitical genealogy does not follow the traditional birth order (Gen. 46:11; Exod. 6:16; Num. 3:17; 26:57; 1 Chron. 5:27; 6:1 [6:1, 16E]; 23:6) but rather the "priests first" order of Numbers 4. The special status of the Aaronic priests creates a double pattern of organization. There are three clan segments, each with two cities of refuge (vv. 13–26, Kohath; vv. 27–33, Gershon; vv. 34–40, Merari). But simultaneously there are also four segments, each with its own summary total (vv. 13–19, Aaron; vv. 20–26, remaining Kohath; vv. 27–33, Gershon; vv. 34–40, Merari).

[1–3] The system is linked into the overall narrative structure of Joshua by vv. 1–3. Eleazar, Joshua, and the tribal heads make up the same group who have appeared in 14:1, 17:4, and 19:51. They will again be at Shiloh in 22:9. The plot is initiated by a request for land, the same situation as 14:12; 15:19; 17:4, 14. This seems to be a literary imitation of the land grant narrative genre (see the commentary on 14:6–15), and 17:4 is likely to be the source of the language used in vv. 2–3.[19] An interest in the Levites has already been raised by 13:14, [33 MT], 14:4. The text's allusion to a command of Moses and Yahweh is problematic if one excludes Num. 35:1–8 from consideration as a text dependent on this one. Perhaps this is an oblique reference to the command for cities of refuge in Deut. 19:1–8.

18. Although it has pre-exilic roots, Nelson, *Raising Up a Faithful Priest*, 7–11.
19. Auld, *Joshua, Moses and the Land*, 94–95.

[4–8] A preliminary outline of the scheme follows. Verses 3 and 8 provide a repetitive framework for this section, and as a "resumptive repetition" may be a sign that it was inserted into the text at a later date. This preview seems secondary to the following list. It scrambles the more rational geographic order of vv. 9–40 by putting half-Manasseh at the end of the Gershon allotment and Zebulun at the end of the Merari section. A repeated formula provides a unifying parallel and coordinates the four family divisions to the tribal territories (literally "to the sons of X from Y," vv. 4b, 5, 6, 7). This prepares the reader for the structure of the upcoming catalog and explains its rationale. The use of the lot as in chapters 14–19 links these levitical possessions to those of the secular tribes and indicates that the resulting system was Yahweh's will.

[9–41] A repetitive rhythm of formulaic elements provides the impression of a thorough and balanced system:

> levitical genealogical headings, vv. 10, 20, 27, 34
> tribal headings, vv. 17, 23, 25, etc.
> tribal sub-totals, vv. 16, 18, 22, etc.
> totals, vv. 19, 26, 33, 40
> grand total, v. 41

For all its character as a catalog, the repetition of "they gave" still keeps alive the notion of a narrative (vv. 9, 11, 13, 21) and provides a link to the upcoming "Yahweh gave" of v. 43. The otherwise orderly pattern is disturbed at the start by v. 9 as a unique tribal heading for vv. 13–16 and the intrusive vv. 10–12. These verses indicate an unsurprising special interest in Judah/Simeon and Aaron and link back to events reported earlier in the book (14:13–14; 15:13–14). Verse 42 reiterates the provision of pasture lands and thus returns in a satisfying way to the concern of v. 2.

[43–45] This theologizing summary statement is of a totally different character from what has gone before. Its theology and vocabulary is deuteronomistic.[20] As a summary statement of DH, its horizon encompasses the themes of chapters 1–12, emphasizing the totality of victory and the gift of the entire land. The word "all" is used half a dozen times. It echoes other optimistic passages asserting total triumph such as 10:40–42; 11:16–20, 23; 12:7–24; 23:1, rather than those notices of incompleteness and the continued presence of alien elements in the land such as 13:2–6; 15:63; 16:10; 17:12–18; 23:4, 7, 12–13. Although to a large degree this inconsistency is a function of the book's history of composition, these are not completely incompatible assertions, as their correlation together in 23:1, 4–5, 7, 12 shows. They are held in dialogical tension in both DH and the final form of Joshua, just as are the correlative themes of God's fidelity and human obedience (cf. 1:5–9). Here, however, the emphasis is strongly on the confession of

---

20. Weinfeld, *Deuteronomy and the Deuteronomic School*, 343–44, 350

Yahweh's total fidelity to all oaths and promises (23:14; 1 Kings 8:56; 2 Kings 10:10) and the provision of "rest" (1:13, 15; 22:4; 23:1; Deut. 12:9–10; 2 Sam. 7:1). Yahweh is the subject of the verb "give" three times and "swear" twice. All that was anticipated in 1:2–6 has been achieved: Yahweh has given the land sworn to the ancestors; Israel has taken possession; no enemy has been able to withstand them. The rest foreseen in 1:15 has been consummated. These verses set the stage for the dismissal of the eastern tribes (22:4) and Joshua's concluding sermon of chapter 23. They are the "good things" to which he will refer in 23:14–15.

A Witness
to Solidarity
Joshua 22:1–34

The Eastern Tribes
Go Home

22:1 Then Joshua summoned the Reubenites, the Gadites, and the half-tribe of Manasseh.[a] 2 He said to them, "You have kept everything that Moses the servant of Yahweh commanded you and have obeyed me in everything that I have commanded you. 3 You have not forsaken your kinfolk this long time up to this day, but have kept the observance of[b] the command of Yahweh your God. 4 And now Yahweh your God has given rest to your kinfolk, just as he promised them. So now turn around and go back[c] to your tents, to the land where you hold property, which Moses [the servant of Yahweh] gave you on the other side of the Jordan.

5 Only be very careful to perform the commandment and law that Moses the servant of Yahweh commanded you—to love Yahweh your God, to walk in all his ways,[d] to keep his commandments, and to cling to him, and to serve him with all your heart and with all your being." 6 Then Joshua blessed them and sent them away, and they went to their tents.

7 Moses had provided for half of the tribe of Manasseh in Bashan, but Joshua had provided for the other half along with their kinfolk across the Jordan on the west. Moreover, when Joshua sent them away to their tents and blessed them, 8 he said to them, "Return to your tents with great wealth and with very many cattle, with silver, gold, bronze, and iron, and with very much clothing. Divide up the spoil of your enemies with your kinfolk."[e]

The Altar of Witness

9 So the Reubenites and the Gadites and the half-tribe of Manasseh turned around and left the Israelites at Shiloh, which is in the land of

Canaan, to go to the land of Gilead, to the land of their own holding, in which they had settled at the command of Yahweh through Moses. 10 They came to the districts of the Jordan that are in the land of Canaan, and there the Reubenites and the Gadites and the half-tribe of Manasseh built an altar by the Jordan, a huge-looking altar. 11 The Israelites heard it said, "The Reubenites and the Gadites and the half-tribe of Manasseh have built an altar towards the front of the land of Canaan, in the districts of the Jordan on the Israelite side." [f] 12 When the Israelites heard,[g] all [the community of] the Israelites gathered at Shiloh to go up to war against them.

13 Then the Israelites sent Phinehas son of Eleazar the priest to the Reubenites and the Gadites and the half-tribe of Manasseh in the land of Gilead. 14 And ten leaders were with him, one leader for the patriarchal house of each tribe of Israel. They were each a head of the patriarchal houses of the contingents of Israel.[h] 15 They came to the Reubenites, the Gadites, and the half-tribe of Manasseh in the land of Gilead, and spoke with them, 16 "Thus says the whole community of Yahweh, 'What is this sacrilege[i] that you have committed against the God of Israel, turning away today from following Yahweh, by building yourselves an altar for your rebellion [today] against Yahweh? 17 Was not the offense of Peor enough for us, from which we have not cleansed ourselves even to this day? Then there was a plague on the community of Yahweh! 18 You are turning away today from following Yahweh. If you rebel against Yahweh today, tomorrow he will be angry with all [the community of] Israel. 19 However, if the land of your own holding is unclean, cross over into the land of Yahweh's holding where the tabernacle of Yahweh stands, and settle among us. But do not rebel against Yahweh or involve us in rebellion[j] by building yourselves an altar apart from the altar of Yahweh our God. 20 Did not Achan son of Zerah commit sacrilege with the things devoted to destruction? Wrath came on the whole community of Israel, and he was not the only one to die for his offense.'"[k]

21 Then the Reubenites, the Gadites, and the half-tribe of Manasseh answered the heads of the contingents of Israel, 22 "Yahweh is God of gods! Yahweh is God of gods! He knows and now let Israel itself know! Do not rescue us[l] today if it was in rebellion or in sacrilege against Yahweh, 23 by building[m] an altar for ourselves to turn away from following Yahweh. If it was to offer a burnt offering or a gift offering upon it, or to perform peace offerings on it, let Yahweh himself exact the penalty. 24 No, instead we did this thing out of a concern that in the future your children might say to our children, 'What do you have to do with Yahweh the God of Israel? 25 For Yahweh has set the Jordan as a boundary between us and you [Reubenites and Gadites].[n] You have no share in Yahweh.' So your

children might make our children stop revering Yahweh. **26** So we said, 'Let us work for ourselves to build an altar,' not for burnt offering or for sacrifice, **27** but to be a witness between us and you and between our descendants after us that we perform the service of Yahweh before him through our burnt offerings and sacrifices and peace offerings, so that in the future your children would never say to our children, 'You have no share in Yahweh.' **28** We thought, If they say this to us or to our descendants in the future, we could say, 'Look at this replica of the altar of Yahweh that our ancestors made, not for burnt offerings or for sacrifice, but to be a witness between us and you.' **29** God forbid that we should rebel against Yahweh and turn away today from following Yahweh by building an altar for burnt offering, gift offering, or sacrifice, besides the altar of Yahweh [our God] that stands before his tabernacle!"

30 Phinehas the priest and the leaders of the community [and the heads of the contingents]° of Israel who were with him heard the words that the Reubenites and the Gadites and the Manassites^p spoke, and it seemed proper in their opinion.

31 So Phinehas [the son of Eleazar] the priest said to the Reubenites and the Gadites and the Manassites, "Today we know that Yahweh is among us, because you have not committed this sacrilege against Yahweh. Now you have delivered the Israelites from the power of Yahweh." **32** Then Phinehas [the son of Eleazar] the priest and the leaders returned from the Reubenites and the Gadites in the land of Gilead to the land of Canaan, to the Israelites, and brought word back to them. **33** The matter seemed proper in the opinion of the Israelites and the Israelites blessed God. They no longer spoke of going up to war against them to destroy the land where the Reubenites and the Gadites were living. **34** The Reubenites and the Gadites gave the altar a name, "for it is a witness between us that Yahweh is God."^q

a. Here the gentilic forms for Reuben and Gad are used. Everywhere else the form is "sons of Reuben and sons of Gad."

b. Follows MT. OG and S have a haplography '[*t mšmr*]*t mṣwt* triggered by the repetition of *t* followed by *m*.

c. For the so-called "ethical dative" of *lākem*, Waltke and O'Connor, *Hebrew Syntax*, 11.2.10d.

d. Follows MT and OG. S has a haplography *wl*[*lkt bkl-drkyw wl*]*šmr* triggered by the repetition of *wl*.

e. Verses 7b–8 follow MT. What in MT is a speech of Joshua with imperatives and second person pronouns, in OG is an indicative statement with third person pronouns: "^7bAnd when Joshua had sent them away . . . ^8they returned to their tents . . . . They divided up the spoil of their enemies with their kinfolk." A case can be made for this as the earliest recoverable reading. To avoid a triple repetition of the return home (vv. 6, 8 OG, 9), MT could have added "he said to them" to v. 8 and recast the sentence

(Holmes, *Joshua: The Hebrew and Greek Texts*, 74–75). OG apparently tried to ease the same problem of repetition by removing the first word "turned around" from v. 9. MT is read here to avoid the awkwardness of three reports of the return and because v. 7b seems to lay the groundwork for direct discourse. The Greek witnesses exhibit several obvious haplographies in the list of goods.

f. Alternatively this may be translated to put the altar on the east side of the Jordan: "an altar opposite the land of Canaan, in the districts of the Jordan, across from the Israelites" (cf. REB, NAB, JPSV over against NRSV, NJB). Both locational designations are ambiguous: *'el-mûl* "opposite, in front of" and *'el-'ēber* "on the side belonging to" or "towards the region across from." But v. 10 seems to require a location "in the land of Canaan" and to delete this phrase there as REB does is unwarranted. The question of location is further obscured by variants reading "Gilgal" (LXX^B in v. 10, S in vv. 10, 11) and "Gilead" (LXX^B in v. 11) for *glylwt* "districts" (cf. the inner-MT variation between 15:7 and 18:17). On issues of translation and text, see N. Snaith, "The Altar at Gilgal: Joshua 22:23–29," *VT* 28 (1978): 330–35.

g. Follows MT. OG, S, and V lack "when the Israelites heard," a haplography triggered by the repetition of *bny yśr'l*.

h. "Patriarchal house" is to be understood in the sense of Num. 17:17 [2E] where the term is effectively synonymous with tribe. S (followed in part by REB) omits the two occurrences here, probably because it failed to understand this.

i. For this translation of *m'l* and the concept in Israel's religious thought, see Milgrom, *Leviticus 1–16*, 345–56.

j. MT has "rebel against [?] us." The problem is more grammatical than textual, since *mrd* "rebel" does not occur elsewhere with a direct object. OG has a doublet "rebel against God and rebel against Yahweh" and lacks "us." Repointing the verb as hiphil is the solution adopted here. This concern with communal guilt prepares for v. 20.

k. Alternate translation taking the last part of the verse as a rhetorical question: "though he was only one person. Did he not die for his offense?" (cf. NJB).

l. Follows MT as the more difficult reading. The versions have "let him not rescue us."

m. Taking the infinitive construct in a gerundive sense explaining "in rebellion or in sacrilege" (Waltke and O'Connor, *Hebrew Syntax*, 36.2.3e). An alternate translation would construe it with v. 23b: "If we built an altar for ourselves to turn away from following Yahweh or if it was to offer . . ." (REB, NAB, NJB, JPSV).

n. MT explanatory supplement not present in S or OG.

o. MT expansion based on v. 14.

p. Here and in v. 31 the form "sons of Manasseh" is used instead of the usual "half tribe of Manasseh."

q. MT is enigmatic, apparently not explicitly expressing the name of the altar. Perhaps the whole of v. 34b is supposed to be the name. Arguably one could translate: "called out in regard to the altar, 'It is a witness . . . .'" OG makes Joshua the one who names the altar, and S supplies the obvious name "Altar of Witness" (cf. NRSV, REB).

After their dismissal by Joshua, an enigmatic act of altar building by the eastern tribes leads to conflict. Dissension centers on whether this altar should be interpreted as evidence of apostasy. The eastern tribes advance an alternate interpretation that evaluates the altar as a sign of fidelity instead. Acceptance of this evaluation by the western tribes leads to a permanent resolution of the conflict.

This chapter divides into deuteronomistic and priestly halves along the hinge of vv. 7 and 8. The language of vv. 1–6 is unquestionably deuterono-mistic,[1] whereas vv. 9–34 exhibit characteristics associated with priestly com-position.[2] Obvious P-like expressions are *'ăhuzâ* "holding" and the niphal of this root (vv. 4, 9, 19), *něśî'îm* "leaders" (vv. 14, 30, 32), *'ēdâ* "community" (v. 16 etc.), and *miškan* "tabernacle" (vv. 19, 29). Joshua abruptly disappears as the main character after vv. 7–8, and Phinehas the priest takes his place. Un-like DH, in whose opinion the eastern territories are genuinely the land of Yah-weh's gift (Deut. 2:31–3:17), vv. 9–34 rest on the assumption that there is something problematic, perhaps even "unclean" about the Transjordan. The same group that are paragons of obedience in vv. 1–6 become objects of sus-picion in vv. 9–34. The deuteronomistic gentilic for Reuben and Gad in v. 1 (Deut. 3:12 etc.) is replaced by the expression "sons of" from v. 9 on. More-over, vv. 1–8 give no hint of the problems of the rest of the chapter, while vv. 9–34 work perfectly well as a story without these initial verses.

Viewed as a completed whole, however, the redactional maneuver of fol-lowing the deuteronomistic dismissal of the eastern tribes with the story of their enigmatic altar works fairly well. The topics of fidelity to the law, settle-ment in the land, and the unity of Israel are brought into focus by vv. 1–8. Sep-arating the eastern tribes "to the other side" (v. 4) prepares for the dialogical tension between geographic division and national integrity in the following narrative. Introducing them as a loyal group who did not "forsake" their "kin-folk" (vv. 3, 8; lit. "brothers") prepares for ambiguity in the interpretation their enigmatic act of altar building. Emphasizing that their separated settlement was authorized by Moses (vv. 4, 7) provides a counterweight to the suggestion that their east Jordan land may be unclean (v. 19) and thus a potential object of destruction (v. 33). Even the intrusive notice about Manasseh (vv. 7a) supports the overall theme, for this tribe is a bridge people, settled on both sides of the Jordan, who embody in their special situation the central narrative dilemma of separation versus solidarity. When the two parts of chapter 22 are read to-gether, vv. 1–6 (7–8) conclude the theme of full participation in the conquest by the eastern tribes (1:12–18 and 4:12–13), and then v. 9 opens the question of future relations among the same cast of characters in the new post-conquest situation. Viewed canonically, this chapter previews the impending intertribal tensions that will be reported in the book of Judges.

1. Weinfeld, *Deuteronomy and the Deuteronomic School*, 332–36, 338, 343.
2. J. Kloppenborg, "Joshua 22: The Priestly Editing of an Ancient Tradition," *Bib* 62 (1981): 355–61. *Něśî'îm* "leaders" and *'ēdâ* "community" also appear in 9:15–27, where a similar P-like redaction is discernible.

Form-critically, this narrative exhibits an oblique affinity to sanctuary legends involving altar erection and naming (Gen. 35:7; Exod. 17:15; Judg. 6:24). There is a more direct narratival connection to Gen. 31:43–54. Both narratives share the elements of a named landmark witnessing to an ongoing relationship between kindred peoples, an etymology involving '*ēd* "witness," and the locale of Gilead. In Joshua 22, however, the stock elements of building (v. 10) and naming (v. 34) have been widely separated in order to provide the framework for a rich literary development of conflict and ideological rhetoric. Literary and theological concerns have overwhelmed whatever traditional narrative may have originally provided the author with inspiration.[3] Thus the name of the altar, having lost any narrative importance, simply remains unexpressed. The potential of civil war against treacherous tribes (Judges 19–21) provides the (presumably fictional) social backdrop. A tradition of east-west intertribal tensions is suggested by the nonparticipation of Reuben and Gilead in Judges 5 and the conflict between Gilead and Ephraim related in Judg. 12:1–6.

The ideological background of the plot is the conviction that no more than one altar can be a place of lawful sacrifice. While this was an axiom of both deuteronomistic and priestly theology, here the single central altar is delineated in a typically priestly mode. It is the altar of the tabernacle, implicitly at Shiloh and tacitly under the administration of Phinehas. The concept of endangering the whole community through cultic trespass is also thoroughly priestly (Nadab and Abihu, Lev. 10:1–7; Korah, Numbers 16). Yet at the same time the relationship of this narrative to the Pentateuchal source P is not absolute. Use of the term '*ăbōdâ* for worship (v. 27) and details of the itemized sacrifices (v. 23) are distinctive features that set this narrative apart from the Penteteuchal source.[4]

Although a nonsacrificial altar might seem to be an oxymoron, altars could be built to mark a god's territory. In 1 Kings 18:30–32 altar rebuilding reclaims Carmel for Yahweh and the twelve tribes. This also seems to be the thinking behind Namaan's proposal to sacrifice on Yahweh's own soil (2 Kings 5:17). Altars could commemorate a divine revelation (Gen. 35:7) or even an established principle (Exod. 17:15). Perhaps closest to the concept advanced here by the eastern tribes is Isa. 19:19–21, where an altar built in Egypt serves as sign and witness of that nation's relationship to Yahweh. Yet in all

---

3. It has been suggested that this narrative reflects conflict between the sanctuaries of Shiloh and Gilgal. See Möhlenbrink, "Die Landnahmesagen des Buches Josua," 246–50; Otto, *Das Maz-zotfest in Gilgal*, 170–71, 392; N. Snaith, "The Altar at Gilgal: Joshua 22:23–29," *VT* 28 (1978): 33–35. Although LXX[B] reads Gilgal for Geliloth (districts) in v. 10, this hypothesis is undercut by the absence of any solid localization for the altar in vv. 10–11. If such a tradition does lie behind this text, it has left so few traces as to be virtually invisible. In any case, the purpose of this narrative as it now stands is not the polemical rejection of a sanctuary, but the assertion of national unity.

4. Kloppenborg, "Joshua 22: The Priestly Editing of an Ancient Tradition," 366–67.

these parallels, sacrifice remains associated with the altar. For this particular altar, however, any sacrificial function was paradoxically but inevitably superseded by its narrative role as a witness to participation in sacrifice at the unique central altar.

The intention of this story is to promote an awareness of and commitment to national unity in the face of opposing attitudes and circumstances. This is done by means of a narrative that mediates disunity and rival viewpoints into solidarity and agreement. The two groups begin the story separated from each other, divided not only by geography, but by differing interpretations of reality that lead them to the brink of war. For one party the problem is the future possibility of losing their acceptance as Yahweh's people; for the other the problem is residency outside Yahweh's territory and what appears to be an act of apostasy. Yet both parties also agree on certain basic assumptions: the Jordan presents a obstacle to national unity (vv. 19, 25), non-central sacrifice is wrong (vv. 16, 18, 19, 23, 26, 29), and the tabernacle is the proper place for it (vv. 19, 27 "before him," 29). As the narrative progresses, unity is achieved as their rival interpretations coalesce into an agreement achieved by effective rhetoric. This is why the embassy seems so easy to convince. They are intended to provide a paradigm for readers to follow. In the end, the altar that begins as the center of the conflict turns out to be an instrument of reconciliation. Geographically it stands as a mediating presence between the two parties (v. 11), while as "witness" and "replica" it symbolizes the eastern tribes' aspiration for a continued "share in Yahweh" (v. 25) and their loyalty to the authentic sacrificial cult.

Curiously, for all its emphasis on the unity of west and east, the narrative itself is told from a thoroughly west-of-Jordan perspective. It is the westerners who are "the Israelites" and "the whole community of Yahweh." It is the westbank territory which is "Yahweh's land." This represents the perspective not only of those who voice the rumor (v. 11) and the delegation (vv. 16, 19), but of the narrator as well (vv. 9, 12–14, 21, 30, 32–33). Rather oddly, therefore, this expression of the ideal of national unity to some degree undermines it.

Attempts to date this story have ranged from the premonarchy period[5] through the exile[6] to the period of the Elephantine temple.[7] Perhaps the view that the land east of the Jordan presented an ideological problem originated with

---

5. Möhlenbrink, "Die Landnahmesagen des Buches Josua," 246–50; O. Eissfeldt, "Monopol-Ansprüche des Heiligtums von Silo." *Orientalische Literaturzeitung* 68 (1973): 327–33. J. Dus, "Die Lösung des Rätsels von Jos. 22," *Archiv Orientální* 32 (1964): 529–46, suggests that the altar was put on the west bank to facilitate access by the cows who supposedly pulled the ark on a cart at intervals to pinpoint the new location of the national sanctuary.

6. A. Menes, "Temple und Synagoge," *ZAW* 50 (1932): 268–76.

7. J. Vink, "The Date and Origin of the Priestly Code in the Old Testament," *OTS* 15 (1969): 73–77.

the imposition of the Assyrian provincial system and Assyria's ethnic exchange policy, which would have added further alien elements to the Ammonites and Moabites already present. However, the notion that the Jordan marks the limit of Yahweh's land first clearly emerges in Ezek. 47:13–48:29, especially in 47:18 where the Jordan divides "Gilead" from "the land of Israel."[8] The concept of an unclean land and questions about who may participate in the sacrificial cult point to the period of restoration. Could Yahwists who lived outside the holy land participate in temple sacrifice or were they unclean (v. 17)? Were the offerings they brought products of an unclean land (v. 19)? This narrative opposes such restrictive and divisive opinions. The view of vv. 9–34 is that of Pss. 60:9 [7E] and 108:9 [8E]: Canaan is Yahweh's land, but Yahweh owns Gilead as well. Jews outside the land have a "share in Yahweh" and the standing to join in temple worship. This principle goes back to an agreement made in the foundational period of Joshua, an agreement approved by none other than Phinehas the Aaronic high priest. What really matters is not one's place of residence, but one's confession that Yahweh is God alone (v. 22) and adherence to the principle of sacrificing nowhere but in Jerusalem. In whatever period this story originated, it must have persuaded generations of readers to hold fast to national unity in spite of geographic separation and the dangers of diverse viewpoints. The unity of Yahweh's people is founded not on geographic proximity, but on shared faith and fidelity in worship.

[1–6] Within the orbit of DH, vv. 1–5 function as a minor transitional speech, a smaller version of those periodic orations at historical turning points through which DH communicates ideology (Joshua 23, 1 Samuel 12, 2 Samuel 7, etc.). This section is a natural next step after the DH summary of 21:43–45 and a culmination of themes launched in 1:12–18. The "rest" promised in 1:13, 15 and asserted in 21:44 becomes the occasion for the return of the eastern tribes (22:4). Complete fulfillment of all promises (21:45) leads to the actualization of Yahweh's commitment to this group (1:13, 15; Deut. 3:18–21). This transitional moment provided DH with an opportunity to commend compliance with the law of Moses (v. 5; 1:7–8). These tribes are held up as examples of obedience (vv. 2–3; 1:17), who experience blessings (vv. 4, 6; 1:13, 15) in accordance with standard deuteronomistic principles. In this way Joshua's speech previews the themes of chapter 23, itself launched by the notion of "rest" (23:1).

The section begins with a vague temporal connection (*'az* with the imperfect, cf. 8:30 and 10:12) indicating that it is contemporary with (and thus an example of) the fulfillment and rest that DH has just described in 21:44. The "long time" of v. 3 takes the same perspective as 11:18. After a review of past loyalty in vv. 2–3, v. 4 makes a disjunctive shift to the blessings and obedience

---

8. The boundary description of Num. 34:1–14 rests on a similar assumption.

of the present. Return to "tents" evokes the dispersal of the national assembly (Deut. 16:7; Judg. 7:8; 1 Kings 12:16). Joshua's act of blessing is paralleled in 14:13.[9] Verse 6 seems to bring this scene to a decisive end.

[7–8] The awkward skip to a bit of delayed exposition in v. 7a can be taken as evidence that Manasseh was added only later to a story that originally involved Reuben and Gad alone. Only these two tribes are mentioned in vv. 32–34 (and the MT of v. 25). Here Moses is invoked as the authority for Manasseh's abnormal situation. The *wĕgam kî* "moreover, when" and the repetition of Joshua's sending and blessing (v. 7b) are needed to restart the plot after this excursus. Rich booty underscores the wonder of Yahweh's blessings showered on the chosen nation. In Joshua, conquest means loot (in harmony with Deut. 20:10–18), and only Jericho is an explicit exception to this. The command to share out the booty conforms to traditional custom (Num. 31:27; 1 Sam. 30:21–25) and highlights the theme of national unity. It may also be a parenetic hint to readers urging generous altruism toward their own "kinfolk."

[9–34] After the scene setting of v. 9 the story is told in an elegant chiastic pattern:[10]

> A. building the altar (vv. 10–11)
> > B. plan to "go up to war" (v. 12)
> > > C. delegation's composition and travel (vv. 13–15a)
> > > > D. delegation's accusation (vv. 15b–20)
> > > > > E. denial of the accusation (vv. 22–23)
> > > > > > X. defense (vv. 21–29)
> > > > > E'. denial of the accusation (v. 29)
> > > > D'. delegation's approval (vv. 30–31)
> > > C'. delegation's travel (v. 32)
> > B'. discontinue plan "to go up to war" (v. 33)
> A'. naming the altar (v. 34)

The exposition of v. 9 (who? where?) immediately introduces the two central dichotomies of the narrative. The eastern tribes stand over against "the Israelites," and the land of Canaan is placed in opposition to Gilead, representing Transjordan as a whole (vv. 13, 15, 32). Shiloh has been the locus of narrative action since 18:1. The noticeable size of the altar ("huge-looking," v. 10) points forward to the rumor it will generate and eventually to its role as a visual "witness." Its identification as an "altar" (literally "place of sacrifice") immediately awakens the suspicion that it may be for illegitimate sacrifice. The puzzle of the altar's significance is further deepened by the enigma of its location.

---

9. Possibly 14:13 is part of a stray piece of DH, as asserted by Noth, *Josua*, 71, 83–85.

10. For this pattern and a structuralist reading, see Jobling, "The Jordan a Boundary: Transjordan in Israel's Ideological Geography."

The generalized term *gĕlîlôt* "regions" (vv. 10, 11; 18:17) cannot be located and the ostensibly abundant geographic data of v. 11 only serves to disorientate the reader further. Is it on the east side or the west side? Have they compounded their error by building it outside of Canaan? Appropriately, the rumor ("heard it said") is somewhat confused and confusing, cluing the reader that perhaps it should not be accepted too uncritically.

Phinehas (v. 12) replaces Eleazar, who had been co-leader with Joshua in 14:1; 19:51; 21:1. "Contingents (*'elep*) of Israel" (v. 14) is used in priestly texts for tribes (Num 1:16; perhaps 10:36) and the priestly word *'ēdâ* "community" stresses the cultic aspect of the nation. Obviously the reader is intended to respect the judgment of such an aristocratic delegation, who clearly have the standing to speak for the "whole community of Yahweh" (v. 16). The rhetoric of their indictment is harsh ("sacrilege," "rebellion"). Reference to the prototypical apostasy of Peor (v. 17; Numbers 25; Deut. 4:3; Ps. 106:28) points both to the dubious status of the land east of the Jordan and to the dire consequences of cultic infidelity (plague, persistent uncleanness). The negative side of national unity is that Yahweh's anger will fall on the whole community (v. 18) and that rebellion by any one group of the community signifies rebellion on the part of the whole people (v. 19). This point is emphasized by the example of Achan (v. 20; verbally linked by the repeated root *m'l* "sacrilege," vv. 16, 20, 22, 31; cf. 7:1). From their perspective that the Transjordan may be unclean (cf. Amos 7:17), the delegation suggests a solution: cross back to Yahweh's land and Yahweh's tabernacle (v. 19). This same notion that the territory east of the Jordan might be impure seems to inspire their plans for a war intended "to destroy the land" (v. 34).

The response of the eastern tribes begins with a doxological exclamation that cuts right to the heart of the matter (v. 22). The coordination of divine designations (El = God = Yahweh) has a cultic origin and is paralleled in Ps. 50:1. There is a strong creedal flavor to this, similar in intention to the phrase uttered in 1 Kings 18:39. The eastern tribes then pile up words and arguments to convince both the suspicious delegation and the reader that the altar means precisely the opposite of what has been assumed so far. To make their point they engage in what is essentially self-cursing (vv. 22–23). They reuse the key words "sacrilege," "rebellion," and "turn away" from the accusation (vv. 22–23, 29; cf. 16, 18–20, 31) in order to refute it. They repeat the standard catalog of sacrifices both to deny any intention to perform them illegitimately (vv. 23, 26, 29) and to assert their desire to offer them in the proper place in Yahweh's presence (v. 27). The matter of Yahweh's potential reaction, so ominous for the west-Jordan group (vv. 17, 18, 20, 31), is discreetly passed over.

The eastern group say they are concerned about anticipated attitudes of the children of the western group and their own children's future as the people of Yahweh (vv. 24–25, 27–28). This echoes the catechetical concerns of 4:6–7, 21–24. As is the case with those passages, this theme directs the impact of the text directly at the readers, who are themselves the "children" under discussion. The potential denial of a "share" (*ḥēleq,* vv. 25, 27) in Yahweh reverberates powerfully with the importance of this root in the book of Joshua[11] and more narrowly with the sharing out of booty in v. 8.

In order to retain reader suspense, key pieces to the puzzle concerning the altar have been held off until vv. 27–28, when the notions of witness and replica are first introduced. The imperative "look at" (v. 28) finally unpacks the potential of "huge-looking" in v. 10. The replica altar certifies that they intend to keep on worshipping at its legitimate prototype. "Replica" (*tabnît*) refers to identity of pattern, often the design according to which something is crafted (Exod. 25:9; 2 Kings 16:10). Thus this is not really an altar after all, but only a facsimile of one. Just as a human witness secures the truth of an asserted claim, often in the context of a legal proceeding, this inanimate "witness" documents and gives legal force to a crucial affirmation. The eastern tribes are indeed faithful in their participation in the cult. They really are part of Israel. The replica altar will attest to these realities even when future generations come onto the scene and the original parties to this consensus are gone (cf. Gen. 31:43–50).

The complete evaluative reversal effected by this rather long-winded justification may leave skeptical modern readers suspicious, but the text clearly intends that this defense should be believed. The reader is supposed to follow the lead of the highly respectable delegation (vv. 30–31). Their assertion that Yahweh is "among us" signals that there is now no danger of Yahweh's departure as a result of cultic impropriety, a key concern of priestly theology (Ezek. 8:6; cf. Num. 35:34). The "power of Yahweh," recalling the potential divine anger of vv. 18 and 20, is not a threat after all. The eventual agreement of "the Israelites" (v. 33) underscores the truth of the text's claim. They give up plans for war. Thus the narrative problem of v. 12 is solved as the misunderstanding of v. 11 is cleared up. The final comment on the altar reiterates the creedal formula of v. 22. It witnesses within the context of a unified Israel that Yahweh is God. This is what really matters to the narrative, not the unexpressed name of the altar.

Joshua's Farewell
Joshua 23:1–16

23:1 A long time afterward, when Yahweh had given rest to Israel from all their enemies all around and Joshua had reached old age, **2** Joshua summoned all Israel, their elders, their heads, their judges and their officers. He said to them, "I have reached old age. **3** You have seen all that

---

11. There are seven occurrences as a verb and nine as a noun.

Yahweh your[a] God has done to all these nations on your account, for it is Yahweh your God who fights for you. 4 I have allotted to you these nations that remain[b] as hereditary property for your tribes from the Jordan (and all the nations I have cut off) and the great Western Sea.[c] 5 It is Yahweh your God who will force them back on your account and dispossess them before you.[d] Then you shall take over their land, just as Yahweh your God has promised you. 6 Be very strong, being careful to do everything written in the book of the law of Moses, not deviating from it right or left, 7 not having dealings with these nations that remain.[e] Do not invoke the names of their gods, do not swear by them,[f] do not serve them, and do not worship them. 8 Instead cling to Yahweh your God, just as you have done to this day.

9 "For Yahweh has dispossessed before you great and strong nations. As for you, no one has withstood you to this day. 10 A single one of you pursues a thousand, for it is Yahweh your God who fights for you, just as he promised you. 11 Be very careful about yourselves to love Yahweh your God. 12 For if you turn away and cling to the rest of these nations with you[g] and intermarry with them and have intercourse with them and they with you, 13 then certainly know that Yahweh [your God] will not continue to dispossess these nations before you, but they will be a snare and a trap for you, a whip on your sides and thorns in your eyes, until you perish from this good land that Yahweh your God has given you.

14 "Today I am going the way of all the earth. You know with all your heart and being that not one of all the good things that Yahweh your God promised concerning you has failed. They all were fulfilled for you. Not one word of them has failed.[h] 15 But just as every good thing that Yahweh [your God] promised about you has been fulfilled for you, so too Yahweh could[i] bring against you every bad thing until he has destroyed you from this good land that Yahweh [your God] has given you. 16 If[j] you violate the covenant of Yahweh your God, which he commanded you, and go and serve other gods and worship them, then the anger of Yahweh will break out against you, and you will quickly perish from the good land that he has given you."[k]

a. OG generally has first person plural throughout.

b. Follows MT as the shorter reading. S supplements with "with you" and OG conflates MT and S. Comparable situations occur in vv. 7 and 12. See the analysis in R. Boling, "Some Conflate Readings in Joshua-Judges," *VT* 16 (1966): 296–97.

c. Follows MT. OG adds *gbwl* "border" as a dittography of *gdwl* "great," resulting in "from the Great Sea, the western border." The parenthesis in this sentence is awkwardly placed and is presumably a misplaced gloss.

d. Follows MT. The evidence offers alternate texts between which it is difficult to choose. Instead of MT "and dispossess them before you," OG has "until they perish and he will send against them wild animals until he destroys them and their kings on your account" (perhaps '*d 'šr y'bdw wšlḥ bm 't ḥyt hśdh 'd 'šr yšmyd 'wtm w't mlkyhm mp-nykm*). This could have been lost by MT by haplography from *mpnykm* to *mpnykm* or *mlkyhm*. Conversely, the MT reading absent in OG could have been a casualty of a skip from *mpnykm* to *mlpnykm*. MT is preferable as less likely to be product of scribal development on the basis of texts such as Lev. 26:22 and Deut. 7:20.

e. Follows OG as the shorter reading. S has a variant that expands with "with you" and MT conflates OG and S into "these nations, these that remain with you."

f. Follows MT. OG lost "do not swear" by haplography triggered by the repetition of *wl'*. S suggests "to swear (niphal). The Masoretic hiphil implies "to cause oaths to be taken."

g. Follows OG (LXX[B]) as the shorter reading. S has the same reading as in vv. 4 and 7 ("these nations that remain with you") and MT conflates OG and S into "these nations, these that remain with you."

h. Follows MT. OG can be explained as haplography through homoioteleuton (loss of "good"), scribal correction (removal of "today" in light of chap. 24), and free translation.

i. "Could bring" takes the verb as a modal imperfect (cf. JPSV, REB). An alternate translation would be the unconditional threat of a simple future: "will bring" (NRSV).

j. Conditional sentence beginning with an infinitive construct, as 2 Sam. 7:14.

k. Follows MT. OG lost the last half of the verse through haplography from *lhm* to *lkm*.

This parenetic speech was composed along the lines of a farewell testament, correlating Joshua with both Moses (Deut. 31:1–8, 24–29) and royalty (1 Kings 2:1–9). Claimed similarities to ancient Near Eastern treaty forms[1] are slight and probably result from a general correspondence in literary and rhetorical purpose. In language and conception, this chapter is wholly deuteronomistic.[2] This characteristic rhetorical and homiletical style, marked by repetition and piling up synonymous expressions, does not lend itself to structural analysis.[3]

Joshua's farewell address is not completely without pattern, however. After the introduction in vv. 1–2, it falls naturally into two sections (vv. 3–13 and 14–16), each beginning with an allusion to Joshua's approaching end (vv. 2b and 14a). Within these two sections can be traced three successive rhetorical movements (vv. 3–8, 9–13, 14–16). Each of these movements leads from a summary statement reviewing the contents of the book of Joshua (vv. 3–5, 9–10, 14) to

1. K. Baltzer, *The Covenant Formulary*, Philadelphia, 1971, 63–65; D. McCarthy, *Treaty and Covenant: A Study in Form in the Ancient Oriental Documents and in the Old Testament*, AnBib 21a, Rome, 1975, 200–203.

2. Weinfeld, *Deuteronomy and the Deuteronomic School*, 320–21, 333–34, 336, 339–44, 347, 350, 357.

3. For a detailed "colometrical" analysis that exposes the "poetic prose" qualities of deuteronomistic rhetoric and highlights important compositional features of this chapter, see W. Koopmans, "The Poetic Prose of Joshua 23," *The Structural Analysis of Biblical and Canaanite Poetry*, JSOTSup 74; Sheffield, 1988, 83–118.

motivational encouragement based on those review statements (vv. 6–8, 11–13, 15–16). The first motivational segment (vv. 6–8) consists only of injunctions. The second one (vv. 11–13) begins in an imperative format and then moves into a conditional threat. The third (vv. 15–16) is entirely conditional and exceedingly ominous (see text notes i and j). Thus there is a clear escalation in the severity of the rhetoric, beginning from imperatives without any mention of punishment (vv. 6–8) through a warning that connections with the persisting alien nations would lead to Israel's extinction from the land (v. 13), to the ultimate threat of Yahweh's anger and personal divine involvement in their destruction (vv. 15–16). Overall, the perspective moves from a focus on the positive potentials in Israel's present and future (vv. 5, 8, 9–10) to the real possibility of disobedience and destruction (vv. 13, 15–16). One way of outlining the chapter would be:

> exposition, vv. 1–2a
> first section opening: "I have reached old age," v. 2b
> review: Yahweh's victory and land allotment, vv. 3–5
> exhortation to exclusive loyalty in regard to alien gods, vv. 6–8
> review: Yahweh's victory, vv. 9–10
> exhortation to love Yahweh and conditional threat in regard to alien nations, vv. 11–13
> second section opening: "I am going the way," v. 14a
> review: fulfillment of all Yahweh's promises, v. 14b
> conditional threat about covenant violation, vv. 15–16

As expected in deuteronomistic style, an interlocking repetition of words and phrases cements the whole. Among these are the positive uses of "to this day" in vv. 8 and 9 that link Israel's fidelity to their military success. A positive use of "cling" in v. 8 is balanced by a negative one in v. 12. The assertion that it is Yahweh who fights for Israel ties together the reviews of divine victory in vv. 3 and 9–10. The word "nations" is repeated seven times, coordinating Yahweh's victory and appropriation of their land (vv. 3, 4, 9) with the dangers of consorting with them (vv. 7, 12) and then in turn with their potential role as agents of punishment (v. 13). The adjective "good" communicates that the "good land" (vv. 13, 15) is parallel to the "good things" or "words" (*děbārîm;* vv. 14, 15) promised (*dābar*) and performed by Yahweh, while providing a counterpoint to the "bad thing" of Yahweh's threatened retribution. "Land" (*'ădāmâ* and *'ereṣ*) correlates Joshua's nearness to death (v. 14) with the conquest (v. 5) and the peril of national destruction. This threat is hammered home with parallel phrases using *'ădāmâ/'ereṣ:*

> "until you perish from this good land that Yahweh your God has given you," v. 13

"until he has destroyed you from this good land that Yahweh
has given you," v. 15
"you will quickly perish from the good land that he has given
you," v. 16

The text urges love for Yahweh (v. 11) and comprehensive obedience to
"everything written in the book of the law of Moses" (v. 6). The spotlight, however, is on two particular issues: avoidance of alien gods and remaining aloof
from alien peoples (vv. 7, 12–13, 16). Although such prohibitions were already
part of earlier legal material (Exod. 23:13, 24–25, 33; 34:12),[4] exclusive loyalty to Yahweh and the success that would result is a constant theme of
Deuteronomy. Joshua's speech picks up the language of texts such as Deut.
6:13; 7:16; 10:20; 11:16–17, 22–25; 12:3; 13:4–5 [3–4E] and especially 7:1–5.

Effective exhortation relies on providing convincing motivation. Certainly
one motive given here for Israel's obedience and love is appreciation for Yahweh's gracious gift of victory and land. However, theology based on Deuteronomy must also speak in terms of the threat of potential punishment (Deut. 6:15;
7:4; 8:19–20; 11:17). Thus Joshua's exhortation is largely motivated by the impending threat of destruction and estrangement from the land, and this threat
increasingly dominates the rhetoric. The period that gave rise to this homily
must have been one of uncertainty over continued national existence in the
land. It was undeniably a time when intermarriage with other ethnic groups
was an active danger (v. 12). On the other hand, this could hardly have been a
period of complete hopelessness, for it still seemed to make sense to challenge
readers to fidelity and obedience. These warnings are in the same spirit as DH
texts such as Deut. 31:24–29; 1 Sam. 12:15, 25; 1 Kings 8:33–34; or 2 Kings
20:17–18, where the threat of national crisis or even exile is a real possibility,
but still only a possibility and one which could be averted by obedience.

Joshua's grim last word (vv. 14–16) pronounces the central warning of the
deuteronomistic program. The classic choice of deuteronomic theology is set
before the representatives of the people: "good" or "bad," life or death, blessing or curse (Deut. 11:26–28; chap. 28). Here the "good" and the "bad" correspond specifically to the gift of the "good land" over against being destroyed
and perishing "from the good land" (vv. 15–16). The supreme apostasy would
be to violate the covenant by serving other gods. The inevitable result would
be Yahweh's anger (Deut. 8:19–20; 11:16–17; 13:14 [13E]), and Yahweh's
anger means destruction (v. 16b; Deut. 6:14–15; 7:4). This language of
covenant violation and divine anger recalls the fate of Achan (7:1, 15, 26). The
gift of the land, the celebration of which is so central to this book, is now made
uncertain, thus launching a theme to be played out in the books of Judges and

---

4. The classic treatment of this prohibition is that of Schmitt, *Du sollst keinen Frieden
schliessen.*

Kings and culminating for the northern kingdom in 2 Kings 18:12 and for Judah in 2 Kings 24:20. Pre-exilic audiences would be all too well acquainted with the grim effects of international alliances and pagan worship, while for later readers these conditional threats would sound more like inevitable predictions.

This chapter serves as one of the periodic addresses and editorials that punctuate DH, looking backward and forward and interpreting events (Deuteronomy 1–3; Joshua 1; 1 Samuel 12; 2 Samuel 7; 1 Kings 8). As such it looks back on Joshua 1–12 to summarize promise, conquest, and allotment, but also forward to the perilous new situation to be described in Judges 2–16. The era of the leadership of Joshua is almost over. A different pattern of leadership is about to emerge. Therefore the careful obedience that was laid upon Joshua as an individual at the start of the book now becomes the duty of the entire people and of their collective leadership (1:7–8; 23:6, 11). If this duty is fulfilled, then the promises made to Joshua could be continued for following generations (1:5–6, 11; 23:5, 9). The "to this day" of vv. 8–9 points to obedience and blessing up to this point, but the warnings and imperatives point to the more somber picture of the upcoming book of Judges. Judges 2 reports that after Joshua's death the people remained loyal only as long as the elders who had witnessed Yahweh's deeds still lived (Judg. 2:7, 10 and Josh. 23:2–3). Then Israel began to ignore the warnings given here by Joshua (Judg. 2:12–13, 19, 20; Josh. 23:7, 16) and suffered some of the consequences he had predicted (Judg. 2:14, 20, 21; Josh. 23:13, 16). In Judges, Israel's subsequent violation of the covenant (Josh. 23:16; Judg. 2:20) would convert the fortunate situation of Josh. 23:9 ("Yahweh dispossessed," "no one has withstood you") into its tragic opposite (Judg. 2:14: "they could no longer withstand their enemies," Judg. 2:21: "I will no longer dispossess").

Read against the background of the other DH portions of Joshua, chapter 23 marks a distinct change in emphasis indicated by the introduction of a new word not previously used for the population of Canaan, "nations." This new topic of the "nations" is here added to the familiar assertions already summarized in 21:43–45: Yahweh has given all the land (1:3; 2:24, etc.; 23:13, 15, 16) and Israel has struck (10:40–41), captured (10:42), taken (11:16, 23), and taken possession of it (*yrš* qal; 1:11; 12:1; 21:43).[5] Up to now all "kings" and "enemies" faced by Israel have been defeated (10:13, 19, 25, 40, 42; 11:12, 17–20; 12:1, 7; 21:44; 23:1) and Yahweh has dispossessed them (*yrš* hiphil; 3:10). The *ḥērem* has been applied with rigor (8:26; 10:40, etc.; 11:11–12, 20–21). Yet at the same time, the continued existence of Rahab and the Gibeonites "among Israel" (6:21; 9:18, 22; 10:1 MT) prevents the reader from completely accepting the notion of a total annihilation of Canaan's inhabitants. Now in 23:4 the

---

5. In sharp contrast to the non-DH passages 13:1 and 18:3 where land "remains to be possessed."

reader encounters a new, and somewhat unexpected factor: besides the nations Joshua has "cut off" exist the "nations that remain." Rather suddenly, the assurances of past success, though not really denied (vv. 9–10, 14), are put in perspective by the challenges of the future. Only continued obedience (vv. 6–8, 11) will lead to continued success in the process of Yahweh's dispossessing the nations (vv. 5, 9, 13; *yrš* hiphil) so Israel can continue to take possession (v. 5; *yrš* qal) of their land.

Thus chapter 23 modifies the totally positive outlook of 21:43–45 to conform to the reality of the rest of Israel's story in the land. One the one hand, these two texts share the same language ("rest," "enemies," "take over," "withstand"), and there is a near total correspondence between 21:45 and 23:14b. But 23:4–5 explains that the possession asserted in 21:44 was not complete, while 23:9 throws a slight shadow over the unqualified military success of 21:44 by adding that this has been true "to this day." The declaration of 21:45 that Yahweh has kept every good promise is repeated in 23:14b, but now as evidence that Yahweh could also be trusted to bring threatened disasters.

Seeing this shift as an intolerable inconsistency, some scholars have argued that this chapter cannot be not part of the original DH, but must be the work of a later redaction.[6] However, Joshua's speech perfectly matches the other summary sections of DH, both in format (compare the farewells of Moses and Samuel) and intention.[7] Rather than representing a totally different opinion that seeks to correct the concept of total annihilation with the notion of "nations that remain," chapter 23 actually witnesses to the mixed and complex ideology inherited by DH from Deuteronomy. According to Deut. 7:1–5, for example, the nations are to be wiped out, yet at the same time are to be carefully avoided. Deut. 11:22–25 asserts that the complete achievement of the conquest would depends on obedience as well as on divine promise.

DH has reached a new place in Israel's story and now must have Joshua speak about the future. The preceding assertions about triumphant and even total victory in chapters 1–12 perform an important theological purpose in the

6. DtrN or the "nomistic" redactor as proposed by Smend, "Das Gesetz und die Völker," 501–504. Smend points to similarities to other passages he assigns to DtrN, in particular 1:7–8, 13:1, 6; Judg. 2:17, 20–21, 23. He sees chapter 23 as a modification of 21:43–45 that emulates chapter 24. He has been followed in this by N. Lohfink, "Kerygmata des Deuteronomistischen Geschichtswerks," *Die Botschaft und die Boten*, Neukirchen-Vluyn, 1981, 87–100; Mayes, *The Story of Israel between Settlement and Exile*, London, 1983, 48–49; and O'Brien, *The Deuteronomistic History Hypothesis: A Reassessment*, 75–77. Dividing chapter 23 between a pre-exilic and exilic author is another possible solution, but even this does not remove the tension completely. See F. Cross, *Canaanite Myth and Hebrew Epic*, Cambridge, Mass., 1973, 287; R. Nelson, *The Double Redaction of the Deuteronomistic History*, JSOTSup 18, Sheffield, 1981, 123.

7. To quote Noth, *The Deuteronomistic History*, 5, it "looks forward and backward in an attempt to interpret the course of events, and draws the relevant practical conclusions about what people should do."

context of conquest. They glorify Yahweh, engender trust in Yahweh's promises, and claim the land for Israel by right of divinely engineered victory (compare Judg. 11:23–24). But now the context has changed. As a good deuteronomist, DH shifts theological gears to lead into the rest of the story, a sequel which is not so triumphant. The more careful and nuanced picture of conquest offered by chapter 23 prepares for the cyclically negative plot of Judges. This is the perspective picked up in the DH introduction to Judges (2:10–23, esp. vv. 21, 23). In the book of Kings as well, the historian admits the continued presence of alien elements (1 Kings 9:20–21), yet faithfully asserts that Yahweh dispossessed them (1 Kings 14:24; 2 Kings 15:3).

To make this transition into the conflicted period of the judges, Joshua's address synthesizes the ideology of total conquest and the troublesome reality of remaining nations. On the one hand "rest" has been achieved, all battles won, and all divine promises kept (vv. 1, 9–10, 14). On the other hand some nations remain. The present form of v. 4 brings together both ideas by asserting that the territory of both remaining and "cut off" nations has been allotted (*npl* hiphil, "apportion by lot" as in 13:6) for eventual possession. The continued presence of alien peoples does not undermine Yahweh's promise, but now the future is open and depends on Israel's obedience. The remaining nations could lead to a positive future (v. 5), but also threaten a negative one (vv. 13, 15). Israel stands at the crossroads, and the choice is theirs alone.

[1–2] In the context of the present form of the book, the location would be Shiloh (18:1). "Rest" signals the end of the settlement program (1:13, 15; 21:44; 22:4). The repetition of Joshua's old age here and in 13:1 demonstrates that chapters 13–21 were subsequently added to the DH version of Joshua, although the details of this literary operation are probably beyond recovery. The statement that the conquest took a long time reflects both the understanding of 11:18 and the tradition of Joshua's great age (24:29; Judg. 2:8). In order to emphasize that "all Israel" is responsible for keeping the law, the catalog of leaders who are present is exhaustive. This list is most clearly paralleled in 8:33 (DH) and 24:1.

[3–8] It is only in this chapter that "nations" is used in Joshua for Israel's enemies, although the usage is common in Deuteronomy and elsewhere in DH.[8] Perhaps this is a sort of cross-reference to Deut. 7:1. The role of a previous generation as witnesses to Yahweh's deeds (v. 3) is typical of deuteronomistic theology (Deut. 4:3, 9–10; Judg. 2:7, 10). The assertion that the Divine Warrior fights for Israel reflects 10:14, 42 and is important for DH (Deut. 1:30; 3:22; cf. Deut. 20:4). Although victories over nations have been won (v. 3), nations still remain (v. 4). Yet they (that is, their territory) are also Israel's "hereditary property (*naḥălâ*), and future deeds of the Divine Warrior to dispossess

---

8. Weinfeld, *Deuteronomy and the Deuteronomic School*, 342–43.

them are in view. Thus complete fulfillment of the promise of Deut. 6:19; 9:3–5 is not denied, but extended into the open future (v. 5, 13), and the historical reality of alien populations (1 Kings 9:20–21) is synthesized with the ideology of total conquest.

A "democratization of obedience" in vv. 6–8 redirects the imperatives first addressed individually to Joshua in 1:6–9 to the people as a whole. This resonates with the public display and reading of the law to the entire nation in 8:31, 34. The deviation warned against in v. 6 is defined by the reiterated prohibitions of v. 7, while the deuteronomistic expression "cling to Yahweh" in v. 8 expresses its antithesis. The first prohibition of v. 7 (lit. "go into") may refer to sexual contacts. To cause oaths to be taken in the name of an alien god would be to acknowledge that god's power and authority (Deut. 6:13; 10:20).

[9–13] The "rout formula" of v. 10 reflects the blessing of Deut. 28:7. To "love" God (v. 11; 22:5) is a classic admonition of Deuteronomy (Deut. 6:5).[9] Crime and punishment in the conditional sentence vv. 12–13 are deftly held together by parallel infinitive absolutes that sharpen both the protasis of v. 12 ("if turning you turn away") and the apodosis of v. 13 ("knowing you will know"). Verse 12 (and to a degree the rest of speech) was composed with an eye toward Deut. 7:1–5, which served as the inspiration for the theme of intermarriage resulting in divine anger. "Cling" (*dbq*) is thus defined by v. 12 in terms of marriage (cf. DH in 1 Kings 11:2, 11). The verb *ḥtn* hithpael denotes becoming related to another family by marriage. Intermarriage threatened Yahwistic loyalty because it involved more than just taking a foreign partner. It established complex and profound relationships between entire families (Genesis 34).[10]

Verse 13 uses striking metaphors to highlight the danger presented by alien nations. The whip may signify political oppression (1 Kings 12:11). The snare and trap have to do with the capture of birds and communicate the loss of freedom and independence of action.[11] Taken together these images threaten limitations on the fullness of life. Numbers 33:55 makes the same point in similar language.

[14–16] The renewed introductory formula of v. 14 (cf. 1 Kings 2:2) reminds readers that what Joshua is delivering is his farewell testimony and sharpens what follows as the very essence of his message. Interlocking the

9. See W. Moran, "The Background of the Love of God in Deuteronomy," *CBQ* 25 (1963): 77–87.

10. Thus in Deuteronomy intermarriage was permitted only with war captives, who had no families and could be fully integrated into the Israelite social system (Deut. 21:10–14). The concern was not the modern notion of racial or ethnic purity, but the need to shield Yahwistic culture and religion from alien influences.

11. For illustrations, see O. Keel, *The Symbolism of the Biblical World: Ancient and Near Eastern Iconography and the Book of Psalms*, New York, 1978, 89–95. A *môqēš* (taken from Deut. 7:16) was originally a trigger stick in a trap and then by extension the trap itself. The otherwise unknown *šōṭēṭ* is usually taken to be an error for *šôṭîm*, "whips" (root *šwṭ*).

themes of covenant, serving other gods, and divine anger (v. 16) is a characteristic of DH (Judg. 2:19–20; 1 Kings 11:7–11), but also typical of the exilic frame which encloses Deuteronomy (Deut. 4:23–26; 29:13–19 [14–20E]; 24–27 [25–28E]; 31:16–18, 20). Verse 16b is a quotation of Deut. 11:17b and also reflects the language of Deut. 7:4. There is a satisfying and sobering rhyming word play in this last verse between the crime (*wa'ăbadtem*, "and you serve") and its punishment (*wa'ăbadtem*, "and you will perish").

Assembly at Shechem
Joshua 24:1–28

Review of Salvation History

24:1 Joshua gathered all the tribes of Israel at Shechem.[a] He summoned the elders of Israel, its leaders, judges, and officers. They presented themselves before God. 2 Then Joshua said to the whole people, "Thus says Yahweh the God of Israel: 'From of old your ancestors—Terah the father of Abraham and Nahor—lived beyond the Euphrates[b] and served other gods. 3 I took your ancestor Abraham from beyond the Euphrates and led him through the whole land [of Canaan] and increased his descendants and gave him Isaac. 4 I gave[c] Jacob and Esau to Isaac. I gave Mt. Seir to Esau as his possession, but Jacob and his sons went down to Egypt. There they became a large, numerous, and powerful nation, and the Egyptians oppressed them.[d] 5 [Then I sent Moses and Aaron.][e] I plagued Egypt according to what[f] I did in it and afterwards I brought you out[g] 6 from Egypt. You came to the sea and the Egyptians pursued your ancestors with chariots and horses to the Red Sea. 7 Then they cried for help to Yahweh and he put darkness[h] between you and the Egyptians. He brought the sea down on them and it covered them. You saw with your own eyes what I did to the Egyptians. You lived in the wilderness for many days. 8 Then I brought you into the land of the Amorites who live on the other side of the Jordan and they fought you.[i] I gave them into your power and you took possession of their land. I destroyed them before you. 9 Then Balak son of Zippor king of Moab set out to fight against Israel. He sent a summons to Balaam [son of Beor] to curse you, 10 but I was not willing to listen to Balaam,[j] so he actually blessed you[k] and I rescued you from his power. 11 You crossed the Jordan and came to Jericho and the masters of Jericho fought against you—the Amorites, Perizzites, Canaanites, Hittites, Girgashites, Hivites, and Jebusites—but I gave them into your power. 12 I sent a hornet before you and it drove them out before you, the two[l] kings of the Amorites. It was not by your [sg] sword or your bow. 13 I gave you [pl] a land on which you [sg] had not toiled and cities which you [pl] had not built and you settled them. You are eating from vineyards and olive groves which you did not plant.'

Challenge and Assent

14 "So now revere Yahweh and serve him honestly and faithfully. Put aside the gods which your ancestors served beyond the Euphrates and in Egypt and serve Yahweh. 15 Yet if it seems wrong in your opinion to serve Yahweh, then choose today whom you will serve—either the gods which your ancestors served beyond the Euphrates or the gods of the Amorites in whose land you live. But my family and I will serve Yahweh. 16 Then the people answered, "God forbid that we ever forsake Yahweh to serve other gods! 17 For Yahweh is our God.[m] He is the one who brought us and our ancestors[n] up from [the land of] Egypt [from the house of bondage and has done these mighty signs in our sight].[o] He has guarded us the whole way we have gone and in all the nations through which we have passed. 18 Yahweh has driven out before us all the nations and the Amorites who inhabit the land. We also will serve Yahweh, for he is our God."

19 Then Joshua said to the people, "You are not able to serve Yahweh because he is a holy God. He is a jealous God. He will not forgive your rebellion and your sins. 20 If you forsake Yahweh and serve foreign gods, then he will turn around and do you harm and exterminate you, after he had done you good." 21 Then the people said to Joshua, "No! Yahweh is the one we will serve."

22 So Joshua said to the people, "You are witnesses against yourselves that you have chosen Yahweh for yourselves in order to serve him. [They said, "We are witnesses!"][p] 23 So now put aside the foreign gods that are among you and bend your hearts toward Yahweh the God of Israel." 24 The people said to Joshua, "We will serve Yahweh [our God] and will obey him."

Joshua Makes a Covenant

25 On that day Joshua made a covenant for the people and established a statute and an ordinance for them in Shechem. 26 Joshua wrote these words in the law book of God. Then he took a large stone and raised it [there][q] under the oak in the sanctuary of Yahweh. 27 Joshua said to [all] the people, "Look. This stone will serve as a witness against us, for it has heard all Yahweh's words which he spoke to us. It will serve as a witness

against you lest you disown your God." 28 Then Joshua sent the people
away to each one's hereditary property.ʳ

a. Here and in v. 25 OG locates the assembly at Shiloh rather than Shechem in order to harmonize with 18:1 and with the presence of the tabernacle in Shiloh (22:12,
29), to which a Greek plus in v. 25 alludes.

b. Alternate translation: "in the territory 'Beyond the River,'" taking this as the Assyrian and Persian designation for the region *west* of the Euphrates (1 Kings 5:4
[4:24E]) that included Haran (Gen. 11:31).

c. Follows MT. OG lacks "I gave," possibly for translational reasons.

d. Follows OG. The precursor of MT, lacking the plus at the start of v. 5 (text note
e), lost a portion of text by haplography from *mṣrym w* to *hmṣrym w*: "There they became . . . the Egyptians oppressed them" (perhaps *wyhyw šm lgwy gdwl wrb w'ṣwm
wy'nw 'tm hmṣrym*). Nevertheless, the language is similar to Deut. 26:5b, so that the
possibility of an OG expansion from there cannot be totally discounted. See Tov,
"Midrash-Type Exegesis in the LXX of Joshua," 59–60.

e. MT supplement, perhaps from Micah 6:4.

f. Follows MT as the more difficult reading. This can be understood as an economi-
cal reference to well-known details left unmentioned. OG (*b'šr* "by means of what") is a
b for *k* mistake that in fact supports MT. LXXᴬ (*b'twt 'šr*, "with signs which"; cf. S and
V) attempts to alleviate the awkward original, perhaps on the basis of Num. 14:11.

g. Follows LXXᴬ. At the end of v. 5 and the beginning of v. 6, MT conflates two
alternate readings: "I brought you out" and "I brought your ancestors out." The first is
found alone in LXXᴬ and other Greek witnesses; the second is LXXᴮ. Of the two, "I
brought you out" is more apt to be original since reference to the ancestors sounds like
a pedantic "correction." From this point on the Greek presents the actions of Yahweh
in the third person and has other differences in pronoun reference, often reading the first
person plural instead of the second person in vv. 5–11, 14.

h. *ma'ăpēl* is otherwise unknown in biblical Hebrew (but see the commentaries on
Jer. 2:31) and may be the result of dittography: *wyšm [m]'pl*. OG may support this by
offering a conflate doublet "cloud and darkness," unless this taken from the Greek of
Ps. 97:2.

i. Follows MT. OG lost "and they fought you" through an inner-Greek haplography.

j. Follows MT. OG ("to destroy you") translates Balaam's name as an infinitive
from the root *bl'*. OG fails to reflect "to listen," perhaps as a result of theological objections to the thought of God listening to a human being.

k. Alternate translation: "kept on blessing you."

l. Follows MT, although this results in a baffling text. OG reflects a revision of
the more difficult "two" into "twelve," altered because Joshua is clearly reviewing
events on the *west* side of the Jordan. Perhaps the number "twelve" was computed on
the basis of the kings mentioned in chapters 10 and 11. The notion of twelve enemy
rulers is also a literary theme in Assyrian royal inscriptions (e.g., see *ANET*, 279–81,
291, 294).

m. Follows MT. OG adds "he is God" *'lhym hw'* by dittography.

n. Follows MT and OG. "And our ancestors" is absent from S, a haplography triggered by the repeated pronoun suffix.

o. MT expansion based on traditional language similar to that of Deut. 6:22; 7:19.

p. The MT expansion adds the expected formula (cf. Ruth 4:11; 1 Sam. 12:5), but interrupts Joshua's speech.

q. MT expansion lacking in both OG and S. OG moved "Joshua" for translational reasons and paraphrased "sanctuary" due to theological disquiet over the presence of a sacred tree.

r. Follows MT and Judg. 2:6. OG has *topon autou*, apparently translating *mqwmw*.

This chapter has been a focus of a great deal of scholarly controversy. There is no consensus about its compositional history, time of origin, or possible relationship to the history or cultic life of Israel.[1] At first attributed to the E source, assignment to J was advocated by others.[2] Although deuteronomistic editing has generally been recognized, contradictory proposals about the text's composition have proliferated.[3] Its relationship to DH and thus to chapter 23 is problematic and has been much discussed.[4] The influence of ancient Near Eastern treaty forms has often been asserted.[5] The chapter has commonly been thought to have grown out of some sort of Shechem-centered liturgical rite associated with Deut. 11:29–32; 27:1–26;

1. For reviews and evaluation of research, see Koopmans, *Joshua 24 as Poetic Narrative*, 7–162; J. Floss, *Jahwe dienen—Göttern dienen*, BBB 45, Bonn, 1975, 334–40; S. Kreutzer, *Die Frühgeschichte Israels in Bekenntnis und Verkündigung des Alten Testaments*, BZAW 178, Berlin, 1989, 183–92.

2. Classically by Rudolph, *Der 'Elohist' als Erzähler von Exodus bis Josua*, 244–52, and most recently by J. Van Seters, "Joshua 24 and the Problem of Tradition in the Old Testament," *In the Shelter of Elyon*, 1984, 139–58 (a post-deuteronomic J).

3. J. L'Hour, "L'Alliance de Sichem," *RB* 69 (1962): 5–36, 161–84, 350–68: a basic text edited to lessen treaty form elements, reducing legal elements in favor of liturgical ones; Floss, *Jahwe dienen—Göttern dienen*, 334–71: seven layers of tradition; Mölle, *Der sogenannte Landtag zu Sichem*, 105–107, 283–99: four levels beginning with a basic Shechem source, elohistic and yahwistic layers, and concluding with two deuteronomistic redactions; Kreutzer, *Die Frühgeschichte Israels in Bekenntnis und Verkündigung*, 193–213: splicing of early (Josianic, vv. 2–15) and late (from v. 16 on) summary materials, the later summary being an amplification of chapter 23; S. Sperling, "Joshua 24 Re-examined," *HUCA* 58 (1987): 119–36: a northern monarchy period composition with no relationship to Deuteronomy.

4. W. Richter, *Die Bearbeitung des "Retterbuches" in der deuteronomischen Epoche*, BBB 21, Bonn, 1964, 45–47, and Smend, "Das Gesetz und die Völker," 501–504, see chapter 24 as the DH conclusion for Joshua and chapter 23 as secondary to it. Fritz, *Josua*, 235–39 holds a similar opinion. The opposite view is advanced by Nelson, *The Double Redaction of the Deuteronomistic History*, 94–98, who understands chapter 23 as the summary speech of a pre-exilic DH, with chapter 24 as the addition of an exilic redactor. Mayes, *The Story of Israel between Settlement and Exile*, 48–57, and M. O'Brien, *The Deuteronomistic History Hypothesis: A Reassessment*, 76–81, maintain that neither chapter was part of the original DH.

5. Baltzer, *The Covenant Formulary*, 19–27, and in a more nuanced way by McCarthy, *Treaty and Covenant*, 221–42, 279–84.

and Josh. 8:30–35, perhaps involving the elimination of strange gods reflected in Gen. 35:2–4.[6] In contrast, others have strongly denied any connection to a liturgical ceremony and have understood this chapter as a purely literary composition with no direct association with the form-critical genres of the cult.[7]

Although theorizing about this chapter has tended to outstrip the available evidence, certain significant points may be made with reasonable confidence. For example, its language reflects that of Genesis–Numbers, but expressions also occur which are at least consistent with deuteronomistic usage.[8] Most would agree that glosses or later expansions are present in v. 2 (the phrase about Terah), in v. 11 (the list of nations), possibly in 12b, and in v. 18 ("all the nations"). Chapter 24 reflects traditions not found in the Pentateuch or elsewhere in Joshua, namely the ancestors' worship of alien gods beyond the Euphrates and in Egypt (vv. 2, 14–15) and a battle at Jericho (v. 11). At the same time, it has close connections with a wide variety of other texts, notably to Exod. 23:20–33 and Deut. 7:12–26, to the Shechem/covenant texts Deut. 11:29–32; 27:1–26; Josh. 8:30–35; and to Judg. 2:1–5; 6:8–10; 10:10–16; 1 Sam. 7:3–4; 10:17–25.[9]

These connections naturally raise the question as to whether any older traditions or genres lie behind this text. Proposed contacts with covenant or treaty genres are undercut by the circumstance that certain key elements expected in a treaty pattern are lacking: oath, stipulations, or curses and blessings. In any

6. Kraus, *Worship in Israel*, 136–41; Schmitt, *Der Landtag von Sichem*, 55–79. A cultic background is also asserted by M. Noth, *Das System der Zwölf Stämme Israels*, BWANT 4/1, Stuttgart, 1930, 133–36 (with reference to the cult of the amphictyony) and G. von Rad, "The Form Critical Problem of the Hexateuch," *The Problem of the Hexateuch and Other Essays*, London, 1984, 3–8 (as an example of the historical credo).

7. Perlitt, *Bundestheologie im Alten Testament*, WMANT 36, Neukirchen-Vluyn, 1969, 239–84; E. Nicholson, *God and His People*, Oxford, 1986, 151–63; C. Brekelmans, "Joshua 24: Its Place and Function," *Congress Volume Leuven 1989*, VTSup 43, Leiden, 1991, 1–9; Fritz, *Josua*, 233–46. M. Anbar, *Josué et l'Alliance de Sichem (Josué 24:1–28)*, BBET 25, Frankfurt, 1992, proposes a post-exilic midrash elevating Joshua and his covenant over Moses and the covenant at Sinai.

8. This is a deliberately circumspect statement. Evaluation of the language in source-critical terms has diverged widely. For a summary, see Koopmans, *Joshua 24 as Poetic Narrative*, 104–41. The maximalist position for deuteronomistic language is that of Perlitt, *Bundestheologie im Alten Testament*, 249–70. Representatives of the minimalist position are McCarthy, *Treaty and Covenant*, 221–34; Sperling, "Joshua 24 Re-examined," 123–33; and Koopmans, *Joshua 24 as Poetic Narrative*, 271–344. A moderate list of deuteronomistic language would be the leadership catalog of v. 1; "saw with your own eyes," v. 7; "took possession of their land," v. 8; the nation list of v. 11; v. 13 as a whole; "fear and serve," v. 14; "forsake Yahweh to serve other gods," v. 16 and probably v. 20; "serve and obey," v. 25.

9. For an analysis of these, see Schmitt, *Der Landtag von Sichem*, 26–28; W. Koopmans, *Joshua 24 as Poetic Narrative*, 370–86; E. Blum, *Die Komposition der Vätergeschichte*, WMANT 57, Neukirchen-Vluyn, 1984, 45–61.

case, the text does not present itself as a transcript of a treaty or covenant, but instead as a report about the making of a covenant.[10] The idea that some liturgical rite may be mirrored here is weakened by vv. 15 and 19a, which seem to be completely at odds with any conceivable liturgical purpose.[11] However, there is some relationship to or memory of rites and objects that are connected with Shechem in other texts (tree, Gen. 12:6; 35:4; Deut. 11:30; Judg. 9:37; tree and standing stone, Judg. 9:6; putting aside alien gods, Gen. 35:1–4). Yet these Shechem traditions are being used in a literary fashion to validate this text. The text does not function as an etiology for them. An analysis of the rhetorical argument shows that this speech has in its conceptual background either the imminent threat or actual experience of exile beyond the Euphrates and perhaps in Egypt and an urgency about choosing for Yahweh and against other gods. Correlations with the ethos and even the language of the Mesha Inscription[12] point to political rhetoric supporting national identity as the loyal people of a victorious god.

Structurally, the unit consists of dialogue framed by narrative. The narrative itself is scant and uncomplicated: the gathering (v. 1), four actions by Joshua (vv. 25–26: "made a covenant," "wrote," "took," "raised"), and dismissal (v. 28). The real weight of the text centers on reported speech. Even Joshua's four actions are actually only consequences of the dialogue, as v. 27 indicates. In the dialogue portion, the indicative of Yahweh's actions (vv. 2–13, 17–18) serves as the foundation ("and now," v. 14) for Joshua's imperative challenges (vv. 14–15) and the people's commitment (vv. 16–18). Yahweh's speech provides the data upon which their decision is made. Repetition drives home the reality of their choice for Yahweh. There are three challenges and three assents:[13]

> historical review: Yahweh speech embedded in a Joshua speech through prophetic formula (vv. 2–13)
>> patriarchs, exodus (vv. 2–7), key word "Egypt" (vv. 4, 6, 7)
>> conquest (vv. 8–13), key word "hand" (translated "power," vv. 8, 10, 11)

10. Weinfeld, *Deuteronomy and the Deuteronomic School*, 61–66.

11. Schmitt, *Der Landtag von Sichem*, 42–43, 80–81; Perlitt, *Bundestheologie im Alten Testament*, 244.

12. Compare v. 2 "from of old" to line 10; v. 4 (restored text) "oppressed" to line 5; v. 8 "you took possession (*yrš*) of their land" to line 7; v. 17 the deity "drove out (*grš*) before you" to line 19.

13. For structural observations see J. Muilenburg, "The Form and Structure of the Covenantal Formulations," *VT* 9 (1959): 357–60. The elaborate structures claimed by C. Giblin, "Structural Patterns in Joshua 24:1–25," *CBQ* (1964): 50–69 and Koopmans, *Joshua 24 as Poetic Narrative*, 165–270, could function only at some nonconscious level, assuming they are actually present.

first challenge, with reference to the past (vv. 14–15)
first assent, with reference to the past: "we will serve" (vv. 16–18)
second challenge: the danger and absurdity of their commitment, with reference to the future (vv. 19–20)
second assent: "we will serve" (v. 21)
third challenge and validation by a witness formula (vv. 22–23)
third assent: "we will serve and obey" (v. 24)

The last two answers are much more succinct than the first, perhaps communicating certainty in face of objections raised and demands imposed. The climactic third assent adds obedience to service. The rhetorical power of threefold repetition impels the reader to go along with assembled Israel and to concur with the text's agenda.

The status of chapter 24 within the book of Joshua is ambivalent because it so closely parallels the function of chapter 23 in the plot structure. Without ever dismissing the assembly of chapter 23, Joshua assembles them again. His anticipated death, which prompts chapter 23 (vv. 1, 14), takes place only after this second gathering (24:29), which is provided with no additional narrative motivation. There is topical overlap between the two chapters: survey of the past (23:3–5, 9–10; 24:2–13), imperative and exhortation (23:6–13; 24:14–15), and the "Yahweh alone" ideology (23:7, 12, 16; 24:2, 14–24, 27). In genre, however, they are rather different. Chapter 23 is a call for obedience to the law and separation from the nations in the form of a testament, while chapter 24 is a challenge to serve (that is, worship) Yahweh crafted in the form of a dialogue. While chapter 23 directs Israel *how* to worship Yahweh (exclusively, vv. 7–8, 16), the question in chapter 24 is not so much how, as *who* ought to be worshiped, and the answer is a resounding "Yahweh." Chapter 23 works well as a summary to the book of Joshua, limiting its review to the occupation of the land. Chapter 24, in contrast, seems designed as a conclusion for the Hexateuch as a whole.[14] It is less focused on the issue of land and operates with a wider horizon, one that includes patriarchs, exodus, and wilderness. Perhaps 23:16, which pulls together the themes of serving other gods, covenant, and the possibility of perishing from the land, served as the topical attachment point for chapter 24, which focuses on these same matters.

Although critical opinion has often insisted that one of these summaries must have served as a pattern for the other, the only unambiguous literary connection is that between 23:2 and 24:1. In light of the retrospective summary found in 1 Samuel 12, it can hardly be said that DH would need a literary model

---

14. Brekelmans, "Joshua 24: Its Place and Function," 4–6.

to produce a conclusion for the Joshua era. Chapter 23 is a better candidate for DH's summary editorial for the end of the conquest era than chapter 24. It is directly motivated by Joshua's impending death and does not reach back into matters earlier than Deuteronomy. In contrast, features of chapter 24 clearly fall outside the DH presentation. The need for a choice of Yahweh and the presumption that alien gods are present in Israel (vv. 14, 23) differ from DH's assertion that the people were perfectly faithful during Joshua's lifetime (24:31; Judg. 2:7, 10). Establishing and writing supplementary law (vv. 25–26) goes well beyond the role of Joshua outlined in chapter 1.

Joshua assembles the tribes at Shechem. As a site connected in tradition with Israel's loyalty to Yahweh and with the concept of the covenant (Gen. 35:2–4; Deut. 27:4–26; Josh. 8:30–35; Judg. 8:33; 9:4, 46), this is an appropriate location. All the people are gathered and addressed, but the leadership is singled out to take their stand "before God," that is in God's cultic presence (1 Sam. 10:19). This accentuates the significance of what is to take place. Joshua begins with a prophetic messenger formula to give authority and weight to a speech of Yahweh reviewing Israel's election traditions. "Yahweh the God of Israel" is unambiguously the initiator of this election relationship, the subject of almost twenty first-person verbs. The review covers the patriarchs (vv. 2–4), exodus (vv. 5–7a), wilderness (v. 7b), and conquest (vv. 8–13).

The patriarchal traditions about Terah and Nahor are similar to those recorded in Gen. 11:27–32. The travels of Abraham and the increase of his "seed" echo the plot of Genesis 12–36. It may not be a coincidence that the first stage of Abraham's journey took him to Shechem (Gen. 12:1–7). Right from the beginning, this review is designed to pilot both audience and reader to a climactic decision for Yahweh. Each of Israel's three alternate options, Mesopotamian, Egyptian, or Amorite gods (vv. 14–15), are prepared for and dismissed as absurd. Abraham was *taken* from the territory of the gods beyond the Euphrates (v. 2). The Egyptians were humiliated by the events of the exodus (vv. 5–7). The Amorites were destroyed, Balaam was coopted, the masters of Jericho and the seven nations were defeated. What they had worked to develop was wrested from them (vv. 8–13). In contrast to their ineffective gods, Yahweh has been consistently in control of events for Israel's sake, graciously leading, increasing, defending, prevailing, and giving. The objects of Yahweh's favor are at first the ancestors (vv. 2–4), but very soon the "you" of the story audience and readership (vv. 5–13). Yet even early in the story there is a hint that election can also mean trouble. Esau was given Seir but Jacob went down to Egypt.

With "now therefore" and a change of speaker, v. 14 turns from saving history to its ramifications for the assembled people. Because the text seeks to have readers explore their religious options, Joshua is represented as giving the nation a choice of gods. His challenge leads to a dramatic dialogue that continues as far as v. 24. Yet the option to choose is really no option at all. Even the way Joshua frames the situation shrewdly advances the choice for Yahweh, for to use the word "choose" (v. 15) recalls the typical use of this verb to express Yahweh's election of Israel (Deut. 7:6, 7; 10:15; 14:2; 1 Kings 3:8). Moreover, the whole notion that a people ought to choose one God to the exclusion of others is in itself distinctive to the "Yahweh alone" ideology. In a real sense, even to agree that such a choice is necessary is implicitly to make the choice for Yahweh.

Three imperatives in v. 14 express the choice of loyalty to Yahweh: "revere" (that is, respect and obey), "serve" (that is, worship and be subject to), and "put aside" rival gods. This last implies eliminating their images (v. 23; Gen. 35:2–4; Judg. 10:16). The verb "serve" provides a unifying focus for the dialogue to follow, where it is used to express both fidelity and infidelity (vv. 14, 15, 16, 18, 19, 21, 22, 24). "Today" communicates the urgency of choice and contemporizes it for the text's readers, for whom the gods of Mesopotamia and Egypt are apparently viable alternatives, along with the local gods of Canaan. Joshua leads the nation to the right decision with his own rhetorically effective statement of commitment, one which clearly intends to call forth a corresponding one from them (v. 15).

The peoples' answering rhetoric (vv. 16–18) is just as impassioned, stressed with an initial asseveration and typically deuteronomistic language ("forsake Yahweh"). They agree that the choice for Yahweh is obvious, based on Yahweh's past saving deeds. The gift of the land obligates the choice of Yahweh, for their possession of the land rests entirely on Yahweh's deeds. Traditional confessional language about plagues, exodus, wilderness wandering, and conquest, summarizes what Yahweh has already proclaimed in vv. 2–13. Verses 17–18 are bracketed by a short confessional formula that wraps the matter up in a nutshell: "For Yahweh is our God . . . for he is our God" (cf. 22:22; 1 Kings 18:39). The choice is no real choice at all. Yahweh will continue to be what Yahweh has always been, our God.

With vv. 19–20 the drama sharpens. Joshua insists that the choice confidently made in v. 18 will prove to be impossible to live out. The rhetorical jolt is sharp and effective. The issue, seemingly closed, is reopened in order to be explored on a deeper level. The new perspective is one that anticipates (or has already experienced) the fateful consequences of "forsaking Yahweh." There are parallels to Joshua's warning in prophetic proclamation, for example Amos 3:1–2; Isa. 6:9–10.

It is not so much Israel's weakness or wickedness that makes their aspiration to serve futile, but the inherent nature of the God they have chosen. Yahweh is holy and jealous and does not forgive rebellion. To speak of a "holy God" is to speak of a dangerous quality in Yahweh (Num. 4:19–20; 2 Sam. 6:6–7; Isa. 8:13–14) that is incompatible with the worship of other gods (Exod.

15:11; 1 Sam. 2:2). Idolatry "profaned" (desanctified) Yahweh's name (Lev. 18:21; 20:3; Ezek. 20:39). Yahweh's traditional title *'ēl qannô'* "jealous God" (Exod. 34:14) also relates directly to the exclusivity of worship that lies behind the demand to "choose." It is often connected to the threat to punish illicit worship (Exod. 20:5; Deut. 4:24; 6:14–15). What Yahweh will not forgive is the "rebellion" (*pešaʿ*) of worshiping other gods (Exod. 23:21), because such worship violates Yahweh's very nature as a holy God, jealous for exclusivity.

The completely negative viewpoint of vv. 19–20 would be compatible with an intention to explain a catastrophe of defeat and exile (2 Kings 17:7–20), but in any case has the effect of urging religious loyalty in the strongest possible terms. It represents the ultimate honing of the "Yahweh alone" ideology and urges all those who undertake to serve Yahweh to count "the cost of discipleship."

Because Joshua has raised the stakes in regard to what it costs to serve Yahweh, Israel's reassertion of their decision in v. 21 is rhetorically powerful, especially for readers who might themselves have experienced the negative consequences of a relationship with Yahweh. The people's role as witnesses, prepared to accuse themselves in case of transgression (v. 22), underscores both the reality of their commitment and its potential dangers. With "so now" (v. 24), Joshua turns to an immediate consequence of their unambiguous choice for Yahweh, the imperative to "put aside" (picked up from v. 14) "foreign gods" (from v. 20; Gen. 35:2, 4; Deut. 31:16; 1 Sam. 7:3). These gods turn out to be not just a matter of their ancestors' former practices or a theoretical option on their part. They are "among" them even now. Moreover, something more than mere outward conformity is required, for Joshua urges an inclination of the heart toward Yahweh (1 Kings 8:58; negatively in 1 Kings 11:2, 4, 9; cf. Deut. 6:5; 10:16). The people's third and climactic assent (v. 24) puts Yahweh in the object-first emphatic position and adds a supplementary commitment of obedience to their previous commitment to worship (cf. v. 18b with v. 21).

Narrative replaces dialogue in vv. 25–26, as Joshua gives structure and effectiveness to the people's agreed-upon commitment with three actions: making a covenant, writing in a book, and erecting a witness stone. He makes a covenant "for them, on their behalf" (dative preposition *l*), formally validating the people's commitment. In association with this covenant, Joshua promulgates ("sets") an otherwise unspecified "statute and ordinance" (Exod. 15:25; 1 Sam. 30:25), which in context must have something to do with the exclusive worship of Yahweh. Joshua records this precept in the "law book of God." This last is a conspicuously non-deuteronomistic phrase (cf. Neh. 8:8, 18), although the act of recording law is familiar from Deut. 31:9, 24. Joshua's third action is to erect a standing stone in the sacred enclosure of Shechem under the famous tree there. Joshua does not write on this stone, in contrast to 8:32 and Deut. 27:2–4. Rather it functions as a second and more objective witness in addition to the witness role of the people. The stone is a witness in the sense of being a visible public reminder (22:27, 34), but also because it has heard the words spoken by Yahweh. This concept seems similar to the role of the Galeed stone heap and the Mizpah pillar as witnesses to the spoken words of an agreement (Gen. 31:48–50; for human earwitnesses, 1 Kings 21:10, 13). The stone is potentially a witness "against," in the juridical sense of supporting an accusation, for there would be no need for a witness unless some apostasy has been charged. This narrative frame ends with a dismissal parallel to that of 22:6. Here as there, the use of *naḥălâ* "hereditary property" signals the end of the land distribution process.

Joshua is a book about national victory and glory, but how was it to be read by those who had experienced defeat and national humiliation? For such readers there was little glory and much pain in being Yahweh's people. The mental horizon of the implied audience for this text includes at least the possibility of settlement in a foreign land such as Egypt or Mesopotamia and the resultant threat to their loyalty to Yahweh. Rueful awareness of Israel's sad history of worshiping "the gods of the Amorites" is also present. Possibly it is still only the threat of national catastrophe that lies behind this rhetoric, and not the reality. Perhaps it is only the looming specter of Assyrian imperialism that tempts readers to worship the gods of Mesopotamia, Egypt, and the Amorites. However, it is more likely that the readers are living through the time of exile or the unheroic period of Persian domination. Since Yahweh has proved unreliable or ineffective as a national god, other gods may be more worthy of allegiance. Possible options include the gods of the victors across the Euphrates or of the Egyptians (Jer. 44:8) or the local gods whose worship it may have been a mistake to abandon (Jer. 44:15–19).[15]

So the author of this chapter calls the people together once again (in a literary sense) to reevaluate their religious loyalty and recommit themselves to Yahweh. The either/or challenge of exclusive Yahweh worship is as old as the traditions of Elijah (1 Kings 18:21), but now the thought-world seems to be closer to that of Second Isaiah (e.g. Isa. 43:10–12). This audience would be a sadder and wiser group than the enthusiastic pioneers in the text, who speak in such glowing terms about the benefits of serving Yahweh. The readers are a people who have suffered at the hands of their God and from the vicissitudes of history. The text confronts them anew with the same challenge once put to

15. Perlitt, *Bundestheologie im Alten Testament*, 274–79, advocates a seventh-century context, pointing to the supposed worship of Assyrian gods in Judah between the reigns of Ahaz and Josiah and the gods introduced into the north by the Assyrians. McCarthy *Treaty and Covenant*, 238, suggests an even earlier origin in the temptations offered by Syria, part of the territory "Beyond the River." Schmitt, *Der Landtag von Sichem*, 32, similarly points to 1 Kings chapter 18 and the time of Elijah, and Sperling, "Joshua 24 Re-examined," 136, proposes the time of Jeroboam II. Suggestions of an exilic origin are more common, for example Van Seters, "Joshua 24 and the Problem of Tradition," 139–58 and Nicholson, *God and His People*, 160–63. Finding indications of tensions between Jews and the inhabitants of the former northern kingdom, Blum defends a post-exilic date, *Die Komposition der Vätergeschichte*, 45–61.

their ancestors. Choose *today* whom you will serve. Will you serve the gods of history's victors who seem to have humiliated Yahweh and now dominate Yahweh's people? Will you worship the gods of Canaan, who might defend their territory better than Yahweh has?

The text inspires its readers to join their ancestors and to decide to remain loyal to Yahweh. It intends to convince them that the choice today is still as obvious as it was then. The reader response is intended to be: "No, we too choose to serve Yahweh. God forbid that we should ever forsake Yahweh to serve other gods. To do so would be to deny our history, heritage, and identity. Looking back over our own recent history of defeat (and perhaps exile and possibly restoration), we must still declare that Yahweh has 'protected us along all the way . . . and among all the peoples through whom we passed (v. 17).'"

The book of Joshua raises the issue of national identity one last time, but now adds a significant twist. Israel is not only a people for whom Yahweh has done many good things, but also a people who have deliberately chosen to serve this perilous God with exclusive loyalty, even though this may mean risk or even extermination. Their identity as the people of "Yahweh the God of Israel" is ultimately not one of security in the land, but one of insecurity, subject to the uncertain forces of history. To be Yahweh's people is to be caught in the vortex of Yahweh's holiness and jealousy, intolerant divine qualities which demand that they serve Yahweh and Yahweh alone "honestly and faithfully," a demand impossible to accomplish. Yet impossible or not, they are the people who have obligated themselves by solemn covenant to serve and obey, and they are responsible for doing so, in accordance with what is written "in the law of God." Their very existence is a witness to the paradoxical nature of their peoplehood: "You are witnesses against yourselves" (v. 22).

[1–7] The catalog of leaders is evidence of a redactional connection of some sort to 23:1–2 and also to the Ebal/Gerizim pericope of 8:30–35 (cf. v. 33). The title "God of Israel" (vv. 2, 23) seems to have been specially connected with Shechem (8:30; Gen. 33:20). The choice of Shechem is unexpected from the perspective of the book of Joshua, but brings with it a rich legacy of an ancient holy place with its sacred tree and pillar (v. 26), traditions of a ceremonial repudiation of gods (v. 23; Gen. 35:1–4), and a long-standing association with the notion of covenant (Baal/El-Berith; Judg. 8:33; 9:4, 46). Shechem also had a political role as a meeting place for making national decisions (1 Kings 12:1, 25).

The historical review of vv. 2–13 is not in the form of a credo taken from tradition, but is a first-person Yahweh speech presented as a prophetic word. It fits its rhetorical context exactly by demonstrating that Yahweh is superior to the gods of Mesopotamia, Egypt, and Canaan. It is thus is more of a literary product than a traditional genre. It has the earmarks of a literary composition created on the basis of some form of Genesis, Exodus, and Numbers for the express purpose of supporting the challenge which follows:

v. 2, Gen. 11:24–32
v. 3, Gen. 12:1–9
    "took," Gen. 24:7
    "increase seed," Gen. 16:10; 17:17
v. 4, Exodus 4–6
v. 5, Exodus 7–13
    "plagued," Exod. 7:27 [8:2E]; 12:23, 27
vv. 6–7, Exodus chapter 14
    "pursued," Exod. 14:9, 23
    "chariots and horses," Exod. 14:9, 28
    "cry out," Exod. 8:8; 14:10, 15; 15:25
    "darkness between," Exod. 14:20, although closer to
        10:22
    "covered" Exod. 14:28; 15:10

These allusions are to both JE and P texts. The Red Sea event is reported only in terms of the inundation of the enemy (Exod. 14:28; 15:10). In contrast, the text is significantly silent about "cutting" apart the water and the dry passage that are emphasized in Joshua 3 and 4. The Mesha Inscription offers a close parallel to the opening phrase indicating immense antiquity: "the men of Gad had always dwelt in the land of Ataroth" (line 10; *ANET*, 320). Terah may have been awkwardly placed into v. 2 to exculpate Abraham as a worshiper of alien gods. For the notion that a change in territory (v. 3) means a change in gods, compare Ruth 1:16 and 1 Sam. 26:19.

[8–13] The story moves into Numbers with the defeat of the Amorites in v. 8 and the Balaam episode in vv. 9–10.

v. 8, Numbers 21
    "in the land of the Amorites" Num. 21:31
    "they fought you," Num. 21:1
    "gave them into your power . . . took possession of their
        land," Num. 21:34–35
v. 9, Numbers chapter 22
    "sent a summons," Num. 22:5, 37
v. 10, Numbers 22–24 (but also Deut. 23:6 [5E])
v. 12, Exod. 23:28; also cf. the "sword and bow" reference
    involving Shechem, Gen. 48:21–22

Parallels in Amos 2:9–10 and Micah 6:4 are evidence that these traditions would have been generally available for rhetorical purposes, so actual dependence on the Numbers text cannot be confirmed. If v. 9 intends to suggest that Balak actually fought Israel, this is not a tradition otherwise known (Deut. 2:9; also Judg. 11:25). Verse 11 presents a version of the Jericho victory at odds with the one in Joshua 6, although perhaps present in some earlier form of the Rahab story. The ungainly inclusion of the nation-list in this verse widens its horizons so that the sentence can refer to the whole conquest. This suggests Jericho's paradigmatic role in the conquest tradition.

Verse 12 contains two classic critical problems in the shape of the "hornet" and the "two kings." The traditional rendering of *ṣir'â* as "hornet" (also Exod. 23:28; Deut. 7:20) rests primarily on the ancient versions and suggests a metaphorical extension to "panic" (REB, supported by the parallelism in Exod. 23:27–28). Less convincing alternate translations are "discouragement" (based on Arabic) and "pestilence" (JPSV; NRSV except in Joshua), apparently grounded on a similarity to *ṣāra'/ṣāra'at* pertaining to "skin disease, leprosy."[16] Perhaps a demon is intended, as suggested by the title "Baal of the Flies" (2 Kings 1:3), something like the animal demons of Isa. 13:21–22.[17] Whatever it is, the "hornet" functions as a classic Divine Warrior weapon (cf. perhaps Isa. 7:18–19), driving out the enemy while Israel's military might played no decisive role (v. 12b). "Two kings of the Amorites" is the preferable reading from a text-critical standpoint (see text note 1), but if the reference is to Sihon and Og it is out of chronological and geographical order. Alternately this may be a reference to an otherwise unknown tradition analogous to the text's mention of a battle with the masters of Jericho, v. 11.

Yahweh's persuasive discourse ends with a summary of conquest ideology in vv. 12b–13: I gave you the fruitful land you now enjoy, without your having had to fight or labor for it. Israel did not have to build city walls and houses or laboriously construct agricultural terraces or plant and tend immature vines and trees for long years. Yahweh alone should be credited for what Israel possesses. The outlook and much of the language is parallel to that of Deut. 6:10–11.

[14–15] Loyalty to Yahweh is a matter of intention and motivation, not just outer compliance. It is to be performed "honestly" (*bĕtāmîm;* with undivided inner coherence, cf. Ps. 15:2) and "faithfully" (*be'ĕmet;* with dependable reliability in holding to agreed-upon decisions). Compare the vocabulary of Judg. 9:16, 19. This is consistent with the deuteronomistic concern for sincerity (cf. v. 23; Deut. 6:5). The tradition that Israel worshiped Egyptian gods is not found in the Pentateuch, but is asserted in Ezek. 20:7; 23:3, 8. The demand to "put aside" other gods may echo a traditional ceremony of burying

---

16. For literature see KB³ 989. For a more literal approach, E. Neufeld, "Insects as Warfare Agents in the Ancient Near East," *Orientalia* 49 (1980): 30–57.

17. A similar case may be the "Destroyer" of Exod. 12:23; 2 Sam. 14:16. Compare the vampire-like leech of Prov. 30:15, a demon in the opinion of F. Vattioni, "Proverbes XXX 15–16," *RB* 72 (1965): 515–16. "Baal of the Flies" is usually understood as an intentional deformation of Baal-*zbl* (the Prince?).

idols practiced at Shechem (Gen. 35:1–4; cf. this language in Judg. 10:16; 1 Sam. 7:4).[18]

The protasis of v. 15 suggests an opinion based on weighing costs and benefits (Gen. 28:8; Exod. 21:8; NIV "if serving the Lord seems undesirable to you"). That Joshua's "house" has already chosen Yahweh has been taken as one key to the "historical kernel" of this episode as the inauguration of the tribal system in an assembly at Shechem.[19] It is more likely to be a rhetorical flourish.

[16–18] Israel's reply picks up selected items from Yahweh's speech: the transgenerational unity of the exodus experience ("us and our ancestors") from vv. 5–7 and "driven out" (*grš*) from v. 12. The notion of being "guarded" from dangers on the way is similar to Deut. 1:31.

[19–24] The radical turn taken by v. 19 has often been taken as evidence of a change in author or editor in vv. 19–24. This view sees v. 18 as the true goal of what has gone before and v. 19 as a secondary taking up of the topic to add a more negative perspective. Verse 25 would thus originally have followed directly on v. 18. This may be true, but the present form of the text makes good rhetorical and structural sense, and the deep paradox introduced by v. 19 adds greatly to the power and theological sophistication of this text.

The call for the people to be witnesses against themselves (v. 22) stresses their own responsibility in the relationship to which they have assented. Just as they would be obligated to accuse the violator of an agreement to which they were formal witnesses, they must now be prepared to engage in self-criticism in the event of infidelity. The rhetorical opposition in v. 23 between *'ĕlōhê hannēkār* "foreign gods" and *'ĕlōhê yiśrā'ēl* is pointed.

[25–28] Israel's formalized self-obligation is termed a covenant in v. 25. This involves the interpreter in controversy about the meaning and place of covenant in Israel. Scholarship has focused much attention on the preposition *l* in the expression "for the people."[20] In this context it is best taken as

18. A. Alt, "Die Wallfahrt von Sichem nach Bethel," *Kleine Schriften* I, 79–89; E. Nielsen, "The Burial of Foreign Gods," *ST* 8 (1954): 103–22.

19. The classical proposal is that of Noth, *Das System der zwölf Stämme Israels*, 65–86, who proposes an agreement between the Joseph tribes and other tribes. A more recent treatment giving greater attention to archaeological and literary critical issues is K. Jaroš, *Sichem: eine archäologische und religionsgeschichtliche Studie mit besonderer Berücksichtigung von Jos 24*, OBO 11, Göttingen, 1976, 148–53. J. Bright, *History of Israel*, Philadelphia, 1981, 168–70, also sees a historical core, but as the extension of the Israelite covenant to the northern tribes. One should note that the present form of the text does not really imply a brand-new allegiance to Yahweh (compare vv. 16–17).

20. According to J. Begrich, "Berit. Ein Beitrag zur Erfassung einer alttestamentlichen Denkform," *ZAW* 60 (1944): 5, 8, this represented the older usage of the unilaterally imposed covenant, but was used in Josh. 24:25 to describe the newer bilateral arrangement. Schmitt, *Der Landtag von Sichem*, 69, proposes an obligation placed on Israel by Joshua as representative of Yahweh. Perlitt, *Bundestheologie im Alten Testament*, 261–62, appealing to 2 Kings 11:4, understands the expression as "Joshua laid an obligation on the people"; similarly E. Kutsch, *Verheissung und Gesetz. Untersuchungen zum sogenannten "Bund" im Alten Testament*, BZAW 131; Berlin, 1973, 22–23.

an "ethical dative"; the covenant was made "for" or "on behalf of" Israel (cf. 9:6). The real question is whether Yahweh is to be seen as a partner in this covenant or whether it is presented as a purely inter-human agreement of national religious policy. Perlitt is probably right (in regard to this particular text) in asserting that what is enacted here is not a covenant in the sense of a two-sided pact or treaty, but rather Israel's own formal validation of its self-imposed promise of allegiance to Yahweh.[21] Within the limits of this text, what is called a covenant is a matter of Israel's solemn self-obligation to serve and obey Yahweh alone, a commitment concretized by a "statute and ordinance" written into a law. What is described here is a formal act of communal assent to the elemental substance of Yahwism. Absolutely nothing is mentioned or implied about any sort of obligation or covenant responsibility on the part of Yahweh. It is Yahweh's *past* favor that constrains Israel's assent and loyalty. For the present and future, however, what is emphasized is Yahweh's sovereign, threatening holiness and jealousy and the distinct prospect of Israel's extermination.

"Statute and ordinance" is found in a similar context in Exod. 15:25b, a passage of uncertain but perhaps deuteronomistic pedigree. The phrase is used elsewhere to refer to an established practice (1 Sam. 30:25; Ps. 81:5 [4E]) and perhaps should be translated "fixed rule." Given the context, this newly established practice can only mean the exclusive worship of Yahweh. The "law of God" may have replaced the standing stone as the medium for recording this "fixed rule," but in the context of the final form of Joshua, the reader must think of the copy of Mosaic law in Joshua's possession (1:8; 8:32). Writing words in a book is a literary strategy for emphasizing their importance and permanent validity (1 Sam. 10:25; Ps. 40:7; Isa. 30:8). Although the notion of a stone that can hear may sound like some kind of archaic animism, it is probably just a literary metaphor. Commentators have suggested that what it is supposed to have heard are the (unreported) stipulations of a covenant or the "statute and ordinance" of v. 25. However, it is said to have heard "Yahweh's words," and the only utterance of Yahweh in the text is the historical review in vv. 3–13 ("Thus says Yahweh," v. 2). Thus the stone is really a witness to Yahweh's deeds rather than to Israel's obligations or agreement. It is the Israelites themselves, rather than the stone, who perform the role of witness to their self-obligation (v. 22). This stone functions in a way similar to the Jordan stones in 4:1–8, which also serve as testimony to Yahweh's deeds. Should Israel "disown" their God, the stone as a reminder of Yahweh's saving deeds would accuse them.

Although some elements in this report stem from a inherited tradition about Shechem, an effort has been made to reduce their offensiveness to orthodoxy.

---

21. Thus for Perlitt, *Bundestheologie im Alten Testament*, 260–70, it is not *Bund* (association) but *Verpflichtung* (obligation); similarly Kutsch, *Verheissung und Gesetz*, 64–65.

Deuteronomy 16:21–22 forbids cultic standing stones, so it is made clear that this one is nothing more than a witness (like the replica altar of chap. 22) and in no way a functioning cult object. Trees with sacred connotations are also problematic from a deuteronomistic viewpoint (Deut. 12:2; 2 Kings 16:4, etc.), but this one is mentioned only as a landmark (cf. Deut. 11:30).

Three Grave
Traditions
Joshua 24:29–33

24:29 After these events Joshua son of Nun, servant of Yahweh, died at the age of one hundred ten.[a] **30** They buried him within the boundary of his own hereditary property, in Timnath-serah [which is][b] in the hill country of Ephraim north of Mt. Gaash. **31** Israel served Yahweh all the days of Joshua and all the days of the elders who lived longer than Joshua and who had known[c] every act Yahweh had done for Israel.

32 The bones of Joseph, which the Israelites had brought up from Egypt, they buried at Shechem in the section of field which Jacob had purchased from the descendants of Hamor the father of Shechem for one hundred qesitahs, and they[d] became a hereditary possession of [the descendants of] Joseph.

33 Eleazar son of Aaron died. They buried him at Gibeah which belonged to Phinehas his son, which had been given to him in the hill country of Ephraim.

a. The Greek of Joshua 24:29–33 preserves a text significantly different from MT. The Greek recensional form is discussed below.

b. This expansion is omitted by OG, Judg. 2:9, and some Hebrew witnesses.

c. Follows MT. OG and Judg. 2:7 have "had seen," which is easier and harmonizes with Josh. 23:3. However, Judg. 2:10 as the antithesis of Josh. 24:31/Judg. 2:7 is a witness for "had known."

d. Follows MT. The idea that Joseph's bones (that is, the site of pilgrimages to venerate his tomb) could be considered as an inheritance for the Joseph tribes was offensive to later orthodoxy. OG avoided reference to the bones with the reading "he gave it," that is, the section of field. Similarly S and V suggest the reading "it [the section] became," which is the translational strategy followed by NRSV and NJB.

Three grave location traditions conclude Joshua. The death and burial formula (vv. 29–30; "died . . . buried") for Joshua provides closure for a career that began with a notice of the death of Moses (1:1–2). Attached to it is a statement (v. 31) that acclaims Joshua's success in leading Israel to obedience, while at the same time indirectly preparing the way for the recurrent disobedience of the Judges generations. The burial tradition about Joseph (v. 32) and the death and burial formula for Eleazar (v. 33) extend the horizon of canonical associations back to Yahweh's promises to the patriarchs in the Pentateuch and to priestly concerns.

The memory of grave sites and veneration of tombs has been a persistent feature of religious life in Palestine.[1] Although the last two notices were certainly attached to the end of the Joshua book late in the course of its formation, they are not alien to the book's purpose and spirit. Remembering burials and land purchases (Genesis 23; 2 Sam. 24:18–19) are ways for a people to claim land and identity, similar in function to battle reports and topographic lists. The words "hereditary property" in v. 30, "purchase, acquire" in v. 32, and "give" in v. 33 all point in this direction. As the book's concluding reports, these brief notices supplement and fortify the preceding conquest stories and geographic catalogs. The tombs of Joshua and Eleazar are located in the hill country of Ephraim, while the tomb of Joseph at Shechem was considered to be a possession shared by Ephraim and Manasseh.

[29–31] The last information reported about Joshua attaches to the close of the Shechem assembly with a generalized temporal connector. His death report is a functional parallel to Gen. 35:28–29 or Deut. 34:5 in that it brings an era to an end. Implicit comparisons with Moses serve to evaluate Joshua. Only here is he given the Mosaic title "servant of Yahweh." Previously he was only "attendant of Moses" (1:1). Locating Joshua's burial place inside the land contrasts with Moses' unknown grave outside the promised land (Deut. 34:5–6). This signals the momentous change in Israel's circumstances that Joshua has brought about. Dying at one hundred ten, Joshua is the equivalent of Joseph, although he still falls ten years short of Moses (Gen. 50:26; Deut. 34:7). He turns out to be the last of those foundational figures whose piety and significance are symbolized by extraordinary life spans. Joshua's success in leading Israel to obedience prepares for the influential role that royal religious leadership would have, for good or ill, in later portions of DH.

Joshua's inheritance and his foundation of Timnath-serah was already covered in 19:49–50. The bestowal of a special family inheritance is paralleled by the endowment of Hebron to Caleb, Joshua's fellow spy (14:6–15). Timnath-serah ties Joshua to Ephraim in tradition history. Apparently readers were thought to require help in locating the site, so it was associated with Mt. Gaash, which today cannot be identified. The name as given here in MT (LXX[B] has "Timnath-s-h-r") and in 19:50 MT is a metathesis of the form Timnath-heres

---

1. Examples are Machpelah, Rebekah's nurse, and Rachel (Gen. 35:8, 19–20; 1 Sam. 10:2), Elisha (2 Kings 13:20–21), and 2 Kings 23:17–18.

(as in Judg. 2:9 MT; Josh. 19:50 LXX). Timnath-heres ("portion of the sun") is usually thought to be the original name, changed to Timnath-serah ("portion which hangs over," "of surplus") to avoid the pagan reference.

The next generation will also be faithful, but their fidelity is coordinated with the circumstance that the elders are directly acquainted with Yahweh's saving deeds (v. 31). This leaves the future under a potential cloud, and the groundwork is laid for a new narrative problem launching the plot of the book of Judges. The overlap between vv. 28–31 and Judg. 2:6–9 indicates that the DH form of Joshua ended at v. 31.[2] Verses 29–31 may be seen as a balancing frame to the introductory 1:1–6.

[32] An object-first sentence redirects attention to a new topic. This verse shows a scribal interest in anchoring the Joseph grave tradition to the stories of Genesis and Exodus. Direct reference is made to Jacob's purchase of Shechem in Gen. 33:18–20. The itinerary of Joseph's bones connects back to Gen. 50:24–25 and Exod. 13:19 (both E). The area around Joseph's grave seems to have enjoyed a certain extraterritoriality as the shared claim of both Joseph tribes. Mention of the price and seller serves as a sort of deed (cf. Gen. 23:15–16; 2 Sam. 24:24), a claim to the land by right of purchase. The value of a qesitah (Job 42:11) is unknown. The claim of Joseph as a whole to Shechem is also reflected by the pun of Gen. 48:22 ("shoulder" or "mountain slope" = Shechem), to which v. 12 alludes with "sword and bow." The site of Joseph's tomb shown today dates at least to early Byzantine times (Eusebius, Madeba map).

[33] The disjunctive syntax of a subject-first sentence changes the topic again. Eleazar has played an important role in Joshua (14:1; 17:4; 19:51; 21:1), so mention of his death and burial is appropriate. Perhaps this is related in some way to the priestly materials found elsewhere in the final form of the book. Whether this town (or hill?) was given originally to Eleazar or to Phinehas is unclear, but its eventual ownership by Phinehas points to the new situation of the post-conquest era in which the land of promise is handed down by inheritance. The location of this Ephraimite Gibeah is unknown.

[29–33B OG] The Greek represents a longer text than MT and is closely associated with Judg. 2:6–10, 13; 3:7, 12, 14.

[LXX 29/MT 31] Israel served Yahweh all the days of Joshua and all the days of the elders who lived longer than Joshua and who had seen every act Yahweh had done for Israel. [LXX 30/MT 29] After these events Joshua son of Nun, ser-

---

2. On the implications of this overlap, see H. Rösel, "Die Überleitungen vom Josua- ins Richterbuch," *VT* 30 (1980): 342–50, who takes the linkage between Joshua chapter 24 and Judg. 1:1–2:5 to be older than that between Joshua chapter 23 and Judg. 2:6–9. M. Brettler, "Jud 1,1–2,10: From Appendix to Prologue," *ZAW* 101 (1989): 433–35, asserts that Judg. 1:1–2:5 was once an appendix to Joshua. Noth, *Deuteronomistic History*, 7–9, points to the overlap as evidence that Joshua and Judges were part of a larger historiographic work.

vant of Yahweh, died at the age of one hundred ten. [LXX 31/MT 30] They buried him within the boundary of his own hereditary property, in Timnath-serah in the hill country of Ephraim north of Mt. Gaash. [LXX 31A] They put there with him into the grave in which they buried him the stone knives with which he had circumcised the Israelites at Gilgal when he led them out of Egypt, just as Yahweh had commanded them. They are still there today.[3]

[32] The bones of Joseph the Israelites brought up from Egypt and they buried (them)[4] at Shechem in the section of field which Jacob had purchased from the Amorites,[5] the inhabitants of Shechem, for one hundred qesitahs, and he gave it as a hereditary possession to Joseph.

[33] After these events,[6] Eleazar son of Aaron the chief priest died. They buried him at Gibeah which belonged to Phinehas his son, which had been given to him in the hill country of Ephraim. [LXX 33A] On that day the Israelites took the ark of God and brought it around among themselves. Phinehas served as priest instead of Eleazar his father until he died. Then they buried him in Gibeah, which belonged to him. [LXX 33B] Then the Israelites each went to his place and to his city. The Israelites revered the Astartes and the Astaroth[7] and the gods of the peoples who were around them. So Yahweh gave them into the power of Eglon king of Moab and he ruled them eighteen years.

There are three major issues involved: the order of vv. 29–31, the flint knives of v. 31A, and the material offered by OG in vv. 33A–33B. Nevertheless, in each case MT represents the earliest recoverable text.[8]

OG and the parallel text Judg. 2:6–9 reflect the order: v. 28 + v. 31 + vv. 29–30. This order also seems to have been known to the Damascus Document (CD 5:3–4). There are two clues that the MT verse order is preferable *in Joshua*. First, the OG of v. 29 retains the words "after these events," which link directly to v. 28, but which make little sense after v. 31. For this reason they are absent in Judg. 2:8. Second, the divergent sequences found in MT Joshua

3. This verse is associated with the OG plus found after 21:42 [LXX 43D] connecting these stone knives with Joshua's town.

4. Understood as though the transfer of Joseph's bones were a contemporary act, not a reference to something that happened during the exodus. According to Margolis, *Joshua in Greek*, 472, this was an inner-Greek development precipitated by the haplography of the relative pronoun referring to "bones."

5. The translator seems to have misunderstood Hamor's name, compare Gen. 48:22.

6. OG eases the transition by leading into the new topic with "after these events," parallel to v. 29.

7. Apparently a conflated doublet.

8. The case for this is made by Rösel. "Die Überleitungen vom Josua- ins Richterbuch," 348–49. For the contrary position, see A. Rofé, "The End of the Book of Joshua according to the Septuagint," *Henoch* 4 (1982): 17–36, who finds in OG the original form of the connection between Joshua and Judges. On the textual relationships between the first chapter of Judges and Joshua also see A. G. Auld, "Judges I and History: A Reconsideration," 261–85. The most influential study of the redaction of the beginning of Judges is that of Richter, *Die Bearbeitungen des 'Retterbuches' in der deuteronomischen Epoche*, 44–49.

and Judges each fit perfectly into their own particular contexts. Because the question of loyalty and apostasy was the key issue for Judges, it was logical to raise this topic immediately after the people's dismissal and before Joshua's death (thus Judg. 2:7 comes before v. 8). In contrast, MT Joshua used the issue of faithfulness as a summary of Joshua's accomplishments and therefore properly mentioned it after his death and burial (thus Josh. 24:31 comes after vv. 29–30). In its recensional development away from MT, OG chose to follow the order it found in Judges as better synchronized with the larger canonical story and as more chronological, in that the death and burial of Joshua now became the very last things reported about him.

Verse 31A reports on the flint circumcision knives. The MT is preferable in not having this sentence. The argument for accepting this verse as part of the earliest recoverable text is that burial of sacred memorabilia in a grave would surely offend an orthodox scribe or reviser. There would be every reason to eliminate this notion if it had been part of the original text. On the other hand, it also represents just the sort of folkloristic, midrashic detail typical of textual expansions. The expanded form of the text depends on 5:4 because the notion of Joshua as the leader of the exodus ("when he led them out of Egypt") is completely inexplicable except in direct reference to the premises of that passage.

Verses 33A and 33B LXX link forward to the story of Judges. If they were taken to be the original ending of Joshua, this would indicate that Judges once had a redactional shape quite different from its present configuration. The OG text suggests a direct junction between the end of Joshua and Judg. 2:6, 12–13, as well as an edition of Judges that lacked the summaries of Judg. 2:14–3:6 and the insubstantial figure of Othniel. The original story line of Judges would have begun with the oppression by Eglon. However, it is much more likely that vv. 33A and 33B are recensional developments that seek to tie the books of Joshua and Judges more closely together. The overlap of Josh. 23:28–32 with Judg. 2:6–10 (the result of the insertion of Judg. 1:1–2:5 into DH) apparently provoked a scribal desire to tighten the connection even more snugly. Thus, as has already been shown, OG adjusted the details of vv. 29–31 in the direction of the presentation given in Judges. Moving material from the early chapters of Judges back into Joshua was part of the same process of intertextual bridge building. Skipping over to Eglon provides a much more interesting reference point than the colorless Othniel. In fact v. 33A actually points all the way forward to Phinehas and the ark in Judg. 20:27–28, from which it has appropriated the formula "on that day." Conversely and decisively, there would be no conceivable reason for later copyists or revisers to remove these OG pluses. These verses are certainly no more discursive or problematic than vv. 32–33. Unless one wishes to postulate damage to the end of a scroll, therefore, MT is preferable.

To recapitulate, the OG text developed in order to connect to the continuation of the national story in Judges. The text tradition preserved in OG adjusted the order of Josh. 24:28–31 to that of Judg. 2:6–10. Mention of Eleazar (v. 33; introduced with the phrase "after these events" repeated from Josh. 24:29) triggered a reference to Phinehas and an allusion to Judg. 20:27–28 (v. 33A). Next the reviser introduced reflections from Judg. 2:6, 11–13, and finally jumped to Judg. 3:12, 14, to touch on the oppression by Eglon (v. 33B). As in the case of the circumcision of chapter 5, the fall of Jericho in chapter 6, and the cities of refuge in chapter 20, the divergence between MT and OG here ought to be conceived of in terms of redactional development. The MT and OG versions of the book of Joshua each represent later redactions or recensions of the earliest recoverable form of the book.

APPENDIX:
SITE IDENTIFICATIONS

Abdon	(MT Ebron) Kh. 'Abdeh, 165272
Acco	T. el-Fukhkhar, 158258
Achshaph	probably T. Kisan 164253
Achzib (Asher)	ez-Zib, 159272
Achzib (Judah)	probably T. el-Beida 145116
Adam	T. ed-Damiyeh 201167
Adami-nekeb	Kh. et-Tell near Kh. ed-Damiyeh 193239
Adullam	T. esh-Sheikh Madhkur 150117
Ai	Kh. et-Tell 174147
Aijalon	Yalo 152138
Almon	Kh. 'Almit 176136
Anab	Kh. 'Anab es-Seghireh 145091
Anaharath	probably T. el-Mukharkhash 194228
Anathoth	Ras el-Kharrubeh near Anata 174135
Anim	Kh. Ghuwein et-Tahta 156084 and el-Foqa 157085
Aphek (12:18)	Ras el-'Ain 143168
Aphek (13:4)	probably Afka 231382
Arab	probably Kh. er-Rabiyeh 153093
Arad	T. 'Arad 162076
Ararah	(MT Adadah) Kh. 'Ar'arah 148062
Aroer (Reuben)	'Ara'ir 228097
Ashdod	Esdud 117129
Ashkelon	'Asqalon 107118
Ashtaroth	T. 'Ashtarah 243244
Azekah	Kh. T. Zakariyeh 144123
Aznoth-tabor	probably Kh. el-Jebeil 186237
Azor	Yazur 131159
Baalath	probably el-Mughar 129138
Beeroth	probably el-Bireh 170146
Beersheba	T. es-Seba' 134072
Bene-berak	el-Kheiriyeh 133160 associated with Ibn-Ibraq
Beten	probably T. el Far near Kh. Ibtin 160241
Beth-anath	probably Safed el-Battikh 190289

Beth-arabah	probably 'Ain el-Gharabeh 197139
Beth-aven	probably T. Maryam 175141
Beth-baal-meon	Ma'in 219120
Beth-emek	probably T. Mimas 164263 near 'Amqa 166264
Beth-haram	T. Iktanu 214136 near wadi er-Rameh
Beth-hoglah	probably Deir Hajlah 197136
Beth-horon, Upper	Beit 'Ur el-Foqa 160143
Beth-horon, Lower	Beit 'Ur et-Tahta 158144
Beth-jeshimoth	T. el 'Azeimeh 208132 near Kh. es-Suweimeh
Beth-nimrah	T. el-Bleibil 210146 near T. Nimrin 209145
Beth-shean	T. el-Husn 197212 near Beisan
Beth-shemesh (Issachar)	probably Kh. Sheikh esh-Shamsawi 199232
Beth-shemesh (Judah)	T. er-Rumeileh 147128 near 'Ain Shems
Beth-tappuah	Taffuh 154105
Beth-zur	Kh. et-Tubeiqeh 159110 near Kh. es-Sur
Bethel/Luz	Beitin 172148
Bether	Kh. el-Yehud 162126 near Bittir
Bethlehem (Zebulun)	Beit Lahm, 168238
Betonim	Kh. Batneh 217154
Bezer	probably Umm el-'Amad 235132
Cabul	Kabul 170252
Carmel	Kh. el-Kirmil 162092
Chephirah	Kh. el-Kefireh 160137
Chesalon	Kesla 154132
Chesulloth	(= Chisloth-tabor) Iksal 180232
Chinnereth	Kh. el-'Oreimeh, 200252
Chisloth-tabor	(= Chesulloth) Iksal 180232
Daberath	Kh. Dabbura, 185233
Dan/Leshem	T. el-Qadi 211294
Debir	(= Kiriath-sannah) Kh. er-Rabud 151093
Dibon	Dhiban 224101
Dor	Kh. el-Burj 142224
Dumah	Kh. Domeh ed-Deir 148093
Edrei	Der'a 253224
Eglon	probably T. 'Aitun 143099
Ekron	Kh. el-Muqanna' 136131
Eltekeh	probably T. esh-Shallaf 128144
En-dor	probably Kh. Safsafeh 187227
En-gannim	probably Kh. Beit Jann 196235
En-gedi	T. ej-Jurn 187097 at 'Ain Jidi
En-haddah	el-Hadatheh 196232

En-rimmon	Kh. Khuweilfeh 137087 near er-Rammamin
En-shemesh	'Ain Hod 175131
Ephrathah/Bethlehem	Beit Lahm 169123
Eshtaol	probably Kh. Deir Shubeib 148134 near Ishwa' 151132
Eshtemoh/Eshtemoa	es-Samu' 156089
Etam	Kh. el-Khokh 166121 near 'Ain 'Atan
Ether	Kh. el-'Ater 138113
Gath-hepher	probably Kh. ez-Zurra' 180238
Gath-rimmon	probably T. Jerisheh 132166
Gaza	Ghazzeh 099101
Geba	Jeba' 175140
Gedor	Kh. Jedur 158115
Gezer	T. Jezer 142140
Gibbethon	probably T. Malat 137140
Gibeon	el-Jib 167139
Golan	probably Sahm el-Jolan 238243
Halhul	Halhul 160109
Hali	probably Kh. Ras 'Ali 164241
Hammath	probably Hammam Tabariyeh 201241
Hammon	Kh. Umm el-'Awamid 164281 near 'Ain Hamul
Hannathon	T. el-Bedeiwiyeh 174243
Hapharaim	probably et-Taiyibeh 192223
Hazor	T. el-Qedah 203269
Hebron/Kiriath-arba	el-Khalil 160103
Heleph	probably Kh. 'Irbadeh 189236
Hepher	probably T. el-Muhaffar 170205
Heshbon	Hesban 226134
Hormah	probably Kh. el-Meshash 146069
Hosah	(= Usu, mainland Tyre) T. Rashidiyeh 170293
Hukkok	probably Yaquq 195254
Ibleam	Kh. Bel'ameh 177205
Ir-shemesh	T. er Rumeileh 147128 near 'Ain Shams
Iron/Yiron	Yarun 189276
Jabneel (Judah)	Yebna 126141
Jabneel (Naphtali)	T. en-Na'am 198235 near Kh. Yamma 198233
Jahaz	probably Kh. el-Medeiyineh 236110
Janoah	Kh. Yanun 184173 or Yanun 183172
Japhia	Yafa 176232
Jarmuth (Issachar)	(= Remeth) probably Kokhab el-Hawa 199221
Jarmuth (Judah)	Kh. el-Yarmuk 147124
Jashub	Yasuf 172168
Jattir	Kh. 'Attir 151084

Jazer	probably Kh. Jazzir 219156
Jehud	el-Yehudiyeh 139159
Jericho	T. es-Sultan 192142
Jezreel (Issachar)	Zer'in 181218
Jokneam	T. Qeimun 160230
Joppa	Yafa 126162
Juttah	Yatta 158095
Kadesh-barnea	'Ain el-Qudeirat 096006
Kain	probably en-Nebi Yaqin 165100
Kanah	Qana 178290
Karem	probably Ramat Rahel 170127
Kedesh	T. Qades 199279
Keilah	Kh. Qila 150113
Kinah	probably Kh. Ghazzah 165068
Kiriath-arba/Hebron	el-Khalil 160103
Kiriath-jearim	Deir el-'Azar 159135
Kiriath-sannah	(= Debir) Kh. Rabud 151093
Lachish	T. ed-Duweir 135108
Lakkum	probably Kh. el-Mansurah 202233
Lebo-hamath	Lebweh 277397
Libnah	probably T. Bornat 138115
Madmannah	Kh. Tatrit 143084 near Kh. Umm ed-Demineh
Mahalab	(MT Mehebel) Kh. el-Mahalib 172303
Mahanaim	T. edh-Dhahab el-Gharbi 214177
Makkedah	probably Kh. el-Qom 146104 near Kh. Beit Maqdum
Manahath	el-Malhah 167129
Maon	Kh. Ma'in 162090
Mareshah	Kh. Sandahannah 140111
Medeba	Madeba 225124
Megiddo	T. el-Mutesellim 167221
Mephaath	T. Jawah 239140
Migdal-gad	probably Kh. el-Mejdeleh 140105
Mizpeh (Benjamin)	T. en-Nasbeh 170143
Moladah	probably Kh. el-Waten 142074
Mozah	probably Kh. Beit Mizza 165135
Naarah	probably Kh. el-'Auja el-Foqa 187150
Neiel	probably Kh. Ya'nin 171255
Nephtoah	Lifta 168133
Nezib	Kh. Beit Nesib 150110
Ophrah	et-Taiyibeh 178151
Parah	probably Kh. 'Ain Fara 179137
Peor	Kh. Faghur 164119

Rakkath	(= Kartan) probably Kh. el-Quneitireh 199245
Ramah (Benjamin)	er-Ram 172140
Ramah (Naphtali)	Kh. Zeitun er-Rameh, 187259
Ramoth-gilead	probably T. Ramith 244210
Rehob	probably T. el-Bir el-Gharbi 166256
Remeth	(= Jarmuth) probably Kokhab el-Hawa 199221
Rimmon (Zebulun)	Rummaneh 179243
Sadud	(MT Sarid) T. Shadud 172229
Salecah	probably Salkhad 311212
Sansannah	Kh. esh-Shamsaniyat 140083
Secacah	probably Kh. Qumran 193127
Shaalabbin	Selbit 148141
Sharuhen	probably T. el-'Ajjul 093097
Shechem	T. Balatah 176179
Shikkeron	probably T. el-Ful 132136
Shiloh	Kh. Seilun 177162
Shim'on	(MT Shimron) Kh. Sammuniyeh 170234
Shunem	Solem 181223
Socoh (15:35)	Kh. 'Abbad 147121
Socoh (15:48)	Kh. Shuweikeh 150090
Succoth	T. Deir 'Alla 208178
Taanach	T. Ti'innik 171214
Taanath-shiloh	Kh. Ta'na el-Foqa 185175
Tappuah (Ephraim)	probably Sheikh Abu Zarad 172168
Tekoah	Kh. Tequ' 170115
Timnah (15:10)	T. el-Batashi 142132
Timnath-serah	Kh. Tibnah 160157
Tirzah	T. el-Far'ah 182188
Zanoah (15:34)	Kh. Zanu' 150125
Zaphon	probably T. es-Sa'idiyeh 204186
Zarethon	probably T. Umm Hamad 205172
Ziklag	probably T. esh-Shari'ah 119088
Ziph (15:55)	T. Zif 162098
Zorah	Sarcah 148131

INDEX OF ANCIENT SOURCES

INDEX OF SUBJECTS